To Ray Hedin

warmest regards,

Christian Moravu

March 2010,

North Carolina

POSTCOMMUNISM, POSTMODERNISM, AND THE GLOBAL IMAGINATION

Christian Moraru, Editor

Introduction by Aaron Chandler

EAST EUROPEAN MONOGRAPHS, BOULDER, CO
DISTRIBUTED BY COLUMBIA UNIVERSITY PRESS, NEW YORK
2009

EAST EUROPEAN MONOGRAPHS, NO. DCCLIV

CONTENTS

PREFACE

CHRISTIAN MORARU

Twenty years after the memorable 1989, the essays gathered in *Post-communism, Postmodernism, and the Global Imagination* set out to examine how post-Cold War accelerated globalization has been reshaping Central and East European literatures, cultures, and theoretical-ideological debates, particularly those aesthetic and cultural practices and representations revolving around experimentalism, the neo-avant-garde, the media, and, most importantly, postmodernism. Questions posed by our contributors include: Which new configurations of theme, form, and ideology have come about in the former communist countries in the post-1989 global world? What is the impact of globalization on cultural traditions, old and recent, in this geopolitically fluid part of Europe? How do these countries' writers, artists, critics, and public intellectuals see themselves in the new, evolving context? More basically, how do they imagine the globalizing planet and themselves in it? How do they picture themselves and their lands in the process of "going global," as individual and communities resist or complicate globalization?

These are, to be sure, only a few of the more insistent interrogations and concerns. Their foci vary, and some of the answers may surprise the reader. What the interventions share is rather a cross-disciplinary, fundamentally comparative approach. On the latter, a couple of quick points are in order. First, as Fredric Jameson notes in his preface to *The Cultures of Globalization*, the topic in his title is "unclassifiable," falling as it does "outside the established academic disciplines" (xi). So is, by and large, our collection's subject. That is why the scholarship addressing such a problematic will conceivably raise questions of expertise, focus, and so forth. In fact, global studies has been going through a perennial "identity crisis" of sorts, much like cultural studies, from which it is basically derived. Second, but in close relation to its ancestry, global studies is still struggling to work out instruments, methodologies, and a vocabulary of its own. It has not managed to reach this important objective yet and probably never will. Instead, it has heavily borrowed from the available repertoires of the debates on modernism, postmodernism, postcolonialism, information technologies, late twentieth-century economics, and so on. Our volume demonstrates, though, that the problems at hand are, in Central and Eastern Europe as much as elsewhere, urgent and worthy of our attention despite the inaccuracy of the tools and idioms we may be utilizing. "It's at the moment when we begin to intellectualize a phenomenon that in reality it disappears," Jean Baudrillard tells Philippe Petit in *Paroxysm* (20). If this is true, then globalization is, one could argue, already a thing of the past. But since we are trying hard to understand what it is and since we still have to find a modality to formulate our understanding, the phenomenon is, more likely, under way. At any rate, in the preface mentioned above and in his own contribution to the volume, "Notes on Globalization as a Philosophical Issue" (54-77), Jameson contends that the whole issue of the subject matter, field of inquiry, and critical vocabularies can be sorted out, and his solution is, I think, worth considering.

There are, he offers, four possible reactions to the global topic: a) given that the nation state is still around, there is no globalization; b) globalization is happening, but it represents just another chapter in the history of modernization; c) globalization is in full swing, fueled by recent phenomena such as the "world market," even though the latter introduces a difference of degree, not of kind, into the evolution of capitalism; c) according to the most interesting scenario (to my mind, at least), one posits "some new, or third, multinational stage of capitalism, of which globalization is an intrinsic feature and which we now largely tend, whether we like it or not, to associate with that thing called postmodernity" (54). The critic also insists that the "now familiar postmodern debate" should be separated from "the matter of globalization, all the while understanding only too well that the two issues are deeply intertwined and that positions on the postmodern are bound to make their way back in eventually" (55). In other words, he is drawing from postmodern criticism—and from his own work on the subject—to conceptualize globalism. This makes sense, I believe, and a number of contributors to our volume seem to agree. Their context—and this is the last point I want to make—is geopolitically and culturally-historically specific: Central and Eastern Europe. In it, unlike in the one Jameson is familiar with, postmodernism and experimental literature and culture have played, more often than not, a quintessentially oppositional, anti-totalitarian (i.e., anti-communist) role. It is this role that, as our anthology's essays variously show, artists and critics struggle to reimagine in a postcommunist world itself calling for a renewed, broader effort of comprehension.

*   *   *

This project would not have been possible without the support of a number of individuals and institutions. My thanks go, first, to Professor Stephen Fischer-Galati, distinguished historian of Eastern Europe and Editor of the Columbia University Press series in which this volume has come out, and to Anne Wallace, Head of the English Department at University of North Carolina, Greensboro. I am also grateful to UNCG's exceptionally dynamic and resourceful Center for Critical Inquiry in the Liberal Arts, as I am to my research assistant, Andrew Meredith, and to Nancy Tyson, who has done an excellent copyediting job.

BIBLIOGRAPHY

Baudrillard, Jean. *Paroxysm: Interviews with Philippe Petit.* Translation by Chris Turner. London: Verso, 1998.

Jameson, Fredric. "Notes on Globalization as Philosophical Issue." In Fredric Jameson and Masao Miyoshi, eds. *The Cultures of Globalization.* Durham, NC: Duke University Press, 1998, 54-77.

INTRODUCTION:
IMAGINATION WITHOUT WALLS

AARON CHANDLER

Twenty years ago, on the afternoon of November 9, 1989, at the tail end of an otherwise routine daily press briefing, GDR Central Committee media spokesman Günter Schabowski read slowly through an announcement of new travel rules.[1] The new regulations—including a provision permitting the orderly egress of GDR citizens with visa and passport via any border crossing—was an effort by the Politburo to defuse an increasingly tense travel issue through a reluctant and (it was thought) temporary easing of restrictions. No one envisioned a massive exodus of people past the city's heavily guarded gates, much less an outright abandonment of the Berlin Wall, a barrier that only months earlier Erich Honecker said would stand for another hundred years. The plan was to concede to public pressure in a way that reduced tensions and further underscored the Politburo's power over how, when, and in what fashion its citizenry could move.[2] The plan went awry.

Schabowski, who had returned from vacation the day before and therefore had not been thoroughly briefed, unwittingly announced the change in travel policies a day too soon. When the baffled press corps asked him when the new rules were to take effect, he rifled through his notes, shrugged, and answered, "so far as I know, um, immediately, without delay."[3] Within hours, the mistaken claim that East Germany had "opened its borders" was broadcast with great fanfare on West German news stations, despite the fact that those borders remained conspicuously closed.[4] Having heard the news from Western broadcasts, hundreds of East Germans began to gather at the city's checkpoints, restively demanding to cross into West Berlin and inundating unprepared border guards. Exhilarated by historic news that was ahead of the facts, these crowds would, by midnight, storm all three major border crossings without casualty.[5] The reformism of GDR citizens' chanting "We are the people" became, famously "We are *one* people" within a month of the wall's collapse, while chucks of concrete alleged to be pieces of the

1

Berlin Wall began to be sold and circulated throughout the world as mundane tokens of the marvelous.[6]

That such a massive, significant movement of people could be occasioned, in an admittedly limited sense, by Schabowski's shrugging slip attests to the fragility of GDR's regime during this period, but it also suggests much of what is characteristic about the twenty years that have followed. As Jean Baudrillard writes of the December 1989 Timişoara massacre, the Berlin accidental triumph suggests that "the street has become an extension of the studio" and that claims to historic truth have become replaced by claims to credibility.[7] Furthermore, the peculiar asymmetry of the event sequence—reminiscent of the clichéd butterfly effect—evokes a persistent pattern of disjunctive connection between individual and global scales of meaning, movement, and agency. Finally, the role played in this moment of history by the amplification, augmentation, and manifold reception of news shows how sanctioned borders fail to hem in variant "mediascapes" and "ideascapes."[8] The permeability of cultural and technological frontiers exacerbates (or enhances, depending on how you look at it) the porousness of physical, economic, and political boundaries, leading to societies in which migration and transnationalism become the norm, not the exception. Thus, embedded in one of the most storied moments of postcommunist era's birth are both the fragmenting undecidability typical of postmodernism (is this a piece of history or of gravel?) as well as the simultaneously agglutinative and migratory forces of what might be called a new (and much contested) global imaginary.

The incisive studies collected by this volume trace this intersection of postcommunism, postmodernism, and globality in the context of Central-East European literatures, cultures, and theoretical-ideological debates. They examine how post-Cold War accelerated globalization has reshaped the intellectual and cultural topography of this region, with a particular emphasis on neo-avant-garde movements, experimentalism, and postmodernism. These essays set out to provide revealing vantages on what has emerged from former communist countries in the post-1989 global context. To do so, they attend to the impact of globalization on the cultural tradition of these countries, their writers, artists, critics, and public intellectuals. Charting how such individuals imagine themselves and their lands in a globalizing world as well as how they seek to resist or complicate globalization's multiple processes is the central ambition of this volume. Taken as a whole, the collection makes clear that, although globalization has at its core a profoundly economic and political set of processes, it is also everywhere a matter of cultural imaginings—often conflictual, always plural. Such global imaginings emerge from specific cultures, sometimes manifesting quite parochial assumptions. Nonetheless, the fact that these ideas of globality bear traces of the conditions of their own emergence does not necessarily mean that they are inseparably tied to specifiable "origins." Indeed, it is the surfacing of local variations of the global that holds the attention of this collection's contributors most intently.

To contextualize these critical interventions, I begin by sketching the relationship between postcommunism and globalization. Grasping these coordinated but distinct occurrences should provide the reader with a general background in some of the macrocosmic shifts, both political and economic, occurring in Central and Eastern Europe over the last two decades. This broad sociological overview is followed by a more focused cultural assessment of the relation between the postcommunist world and postmodernism. With this section, I do not propose to establish a rigorous correlation between the two—the definitions of postmodernism are too numerous and the essence of postcommunism too nebulous—but to offer instead a suggestive survey of trends in the literary, cultural, and aesthetic milieu of these societies just before and after the emancipations and contestations of 1989. In attending, next, to the possible meanings of "the global imaginary," I offer several thoughts on how the macrocosmic and the cultural have been linked in recent years. I close with a preview of the essays included in the book.

1. *Postcommunism and Globalization*

In the spirited contests over how best to periodize globalization, it has become a mark of unsophistication to link its development too strongly to the multiple collapses of communism. Indeed, many of the most prominent and influential theorists of globalization date its first appearance much earlier, though few agree on *how* much earlier. For world-system theorists following Immanuel Wallerstein, globalization is a process not begun but *completed* in the twentieth-century, having been initiated much earlier by the crisis of feudalism in the late-fifteenth and early sixteenth centuries.[9] This view is at odds with the chronology

offered by Manuel Castells, who argues that the interconnected globalization of economy, technology, and communication that began to take
shape in the 1970s and accelerated in the 1980s represents a mode of
social organization qualitatively different from those that preceded it.[10]
At any rate, as Schabowski's example makes clear, the political dimin-
ishment of communism, the economic deterioration of democratic
socialist states, and the rising public sense of transnational belonging
precipitated rather than followed the tumults of 1989.

Whatever the elusive moment of globalization's inception, none
can doubt the power of the dizzying upheavals of that year: the election
of Solidarity in Poland, the opening of Hungary's border with Austria,
the Soviet abandonment of East German hardliners, the "singing revolution" of the Baltic states, the Velvet Revolution in Czechoslovakia, the
collapse of the Berlin wall, the resignation of Zhivkov in Bulgaria, and
the violent demise of Ceauşescu, to name only the most obvious.[11] As
they crashed on one another consecutively, these events helped to initiate
a set of profound economic and cultural changes that transformed far
more than just the vast swathe of territories and populations struggling
under repressive and sclerotic governments. The OECD economies were
only able to enter the recent period of intensive deindustrialization when
outsourcing to transition economies in Central-Eastern Europe, as well
as newly industrialized countries in Latin America and Asia, became
feasible.[12] Just as importantly, these revolutions brought into question
the imaginary boundary of East and West, transformed how Europe
could be conceived, produced the sometimes-destabilizing unipolarity of
American power, and drastically augmented the circulation of ideas and
competition of ideologies both in the Global North and South. The very
monumentality of these many changes makes their mention seem banal.

Such a brief and broad-stroked inventory of that *annis mirabilis*'s
reverberating effects risks repeating an unfortunate tendency—one not
uncommon among Western observers—to treat the fall of communist-
led governments in 1989 as a diacritical marker separating the end of a
political system in the East and the beginning of accelerated Western
transformations.[13] This historiographic punctuation is objectionable
because it defines what and who belongs to the future instead of marking
the several futurities contesting in the present. Furthermore, the conceit
of periodization dangerously occludes the reality of cultural and political
continuities in the former Soviet sphere and distracts from the numerous

transformations, struggles, and experiments that have continued to occur within and across the postcommunist world.

The changes have been multi-tiered and profound. Economically, the opening up of Eastern Europe meant an often-painful engagement with an already highly integrated global market. The abrupt release of price controls, removal of subsidies, and privatization of public enterprises collectively known as "shock therapy" failed miserably in many post-Soviet states, resulting in the collapse of industry, soaring inflation, and mass unemployment.[14] Even successful stabilization and entry into the European Union meant coping with an erosion of social protections and the limitation of genuine political alternatives, as well as what George Ritzer terms the McDonaldization of nearly every sector of life.[15] The most traumatic economic agonies were endured in the 1990s, and many Central and East European states have had their standards of living rebound in the years that have followed, including the Czech Republic, Hungary, Poland, Romania, Slovakia, Slovenia, as well as the "Baltic Tiger" economies. However, this newfound prosperity has been unevenly spread, eluding several postcommunist nations—Moldova, Serbia, Ukraine, for example—that are poorer today than they were under communism.

The political and cultural vicissitudes have been just as distinct as the economic pains former Warsaw Pact nations suffered. Indeed, for most of these states the fall of communism represented a shift in political polarity from being behind the Iron Curtain to being somewhere within a second *Mitteleuropa*.[16] In the communist world's southern tier, from Tajikistan to the former Yugoslav Federation, the end of communism meant the unleashing of ferocious ethnic, religious, and nationalist factionalism. These processes reflected imaginary investments legitimating claims to state power shifted from those licensed by old regimes to those salient in more fragmented civil societies. The emergence of new revanchisms and of "defensive" or "predatory identities" has occurred alongside subtler cultural changes as well as parallel to cultural continuations, political holdovers, and nostalgias for the past order.[17] Finally, the social experience of being entangled in the ideological and economic *doxa* of distant world powers—Comecon and the IMF—and of coping with the threat (and occasional reality) of military invasions by these powers, suggests that postcommunism may be a specific kind of postcoloniality, especially since these exogenous cultural and economic

pressures have, in every case, hybridized with national and ethnic specificities. A postcolonial comparative approach undoubtedly offers much
critical value, but one must avoid the temptation to emplot these cultures
in a comprehensive narrative trajectory, a temptation many have failed to
resist.

For some its Western observers, the fall of communism heralded
the promise of liberal democracy's universal ascendancy, proposed in a
particularly mechanistic way by Francis Fukuyama's neo-Hegelian "end
of history."[18] No matter how one wishes to construe the relative failures
and successes of these states, economies, and communities, it would be a
mistake to infer that the result was in any sense *uniform* or *utopian*, as
Fukuyama's line of thinking tends to imply. Instead, the region and its
cultures have been characterized by an ever-increasing "heterogeniza-
tion"—disjunctive fragmentation of media, art, architecture, language,
religions, and ethnicity, a trend compounded by the diasporic movement
of its populations.[19] Moreover, just as life under communism often
required the cynical "we pretend to work, and they pretend to pay us," so
too does political life in present-day Central-Eastern Europe seem to
encourage a diminished credulity in political promises and a withering of
explanatory templates.[20] Thus, in an intriguing way, the most recognizable banner of the 1989 movements—the Romanian flag with the coat of
arms cut from its center—already foretold the revolution's future. This is
true not in the sense of establishing a society purified of its unwarranted
elite, but rather of producing an elusive, "piecemeal" kind of cultural
identity which is nonetheless (torn) "open" to other possibilities. This
sense of remaining unfinished, contingently incomplete, or heteroge-
neously fragmented can be usefully reviewed under the rubric of postmodernity.

2. *Postcommunism and Postmodernism*

Postcommunism's relation to postmodernism is an open question, laden
with accompanying problems and difficulties, not least how one is to define postmodernism. Following Lyotard, we can formulate postmodern
sensibility as one of suspicion toward global explanatory matrices,
grounded epistemologies, ideas of progress, or metanarratives.[21] Such a
definition implies the politically inimical status of postmodernism to
Central-East European communism, which claimed legitimation on the

basis of progressive socialist science. Attempting to escape the pull toward transcendence, hypostasis, or totalizing claims entails rejecting, in one form or another, all claims of totalitarianisms as well. However, the doubts usually deemed characteristic of postmodernity—doubts about the claims of "universally" applicable to frameworks of knowledge and narratives of progress—seem to be what Marxist thinkers like Fredric Jameson and David Harvey criticize most about postmodernism.[22] For such influential thinkers, embracing postmodern suspicions risks vitiating any possible critique of capitalism and commodity culture. Consequently, one would surmise that postmodernism might have served as an effective tool of critique for dissident intellectuals during communist rule but a less sharpened weapon after its collapse, and yet this is far from clear. Postmodernism is indeed acidic to socialist realism, the representational and teleological assumptions of which are anathema to postmodern playfulness, reflexivity, and dedication to intertextuality. But postmodern art is also capable of critically engaging with neoliberal orthodoxies. Linda Hutcheon's response to Jameson and others helpfully complicates too-easy dismissals of postmodernism's sociocultural import and also brings us more directly to the intersection of political and aesthetic postmodernisms. She claims that postmodern*ity* as a social and philosophical condition characterized by a "universal, diffuse cynicism" ought to be distinguished from cultural and aesthetic postmodern*ism*, which engages the postmodernity in a "complicitous critique."[23] Allowing for the possibility of critical agency within postmodern aesthetics means that one should consider its characteristic patterns—its emphasis on play, difference, otherness, and contingency, its stylistic eclecticism, its admixtures of the high and serious with the low and parodic—as something more than a straightforward capitulation to commodity capitalism's underlying assumptions.[24]

So what is postmodernism's place in Central and Eastern Europe, where socialism and capitalism have so dramatically tangled? Although postmodern, avant-garde, and experimental writers and artists have been in bountiful supply in Eastern Europe since 1989, it is a mistake to suggest that postcommunism produces postmodern art. Such experimental, reflexive, and highly playful work has been enriching and complicating the region's imaginaries not only in the decades since the revolutions of 1989, but also in the decades before as well. A means of departing from Soviet-style socialist realism, postmodernism represented a form of aesthetic resistance to the homogenizing force of compulsory aesthetics and in at least this sense was an anti-imperial, quasi postcolonial, aesthetic gesture. Indeed, some of the region's early postmodern works, such as Péter Esterházy's 1979's *Termelesi-regeny* (A production novel), were parodies of then-unavoidable socialist realist fiction. In many Central-East European intellectual circles prior to 1989, postmodern poetics was an aesthetic choice with political resonances, an implicit call for greater liberalization and democratization.[25] This historical circumstance ought to augment our reading of the formalist experimentation, unreal games-manship, and intertextual playfulness of much contemporary Central and East European literature, art, and performance.

In short, if critical observers of Western postmodernism have been often concerned with its status as a mode of capitulation to and complic-ity with the standing power structure, the postmodernisms that devel-oped behind the Iron Curtain usually carried with them the aura of dissent, even if it was an explicitly depoliticized mode of opposition. Here, one may helpfully align aesthetic postmodernism to what György Konrád called "antipolitics," the utter rejection of the pursuit of power by opposition forces as a repudiation of the generalized politicization of life under communism.[26] It is too rarely acknowledged that significant tensions exists between the liberal democracies that have been instituted in the former communist bloc post-1989 and the ambitions and objec-tives of those struggling against communism. The fall of communism offered a utopian interim in which such antipolitics could be more than opposition, could in fact bear political fruit, but that moment has not survived into the present. Thus, a crucial postmodern continuity between pre- and post-1989 Central-Eastern Europe is between the antipolitical politics that led to many of the massive uprisings and the decline in political credulity of many East Europeans today. Moreover, if, as Zygmunt Bauman has claimed, postmodernity is "modernity without illusions," a mode of self-understanding that demands living with ambivalence and contingency, then one would expect postmodernism's continued, perhaps invigorated appeal to occur in the postcommunist world where ambivalence and contingency abound.[27]

Given the massive amount of literary and artistic postmodernism that Central and Eastern Europe has actually produced before and after the fall, this volume divides the task by including analyses of broad-spectrum trends (Cornis-Pope), discussions of major figures and their works (Peter Morgan on Ismail Kadare, Christian Moraru on Mircea Cărtărescu), and examinations of specific literary and intellectual enclaves (for example, Almantas Samalavicius on the relation between the Vilnius of Ričardas Gavelis and the postcommunist present). I wish here only to supply the briefest sketch of the Romanian and Serbian postmodernist scenes in order to suggest the richness and multiplicity of much Central and Eastern European avant-garde literature. In Romania, postmodernism developed early and vigorously. Drawing inspiration from surrealist modes dating back to World War I, a discernibly postmodernist avant-garde emerged as early as the 1960s with the work of Mircea Horia Simionescu, Ştefan Agopian, Dumitru Tsepeneag, and Leonid Dimov.[28] No account of Romanian postmodernism, however, can overlook the dominant force of Mircea Cărtărescu, whose poetry (the epic *Levantul*, 1990), novels (*Visul*, 1989, recently translated into English as *Nostalgia*), and academic work (*Postmodernismul românesc*— Romanian Postmodernism) all continue to prove exceptionally influential. Cărtărescu is a relative recent arrival when compared to Serbian writer Milorad Pavić, whose 1984 *Roman-leksikon u 100,000 reci* (Dictionary of the Khazars: a Lexicon-Novel in 100,000 words), with Borgesian gusto, takes the form of three cross-referenced encyclopedias of the disappeared Khazars (one Jewish, one Christian, one Muslim). Beside the enigmatic and decentered work of Pavić should be placed Svetislav Basara, who has sustained his iconoclastic, sardonic voice from *Kinesko pismo* (The Chinese Letter, 1984) and the much-lauded *Fama o biciklistima* (Fuss about Cyclists, 1985) to his two-part "Manic-Paranoiac History of Serbian Literature" (1997, 1998). These are but a handful of the novelists, poets, essayists, performance artists, and intellectuals, who have shaped postmodern work imaginatively, contesting the official line no matter how it is drawn or who draws it.

The ludic experimentation exemplified by these writers—with its more of less tacit opposition to the prevailing truisms—sets itself up in tension with the embrace of "lower" and popular forms by postmodernity in the arts and in broader cultural formations. As globalization preceded and shaped the twilight of communism, arguments over the appropriate role of consumer culture within Central and East European cultures go back even further. Indeed, the deep background of the trauma endured by Hungary in 1956 was a contest between Mátyás Rákosi's Stalinist focus on industrial goods and Imre Nagy's reformist push for

increased consumer commodities.[29] That the generation of young Romanian writers in the 1980s were dubbed the "Blue Jeans Generation" again
indicates the extent to which subversion was associated with Ameri-
canization and consumer culture. In the postcommunist context, the
embrace of consumer culture obviously signifies differently. Moreover,
the decreasing cultural power of print culture is the result, at least in part,
of the elimination of state subsidies but also of the immense influx of
West European and American consumer commodities, television, music,
and film. This creates a pressing and as yet unsolved question for intellectuals in postcommunist countries (a problem explored here most
clearly in the essays of Kos and Imre), namely, are the margins condu-
cive to greater richness or are they a space for an exile into irrelevance?
This may be another way of asking, who writes in the global imaginary?

3. *Imagining the Global*

The use of the phrase "the imaginary" in a broad sociological sense has
its most important antecedent in the psychoanalytic theory of Jacques
Lacan. Lacan developed it as part of his triptych of terms disentangling
discrete aspects of psychic life. In a Lacanian sense, the imaginary is an
order of experience established by a fundamental narcissism whereby a
human subject creates fantasy images of himself and his object of
desire.[30] In the decades since, a number of thinkers have modified this
notion to suggest the existence of a set of shared identificatory understandings and projections—neither mere fantasy nor materially given—
that enable publicness.[31] In Charles Taylor's words, a social imaginary is
made up of the "ways people imagine their social existence, how they fit
together with others, how things go on between them and their fellows,
the expectations that are normally met, and the deeper normative notions
and images that underlie these expectations."[32] A sense of natural, given
interconnectedness, of spatio-temporal uniformity, and of peer legibility
co-function with one another to provide a salient scale of "us."

So then, what does it mean to partake of a global imaginary? Following Lacan, we may say that it is a way of *seeing* "ourselves" from a
drastically alienated distance—the "Earthrise" photograph of the 1968
Apollo 8 mission—that sharply devalues heretofore crucial aspects of
"our" self-image and produces new concerns. Or, following Taylor and
Anderson, we can find the global imaginary in the nearness of cross-

continental, transnational proceedings and events, contingent on technology and assuming a modicum of shared norms. These two ways of
imagining the global—as total and as present—may serve as paradigmatic ends of a tension I take to be prevalent. Sharing in the global
imaginary is always a negotiation of such boundaries—between a general, perhaps chilling transcendence of local space and the imminence of
available plenitude of competing information, styles, and variant
histories. Extremities of distance and proximity—nested within one
another in a dizzying *mise en abyme*—characterize any possible global
imaginary. Thus, one feature of "feeling global" (paradoxically enough)
is a sense of disjunction—between the particular and the enormity of the
total, the individual and the collective, and the single and the plural.

It goes without saying, the models on which I constructed my
sketch of oppositions are not the only possibilities, for the global imaginaries cannot be separated from the social theories employed to articulate them. Consider how these dimensions are at play in three subtly
differing interpretations of the global now. British sociologist Roland
Robertson considers the global and local as two sides of the same coin,
clearly seeking to transcend the opposition by sublating it and treating its
interpenetration as a *fait accompli*.[33] This approach can produce un-
wieldy portmanteau words such as "glocalization" and "globalocal," but
it also enables substantial and innovative initiatives, such as Fair Trade
labeling.[34] Likewise, the explosive growth of Internet access in postcommunist "Cyberia" has spectacularly transformed the reception and
dissemination of cultural texts.

Just as this interpenetration of local and global is not a given,
Anthony Giddens would note, so too are its consequences unpredictable.
Our experience of the global has been produced often at the expense of
earlier imaginaries but also with the tools provided by them. Much as it
previously disembedded individuals from their traditional locations,
modernity, Giddens argues, has now also all but dissolved territorially
bounded societies and re-embedded these members in social systems
organized and spread across global spaces.[35] The resulting social reality
deeply affects individuals, whose identities—in the face of multiple
choices—increasingly become a reflexive project of self-creation rather
than of static inheritance.[36] This salutary promise was for many Central
and East European nationals in obvious contrast to top-down identities

provided for them under communist regimes. But such autonomy was not everywhere substantially available, nor has it come without costs.

The recent emergence of global scales of belonging does not necessarily subordinate or annul smaller-scale imaginings. Contesting global imaginaries as well as competing national imaginaries increasingly define our present historical moment, and perhaps this is true nowhere more than in the postcommunist world. Over the last two hundred and fifty years, national imaginaries of differing varieties have emerged, strengthened, and, in many cases, ultimately diminished in consequence. Following Benedict Anderson's powerful argument, we might say that the creation of such imagined communities are tied to the emergence of media technologies securing a sense of shared simultaneity.[37] Their establishment therefore is always tied to the new, yet within the imaginary itself the community is seen as an ancient if not primordial given. Perceptible shifts in the scale of imaginaries are experienced as moments of revealed truth. This introduction's opening example—West German television sparked a mass gatherings in the GDR; demonstrators shifted from declaring "We are the people" to "We are ONE people"—shows how the sense of a naturally interconnected place involves the technologically complex and historically contingent circulation of messages. The swift dilation of social imaginaries that characterized the self-creating of *die Wende* is the counterpart to, not the opposite of, the contraction and contested fragmentary self-creations of the former Yugoslav Federation. Both are moments in which the choice between competing social imaginaries radically altered the shape of the nation with immeasurably different effects.

Moreover, global effects on the local are not always a matter of choice. Instead, as Ulrich Beck has noted, they are often reactions to involuntarily incurred risks.[38] Risks such as terrorism or environmental collapse "endow each country with a common global interest…[so that] we can already talk about the basis of a global community of fate."[39] That the global imaginary may obtain in local answers to comprehensive problems is of particular interest for Central and Eastern Europe. During the 1980s, grass-roots movements arose in communist nations in response to the employment of nuclear power and to the severe pollution and ecological havoc caused by state industrial planning.[40] For many, such movements gave focus to social discontent in the period leading up to the late-1980s upheavals and played a significant role in bringing about political change in Czechoslovakia, Hungary, and Bulgaria.[41] There are, therefore, reasons to be hopeful that global imaginaries can stem from civic solidarities and mold participation in the face of oppression, helping to break down the monological agency of authoritarian states and transnational corporations alike.

At the time of writing, the global financial crisis of 2008-2009 threatens to obliterate the hard-won successes of the Central-East European nations that have advanced in recent years and to further impoverish the nations that have not. Some of the staunchest advocates of market globalism in the West, leaders who have promoted a global imaginary based on trade liberalization and trust in markets, have repeatedly resisted debt relief to the nations most vulnerable to the crisis.[42] In so doing, they risk echoing Neville Chamberlain's notorious assertion that Czechoslovakia was "a faraway country...of which we know nothing."[43] It is thus now more critical than ever to seek out greater knowledge of the global visions, opportunities, disenchantments, and promises produced by postcommunist cultures, and to attend more carefully to the new ways in which we have come to say "we."

4. *Central and East European Imaginings*

In this volume's first essay, "Shifting Paradigms," Marcel Cornis-Pope offers a wide-ranging overview of East European postmodern literature and tackles some of the most pressing questions of this literature. Showing that East European postmodernism has been, from the beginning, different from postmodernisms of the West, Cornis-Pope proposes that the former should be understood as a postmodernism of contestation keen on problematizing "the very distinction between historical representation and falsification." He argues forcefully for the efficacy of *postmodern theory* in testing and contesting the fragmentation characteristic of the *postmodernity* of the former Soviet empire. His essay also weighs the appropriateness of postcolonial theory in the case of postcommunist cultures. Given Central and Eastern Europe's Russification and its place at the historical intersections of the earlier Ottoman and Austria-Hungarian empires, postcolonial theory provides an illuminating lens to examine certain aspects of the postcommunist experience. Nonetheless, Cornis-Pope suggests that a postcolonial approach ignores the relative autonomy that many of these nations and cultures enjoyed if compared to the colonies of West European empires. He deliberates whether the diversification of post-1989 East European literatures constitutes a hybridization (of media forms, levels of taste, and so on) or a state of confusion, concluding that their most striking feature, along these lines, is their profoundly dialogic cultural belongings, most obviously in the work of globally peripatetic, émigré writers—"the shuttlers between East and West."

To this itinerancy one might oppose (or appose) the imaginative capacity to uncover the world without leaving home. The difficulty and promise of this uncovering are the subject of our collection's second essay. With "Cosmallogy: Mircea Cărtărescu's *Nostalgia*—The Body, the City, the World," Christian Moraru works out a reading of Cărtărescu as a kind of magician of a global imagination that encloses the world into a single city, Bucharest, or that *produces* rather the world from the city as if pulling a rabbit from a hat. In so doing, Moraru maintains, Cărtărescu's novel *Nostalgia* reveals Bucharest as "a site of astonishing otherness, a strange and vast place locked inside the nation-state's body." The stress on otherness here is crucial, for Cărtărescu does not accomplish his trick of time-space compression by recourse to the tropes of humanist universalisms. Instead, Moraru observes, the novel's narrative splinters set forth homologies "that safeguard and honor difference wherein self and other…retain their distinctive contents yet communicate because those contents are not incompatibly structured." Reading intertextually through Cărtărescu's "Bookarest," Moraru encounters not only Kafka, Borges, and García Márquez, all of whom one might expect to populate such a fantastic city, but also Rushdie and Pynchon. The diaphanous layers of dreams, absurdities, and impossibility in Cărtărescu's multi-part work were not just an aesthetic diversion from the official culture of Romanian communism, Moraru's argument demonstrates, but also constituted (and continue to offer) an opening up to a strange futurity that is the city's own.

A different kind of unveiling of the urban occurs in Alexander Kiossev's essay "The Screen of the City," which chips through the visual and temporal strata of Bulgaria's capital city to reveal its self-staging as a "private," "neo-capitalist" city with no rules. Attending to the politics of the visible and invisible within the shifting urban spectacle of Sofia, Kiossev reveals how "the screaming images" of its contemporary advertisements and signage—denoting market superfluity, heterogeneity, and chaos—stage themselves as boisterous refutations of an impersonal collectivist and panoptical city of the past, a city that only partially existed as such in the first place. This "Babel of private perspectives and interests" at first supplemented and then substituted for the carnivalesque celebrations of the city in the immediate aftermath of Zhivkov's fall. But Sofia's commercial bedlam shares the stage with "signs" of weakened and corrupt municipal authority. To these multiple visibilities, Kiossev adds the triumphal self-announcements of organized crime, which aggressively impresses its own territorial and authorial claims on Sofia's *flaneur* and in so doing, partially justifies itself by imparting the sense that the vitality of indiscriminate enterprise is irreversibly intertwined with such (black) market risks and hazards.

Almantas Samalavicius performs a comparable reading of the urban palimpsest of Vilnius in his essay "Facing Globalization" as part of an ongoing elucidation of "high postcommunism," that is, of the "liminal state of societal transition that started with the collapse of the Soviet era and continues up to the present moment." Samalavicius's essay elucidates the various imprints of cultural epochs in the urban built environment, from the distant Baroque and late Gothic past, through the forceful industrialization during Soviet colonization, to the latest wave of globalized urbanization and sprawl. Returning to Ričardas Gavelis's *Vilnius Poker,* which conjured Vilnius as a city castrated by both Soviet control and Lithuanian passivity, Samalavicius argues that today's capital, though much changed by the embrace of globalization, is still laden with metaphorical ironies intimating new forms of alienation. He finishes with an anti-conclusion of sorts, seeing in the story of the aborted Guggenheim-Hermitage Museum an argument against Lithuania's continuing inertia and its willingness to allow others—here, the global tourist industry—to imagine its best shape rather than taking up that difficult task itself.

The overrun autonomy of Central and East European states confronted with market globalism and Western governmental mandates is a theme recurring throughout this volume, and our fifth essay demonstrates how the resulting frustration can be inscribed in the very heart of invading universalism. Marcela Kostihová's contribution, "Shakespeare after Shock Therapy," considers how productions of works by Shakespeare in the postcommunist Czech Republic have changed in response to the vicissitudes of neoliberal "shock therapy" and the double standards at play in the non-negotiable EU accession conditions. It has not been uncommon to encounter adaptations and modifications of the Shakespeare canon by colonial subjects, who use his texts to argue, sometimes implicitly but often explicitly, for their cultural and ethical equivalence. Similarly, Kostihová claims that, through both productions and reviews, the Czechs have wielded Shakespeare's cultural capital as a site of perceived universality to express frustration with the cultural and political hierarchies of the postcommunist era. It is only fair that these disappointment, angers, and claims to legitimacy—too frequently pressed back to shadowy curtains—have been given center stage in the theaters of the Czech Republic.

If Kostihová's article shows how some Czech artists have appropriated Shakespeare to culturally *contest* the process of European political unification, our sixth essay concerns an esteemed author who is wielding his influence to argue *for* the political and cultural coherence of New Europe. Peter Morgan's "Kadare after Communism" provides a compelling review of one of East European literature's major figures, world-renowned Albanian novelist Ismail Kadare. Best known in the West for his novel *The General of the Dead Army,* Kadare has become "the grand old man of Albanian letters," writes Morgan, exhorting "his countrymen to reject aspects of their history and rejoin Europe." Morgan outlines the shape of Kadare's work in the years following the collapse of Albania's dictator Enver Hoxha, focusing especially on texts such as *Spiritus* and *The Successor,* in which Kadare deals most openly with the past regime. Against critics who renounce Kadare as complicitous with Hoxha's government, Morgan remarks that the writer's Aesopian fabulation and myth-making have to be read in the context of an "Albanian socialism [that] was Stalinist to the end." Morgan sees Kadare's interventions in Albanian identity in the years since 1990 as an effort to reestablish (to, in fact, imaginatively re-invent and construct) it as a European nation that has been historically subjected to Byzantine, Ottoman, and Soviet ambitions.

The way in which imaginative (re)constructions of past enable and construct the political unities of the present is also the subject of Jennifer Ruth Hosek's contribution. In "Postcommunist Spectacle," she asks how the Western mythology surrounding the 1990 German *Wende* has come to be the most dominant narrative. While Hosek notes that the absence of *the* definitive reunification text licenses an enduring search for it (with corresponding publicity), it also conveys "the multiplicity of *Wende* experiences." That multiplicity is belied, however, by the oversimplification of the *Wende* mythology, which, Hosek reaffirms, normalizes the GDR's merger with the FRG as "the cathartic embrace of an estranged family or as a heterosexual marriage, with the West as strong male provider." While the popular films *Das Leben der Anderen* and *Good Bye, Lenin!* may be symptomatic of "Ostalgia," Hosek maintains that they also reaffirm reunification logic. Her thoughtful reading of the latter film shows how its deployment of humor and its focus on consumer choice ultimately diminish political choice and the East's hope of traveling a "third way" in the postcommunist era.

The role played by consumer culture and democratic freedom in postcommunist Central and Eastern Europe is also the subject of the volume's eighth piece, though in it, the predominant concern is not with its relation to political identity but instead with its effect on aesthetic freedom. Matevž Kos's "The Anxiety of Freedom" sketches out a literary-historical narrative to conceive shifts in Slovenian literature from the postwar period to the present, culminating with a challenging claim about the relationship between political freedom and artistic autonomy. From the break with the Soviet Union and its prescribed aesthetic line in 1948 until the early 1970s, asserts Kos, a mix of dark modernist formalism and thematically existentialist literature developed in Slovenia, replete with concerns of Sartrean freedom and commitment. This was literature laden with "added" meanings capable of subtly speaking against the non-democratic Yugoslav federation, and thus of expressing a kind of *symbolic* freedom. Following the exhaustion of this aesthetic's possibilities, the decade from 1975 to the collapse of communism saw the flowering of postmodernism, first as a politically critical trend and then as an intertextual and autoreferential phenomena. Kos concludes by noting that the threat to Slovenian literatures posed by state repression in the decades following World War II has been replaced by the obligations of market conditions, which endangers the viability of less commercial texts. "What suggests itself," the critic argues, "is a provocative thesis," namely that "the political freedom brought by liberal democracy is less *liberating* than the lack of this freedom."

This anthology's ninth essay examines two avant-garde collectives that, far from moving amiably between cultural spaces, ventriloquize familiar elements within their respective cultures and reveal them as monstrously other. In "Late Communist and Postcommunist Avant-Garde Aesthetics," Nataša Kovačević reminds us that narratives treating Eastern Europe "as a democratic apprentice gradually waking up from the nightmare that was communism" have been exposed as simplistic by a wealth of avant-garde art, performance, and film. Kovačević demonstrates how groups such as Slovenian artist collective Neue Slowenische Kunst and Russian artist collective Necrorealists create an implicit utopian opening by collapsing the differences between socialist and neoliberal rhetorics and "reserv[ing]" the artists' "right to incomprehensibility" in the process. The first of these groups, the NSK, relies on "an overidentification with dominant political and cultural discourses that effects its own manipulation of signs" rather than openly contesting the hegemonic styles supplied by globalization. In so doing, NSK subtly subverts power's style of self-legitimation. The second group she considers, the Necrorealists, accomplish something similar, but this time the target is everyday life itself, which, Kovačević explains, the Necrorealists defamiliarize by staging, filming, and exhibiting brawls, producing grotesque death and zombie imagery, and simulating as spectacle violent homosexual sex. Kovačević examines the degree to which such Situationist-like interventions travesty socialist realism, nationalist models of masculinity, and—perhaps more importantly—the limits of what can be appropriated by a society understood in biopolitical terms.

If, as Kovačević observes, NSK and Necrorealists embrace a marginal position in their cultures, Anikó Imre's article touches on the increasingly marginal role of intellectuals in the postcommunist era, though in a much different capacity. In "Global Media and National Value: Postsocialist Negotiations," Imre examines how the efforts of national elites to build democratic public spheres in their countries following the collapse of the Soviet empire have been undermined by the transformations wrought by new media. Offering a glimpse at the role played by both the Internet and Western-influenced commercial television in postcommunist societies, Imre gauges both the archly withering rejections issued from the intellectual classes and the powerful but politically ambivalent phenomena embodied by "fandom." She insightfully traces the bifurcated reactions to the Hungarian reality program *Győzike Show*, which revels in the lurid conduct of Roma pop singer Győző Gáspár and his family. A lightening rod for attacks by both native cultural critics, who reject it as a coarsening, "foreign" form, and by many of its regular viewers, whose most racist ideas about Roma culture it confirms, the show exposes many of the rawest nerves laid bare by globalization. Furthermore, writes Imre, the show provides an outlet particularly suitable for what she terms "traumatic citizenship," that is, for the venting of affects in cultures "where public emotional expression has been suppressed by decades, if not centuries, of collective trauma."

Though it is also highly mediated and deeply ambivalent, a nonetheless very different kind of emergent citizenship is at play in Phyllis Whitman Hunter's essay "Love Game." Building on Eric Hobsbawm's claim that the institutionalization of sports on (inter)national scales of competition represented an "invention of tradition," Hunter examines the double cultural status of tennis mega-stars from the former Yugoslav Federation. Players such as Goran Ivanisevic, Novak Djokovic, Ana Ivanovic, and Jelena Jankovic are, Hunter points out, members of a global "cosmopolitan elite," but they also epitomize the nationalist confrontations that have enmeshed their birthplace in the postcommunist era. The duality of their role—at once supernational and *super* nationalist—discloses, for Hunter, the double move whereby the global imagination intensifies and gives shape to the local, often with pernicious consequences.

The tension between centrifugal and centripetal forces in Central and East European identificatory orbits continues to get significant play in our volume's concluding intervention. In her essay "Nomadic Homes, Postmodern Travel, and the Geopolitical Imaginary in the Post-Totalitarian Cultures of Poland and Ukraine," Irene Sywenky supplies a fittingly heterogeneous account of Central and East European efforts to reimagine the space of Europe. The essay seizes on Poland and Ukraine as "important loci of cultural displacement through the change of political regimes and borders," and as cultural sites deeply conscious of their historical peripherality. Sywenky deals with the problematic of these contested cultural spaces by reading tropes of travel and what she terms the "literary cartography" of prominent contemporary writers such as Poland's Andrzej Stasiuk, Manuela Gretkowska, and Olga Tokarczuk and Ukraine's Yuri Vynnychuk, Yuri Andrukhovych, and work appearing in the journal *Potiah 73*. What emerges is a nuanced and captivating set of postcolonial and space theory-informed approaches to cultural liminality and migration. In keeping with much postmodern theorizations, some of these authors, *contra* the widespread tendencies to treat

Europe as a stable subject of history, conceive of Europe as a dislocated, in-between space, a nomadic field, or a kind of home on the road. Distinct from this view of Europe but equally intriguing are efforts to recenter the cartographic imaginary map on heretofore marginal sites, taking up, for example, the Carpathian Mountains as the central object of Central Europe (see, e.g., Andrukhovych). Both kinds of imaginative agency suggests that, if the founding myth of Europe is one of abduction and resettlement (Europa and Zeus) the percolating myths of New Europe may be stories of cosmopolitan wandering and rediscovery.

NOTES

1. Frederick Taylor, *The Berlin Wall: A World Divided, 1961-1989*. (New York: Harper Collins, 2006), 422.

2. Ibid., 420-424.

3. Ibid., 424.

4. Ibid., 425.

5. Ibid., 427-428.

6. Ibid., 431.

7. Jean Baudrillard, *The Illusion of the End*. Trans. Chris Turner (Stanford, CA: Stanford University Press, 1994), 56.

8. Arjun Appadurai, *Modernity at Large: Cultural Dimensions of Globalization* (Minneapolis, MN: University of Minnesota Press, 1996), 35-36.

9. Immanuel Wallerstein, *The Modern World-System: Capitalist Agriculture and the Origins of the European World-Economy in the Sixteenth Century* (New York: Academic Press, 1974), 15.

10. Manuel Castells, *The Rise of the Network Society* (Malden, MA: Blackwell, 1996), 33.

11. Daniel Chirot, "What Happened in Eastern Europe in 1989?" *The Revolutions of 1989: Rewriting Histories*, ed. Vladimir Tismaneanu (New York: Routledge, 1999), 33.

12. David Held and Anthony McGrew, "The Great Globalization Debate," *The Global Transformations Reader: An Introduction to the Globalization Debate*, eds. David Held and Anthony McGrew. 2nd ed. (Malden, MA: Blackwell, 2002), 26.

13. Under this category would be the assumptions characteristic of what Michael D. Kennedy calls "transition culture." See Michael D. Kennedy, *Cultural Formulations of Postcommunism: Emancipation, Transition, Nation, and War* (Minneapolis, MN: University of Minnesota Press, 2002), 8-14.

14. See Richard Carter, *The Silent Crisis: The Impact of Poverty on Children in Eastern Europe and the Former Soviet Union* (London: European Children's Fund, 2000), 8, as well as Ben Fowkes, *The Post-Communist Era: Change and Continuity in Eastern Europe* (New York: St. Martin's Press, 1999), 132.

15. George Ritzer, *The McDonaldization of Society*. New Century Ed. (Thousand Oaks, CA: Pine Forge, 2000).

16. Jorg Brechtefeld, *Mitteleuropa and German Politics: 1848 to the Present* (New York: St. Martin's Press, 1996). As Brechtefeld notes, "the concept 'Mittelleuropa' is

closely related to German nation-building and national identity. While Mitteleuropa was prominent in German rhetoric and thought between 1914 and 1918, German history since Frederick the Great has been interpreted as a continuous drive for German domination of Central Europe. Moreover, Germany's imperial aspirations were often presented as part of its national identity" (12-13).

17. For "defensive identities," see Manuel Castells, *The Information Age: Economy, Society and Culture – The Power of Identity* (Malden, MA: Blackwell, 2000), 66. For "predatory identities," see Arjun Appadurai, *Fear of Small Numbers: An Essay on the Geography of Anger* (Durham, NC: Duke University Press, 2006), 51. As an example of a subtler cultural change, consider Michael D. Kennedy's discussion of the "loss of civility" in postcommunist cultures. See Michael D. Kennedy, *Cultural Formulations of Postcommunism: Emancipation, Transition, Nation, and War*, 216-220.

18. Francis Fukuyama, *The End of History and the Last Man* (New York: Penguin, 1993).

19. I borrow the term from Appadurai, *Modernity at Large*, 32. For a brief account of the fragmentation emerging directly from the 1989 upheavals, see Ken Jowett, "The Leninist Legacy," *The Revolutions of 1989: Rewriting Histories*, ed. Vladimir Tismaneanu, 220-227.

20. Fowkes, 150-151.

21. Jean-François Lyotard, *The Postmodern Condition: A Report on Knowledge*, trans. Geoff Bennington and Brian Massumi (Minneapolis, MN: University of Minnesota Press, 1984), xxiv.

22. Fredric Jameson, *Postmodernism, or, the Cultural Logic of Late Capitalism* (Durham, NC: Duke University Press, 1991), and David Harvey, *The Condition of Postmodernity: An Enquiry into the Origins of Cultural Change* (Cambridge, UK: Blackwell, 1989).

23. Linda Hutcheon, *The Politics of Postmodernism* (New York: Routledge, 2002), 23-25.

24. Stuart Sim, *Irony and Crisis: A Critical History of Postmodern Culture* (Cambridge, UK: Icon, 2002).

25. Harold B. Segel, *The Columbia Literary History of Eastern Europe since 1945* (New York, Columbia University Press, 2008), xii.

26. George Konrád, *Antipolitics: An Essay* (New York: Houghton Mifflin Harcourt, 1984).

27. Zygmunt Bauman, *Postmodern Ethics* (Malden, MA: Blackwell, 1993), 32-34.

28. Segel, 198-199.

29. Charles Gati, *Failed Illusions: Moscow, Washington, Budapest, and the 1956 Hungarian Revolt* (Stanford, CA: Stanford University Press, 2006), 24.

30. See Jacques Lacan, *Freud's Papers on Technique, 1953-1954, Book I, The Seminars of Jacques Lacan*, ed. Jacques-Alain Miller, trans. John Forrester (New York: W. W. Norton, 1991), and "The Mirror Stage as Formative of the Function of the I as Revealed in Psychoanalytic Experience," in Jacques Lacan, *Ecrits: A Selection* (New York: W. W. Norton, 2002).

31. The earliest of these—Cornelius Castoriadis's *The Imaginary Institution of Society* (1975), Pierre Bourdieu's *The Logic of Practice* (1990), and Arjun Appadurai's *Modernity at Large* (1996)—employ the term without reference to each another, but more recent theoretical efforts, especially Manfred B. Steger's *The Rise of the Global Imaginary* and Charles Taylor's *Modern Social Imaginaries*, both make reference to Benedict Anderson's notion of imagined communities.

32. Charles Taylor, *Modern Social Imaginaries* (Durham, NC: Duke University Press, 2004), 23.

33. Roland Robertson, "Globalization: Time-Space and Homogeneity-Heterogeneity," in *Global Modernities*, eds. Mike Featherstone, Scott Lash, and Roland Robertson (London: Sage, 1995).

34. See David Howes, *Cross-Cultural Consumption: Global Markets, Local Realities* (New York: Routledge, 1996).

35. See Anthony Giddens, *The Consequences of Modernity* (Cambridge, UK: Polity, 1990).

36. See Anthony Giddens, *Runaway World: How Globalization is Reshaping Our Lives* (London: Profile, 1999).

37. Benedict Anderson, *Imagined Communities: Reflections on the Origin and Spread of Nationalism*, rev. ed. (London: Verso, 1991).

38. See Ulrich Beck, *World Risk Society* (Cambridge, UK: Polity, 1999).

39. Ulrich Beck, "The Terrorist Threat: World Risk Society Revisited," *Theory, Culture, and Society*, 19 no. 4 (2002), 40.

40. See *Environmental Action in Eastern Europe: Responses to Crisis,* ed. Barbara Jancar-Webster (Armonk, NY: M.E. Sharpe, 1993).

41. See Duncan Fischer, "The Emergence of the Environmental Movement in Eastern Europe and its Role in the Revolutions of 1989," in Jancar-Webster, 89-113.

42. In March 2009, European Union leaders led by German Chancellor Angela Merkel rejected Hungarian Prime Minister Ferenc Gyurcsasy's call for a bailout package to minimize the damage to vulnerable Central and East European economies.

43. Qtd. in David Reynolds, *Summits: Six Meetings That Shaped the Twentieth Century* (Jackson, TN: PublicAffairs, 2009), 83.

BIBLIOGRAPHY

Anderson, Benedict. *Imagined Communities: Reflections on the Origin and Spread of Nationalism,* rev. ed. London: Verso, 1991.

Appadurai, Arjun. *Fear of Small Numbers: An Essay on the Geography of Anger.* Durham, NC: Duke University Press, 2006.

_____. *Modernity at Large: Cultural Dimensions of Globalization.* Minneapolis, MN: University of Minnesota Press, 1996.

Basara, Svetislav, and Ana Lucić. *Chinese Letter: a Novel.* Normal, Ill: Dalkey Archive Press, 2004.

Basara, Svetislav. *Fama o biciklistima.* Beograd: Prosveta, 1989.

_____. *Looney Tunes: manicno-paranoicna istorija srpske knjizevnosti u periodu od 1979. - 1990.* Beograd: Dereta, 1998.

Baudrillard, Jean. *The Illusion of the End.* Translated by Chris Turner. Stanford, CA: Stanford University Press, 1994.

Bauman, Zygmunt. *Postmodern Ethics.* Malden, MA: Blackwell, 1993.

Beck, Ulrich. "The Terrorist Threat: World Risk Society Revisited," *Theory, Culture, and Society* 19, no. 4 (2002): 39-55.

_____. *World Risk Society.* Cambridge, UK: Polity, 1999.

Bourdieu, Pierre. *The Logic of Practice.* Stanford, CA: Stanford University Press, 1990.

Brechtefeld, Jorg. *Mitteleuropa and German Politics: 1848 to the Present*. New York: St. Martin's Press, 1996.

Cărtărescu, Mircea. *Levantul*. Bucureşti: Humanitas, 1998.

Cărtărescu, Mircea. *Nostalgia: a Novel*. Translated by Julian Semilian. New York: New Directions, 2005.

_____. *Postmodernismul romanesc*. Bucureşti: Humanitas, 1999.

Carter, Richard. *The Silent Crisis: The Impact of Poverty on Children in Eastern Europe and the Former Soviet Union*. London: European Children's Fund, 2000.

Castells, Manuel. *The Power of Identity (The Information Age)*. Malden, MA: Blackwell, 2003.

_____. *The Rise of the Network Society*. Malden, MA: Blackwell, 1996.

Castoriadis, Cornelius. *The Imaginary Institution of Society*. Cambridge, MA: MIT Press, 1987.

Chirot, Daniel. "What Happened in Eastern Europe in 1989?" *The Revolutions of 1989: Rewriting Histories*. Edited by Vladimir Tismaneanu. New York: Routledge, 1999. 19-50.

Esterházy, Péter. *Termelesi-regeny*. Budapest: Magveto, 1979.

Fischer, Duncan. "The Emergence of the Environmental Movement in Eastern Europe and its Role in the Revolutions of 1989." *Environmental Action in Eastern Europe: Responses to Crisis*. Edited by Barbara Jancar-Webster. Armonk, NY: M.E. Sharpe, 1993. 89-113.

Fowkes, Ben. *The Post-Communist Era: Change and Continuity in Eastern Europe*. New York: St. Martin's Press, 1999.

Francis, Fukuyama. *The End of History and the Last Man*. New York: The Free Press, 1992.

Gati, Charles. *Failed Illusions: Moscow, Washington, Budapest, and the 1956 Hungarian Revolt*. Stanford, CA: Stanford University Press, 2006.

Giddens, Anthony. *The Consequences of Modernity*. Cambridge, UK: Polity, 1990.

_____. *Runaway World: How Globalization is Reshaping Our Lives*. London: Profile, 1999.

Harvey, David. *The Condition of Postmodernity: An Enquiry into the Origins of Cultural Change*. Cambridge, UK: Blackwell, 1989.

Held, David and Anthony McGrew. "The Great Globalization Debate," *The Global Transformations Reader: An Introduction to the Globalization Debate*. Edited by David Held and Anthony McGrew. 2nd ed. Malden, MA: Blackwell, 2002. 1-49.

Howes, David. *Cross-Cultural Consumption: Global Markets, Local Realities*. New York: Routledge, 1996.

Hutcheon, Linda. *The Politics of Postmodernism*. New York: Routledge, 2002.

Jameson, Fredric, *Postmodernism, or, the Cultural Logic of Late Capitalism*. Durham, NC: Duke University Press, 1991.

Jowett, Ken. "The Leninist Legacy." *The Revolutions of 1989: Rewriting Histories*. Edited by Vladimir Tismaneanu. New York: Routledge, 1999. 207-224.

Lacan, Jacques. *Ecrits: A Selection*. Translated by Bruce Fink. New York: W.W. Norton, 2002.

_____. *Freud's Papers on Technique, 1953-1954, Book I, The Seminars of Jacques Lacan*. Edited by Jacques-Alain Miller. Translated by John Forrester. New York: W.W. Norton, 1991.

Kennedy, Michael D. *Cultural Formulations of Postcommunism: Emancipation, Transition, Nation, and War.* Minneapolis, MN: University of Minnesota Press, 2002. 8-14.

Konrád, George. *Antipolitics: An Essay.* New York: Houghton Mifflin Harcourt, 1984.

Lyotard, Jean-François. *The Postmodern Condition: A Report on Knowledge.* Translated by Geoff Bennington and Brian Massumi. Minneapolis, MN: University of Minnesota Press, 1984.

Pavić, Milorad. *Dictionary of the Khazars: A Lexicon Novel in 100,000 Words.* New York: Knopf, 1988.

Reynolds, David. *Summits: Six Meetings That Shaped the Twentieth Century.* Jackson, TN: PublicAffairs, 2009.

Ritzer, George. *The McDonaldization of Society: An Investigation into the Changing Character of Contemporary Social Life.* Thousand Oaks, CA: Pine Forge Press, 1996.

Robertson, Roland "Globalization: Time-Space and Homogeneity-Heterogeneity." *Global Modernities.* Edited by Mike Featherstone, Scott Lash, and Roland Robertson. London: Sage, 1995.

Segel, Harold B. *The Columbia Literary History of Eastern Europe since 1945.* New York: Columbia University Press, 2008.

Sim, Stuart. *Irony and Crisis: A Critical History of Postmodern Culture.* Cambridge, UK: Icon, 2002.

Steger, Manfred B. *The Rise of the Global Imaginary: Political Ideologies from the French Revolution to the Global War on Terror.* Oxford, UK: Oxford University Press, 2008.

Taylor, Charles. *Modern Social Imaginaries.* Durham, NC: Duke University Press, 2004.

Taylor, Frederick. *The Berlin Wall: A World Divided, 1961-1989.* New York: HarperCollins, 2006.

Wallerstein, Immanuel. *The Modern World-System I: Capitalist Agriculture and the Origins of the European World-Economy in the Sixteenth Century (Studies in Social Discontinuity).* Toronto: Academic Press, 1980.

Zinoviev, Alexander. *Homo Sovieticus.* Berkeley, CA: Grove/Atlantic, 1986.

SHIFTING PARADIGMS:
EAST EUROPEAN LITERATURES
AT THE TURN OF THE MILLENNIUM

MARCEL CORNIS-POPE

1. Local and Global Frames in Recent East European Literatures:
   Postcommunism, Postmodernism, and Postcoloniality
The changes undergone by East European literary cultures after the events of 1989 have been described differently as a political "liberation" ("decolonization" in the case of the Baltic states), cultural "emancipation," and rediscovery/retrieval of national traditions. Conversely, after the Cold War, East European literatures have rediscovered their bonds and relevance to broader cultural circuits, not only European but also global. To be sure, certain features of post-1989 literary culture were anticipated in the work of dissident and resisting writers as early as the 1960s. These writers made possible the emergence of a range of alternative literary styles, from poetry that exposed the falseness of both totalitarian existence and its apparent normalization after 1989 (Ewa Lipska, Jana Bodnárová, Milán Buzássy, Michal Habaj, Endre Kukorelly, Mircea Dinescu, Ruxandra Cesereanu, Bisera Alikadić, Ani Ilkov, Kiril Merdzhanski, Georgi Gospodinov, Plamen Doinov), to fiction that deconstructed the grand political narratives of the communist age and of the transition period (Bohumil Hrabal, Vládimir Paral, Jáchym Topol, Peter Pišťanek, Ján Litvák, Péter Esterházy, Imre Kertész, Lajos Grendel, Norman Manea, Mircea Cărtărescu, Ádám Bodor, Saulius Tomas Kondrotas, Alek Popov, Ismail Kadare), and to innovative women's literature concerned with "giving voice" to specific female experiences (Andra Nieburga, Gabriela Adameşteanu, Dubravka Ugrešić, Jana Juráňová, Miglena Nikolchina, Emilia Dvoryanova, etc.). The past two decades have also brought back forms of popular and consumerist literature (both Western and East European) censored under communism. These momentous changes occurred in cultures that for the most part lacked a functional public sphere and a successful civil society.

As a consequence of these changes, the post-1989 literary scene in Eastern Europe has appeared muddled for a while, a hodgepodge of conflicting trends. The underground forms of "alternative" art were recovered and integrated into the mainstream, but—as Alexandr Zinoviev remarked in a post-1989 interview—this integration came in many cases too late: "[T]he time when such works would have exploded their intended readers' orthodox values was two or three decades ago" (qtd. in Clowes 17). The literature of "meta-utopian" resistance that Zinoviev and others had been writing could appear out of place in the contradictory ideological environment of postcommunist Europe, which called into question the political significance of intellectual and aesthetic resistance, including that of the former dissidents. Critics have talked with some justification of a post-revolutionary syndrome that included new ethnic and national tensions, sociocultural resentments, and a "regression of the civic consciousness" (Popescu 11) of the former intelligentsia, which after 1989 was preoccupied more with its own survival in a global world dominated by little understood market forces. In the absence of a genuine "culture of freedom" (Popescu 15), the expansion of creative freedoms after 1989 led paradoxically to a partial disorientation and fragmentation of cultural production. The challenge facing artists in the decade following the 1989 changes was not the "end of history," as some Western theorists have argued, but rather "the end of culture," the perceived erosion of their capacity and "right to express [themselves] through sound, motion, and word" (Popescu 78).

Therefore, the debate around the viability of contemporary East European literature, especially the kind that stretches traditional boundaries and expectations, mixing local and global interests, remains very useful. As the corpus of translations and East European contributions to the theory and practice of postcommunist literature increases, this debate can return to normalcy, helping us understand the new features of postcommunist societies and the role that innovative literary and cultural theory can play in response to them. One of the questions raised by critics is to what extent can there be an East European postmodernism "in the absence of a postmodernity specific to Western societies? Can we talk about a *sui generis* or atypical postmodernity [there]?" (Lungu 5). Bust as Dan Lungu argues, postmodernism could develop in "(pre) modern/totalitarian" contexts (9) because the communist culture was perceived as rhetorically "exhausted" and "artificial," needing a revolution in "sensibility," taste, and attitude (6). That is why East European postmodernism was from the beginning a postmodernism of "contestation" (7) but also one of "anticipation" (8), acclimatizing the region's cultures to Western democratic values and attitudes.

In articulating the paradigm of international postmodernism primarily around Western experiences, Western theorists ignore the historical experience of the former communist countries or exhibit a simplistic understanding of the fate of culture under totalitarian communism, as Terry Eagleton does when he argues that "Mao was about as far from socialism as Newt Gingrich" (6), likening Maoism to Gingrich's new conservatism. The sociocultural conditions in Eastern Europe, both before and after 1989, were substantially different from those in the First World. A number of East European countries did not have a full-fledged modernism that postmodernism could react to; nor was there a developed consumer society and information industry that could support the emergence of postmodernity. Even if we limit our analysis to those East European countries that can claim an important avant-garde legacy as well as a market economy, the differences in literary experiences seem striking. In the former communist countries the rewriting of popular genres (the Western, the detective novel, science fiction, pseudo-historical fiction) was far less widespread. Works like *Enciklopedija Mrtvih* (1983; *Encyclopedia of the Dead,* 1989) by Danilo Kiš or *Khazarski recnik* (1984; *Dictionary of the Khazars*, 1988) by Milorad Pavić do not simply foreground the artificiality of narrative conventions; they problematize the very distinction between historical representation and falsification. These and other postmodern histories remind us that for some Croats Serbian history is pure fiction; the history of the Soviet Union, Czechoslovakia, and Yugoslavia has lost its credibility since the dissolution of those states; and the Hungarian and Romanian versions of Transylvanian history are irreconcilable. We take for granted that the communist representation of the past is a willful distortion, but it is still difficult to see what might replace it.

Still, the theoretical concepts of Western postmodernism are illuminating if applied guardedly to the post-1989 changes. Many of the features we associate with the postcommunist societies can be summed up under the paradigm of postmodernity as defined, for example, by Fredric Jameson: the integration of art "into commodity production, the frantic economic urgency of producing fresh waves of ever more novel-seeming goods," the "coexistence of a host of distinct [sociocultural] forces whose effectivity is undecidable," the breakdown of boundaries between high and low aesthetics and between creation and mechanical reproduction, the replacement of stylistic innovation with "blank parody" or pastiche, the mediafication and politicization of every aspect of cultural production, and the emergence of "a whole new culture of the image or the simulacrum" (*Postmodernism*, 4, 6, 15, 19). If we add to this the breakdown of people's sense of the "real"—already badly compromised by communist propaganda but subsequently diluted even further by the "hysteria of production and reproduction of the real" (Baudrillard 44) pursued by some transitional post-communist governments—it is not surprising to find that Baudrillard is "the most popular postmodern theorist among contemporary Russian intellectuals" since the televised 1991 coup attempt described by some participants as a "typical postmodern revolution," a "carnival and corrida" (Boym 220, 221, 222). In Romania, Baudrillard's relevance goes back to the lavishly televised war game against "terrorists" during the Iliescu takeover of the 1989 anti-Ceauşescu revolution, reminding us that "the condition of simulation," which dominates many aspects of post-communist life, "makes it particularly difficult to think about historical change, crisis, disaster or catastrophe" (Boym 220).

Svetlana Boym relates the eruption of postmodernity in the former Soviet empire to the breakdown of the "Soviet master narrative, which produced a distinct kind of conformism as well as a distinct form of dissidence" (224). The place of such master narratives has been taken by a hodge-podge of ideological positions in which "the postcommunist romance with the West" (276) coexists with some form of resurrected nationalism, a nineteenth-century notion of market capitalism overlaps with a distrust of mass consumerism, and over-politicized modes of cultural production vie with unabashed aestheticism and cheap entertainment. I would argue, however, that this ideological jumble that marks an East European moment of *postmodernity* demands a critical reevaluation such as theoretical *postmodernism* can offer. Postmodern theory and literature can challenge the fragmentation of the social sphere into self-interested local stories, but also the counter call for "a single, all-embracing narrative—national, religious, historic, political, or aesthetic—[...a] single dramatic plot with devils and angels, black and white swans, hangmen and victims" (Boym 228).

From the perspective of postmodern theory, the utopian push of orthodox Marxist-Leninism and the nostalgic pull of nationalistic/ ethnocentric interests are equally harmful because they rely on essentialist definitions and rigid teleologies. While exposing the vestiges of totalitarian thinking, postmodern theory and literature can offer suggestions for a post-essentialist sociocultural practice that would recognize local specificities but in a way that would interplay rather than segregate them. The essays published in the special issues of the Romanian journals *Contrapunct* (2.38 [20 September 1991]), *Euphorion* (5.2 [1994]), and *Euresis* (1-2 [1995]) on postmodernism, in *Xenopoliana* (2.1-4 [1994]) on postmodernism, postcommunism, and posthistory, and in the first volume of *Caietele Echinox* (The *Echinox* Notebooks, 2000) on postcolonialism and postmodernism, have taken a step in that direction, emphasizing the role that postmodernism can play in the postcommunist articulation of a "'politics of acknowledgement' that does not leave room for discriminatory interpretations and policies" (Neumann 65).

By reframing discussions of present-day East European cultures through the Western concept of postcoloniality, recent theoretical interventions (see esp. the vol. *Postcolonialism & Postcommunism*) have helped reposition postmodern innovation, giving it a new role in postcommunist societies, namely, that of reconstructing and pluralizing cultural and political institutions, emphasizing "multiple identity" and multicultural/transcultural communication. The postcolonial framework can be helpful to several East European cultures, especially to those located at the intersection of three imperial systems (Ottoman, Habsburg, and Tsarist/Soviet) at least in a symbolic sense: it helps them understand the postcommunist phase as "decolonization," an attempt at liberating their genealogy and traditions not only from the domination of the Soviet paradigm, but also from older colonial vestiges (Ottoman and Austro-Hungarian). Nonetheless, some analysts have objected to the application of a postcolonial framework to Eastern Europe pointing out that, with the exception of the Baltic States and Bessarabia, these countries were never fully "occupied" or considered themselves "colonies" of the Soviet Union. They benefited of a certain "autonomy"—economic, cultural, and eventually political—obtained with great efforts at the end of the Stalinistic period. Still, the majority of the East European countries remained within the ideological sphere of Soviet influence; many of them underwent a process Russification at one time or another, and their cultural and economic production was strictly controlled from Moscow through the canons of socialist realism and forced economic "cooperation" in the Warsaw Pact. Even without Soviet military occupation, the countries of Eastern Europe shared a subaltern position. In that sense at least the status of a "semi-colony" applies to them (see Lefter 118-19). While not "postcolonial" in the sense experienced by the former British, French, Portuguese, or Dutch colonies, the "postcommunist transition" undergone by East European countries has entailed "leaving behind a certain political and cultural 'occupation.' The specific differences are eloquent, but the examination of the *genus proximus* can be useful" (Lefter 119).

Even without adding to it a "postcolonial" facet, the postmodern/ postcommunist condition is fraught with difficulties. As Zygmunt Bauman argued in the eighties, "The ethical paradox of the postmodern condition is that it restores to agents the fullness of moral choice and responsibility while simultaneously depriving them of the comfort of the universal guidance that modern self-confidence once promised" (xxii). And yet, the very absence of universalist solutions encourages the search for a new type of mediator between political and cultural imagination. According to Bauman himself, the late twentieth-century world of irreversible pluralism, in which "a world-scale consensus on world-views [is] unlikely, and all extant *Weltanschauungen* [are] grounded in their respective cultural traditions," demands "specialists in translation between cultural traditions" (5).

There are some hopeful signs that the work of such "translators" between and inside cultures is gaining new momentum. The input of a pluralistic, mediative type of thought is reflected today in the political programs of those democratic governments that have managed to replace the more ambiguous transition governments of the "postcommunist" phase (1989-1995). A host of journals have devoted issues to the analysis of nationalism and ethnic essentialism, but also to the presentation of alternative models of East European "multiculturalism," from the regional coexistence of parallel cultures in the eighteenth and the early nineteenth centuries, to more direct intercultural exchanges that demarginalize minority cultures. While this type of analysis has advanced our awareness of the causes of ethnic fundamentalism in pre- and postcommunist Eastern Europe, it still needs to achieve a more nuanced understanding of national identity, distinguishing between "open" or inclusive and "closed" or exclusive national definitions. Once the multiple linguistic and communitarian roots of East European populations are recognized, national identity can no longer be viewed as monologic but rather as dialogic, a form of "multiple cultural identity" (Neumann 66). As Victor Neumann argues, this view of national identity allows us simultaneously to recognize the "similitude of human values, their common origin," and to "assume pluralism by claiming participation in more cultural identities" (68). A similar dialogic understanding underlies Neumann's concept of multiculturalism: "Multiculturalism is legitimate when it accepts both the ideals derived from cultural specificities and those that refer to two or more cultures simultaneously" (62).

2. *Post-1989 Literatures: Crossing and Redefining Boundaries*

The literature published since 1989 has broached some of these issues, revising traditional definitions of national identity, gender, and race, and blurring the boundaries between high culture and low culture, politics and literature. At this point it is still difficult to anticipate what directions the creative work of Eastern Europe will take. A common post-1989 complaint is that "literature" in the narrow, aesthetic sense, has been largely supplanted by event-oriented and market-driven writing. A retrospective of the editorial year 1990 in Romania began with a characteristic lament—"At no other time in our history have we experienced such a crisis in publications" (Ungureanu 10)—and went on to explain that pre-revolutionary literature was marked by an oppositional and recreative vocation: "the success of December 22 [1989] was also [literature's] own success." The post-revolutionary culture was by contrast plagued by a "self-devouring vocation" (Ungureanu 10). At the end of the 1990s, the poet and novelist Mircea Cărtărescu similarly deplored the fact that "nothing will be as before: the *system* has become unrecognizable, making impossible the reference to the same literary paradigm" (*Postmodernismul românesc* 462). According to Cărtărescu, his own 1980s generation "closed an important literary loop begun two centuries ago that defined a system, that of modernity" (461). After the collapse of the Soviet-backed communist system, East European cultures underwent "[a] chaotic diversification and dissipation of texts, a hybridization of media, [...] an increasing virtualization of 'possible worlds' [that] will turn literature into a form of generalized *mind game*" (462). The main question, asked already at the beginning of the 1990s in the Polish monthly *Dialog* (see "Czy postmodernizm"), was whether this diversification led to a significant restructuring of our understanding of literature or if it simply represented the confusion that attended a prolonged period of transition.

Judging from the fact that much of recent East-Central European literature is still in some form of amorphous transition, there are no simpler answers to this question. The very definition of literature has been diversified, split into conflicting cultural styles, high and low, experimental and traditionalist. Bulgaria now has more than 50 cultural periodicals and about 20 research journals for the humanities, many of them short-lived. It can be argued that Bulgarian literature has broken into several micro-literatures with no common public field. Literature as a whole has been pushed to the periphery: while its "national tradition" has been turned into a list of compulsory school readings, its contemporary experimental branch has been condemned to quasi-irrelevance, having to compete with versions of pulp literature and the "alternative worlds" of music, drugs, and digital networks. The deaths of prominent East-European writers like Danilo Kiš, Bohumil Hrabal, and Heiner Müller has created a significant gap in experimental literature that younger innovative writers have not been able to fill. A host of East-Central European writers have exchanged fiction for journalism in recent years. In "Post-New China," the dominant literary style is a "combination of 'socialist realism' and American pop" (Lu 119), and in the former Soviet Union post-1990 art is caught in debilitating paradoxes: "while the 'high art' of cinema, experimental fiction, and conceptualism replays the history of kitsch and recovers everyday life, the galleries of the new merchants make a scandal out of art and life, and the born-again commercial culture aspires to the good taste of old and new Russia, developing reverently its own mythical history in pseudo-Russian style" (Boym 225).

But what to some may appear as insuperable incongruities, others may take as signs of a new inclusiveness, proving the versatility and adaptability of contemporary literature, rather than its "exhaustion." The present literary map is not only more diverse, but also richer in transitional and cross-genre forms. The growing editorial interest in previously censored manuscripts and translations from the work of the diaspora has filled important gaps, expanding and restructuring the corpus of East-Central European (post)communist literatures.

In Romania, the questioning of specific political and literary agendas was central to the debates that emerged in the 1990s, affecting the aura that both postmodernism and dissident writing had during the previous decade. To Gheorghe Grigurcu, for example, postmodernism was a bastardly and "immodest" trend, especially in its programmatic manifestations (6-7). Across the Prut River, in the former Soviet Moldova that in the 1980s had its own group of innovative poets writing in Romanian (Ștefan Baștovoi, Emilian Galaicu-Păun, Dumitru Crudu, Vasile Gârbeț), postmodernism was rejected in more strident terms, as the expression of a "diabolic" and "pornographic" deviation from true cultural traditions. Leaving aside such intolerant reactions that were fortunately rare, the debate about postmodernism included a reexamination of the complicated strategies (metaphoric indirection, rhetorical mystification, etc.) that writers had to resort to in order to bypass communist censorship. By contrast, post-1989 literature broached many previously tabooed subjects with a direct, unadorned approach. Whole thematic areas (such as the Soviet concentration camps, life in the Warsaw ghetto and the Warsaw uprising, the post-war Soviet occupation, émigré issues) were rediscovered and tapped into at the end of the eighties and the nineties. Some of these works have a particularly poignant humor, such as Nicolae Esinencu's *Un moldovean la închisoare* (A Moldavian in Prison; 1989) that insinuates ironically that life in prison was not worse than life lived in the "freedom" allowed by the Soviets. Another topic that had to wait several decades for an honest representation was ethnic persecution under the Nazi and the Soviet totalitarian regimes (for example, both Mihail Sebastian's anti-Nazi journal and Ion D. Sârbu's anti-Stalinistic memoirs could only be published after 1989). World War Two itself was approached in a new, unsparing light that did not distinguish between losers and victors. Matei Vișniec's short plays in *Caii la fereastră* (Horses at the Window, performed in Romania and France in 1992), and *Teatru descompus, sau, Omul-lada-de-gunoi; Femeia ca un câmp de luptă* (Decomposed Theater, or Man-as-a-Dumpster; Woman as a Battlefield; 1998) focus on heinous forms of behavior during war—cowardice, bestiality, greed, violence against women. The war is de-ideologized, presented in a light that deprives it of any justification or positive resolution. Patriotic slogans, national interests, and geopolitical reasons pale before the crude reality of carnage, persecution, and inhumanity.

A new generation of writers emerging in the 1990s redefined the relationship with postmodernism in ways that have weakened its hold on the literary field even further. A 1994 issue of the magazine *Luceafărul* (The Morning Star) described this post-1989 generation as less experimental and aesthetically programmatic (see especially Ulici and Stanca). The urban-ironic aestheticism of the previous generation, they argued, had been counterbalanced by an integrative type of literature that mapped broader geocultural areas (not only metropolitan cities, but also small towns, not only the "center" but also the periphery). A certain "Adamic" candor intertwined with a dark surrealistic strain was claimed by the poets featured in a collective anthology entitled *Sfâșierea lui Morfeu* ("The Dismemberment of Morpheus" 1994), edited by Dan-Silviu Boerescu in polemical response to Ihab Hassan's *The Dismemberment of Orpheus: Toward a Postmodern Literature* (1971). In his introduction, Boerescu constructs a mythic genealogy for this dark Adamic poet: he is said to be "born from the rib of a negating Robinson," the latter metaphor designating the poet of the 1980s stranded on the shores of an incomprehensible history. By contrast to his deconstructive predecessor who tried to survive by subverting history, the new Adamic poet is more interested in "integration and structuration." His approach is expansive rather than "recessive," androgynous rather than androcentric, accepting rather than rejecting, and so on.

It is true, however, that postmodernism itself has promoted a hybridization and problematization of literary categories that can lead to its own unraveling. This is clearly illustrated in the work of Romania's most important contemporary writer, Mircea Cărtărescu. Cărtărescu's recently translated novel, *Nostalgia* (2005), contains elements of the "*mixtum compositum* of antimodernism (understood primarily as *anti-lyricism*), nonmodernism (post-avant-garde, surrealism), late modernism, and postmodernism" that Cărtărescu himself attributes to post-World War Two Romanian literature (*Postmodernismul românesc* 137). But Cărtărescu's prose complicates/rewrites these earlier paradigms, illustrating the radical potential of hybridity and polymorphism. Each of the five interlaced novellas that compose *Nostalgia*—"The Roulette Player," "Mentardy," "The Twins," "REM," and the Epilogue ("The Architect")—dramatizes the liberating potential of innovative narration, but also the political and poetic constraints that regulate the work of narrators and their audiences. Rich and protean, mixing high and low styles (narrative of growth, autobiography, philosophic parable, science fiction, gothic horror, erotic narrative), these stories contribute to the post-communist/postmodern diversification of the East European narrative production, calling into questions pre-1989 fictional categories. Significantly, the first Romanian edition of *Nostalgia* (titled *Visul/ The Dream*) was published in the cusp year 1989, after being circulated in manuscript through the eighties. The book's various narrators dramatize the difficulties of creative narration under communism but also the new opportunities for a self-problematized concept of literature at a time when the grand ideological narrative of communism was approaching dissolution. The metaphor used by Cărtărescu to describe the narrative structure resulting from this conflict of conditions is that of a web of "chaotically placed loops and holes," created by "a spider under the influence of a drug" (263). The spider web functions alternatively as a deterministic metaphor, suggesting the inescapable economy of destiny and plot; but also as a metafictional metaphor emphasizing the self-propelled nature of narrative, with characters gaining provisional release from the constrictions of the web, but only to the extent they become weavers of their own stories.

The Czech writers and critics of the post-1989 period have been similarly involved with questions of literary experimentation and revision. As Lubomír Machala points out in *Literární bludiště* (Literary Labyrinth; 2001), postmodernism became a fashionable term in the Czech discourse of the first half of the 1990s, even if it was not always attended by a "systematic reflection on the problems of postmodernism" (20). A dazzling example of Czech postmodernism, published four years after the "Velvet Revolution," is Jáchym Topol's *Sestra* (1994; *City Sister Silver*; 2000). Topol's own biography as the son of the playwright Josef Topol, grandson of the writer Karel Schulz, lyricist for his rock performing brother Filip Topol, and the youngest signatory of the Charter 77, is a remarkable illustration of the transition between generations and cultural paradigms. Before 1989, Topol participated in the creation of samizdat publications, contributing to the *Revolver Revue* and *Respekt* and publishing a collection of poems in samizdat. After 1989, he published a number of innovative works, including *City Sister Silver*, winner of the Egon Hostovský Prize for best book of 1994. This novel offers a dizzying picture of the postcommunist urban scene populated by pleasure-loving and semi-criminal hustlers, whose exploits are chronicled by a first-person narrator, appropriately named Potok ("stream" in Czech), because he shifts identities (actor, detainee, psychiatric hospital inmate, etc.). Topol's novel recalls Anthony Burgess's _A Clockwork Orange_, but also Cărtărescu's _Visul/Nostalgia_: as in the latter novel, characters get involved in telling and analyzing dreams, to the point where reality and dream can no longer be extricated. Also like in Cărtărescu's novel, Potok searches for his "sister" or female soul mate, finding her eventually in the character of Černá ("black" in Czech), a Madonna avatar. Not only thematically, but also structurally and stylistically, the novel breaks out of traditional molds, experimenting with a polyphony of languages and codes, from Standard Czech to slang, with elements of foreign languages mixed in (Russian, German, newly created words).

Another novel that exploits the incongruities of language and form, as the Czech Republic shifted into postcommunism, is _Výchova dívek v Čechách_ (1994; _Bringing up Girls in Bohemia_; 1997) by Michal Viewegh. The narrator wants to write a postmodern novel, but his story of the relationship between an impoverished young teacher and the free-spirited daughter of a postcommunist crime boss fits better a "transition novel," focused on the tragicomic disparities between the post-1989 capitalist world and pre-1989 Prague (see also Cornis-Pope and Neubauer, _History of the Literary Cultures of East-Central Europe_ 1: 80-81). Viewegh divests his novel of linguistic and narrative complications, offering a slightly sensational plot that leads to a tragic denouement. Like other novels of transition, this book is generously populated with socialist goons, religious cults, and money grabbers who represent the new breed of postcommunist "entrepreneurs." Interestingly, in this novel the new capitalist is female, Králová. Predictably for a character in "transition," she dies in a car crash caused by a suicidal urge to experience the limits of her new "freedom." While there is no postcommunist nostalgia in Viewegh's fiction—his previous novel, _Bájecná léta pod psa_ (The Blissful Years of Lousy Living; 1993), confirmed this— _Bringing up Girls in Bohemia_ offers an unsentimental view of both communism and of the transition away from it.

A noteworthy category of writers, specific to the post-1989 period, is that of the shuttlers between East and West. With the access to the West increased and the possible interconnections diversified beyond the traditional categories of exile, émigré, and refugee, a number of East-

Central European writers have become again travelers between cultures, much like some of the late nineteenth- and early twentieth-century multilingual and avant-garde writer-artists. In the recently published *Columbia Literary History of Eastern Europe since 1945*, Harold B. Segel devotes Chapter 10 ("Glimpses of Other Worlds") to East European writers traveling abroad, especially to the US. The chapter discusses briefly the literature of the Romanians Liliana Ursu and Daniela Crăsnaru, the Slovene Tomaž Šalamun and Drago Jančar, the Serbs David Albahari, Nina Živančević, and Vladimir Pištalo, the Bulgarians Bozhidar Bozhilov and Lilyana Stefanova, the Poles Kazimierz Brandys, Ewa Lipska, Marzena Broda, and Adam Zagajewski, the Czechs Miroslav Holub, and the East Germans Günther Kunnert, who at different times before and after 1989 focused on "contact zones" and crosscultural experiences. Their works range from personal reportage and realistic fiction to poetry of reflection, but most often they mix genres as in Albahari's *Cink* (1995; *Tsing*, 1997), a complex work that blends autobiography (memories of his father), with travelogue and fantasy, pursuing a personal history and the history of America. Likewise, Pištalo's *Tales from the Whole World* views America from the conflicting perspectives of the immigrant and the traveler, resulting in an ironic and sometimes confusing narrative.

Equally productive is the category of East-Central European writers who have migrated to the Mediterranean area after 1989 (see Mauceri, "Writing outside the Borders: Personal Experience and History in the Works of Helga Schneider and Helena Janeczek"; also her articles on Sarah Zuhra Lukanic, Mihai Mircea Butcovan, Ornela Vorpsi, and Edith Bruck). Particularly intriguing are the cases of the Albanian writer Ornela Vorpsi, who lives in France but who writes in Italian; or of Barbara Serdakowski, born in Poland, growing up in Morocco, transferred to Canada, married to an Italian artist who emigrated to Venezuela, finally to settle in Italy and write in a plurilinguistic/multicultural mode that translates her own existence. Another paradigmatic example in Mauceri's work is the Romanian Mihai Mircea Butcovan, born in Transylvania and who emigrated to Italy at the age of twenty to reinvent himself as a transcultural writer. His recent *Allunaggio di un immigrato inamorato* (The Moon Landing of an Immigrant in Love) is a novel-diary that recapitulates a failed love relationship with a rich Italian lawyer-activist while at the same time narrating a story of cultural uprooting and readjustment to the metropolitan West, Milano in this case (the novel reminds of Raymond Federman's *Smiles on Washington Square*, where a French-Jewish immigrant experiences in similar ways love and disappointment with both the New World and with an activist lover who introduces him to it).

Maria Mauceri has also offered the first synthesis on East European émigré writing in Italy, "L'Europa venuta dall'Europa (dall'Albania alla Russia)" (The Europe Arrived from Europe [from Albania to Russia]) published in Armando Gnisci's *Nuovo Planetario Italiano* (New Italian Planetarium). Subtitled, *Geografia e antologia della letteratura della migrazione in Italia e in Europa* (Geography and Anthology of Migration Literature in Italy and Europe; 2006), Gnisci's historical-theoretical anthology attempts to canonize the new immigrant literature but also to redefine Italian literature as multicultural. Drawing on multicultural authors like Salman Rushdie, Joseph Brodsky, and Derek Walcott, Gnisci's general introduction emphasizes a number of favorite themes: the poetics of worlds, the creolization and decolonization of Europe (see also Gnisci's other work, *Creolizzare l'Europa*/The Creolization of Europe), and the anthropological nature of migration and its literary expression (*Nuovo Planetario Italiano* 13-39). While quoting Joseph Brodsky's comments on the drama of multiethnic emigration, Gnisci acknowledges the global human dimensions of migratory trends. His entire discussion is framed by the concepts of "dispatrio" (dispatriation) as the defining condition of being human in the twentieth-century, and of "Patrie imaginarie" (imagined homelands) borrowed from Salman Rushdie, as an antidote to uprooting.

Mauceri's own argument in the chapter "L'Europa venuta dall'Europa" (The Europe Arrived from Europe) and in the one that precedes it ("Scrivere ovunque"/Writing Everywhere) builds on Gnisci's key concepts but adapts them to the situation of migrant East-Central European writers. According to her, the new immigrant writers from Eastern Europe and the Third World do not fit the traditional paradigm of cross-cultural writers like Joyce or Beckett, whose mobility did not take them out of the "Western literary canon." The

> current migrant writers are viewed with indifference by the institu-
> tionalized literary world, being considered an exotic ethnic
> phenomenon that some publishers exploit according to the fashion
> of the moment; they are ignored even in their countries of origin

for which they represent writers without a home country. In effect, they do not have a unique home, if by this term one understands a country of origin; in reality they have found a common home without boundaries: literature itself" ("Scrivere ovunque," *Nuovo Planetario* 49).

The writers who illustrate this changed condition in Mauceri's "L'Europa venuta dall'Europa" chapter of Gnisci's anthology include the Albanian Gëzim Hajdari and Ron Kubati, the Croat Vesna Stanić, the Bosnian Bozidar Stanisić and Tamara Jadrejcić, the Romanian Mihai Mircea Butcovan, the Slovak Jarmila Ockayova, and the Polish Barbara Serdakowski. The condition of migration, oneiric and mythic at the same time, is well summed up in Jarmila Ockayova's dream-like narrative, appropriately titled *L'essenziale e invisibile agli occhi* (The Essential is Invisible to the Eyes).

Franca Sinopoli, who is coeditor with Gnisci of a theoretical volume on comparative literature, *Comparare i comparatismi* (Comparing and Comparatisms; 1995), has also contributed significant articles and papers to the discussion of post-Cold War literature from a multicultural-comparative perspective. Her very definition of comparatism has changed over time, influenced both by an increased awareness of globalization and by the counter-trend of multicultural diversification within a national literature such as the Italian. One of the effects of Italy's recent transformation from a country of emigration into one of immigration has been the publication of literary texts by migrant writers coming from European and non-European countries (the Balkans and the countries of the former socialist block, the Magreb area and the former Italian colonies in Africa, the Middle East and the Far East, and Latin America). A special conference on Italophone migrant literature was held at the Università di Roma "La Sapienza" (where both Gnisci and Sinopoli teach) in March 2005. Its theme, "Il dispatrio e i confini letterari" (Dispatriation and Literary Borders) suggests very well the paradoxical dialectic of deconstructing/reconstructing the boundaries of a national culture through immigrant transplants.

The research carried out by Gnisci, Mauceri, and Sinopoli relies on a rich data bank created in 1997 at Sapienza University's Department of Italian Studies (see BASILI). This online data base records bibliographical information for about 300 Italian-speaking migrant writers with 693 recorded works, a number of East European writers included. The

"LettERANZA" website (http://letterranza.org/autori/paesi.html) is another useful archive focused on writers from East-Central Europe (seven from Albania, two from the former Yugoslavia, four from Romania, two from Slovakia, one from the Ukraine), who have settled in Italy, writing poetry, fiction, and nonfiction mostly in Italian. The Albanian writers Gëzim Hajdari, Ron Kubati, and Gino Luka have considered Italy their home for almost two decades. Other ethnic writers have established themselves there more recently. In their poetry, one still hears the desperation of the uprooted:

[N]on tengo niente	I have nothing
né case né terre	no house, no land
nemmeno	not even a current
un conto corrente	account in a bank
mi affido al vento	I entrust myself to the wind
incostante stridente	inconstant and loud
ormai non mi spavento	no longer scared of it
… non bevo non fumo	… I don't drink, I don't smoke
faccio poco all'amore	I seldom make love
sono un nulla facente	I'm a do-nothing
non spero	without hope
e non credo più in niente	no belief in anything
cavalco la vita	Life gallops ahead
… cavalco cavalco	… I ride it and ride it
ma domani la smonto	but tomorrow I'll dismount
me ne vado in banca	and go to the bank
e mi faccio un conto	to open an account

(Viorel Boldis, "Il Conto"/The Account)

The Albanian émigré writer Hajdari, considered one of the best poets in Italian, winner of the Montale prize, defines memorably the effort to recreate a home in exile: "Ogni giorno creo una nuova patria / in cui muoio e rinasco quando voglio" (Everyday I invent a new homeland / in which I die and come alive whenever I want). In her own article on Hajdari, Franca Sinopoli emphasizes his two related themes: exile and absence, vision and blindness, or as Hajdari himself put it in a poem from 1993, "Il mio corpo / nato in un paese povero / è un verso cieco / senza memoria" (My body / born in an impoverished village / is a blind verse / without memory; *Sasso contro vento* 25). Sinopoli describes accurately Hajdari's transformation of the themes of exile and absence, moving from autobiography (his own deracination) to a mode of feeling and knowing that transcends the circumstances of migration. The poetic symbols become more complex, linking important archetypes together (stone, shadow, songs of water and fire), but the emotion continues to darken ("perché sempre più tenebrosi / i miei pensieri / in Occidente?"— why are my thoughts/ increasingly darker / in the West?; *Pietre al confine* 31). The realization of being an "other," caught between cultures, is very much part of the literature written by Hajdari and other of his transcultural colleagues (see in this sense the volume on *Representation of the "Other/s" in the Mediterranean World*, edited by Kuran-Burcoglu and Miller).

In an article-talk presented in Santiago de Compostela in 2007, "Virtual Spaces: Hypotheses for a Mediterranean Model of Diaspora Literary Studies from the Italian Point of View," Sinopoli expanded her interest in Mediterranean migration and diaspora literary studies into a Euro-Mediterranean model of literary studies. Drawing on the intercultural work carried out by members of the Institute of World Literature at the Slovak Academy of Science and by a comparative research team at Sapienza University during 1995-2000, her proposal emphasized the idea of a Euro-Mediterranean "trans-continentality" as an alternative model of European identity. Inspired also by two multinodal/regional literary histories, one on East-Central Europe (ed. Marcel Cornis-Pope and John Neubauer), the other on the literatures of the Iberic peninsula (in preparation), Sinopoli argued in the "Virtual Spaces" talk that the wave of immigrant writers from Eastern Europe and other cultural areas virtualize the space of Italian literary culture, deconstructing the national historiographic discourse by opposing to it the porous literary spaces shaped by transcultural writers. The literary production contributed by immigrant writers hybridizes the host culture, calling into question the concept of a stable monolingual national tradition based upon the coincidence of language, people, and national state.

However, we can take this argument further, as Stephen G. Kellman does, to emphasize the code-switching and *Translingual Imagination* of immigrant writers, which problematize any medium of communication, including that of the native culture of the immigrants. Writers themselves have often understood translingualism as a more conflicted condition, as when Assia Djebar defines herself as a "writer of the passage" between languages (32) or when the Ukrainian Marina Sorina tries to find a home in an interplay of languages, translating her own message and those of others between Russian, Ukrainian, Hebrew, and Italian. Her first novel, *Voglio un marito italiano* (I Desire an Italian Husband), written directly in Italian, promises to stop the cultural and linguistic "errancy" and find some mooring (in seriousness or in jest) in the new culture, but even this work shifts language registers and codes. To use Sinopoli's terminology ("Migrazione/letteratura"), in straddling languages, cultural experiences, and geopolitical boundaries, "translingual" East European writers promote a "poetics of intercultural translation," "transition," and "transitoriness."

WORKS CITED

Albahari, David. *Cink.* Belgrade: Dereta, 1995. Trans. by the author as *Tsing.* Evanston, IL: Northwestern University Press, 1997.

BASILI – Banca Dati degli Scrittori Immigrati in Lingua Italiana (Data Bank of Immigrant Writers in Italian Language): www.disp.let.uniroma1.it/basili2001 (Sapienza Università di Roma).

Baudrillard, Jean. *Simulations.* Trans. Paul Foss, Paul Patton, and Philip Bleitchman. New York: Semio-text(e)/Columbia University, 1983.

Bauman, Zygmunt. *Legislators and Interpreters: On Modernity, Postmodernity and Intellectuals.* Cambridge: Polity Press, 1987.

Boerescu, Dan-Silviu, ed. *Sfîșierea lui Morfeu: O antologie* (The Dismemberment of Morpheus). Bucharest: Phoenix, 1994.

Boym, Svetlana. *Common Places: Mythologies of Everyday Life in Russia.* Cambridge: Harvard University Press, 1994.

Butcovan, Mihai Mircea. *Allunaggio di un immigrato inamorato* (The Moon Landing of an Immigrant in Love). Nardò: Besa, 2006.

Burgess, Anthony. *Earthly Powers.* London: William Heinemann, 1962.

Cărtărescu, Mircea. *Nostalgia.* Trans. Julian Semilian; introduction Andrei Codrescu. New York: New Directions, 2005. Trans. of *Visul* (Dream). First, censored edition, Bucharest: Cartea Românească, 1989. Second, restored edition, Bucharest: Humanitas, 1993.

Cărtărescu, Mircea. *Postmodernismul românesc* (Romanian Postmodernism). Bucharest: Humanitas, 1999.

Clowes, Edith W. *Russian Experimental Fiction: Resisting Ideology after Utopia.* Princeton: Princeton University Press, 1993.

Cornis-Pope, Marcel, and John Neubauer, eds. *History of the Literary Cultures of East-Central Europe: Junctures and Disjunctures in the 19th and 20th Century.* Vol. 1.

Amsterdam/Philadelphia: John Benjamins, 2004. Vol. 2: Amsterdam/Philadelphia: John Benjamins, 2006. Vol. 3: Amsterdam/Philadelphia: John Benjamins, 2007.

"Czy postmodernizm jest dobry na postkomunizm" (Is Postmodernism a Cure to Post-communism?). *Dialog* 11 (1991): 113-23.

Djebar, Assia. *Queste voci che mi assediano. Scrivere nella lingua dell'altro* (Voices that Besiege Me: Writing in the Language of the Other). Trad. Roberto Salvadori. Milano: il Saggiatore, 2004.

Eagleton, Terry. "The Contradictions of Postmodernism." *New Literary History* 28.1 (Winter 1997): 1-6.

Esinencu, Nicolae. *Un moldovean la închisoare* (A Moldavian in Prison). Chişinău (Kishinev): Literatura artistică, 1989.

Federman, Raymond. *Smiles on Washington Square (A Love Story of Sorts)*. New York: Thunder's Mouth, 1985.

Gnisci, Armando. *Creolizzare l'Europa. Letteratura e migrazione* (The Creolization of Europe: Literature and Migration). Roma: Meltemi, 2003.

_____., ed. *Nuovo Planetario Italiano. Geografia e antologia della letteratura della migrazione in Italia e in Europa* (The New Italian Planetarium: Geography and Anthology of Migration Literature in Italy and Europe; 2006). Troina: Città Aperta Edizioni, 2006.

Gnisci, Armando and Francesca Sinopoli, eds. *Comparare i comparatismi. La comparatistica letteraria oggi in Europa e nel mondo* (Comparing and Comparatisms: Literary Comparatism Today in Europe and the World). Roma: Lithos, 1995.

Grigurcu, Gheorghe. "Postmodernismul, un clasicism corupt" (Postmodernism, a Corrupted Classicism). *Euphorion* 5.2 (1994): 6-7.

Hajdari, Gëzim. *Sasso contro vento / Gurë kundër erës* (Stone against the Wind). Milano: Laboratorio delle Arti, 1995.

_____. *Pietre al confine* (Stones at the Border). Ancona: Assoc. culturale "E-ssenza" Metrica," 1998.

Hassan, Ihab. *The Dismemberment of Orpheus: Toward a Postmodern Literature*. Madison: University of Wisconsin Press, 1971. 2nd ed. rev., 1982.

Jameson, Fredric. *Postmodernism, or, the Cultural Logic of Late Capitalism*. Durham: Duke University Press, 1991.

Kellman, Steven G., ed. *Switching Languages. Translingual Writers Reflect on Their Craft*. Lincoln and London: University of Nebraska Press, 2003.

_____. *The Translingual Imagination*. Lincoln and London: University of Nebraska Press, 2000.

Kiš, Danilo. *Enciklopedija mrtvih*. Zagreb: Globus, 1983. Trans. Michael Henry Heim as *The Encyclopedia of the Dead*. Evanston: Northwestern University Press, 1997.

Kuran-Burcoglu, Nedret, and Susan Gilson Miller, eds. *Representation of the "Other/s" in the Mediterranean World and Their Impact on the Region*. Istanbul: The Isis Press, 2005.

Lefter, Ion Bogdan. "Poate fi considerat postcomunismul un post-colonialism?" (Can Postcommunism Be Considered a Post-Colonialism?). *Postcolonialism & Post-comunism*, 117-19.

Lu, Sheldon Hsiao-peng. "Art, Culture, and Cultural Criticism in Post-New China." *New Literary History* 28 (Winter 1997): 111-33.

Lungu, Dan. "Postmodernism, România, postmodernitate" (Postmodernism, Postmodernity and Romania). *Amphion* 3 (2002): 5-9.

Machala, Lubomír. *Literární bludiště. Bilance polistopadové prózy* (Literary Labyrinth: Post-November Prose in the Balance). Prague: Brána, 2001.

Mauceri, M. Cristina. "L'Albania è una ferita che brucia ancora. Intervista a Ornela Vorpsi, scrittrice albanese che vive in Francia e scrive in italiano" (Albania is a Wound that still Hurts: Interview with Ornela Vorpsi, Albanian Female Writer who Lives in France and Writes in Italian). *Kuma. Creolizzare l'Europa,* n. 11, 2006. www.disp.let.uniroma1.it/kuma.htm

_____. "Dove abito è il mio villaggio. A colloquio con Edith Bruck" (Where I Live Is My Village: A Dialogue with Edith Bruck). *Kuma. Creolizzare l'Europa,* n. 11, 2006. www.disp.let.uniroma1.it/kuma.htm

_____. "L'Europa venuta dall'Europa (dall'Albania alla Russia)" (The Europe Arrived from Europe [from Albania to Russia])." In Gnisci, *Nuovo Planetario Italiano.* 113-54.

_____. "Helga Schneider: la scrittura come testimonianza" (Helga Schneider: Writing as Testimonial). *Kuma. Creolizzare l'Europa,* n. 6, Aprile 2003.

_____. "Scrivere per non perdersi: Mihai Mircea Butcovan, osservatore 'romeno'" (Writing to Avoid Getting Lost: Mihai Mircea Butcovan, "Romanian" Observer). *Kuma. Creolizzare l'Europa,* n. 11, 2006.

_____. "Writing outside the Borders: Personal Experience and History in the Works of Helga Schneider and Helena Janeczek." *Across Genres, Generations and Borders: Italian Women Writing Lives,* ed. Susanna Scarparo and Rita Wilson, 140-51. Cranbury, NJ: Fairleigh Dickinson University Press, 2004.

Neumann, Victor. "Perspective comparative asupra filozofiei multiculturale" (Comparative Perspectives on Multicultural Philosophy). *Postcolonialism & Postcomunism,* 55-70.

Ockayova, Jarmila. *L'essenziale e invisibile agli occhi* (The Essential Is Invisible to the Eyes). Milano: Baldini Castoldi Dalai, 1997.

Pavić, Milorad. *Hazarski rečnik: roman leksikon u 100.000 reči.* Belgrade: Prosveta, 1984. Trans. Christina Pribićević-Zorić as *Dictionary of the Khazars: A Lexicon Novel in 100,000 Words.* New York: Knopf/Random House, 1988.

Pištalo, Vladimir. *Priče iz celog sveta* (Tales from the Whole World). Belgrade: Stubovi kulture, 1997.

Popescu, Marius. *Oglinda spartă: Teatrul românesc după 1989* (The Broken Mirror: Post-1989 Romanian Theater). Bucharest: Unitext, 1997.

Postcolonialism & Postcomunism. Caietele Echinox (Postcolonialism and Postcommunism. The *Echinox* Notebooks), vol. 1. Cluj-Napoca: Dacia, 2001.

Sârbu, Ion D. *Jurnalul unui jurnalist fără jurnal* (The Journal of a Journalist without a Journal). 2 vols. Craiova: Scrisul Românesc, 1991–93.

Sebastian, Mihail. *Jurnal 1935–1944.* Bucharest: Humanitas, 1997. Trans. Patrick Camiller as *Journal, 1935-1944.* Intro. Radu Ioanid. Chicago: Dee, 2000.

Segel, Harold B. *The Columbia Literary History of Eastern Europe since 1945.* New York: Columbia University Press, 2008.

Sinopoli, Franca. "Hajdari, due versioni di 'Campana di mare'" (Hajdari, Two Versions of "The Sea Bell"). *Kuma* 3 (Jan. 2002).

_____., ed. *La letteratura europea vista dagli altri* (European Literature as Seen by Others). Roma, Meltemi, 2003.

_____. "Migrazione/letteratura: due proposte di indagine critica" (Migration/ Literature: Two Proposals for Critical Research). http://www.alef-fvg.it/immigrazione/temi/ culture/2003/sinopoli.pdf

_____., ed. *Il mito della letteratura europea* (The Myth of European Literature) Roma: Meltemi, 1999.

_____. "Virtual Spaces: Hypotheses for a Mediterranean Model of Diaspora Literary Studies from the Italian Point of View." Paper presented at the Conference of the ICLA Publication Committee, Santiago de Compostela, June 8-9, 2007.

Sorina, Marina. *Voglio un marito italiano* (I Desire an Italian Husband). Vicenza: Ed. Punto d'Incontro, 2006.

Stanca, Dan. "Generația '90, necesara ruptură de optzecism" (The 1990s Generation: Its Necessary Break with the Generation of the 1980s). *Luceafărul* 9, new series (3 August 1994): 15.

Topol, Jáchym *Sestra* (Sister). Brno: Atlantis, 1994. Trans. Alex Zucker as *City Sister Silver*. North Haven, CT: Catbird, 2000.

Ulici, Lucian. "A șaptea generație: o introducere" (The Seventh Generation: An Introduction). *Luceafărul* 9, new series (3 August 1994): 3.

Viewegh, Michal. *Bájecná léta pod psa*. Prague: Český spisovatel, 1995. Fragment trans. O. T. Chalkstone as *The Blissful Years of Lousy Living*. http://www. arts.gla.ac.uk/ Slavonic/Viewegh.htm

Viewegh, Michal. *Výchova dívek v Čechách*. Prague: Český spisovatel, 1994. Trans. A.G. Brain as *Bringing up Girls in Bohemia*. London: Readers International, 1997.

Vişniec, Matei. *Caii la fereastră* (Horses at the Window). 1992. Bucharest: Aula, 2001.

Vişniec, Matei. *Teatru descompus, sau, Omul-lada-de-gunoi; Femeia ca un câmp de luptă* (Decomposed Theater, or Man as a Garbage Can; Woman as a Battle Field). Bucharest: Cartea Românească, 1998.

COSMALLOGY:
MIRCEA CĂRTĂRESCU'S *NOSTALGIA* —
THE BODY, THE CITY, THE WORLD

CHRISTIAN MORARU

The city that you live in is the world.
— Marcus Aurelius, *Meditations*

1. *All, Aleph,* álloi

Here comes the world of bodies.
— Jean-Luc Nancy, *Corpus*

I truly love my world, the world of Bucharest, yet I am fully aware that Bucharest is concomitantly *all*, the Aleph.
— Mircea Cărtărescu, "Realismul poeziei tinere" (Young Poets' Realism)

I used to imagine myself spreading out, by an act of will, at least as far as Bucharest's outskirts, all the way to the railway tracks and beltways surrounding the city like a membrane wrapped around a cell.... [T]he city would thus become my own artificial body, and so I could give the city my own name, I could soak it in my own desires.
— Mircea Cărtărescu, *Orbitor* (Dazzling)

"The world is one; and it is more interesting than Budapest," Hungarian writer György Konrád intimates in his 1984 book *Antipolitics.*[1] Around the same time, a few hundred miles East of Konrád's Budapest, Romanian writer Mircea Cărtărescu has a similar insight, with a difference: the world is one, but its globality can be experienced as such locally, in and as Bucharest. If the communist regime sought to remove Romania's capital from the world's cultural and political arena and make it into the place the dissidents of the 1980s called "internal exile," Cărtărescu fights off the twin incarceration of the city and of himself in it by opening Bucharest out onto what his 1985 poetry volume calls the "All" (*Totul*).[2]

Drawing from this and other earlier works, his 1993 novel *Nostalgia* lays out this holistic vision with astounding method.[3] Forlorn and dilapidated, plagued by all kinds of shortages and blackouts, Cold-War Bucharest is, literally and allegorically, written by the book back into the wider world and so rendered "interesting" as a site of worldly "oneness." Conversely, in Cărtărescu's work the city and its people reclaim their place in the global world: they are, we gather, part and parcel of the planet's living body while the latter, in all its irreducible strangeness and complexity, is here, with them. Thus, from beneath the defaced surface of Ceau□escu's "golden-age" Bucharest, the writer summons strange faces and the very face of worldly strangeness. From within the maze of concrete ghettoes, he conjures up mind-blowing, cosmic panoramas by bridging physical and metaphysical gaps. In dialogue with E.T.A. Hoffmann, Franz Kafka, Gabriel García Márquez, Jorge Luis Borges, and other classics of the fantastic, the absurd, the oneiric, and magical realism, he unearths a maimed metropolis whose heart throbs in the world's wider body and whose idiosyncratic mix of socialist squalor and "Paris of the Balkans" charm he flips over to display unsuspected depths, passageways, and ramifications into the hidden, the elsewhere, and the otherwise—into the world's larger corporeality. Where the Western mind relegates his city to an alien and cloistered geography overrun by vampires and ruled by dictators razing entire cities to make room for their sepulchral head-quarters, Cărtărescu unfolds a borderless dreamland.

The oneiric politics of *Nostalgia's* urban imaginary was lost on Cărtărescu's readers neither when the book first came out in spring 1989, under the title *Visul* (The Dream) and butchered by censorship, nor a few years later, when it was reissued in unabridged form. Its stag-geringly holistic vision went against officially upheld "tradition," an exceptionalist-solipsistic notion derived from early twentieth-century, agrarian-Orthodox and nationalist-chauvinistic doctrines, on which the Communist Party was falling back in the late 1980s to legitimate its rejection of perestroika and generally reauthorize itself. The novel sym-bolically liberates the city's body politic by linking it up with other urban bodies and bodies of work, with other places and contexts, with their texts, and styles. A *mise en abyme* of this stylistic and intertextually postmodern overhaul of nationalism, the characters' bodies are set free, allowed to enjoy their ambiguous and multifaceted physicality, to cele-brate their fluidity, to evolve, mutate, and otherwise overflow preset taxonomies and codifications. Since the body of the nation, "cultural identity," and tradition as this identity's genealogy are collective constructs not only structurally homological to the private person's identity but also bound up with it, the communal and the personal are *both* reconstructed as either undergoes this sort of magical reimagining. Thus, redrawing the boundaries of this multidimensional corporeality, Cărtărescu fleshes out a worldview of cross-cultural connections, conversations, and affinities that cast the nation's bodies and minds amidst others in the world, in a radically de-fining, politically and intellectually emancipating situation. By the same token, he brings to the fore an unsettling dynamic of self and other that eats into the traditionally prevailing monolithic view of identity by highlighting the role others and alterity in general *already* hold in the structure of the nation's selves regardless of how painstakingly policed the national frontiers are and, inside them, no matter how strict the enforcement of body and mind boundaries purports to be.

The crossing of both political and corporeal lines, travel abroad as well as transsexuality, the natives' dealings with alien bodies ("foreigners") no less than with their own, with that which inside them was poised to unsettle the self-assuringly stable picture of being, were in communist Romania strictly monitored and regulated. "Unauthorized" frontier crossing and homosexuality were equally—and politically— transgressive. Both threatened the perceived homogeneity and the stability of the nation's body, which explains why in a country where political dissent was officially inexistent, "straight" dissidents were routinely charged with "sexual deviance." Nor did people enjoy more freedom as far as nationality or faith went. What they could be and identify themselves as, ethnically, racially, confessionally, and otherwise, in public or private, made up for a meager, selfsameness-bound repertoire. Not only does Cărtărescu expose this restrictive and ruthless identity management; he valiantly emendates and expands the catalogue of possibilities, shuffles and multiplies its formulas like a latter-day alchemist under whose magical wand the me/you, we/they, male/female, here/ there, now/then, and related dualities swap places unexpectedly or become part of bigger ensembles and networks that spill over into fabulous territories beneath Bucharest's urban drabness.

An other to the city and its "official" corporeality thus coalesces beyond the closed-off self, community, and place, an other into whose capaciously agglutinating fabric *Nostalgia*'s main first-person narrator weaves himself and his kin. As Marcel Cornis-Pope observes in this collection's opening essay, the spider web is Cărtărescu's master trope. A motif *in* the story, it also designates, metafictionally, the novel's multiply intertextual fabric and, inside it, the net of Kabbalah-like copulas between stages and levels of existence where the individual brain is plugged into others' and their projections into other worlds and the worlds behind those, *ad infinitum*. As in "REM," one of the novel's sections, our narrator, the writer-in-the-novel, plays the spider sliding up and down the threads of plots and characters. He gets in and out of his dramatis personae's minds, morphing into them while telling us about their own changes into others (as in the "Twins" chapter). At the same time, he shows how the phylogeny of these individual metamorphoses, a Cărtărescu trademark, rehearses cosmic ontogeny by recapping a whole cosmology—an entire cosm*all*ogy, I might say. For what he puts up is a colossal spectacle of the All and those without whom the latter's wholeness would fall short, a spectacle of self and—and necessarily with—others (*álloi* in Ancient Greek).[4]

People's bodies, Bucharest's crumbling body, the nation's body, and at last, the world's: these are *Nostalgia*'s concentric circles, the Kabbalistic web in which what happens in one world occurs or can occur in the rest of them as a show of "Allness," of quasi-mystical participation in the life of the All. Everything—this very All—is here a matter of scale, scope, and perspectives. Substance is defined by extension and location in a space where all locations communicate and so make up a flowing continuum. How things are and what they are depends on where they are, but they can change abruptly because their places are (or are not) theirs insofar as they are spliced together or border on other places next to them, beneath, or above. Ontology *is* here topology. In other words, position, a spatial coordinate, ultimately turns into an ontological category while ontology becomes, as Edward Soja would say, "spatialized."[5] Therefore, one can shuttle back and forth between different levels of life. One can in fact "overcome" ontological difference, run the whole gamut of being—one can be, that is, in various, "other" ways and worlds—by simply changing one's place.

Embedded in this capacious panorama of endless ramifications, imbrications, and juxtapositions, this ontology is also political. For it organizes being by reshuffling the saliently segregationist geography of late-communist Romania metonymically, by setting people and objects next to people and objects in whose vicinity they have neither been nor are supposed to be, or synecdochically, according to a *pars pro toto* logic that renders characters and locales subsets of larger entities above and against the Party-State's immediate, totalitarian totality. Either way, Cărtărescu's dramatis personae act out a drama of being—they *are*—as they are in relation to others, thence de-termined, at the same time bounded and freed by the proximity to others and to their modes of being in culture and history. The self's vicinity, the terminus that both limits and assigns the self a contiguous meaning, also liberates it, brings it forth. Political through and through, topological and cultural relatedness is thus *Nostalgia*'s *modus essendi*. Bucharest's "little context" reflects the shape of bigger places and units or feeds into them unexpectedly. The small and large worlds are similarly built, yet they are neither repetitious nor opposed. In broader bodies, venues, and sequences, the self does not run into versions of itself but, as noted, into others. The All's structure is inherently non-*all*ergic, comprises *álloi*. Like the nation yet unlike how it has been usually pictured, this structure consists of others and calls upon the self to acknowledge them both outside and inside itself. Further, if the All is indeed the alpha and omega of "little" existential forms and, further, if these forms mirror the whole's own form, then they are its microcosm and, because the levels of this ontology interface and overlap, the microcosm is not only analogical and juxtaposed to the macrocosm but also a portal to it, an *Aleph*.

2. *The Borges Connection*

> There is nothing in the world but other people.
> — Don DeLillo, *Cosmopolis*

In calling the small, the local, the isolated, the cloistral, the incarcerated, the city and its bodies Alephs, the Romanian writer also calls out to Borges, interpelates and interpolates the Argentine writer's famous "Aleph." Another homology obtains here via Cărtărescu's engagement with Borges's holistic model of universal intertextuality. This is the Babel Library, in which literature and place are infinite in number and extent and so coextensive, one. Therefore, the universal library and the universe overlap too. In "The Library of Babel," "The Book of Sand,"

"The Total Library," and other Borgesian *ficciones*, the library, the book, and the textual foreground the universe qualitatively, best illustrate its fabric, its "textile" makeup. Conversely, they also hint that, if the cosmos is like a book, all books are infinite. That means that every book holds the rest of the holdings, is an Aleph, "one of the points in space that contains all points."[6] What de-fines book-ness is in-finitude as well as inter-textuality, cosmic boundlessness *and* boundedness. Underlying the latter is, fundamentally, otherness, the others and their books' presence in a particular book. This book does not only "put up" with a "parasitic" other to it within itself; the book simply cannot have a self, an identity, cannot be "original," in short, cannot be what it is without that "alien" presence inside it, without having its roots, its origin, somewhere else, in another text. It follows, then, that the Aleph is not just unlimited and intertextual—and intertextual because unlimited, transgressive, liable to cross over to the other side over and over again—but also "alterial." It is a repository of alterity. It is being that *is* while also being what it is not, its other, much as the Aleph includes its "counterpart," the Zahir, and everything else between the A (alpha) and Z (omega) of existential, cultural, and political "alternatives."[7]

In this sense, Borges's "Aleph," to which *Nostalgia* alludes repeatedly, is not only the novel's primary intertextual ingredient, the closest literary connection. The Aleph also designates the cosmological trope and cultural stratagem through which Cărtărescu reveals his cosmology as cosm*allogy* and Bucharest as an Aleph, a site of astonishing otherness, a strange and vast place locked *inside* the nation-state's body. This vastness is *"une ville devenue monde"*[8] or, more exactly, a polis made into world by the writer's cosmo-imaginary. Describing Los Angeles as "world-city" and utmost sample of postmodern urban geography, Soja notices that the metropolis is also a cosmopolis because it "reproduc[es] *in situ* the customary colours and confrontations of a hundred different homelands." A microcosm of the limitless and itself without limit, bursting with "fulsome" heterogeneity, Soja's LA is, in his own formulation, a Borgesian "LA-leph," at once "everywhere" and "the only place on earth where all places are." And they are here because, as the critic implies apropos, again, of Borges's Aleph, this is a "radical[ly] open," "all-inclusive simultaneity" harboring a whole panoply of otherness,[9] which is also what makes the Aleph ultimately in-comprehensible. Indeed, "global in the fullest sense of the word," the immeasurable Californian Aleph defies critical survey, and this, the critic admits, renders his account fatally incomplete.[10] What "limits" Soja's account is the Aleph, the illimitable itself; this has arrived: the elsewhere and everywhere are here and boggle the mind. In Cărtărescu, quite the contrary, the Aleph stimulates and entices, leads on and out of the all-too-limited. Not the Balkans' Paris any more, Bucharest is not their LA either—or not yet, for *Nostalgia* is already stealing glances at its *other*, "angelic" face.

It bears reiterating: internally, this worldly imaginary gives back to the agonizing corpus of Bucharest and its inhabitants what official policies deny; externally, whereas said policies write this corpus out of the world, the novel rewrites it back in and thus heals the cosmic body's political wound, abolishes an "unnatural" division, "wall," or "curtain" by launching links across them. So the inside and the outside, the below and the above, the microcosm and the macrocosm, the individual body or text (such as *Nostalgia*) and the collective body or body of work (such as national literature or tradition), then national letters and *Bibliotheca Universalis* itself, people's bodies roaming Bucharest's labyrinth and the world's cobweb are all connected because they constitute particles and reflections of the All: homomorphic and intertwined, each other's "counterparts" and containers simultaneously, side by side and inside one another, responding and corresponding to their Zahirs, to their others concomitantly "out there" and "in here." The local partakes of globality and vice versa. Distinct as they are—as they *must* be, according to this "all-ephic" ontology—they are nonetheless united by a "linking" fervor, by a political mysticism of ties, compatibilities, and references.

Undoubtedly genuine, this synthetic élan is fueled by Borges and his "Aleph." In Borges himself, the fervor of analogisms, imbrications, and networks stems directly from the Kabbalah and Judaic tradition (*Kabbalah* itself means "reception," "tradition," he reminds us).[11] Influenced by Gnosticism, Kabbalistic cosmology views the universe as a chain of "emanations" (the Sefirot) issuing out of a center in ever broader life circles, each new circle reproducing on a smaller scale the energy and form of the previous one all the way to our level. "The ten emanations," Borges explains in his essay "The Kabbalah," "form a man called Adam Kadmon, the Archetypal Man," who "himself emanates a world, which emanates another," which then sends forth ours. Thus the latter already lies in previous and superior emanations and in Adam

Kadmon, in whom, coming out of him and after him, "all things,"—
"man and its microcosm"—are "included."[12] The "microcosm" is both
humans' surrounding environment but also the inner space of the body
and mind, with the "little" cosmos of the brain at the core of this inte-
riority.

But, as Konrád also proclaims around the time Cărtărescu was at
work on *Nostalgia*, "the cerebrum is liberating itself." To be sure, the
brain, the life of spirit more generally, is not cutting itself loose from
outer loops of life. On the contrary, it is shaking off the yoke of the
communist nation-state, breaking out of the small circle of the prescrip-
tive political embodiment to join something greater. Thus, "the imagination" is taking off the "clerical-military uniform" it had to wear as a
"Grand Inquisitor for the state," "expert advisor available for hire to
some political leader," and otherwise "commissioned" by national
"bureaucracy." What the brain wants now is "serve itself," the "cause of
independent thinking," that is.[13] This is precisely what the Romanian
writer means when he insists in the title of a widely circulated 2003
essay that "Europe Is Shaped like My Brain"—another way of saying
that he is a European, shaped "like" and *by* Europe, and so he carries its
cultural memory inside him as a *forma mentis* while, precisely due to
this homology, Europe's form and essence, its whole "profile" in turn
reflect and contain his.[14] The artist's brain, on one side, and, on the
other, the continent and the whole world's cultural body are at once each
other's Alephs, one another's parts and wholes. Europe is "relational,"
and so is the "cerebrum," which in the first volume of his novel *Dazzling*
(Orbitor) Cărtărescu calls a "relation" organ.[15] The brain designates the
homological matrix of his cosm*allogy*, the controlling, geometrical figure of this liberating, ever-expanding universe where the self and its "inside" and "here" open onto "outside," "out there." An always provisional
totality and a progressively manifold alterity meet in this heterogeneous
cosmos where the many rejoice in their oneness with one another without fading into each other. This is both a frame of mind, an "outlook" of
(or *in*) the "cerebral" microcosm, and the makeup of the macrocosm, as
a quasi-Borgesian character in *Dazzling* hints by pointing out how the
world's "[secret] services, sects, and cabals are all connected like neuron
networks."[16] Not only are all things linked up horizontally, on their particular life level, inside their worlds; since these worlds or circles have
been spun from one another, they also retain some of each other's form,

and so they are also intermeshed "vertically," across existential planes. The two axes speak to the same, at once metonymic and synecdochic integration of Cărtărescu's cosmos. For here the self and its point in space tie into others and into a wider world "shaped like" the self's world and fitting inside it as much as the self and its neck of the woods have the form of the All and thus belong to it.

Nowhere is this Alephic solidarity of the "macro" world, this cosm*allogical* web of linkages, Baudelairian *correspondances*, and reciprocities more firmly anchored in the "micro" universe of the individual mind, and nowhere in Cărtărescu's work is this ontology more intertextually Borgesian than in *Nostalgia*'s "REM" section. "REM" is Cărtărescu's "Aleph," with Egor, another writer in the story, a true "Aleph weaver."[17] Egor pictures REM as a

> trap set everywhere and endowed with infinite presence, a place of passage that waits for many years to be discovered and then many more years until it is found by the being who can penetrate it.... Some maintain that REM is an infinite machine, a colossal brain that regulates and coordinates, after a certain plan and for a certain purpose, all the dreams of all living beings, from the unconceivable dream of the amoeba and the colchicum to the dreams of all people. The dream, according to them, is the true reality, in which the will of the divinity hidden in REM reveals itself. Others see in REM a kind of kaleidoscope in which you can read all at once the entire universe, with all the details of each moment of its development, from genesis to apocalypse. Not long ago, I read a book in Spanish where REM was perceived the same way but was called *El Aleph*. (*Nostalgia*, 250)

At once in another's work (Borges's) and in Cărtărescu's own, the latter's REM also provides a "passage" into the former. It designates, on the one hand, the realm of all things ever born basking in each other's co-presence, where small and big, incipient and advanced, ontogeny and phylogeny, local and global are concurrently distinct and akin. On the other hand, REM marks the "Entrance" (276) into this realm; it is grandiose vision as well as gateway to it. This holistic—*All*istic—worldview is, Egor submits, what makes "true" writers more consequential than "great writers" not only because this solidarity ideal bears out the former's awareness of the whole and their place in it but also because inside this cosmically centripetal ensemble object and image, reflected and reflection, thought and action, poetics and politics also tend to become one or at least share common features. This is why Egor does not solely "describe" REM. He knows that once he has put that de-scription in writing—once he has *written* REM—he has done more than "just" represent the All. Here representation is both mimesis and praxis. To represent means to intervene, to reach out to others and touch their lives no matter how local the representing agent's abode. Writing writes the world over, carries itself into this world and "substitutes" the author's vision for it. "I don't wish," Egor confesses, "to reach the point of being a great writer, I want to reach *The All*. I dream incessantly of a creator who, through his art, can actually influence the life of all beings, and then the life of the entire universe, to the most distant stars, to the end of space and time. And then to substitute himself for the universe, to become the World itself" (251). "Most writers," he adds, "will never reach *The All*," yet they will have irremediably failed only if they have not given it a try. For the plenitude of the All shines forth already in the try and its trials. The attempt, the pathway, the door ("trap"), and their place are both this and that side of the part/whole divide, "here" as well as "there," *urbis* and *orbis*, of this world and an alternative to it, a mark of the nation and an alter-nation, a "no" to the surrounding "yes." And this is exactly what Egor puts on paper, over and over again, for hundreds of pages: the word "no."

3. *"A Confederation of Egos"*

> The city was hers, as, made up and sleeked so with the customary words and images (cosmopolitan, culture, cable cars) it had not been before: she had safe-passage tonight to its far blood's branchings, be they capillaries too small for more than peering into, or vessels mashed together in shameless municipal kidneys, out on the skin for all but tourists to see.
> — Thomas Pynchon, *The Crying of Lot 49*

> [T]he city's denuded streets, buildings, bridges, monuments, squares and roads are also the contested sites of historical memory and provide the contexts, cultures, stories, languages, experiences, desires and hopes that course through the urban body.
> — Iain Chambers, *Migrancy, Culture, Identity*

In Egor's negative "vision," the dreary quotidian is symbolically annulled, but alternatives take root "negatively" too. He never bodies them forth as positive projections and dreams. He does have insights into the dreamworld, the ability to "penetrate the dream and become a citizen of the dream" (277), but never acquires this oneiric citizenship fully— never quite "projects a world," to quote Pynchon's Oedipa Maas.[18] Therefore, his REM remains "partial." Through him though, stirred by his incomplete yet arresting fantasy, others dream their way into the All. In fact, Cărtărescu's homologism requires that REM reveal itself in dreams, in the brain, if the cosmic whole is indeed shaped like one, and above Egor reminds us that some believe that this is exactly the case (250). Nor does Cărtărescu imply something else by using the "Rapid Eye Movement" acronym to designate a reality comparable to the Borgesian Aleph. This explains why *Nostalgia* teems with dreams and dreams inside dreams, is one big dream machine that reworks the everyday into a fantastically limitless space populated by an oneiric citizenry.

Intriguingly enough, most of it are children. As Egor suggests, the child's body is germane to the boundless All, for, like the latter, it is still a process, has not crossed into adulthood and its symbolic world of more inflexible boundaries, categories, affiliations, and behavioral patterns. As in Jeffrey Eugenides's *Middlesex*, the young, adolescent bodies are shiftier, less stabilized and sexually "settled in"—still a "harmonious jumble, a cosmos" (*Nostalgia*, 161), hence more apt cosm*allogically*. No longer a child despite his body's "retarded" development, Egor recognizes childhood as an ideal, as a multiply transgressive stage and state of being. Less incorporated into a girl's body, female sexuality nevertheless allows the pre-menstrual-age child experiences from which she may hold back as an adult. No wonder Egor thinks "REM"'s lead character, a girl, should keep "dreaming"—dreaming for the REM. Not only are children's brains and in particular girls' brains still open to passions, dreams, and possibilities later on foreclosed, as Cărtărescu implies in his essay "We Love with a Child's Brain"[19]; a girl's awake body too is particularly suited to "reach across" as it blurs lines of sexual conduct that later on may remain uncrossed. And what the little girl crosses over to is simultaneously the other side of sexual norm, of the normative, "controlled" self—the *other*'s side. Thus, "los[ing] any control," she "kisses her [girlfriend Ester] lightly on the lips" (276) during a children's wedding game. What is more, in *Nostalgia* and elsewhere in Cărtărescu,

"Ester" ("Estera" in *Dazzling*) signifies Jewishness. Among the *álloi* roaming his Bucharest, Ester/a represents a *hétera*, a "radical" counterpart, not "just" another self or like it—"more of the same"—but more like an other to it.[20] As such, she occupies a symbolic place in his oeuvre's ethnic, racial, religious, and corporeal/sexual panoply alongside the body politic's disenfranchised "no-bodies": the retarded, the disabled, freaks and "melancholy monsters from another world" like Egor himself (277), displaced peasants turned working-class paupers, brutalized women, the ethnically, racially, and spatially unstable, "nomadic" (the Gypsies), bisexuals, transsexuals, and otherwise sexually "labile," "untrustworthy." These lie outside but also inside our self and so render it, as the author describes it in an interview, "not a despotic and autarchic empire clustered around a central ego ruling over the 'little' and 'submissive' ones," but a "confederation of egos."[21] These lend identity a subversive impermanence that unsettles the mythical homogeneity and steadiness of the national body. Along these lines, in *Dazzling* Cărtărescu looks for the "Bulgarian" inside himself, and, in his 1994 novel *Travesti* (Disguise) he seeks to "set free my inner sister, to help the woman inside me speak out" and thus show off not just an *other* to his self but also another of his own "selves."[22]

Twice marginal as female and child in the exclusivist economy of the collective body, Ester is also cast out by what Cărtărescu aptly deems Romania's "historical guilt": anti-Semitism.[23] The nationalist 1980s solidified the Jew's position as an epitome of the excluded in the country's identitarian imaginary. It is over against this imaginary that the writer turns to Ester and reinscribes her back into the nation's body in intertextual dialogue across and above domestic tradition with Borges and his own, Kabbalistic-Judaic imagination of the All. That is to say, derived from Borges, "Jewishness"—at most an "extra" in the nation's "official" drama of selfhood—supplies both the formal and the thematic context for a non-allergic reconstruction of the individual and national self as the little girl "weds" Ester and thus joins in something far vaster. "My REM," she confesses, "had been the kiss I had given to Ester. In that moment I had the All" (276). Like REM itself, Ester is a way to the All and, as an *altera* herself, also part of it, equally a splinter of humanity, humanity itself, and a chance for the self to discover its own humanity as one form of humanness among other types rather than as the generic, outward expanding yet egocentric category of traditional humanism. Quite apropos, *Dazzling*'s narrator compares "humanity" to a "disseminated brain that desperately struggles to regain its unity."[24] This "unity" is not necessarily homogeneous even though the novel sees in every object an "example of universal homogeneity" in which each thing is, Kabbalah-like, the All—everywhere, every moment, and at the same time. Unity is here not homogeny but homology, symmetry that safeguards and honors difference wherein self and other, "the male and the female, sulfur and mercury, yin and yang" retain their distinctive contents yet communicate because these contents are not incompatibly structured.[25] Unlike recent appeals to "universalism," homologies of this sort need not, and they do not, scale back difference. On the contrary, they preserve it; they presuppose it, actually. Ester opens up the world to the other girl because Ester remains this other girl's other and so prompts her friend's own becoming-other along the lines of a new division: sexuality. Right after the "same-sex" episode that, on the face of it, seems to buttress a sameness fantasy, Ester's playmate falls asleep, dreams of REM, and has her first period (284). What she appears to have lost in her oneness with her other she makes up for in becoming a woman different both from the girl she was and from the woman she is about to be taken for by men in a "real" world where sexual difference is mechanically predicated on heterosexuality.

I use quotation marks advisedly. For reality is no more than "a particular case of the unreal," as much as we all are, "no matter how concrete we may feel, nothing else than the fiction of who knows what world, which creates and comprises us," as Cărtărescu writes in *Dazzling*'s first volume (323). In the 1996 novel, this *fervor homologica*—also a *fervor* hom*allogica*, feverish yearning for this *Totul* (343), the *totum* in which "all corresponds with all" (188) —is fueled by the Pauline vision of the "whole" and the "whole knowledge." This vision supersedes mundane, pre-revelation, and irredeemably "partial" knowing and being, as much as it is spurred by the Kabbalah and magical realism. In fact, the writer uses the *locus classicus* from Saint Paul featuring the distinction between part and whole (1 Corinthians, 13, 9-12) as a motto to *Dazzling*, and this clue is as relevant as "The Library of Babel"-like "cosmos" depicted in "REM"'s first paragraph (*Nostalgia*, 161). In other words, what the New Testament epigraph suggests about *Dazzling* Borges's "Aleph" implies with regard to "REM" and the All of which "REM" is part, *Nostalgia*: the fragment, the self, and the self's "real" here and now are tied into bigger and different bodies, into broader spaces, elsewhere and otherwise, spaces unreal and in an *other* temporality, "before," "after," and at on(c)e with the self's presence and present. Therefore, REM may just as well be a matter of memory, "a memory of memories"—or, as it has been called via another Borgesian reference, "memorious"[26]—and so "perhaps nostalgia" itself, as a narrator ventures (286). Or, it may as well be a future matter, a leap ahead. Either way, retrospectively or prospectively, it is "unreal" yet concurrently hardly so or solely so because, as we have seen, reality itself is a "particular case" of unreality, feeds into the mind and is in turn stirred up by mind events such as recollections and projections, by what has happened in the past or could happen in the future or in a dream. All these representation forms hang together and therefore help build up—in whatever form—the togetherness and many-sidedness of Cărtărescu's cos*mallogy* even after his characters leave the miraculously visionary age of childhood behind.

　　In this view, all Bucharest situations, places, and characters reenact the Ester episode. Not only the self's past, current, and future hypostases are inside one another yet objects distinct from each other like so many Russian dolls, as we learn in *Dazzling* (234) or in the "Mentardy" section of *Nostalgia* (45). So are too self and other, the nearby and the faraway, the individual, urban, and national body on one side, and the cosmic bodies on the other—bodies of people and places, small and big, awake or asleep, daydreaming or sleepwalking. They nest inside one another, reflect each other's form, which helps them shed their own forms and mutate. Like Saleem Sinai's body in Salman Rushdie's *Midnight's Children*, the main narrator's body in *Dazzling* and *Nostalgia* is not simply "entwined with his world" or structurally analogous to it, but *is* that world, its center, part, and matrix, its model, module, and mode at the same time—a litotes to the city's and the nation's hyperbolically anthropomorphized corpus.[27] Also like in Rushdie's "incorporation" and integration of private and public bodies, the narrating hero's anatomy and physiology spill over into broader topography and politics. What happens to one (Saleem) in his private world and most private, oneiric or awake moments happens publicly to the many (India) because, as Saleem keeps stressing, he too "contains multitudes."[28] Cărtărescu's storytelling protagonists are equally capacious inside and similarly inset into even more voluminous realities outside. Their bodies' birthmarks are cosmic cartographies. They resemble constellations, and their dreams "communicate," form "urban arteries" that "merge with reality's highways" and result into corporeal writing, a "tattoo" of sorts that a cosmic reader high up above the city would decipher while a city dweller would feel painfully on her own skin down below. These bodies "expand" fantastically so as to *become* Bucharest's body (*Dazzling*, 212), scale themselves down and crawl inside other bodies' brains (*Nostalgia*, 166), or build gargantuan, golem-like androgynous bodies (239-41).

4. *Nostalgia for the Future: The Ethics of Vision*

> The "in-itself" is even an absurd conception; a "constitution-in-itself" is nonsense; we possess the concept "being," "thing," only as a relational concept.
> — Friedrich Nietzsche, *The Will to Power*

Androgyny is one of the 1993 novel's axial themes. For, in it, nostalgia itself is nothing else than reembodiment desire, desire longing for a more complete, "androgynous" world to come. As in Plato's *Symposium*, this would be a world *again* whole, reunited with itself as the self reunites with its other after and against the disjunctive politics of walls and barbed-wired borders. In that, nostalgia amounts to a provocation to the present and a "return" to the future, or a turn, rather. Indeed, it inheres in a turn toward other bodies and more broadly toward otherness, toward that other self and body that we have lost or to the selves and bodies we have been cut off from. In rejoining its long lost "half"—not its "other self" but an *other* self, place, and *Weltanschauung*—the self recasts its lot with the All, the world's "animal" body to which we were once "glued" (*Nostalgia*, 45). Even more emphatically than in Milan Kundera's *Ignorance*, in Cărtărescu's novel nostalgia is not a "return." It does not hark back to a bygone, pseudo-ideal time, and because of that it does not preclude political change. In other words, Cărtărescu's *nostos* is a cultural and ontological rather than a temporal dimension of being. According to Fredric Jameson, postmodernism's "nostalgia for the present," for a present as re-presented past, as intertextual regurgitation and presentification of a past stuck in itself and thus without a future, "blocks and forestalls any global vision of the latter as a radically transformed and different system."[29] Complicating postmodern nostalgia,

Cărtărescu does something else. On the cusp of a future that critics like Jameson hardly make any provisions for, the book summons up that very temporality, looks ahead, as it were. Cărtărescu's "nostalgic" imagination does not "contest" the "oppositional," to quote Jameson again, but enacts an opposition by disputing the "system"'s own, brutal contestation of the dissenting and the oppositional.[30] Taking on the totalitarian body politic and policies no less than on the nostalgia for regressive homogeneity driving them, this imagination imagines, "yearns for" a "different system."

Yearning for this difference, for an other to *hic et nunc,* is the novel's "plot." The whole book stages this nostalgic turn outward and elsewhere, this search for the other half, for the "more" that, albeit "in here," leads to the All because it is "otherwise" than the self. This process invariably starts off with bodies. A fundamentally *embodied* ideal, difference is here incorporated at once literally and allegorically— mystically, that is. It is bodied forth, as I have said, both in children's bodies, before sexual difference is marked and begins to be publicly policed as such, and following its advent, in adult, sexually "dimorphic" and gender-segregated bodies. As the *Doktor Faustus* motto to *Nostalgia*'s "Epilogue" hints, these are either the "chrysalis," pre-metamorphosis type of bodies, theoretically at least undifferentiated, and bodies of the "butterfly" kind, namely, bodies within stricter, more stable limits that confine what we can be to what we are inside them.[31] Yet whether invisible or all-too-visible, the ensuing bodily boundaries and molds are in the novel broken repeatedly, which results in multiple rein-corporations, metamorphoses, expansions, and couplings. Cărtărescu's stunningly somatic vision shrinks bodies so they can and creep into others, like the narrator-spider (*Nostalgia*, 263), or dilates them, so much so that they form "Bucharest's spider web" (139) if not the entire cos-mos (316). They "echo" and "repeat" each other when everything seems to consolidate their differences (141) and keep them apart. But these bodies manage to cast aside the consuetudinary bio-somatic categories and discover in the catacombs underneath "Bucharest's foundations" (143) a richer "taxonomical paradise" (145). Here species and genders swap forms and organs, mutate into one another while the hero himself makes love to Gina, his lover, "enter[s]" her body and literally ends up in it, and in her stead. Once the corporeal "transfer" (153) has been carried out and he finds himself in "her" place, becomes his other and his own twin, his (old) self and double at the same time, he "ha[s] a sense of the All" (153). Gina undergoes a similar transformation and has an identical revelation. This way, they trade places and physiques, "connect" as bodies and visions. For, as Egor stresses, having access to an other's embodiment is as essential as dreaming your way into somebody else's dream; both are windows into *Totul* (225).[32]

Throughout his work, Cărtărescu argues for a "worlded" Bucharest, Romania, and Eastern Europe. And yet, he notes, more than half a century after the infamous Yalta summit, these all are still *projects* rather than realities—counterprojects, more exactly. For, on the one hand, Western Europe continues to project—construe and push out, outside itself—the "East" as its negative investment at the same time that it struggles to integrate it. What critics from Slavoj Žižek to Maria Todorova have noted with regard to the Balkans largely applies to the entire East: this part of the continent is still the West's symbolic dumping ground, a cultural landfill of "externalized frustrations." Both inside and outside Europe, the East constitutes the "other within" and the dark double cast out on the *other* side of an obsolete yet culturally reinforced divide, an "alter ego" that historically, geopolitically, and otherwise remains, inescapably if unconsciously, "inside," part of the whole.[33]

In *Nostalgia* as in *Dazzling*'s fourteen hundred pages, in *Forever Young, Wrapped in Pixels*, and elsewhere, Cărtărescu pulls, however, this unconscious presence to the surface by "counterimagining" Bucharest as a segment of something much greater. Yet he is careful not to "transcend" his city. Instead, he develops it like a photograph. In the dark room of his imagination, he blows up the city's "negative," a negative that negates Europe's own imaginings of the East. He realizes that identity—the city's and its people's—pivots on the capacity to relate to an other, and that this aptitude has withered. For Bucharest came out of the 1980s completely disfigured, with most of his monuments and churches knocked down and many of the old neighborhoods leveled. Ceausescu's mammoth "People's House" is the better-known episode of the regime's brutal war against the city. With its *belle-époque* landmarks pulled down, its streets torn up or absurdly renamed, buckling under its hastily donned concrete adornments, slowly drowning in a sea of melting asphalt in summer, freezing to death in its working-class housing complexes in winter, Bucharest was becoming at the time Cărtărescu was working on *Nostalgia* more and more inhospitable, anonymous, and impersonal. The grayish, impersonal panopticon was not an urban forum of civic performance any more because its crude geometry, its volumes, proportions, and intervals were by no means geared toward culturally and politically open transactions. The old Bucharest was being supplanted by a new architectonics of surveillance and control that canceled out the city as habitat. It had been Bucharest's multiple locations, agoras, arteries, and nodes that together had spawned, nourished, and channeled a remarkably rich and diverse life, but now all these were demolished, falling apart, or grotesquely retrofitted. Cut off from one another and, together, from the common history of their *civitas*, deprived of its hitherto civilizing spatial arrangements, distributions, and distances, the citizens were less and less experiencing life as neighborly event and self as interplay, nexus, give-and-take.

In a way, *Nostalgia* makes such an experience again possible by fancying a whole other world wherein relation, reaching out to an other to the self and drawing from this generous vicinity still prove determinant, hold a socializing function. And so a parking lot becomes the universe, infinitely wider and "other" at once. You open a door, and you step into all places at once. You go down the stairs into a basement, then through a secret passage into an underworld where you watch the ultimate, "wholistic" peepshow: the rebirth of the cosmos and its life forms. Hidden inside the visible, the dismally "small," the non-descript scarcely worth describing lie the whole and its wholly different world. Cocooned inside the here and the same is the there, the other, and another time. Bucharest's body and the bodies roaming it communicate with other bodies and, through the differences these bodies incorporate, partake of the alien, the remote, and the invisible.

This magical remapping of the city proves uniquely keen on heterogeneity, on the repressed and secluded. The resulting map and the territory overlap like in the Borges short story Jean Baudrillard draws from in *Simulations*.[34] *Nostalgia*, in particular, unfurls a world—provides what its author calls an "Entrance"—and is itself that world. Yet this is not a simulation. The writer cuts open Bucharest's body in search of what Pynchon identifies as the "underlying truth." This urban truth, this "counter-city" à la Pynchonian "counter-Venezia" Pynchon himself hypothesizes in *Against the Day*, the "dreamer" can reach, still in Pynchon's words, by digging "shafts" and "tunnels of truth" under the actual city.[35] The San Narciso of Pynchon's *The Crying of Lot 49* has no boundaries or, if it does, "no one knew yet how to draw them."[36] They shift depending on the observer's position, "inside" or "outside" the insightfully—or just "paranoically"—"projected" system.[37] Cărtărescu's Bucharest does have firm, confining contours, but the point is to break through them, to "project" a world beyond them, a space, a text, a cosmic library beyond (albeit some of its holdings are already inside) "Bookarest"'s "arrested book."[38] Pynchon's neural network of interconnected circles neatly fitting inside one another may well be, after all, a paranoid deconstruction of the "system." Cărtărescu's, on the other hand, is a deliberate construction, a leap into a within in order to reach a beyond where the self's, the city's, and the nation's "truth" is certainly not some finally retrieved and circumscribed meaning but "confederations" of meanings, truths, and possibilities. His "underlying truth" is essentially this vision of the many things that Bucharest, Romania, and Romanianness can be and mean because, in a sense—in an "Alephic" sense—they already are and mean all those things.

The crux of this vision is the notion that being and meaning arise with others, that is to say, the ontology, epistemology, and culture of a place and its people are all founded ethically, in an ethics of the nexus and the indebtedness that follows from it. Even in our "little" circle we can *be* more authentically if we acquire and live up to our membership in, and to our responsibilities to, "outer circles." Thus, Cărtărescu's cosm*allogically* integrated visionarism amends Theophrastus's fourth-century BC famous view of kinship, friendship, and allegiance as relationships tying us into other worlds in circles growing wider and wider from the self, its family, and country outwards.[39] The Romanian writer's Chinese-boxes cosmos is, like Borges's and Pynchon's, circular, but its circles of being and culture do not necessarily make up an ontological and cultural hierarchy. Or, if they do, this is fluid, tentative, a debatable convention as bodies touch on other bodies and their circles, morph into one another, and belong to multiple spheres of existence concurrently. Fascinated by a bigger elsewhere, by an other to fragmental and closed-in topologies—by the All—the writer sees imprisoned, de-spatialized space as a gateway to them, already affiliated with, and part of, them. The elsewhere and otherwise are already here yet unrevealed. As noted apropos of Konrád's Budapest, the world does not end with Bucharest, but it can definitely begin with it. It is just a matter of viewing the body of the capital and, more broadly, the nation's ethno-cultural corpus differently, of seeing, that is, beyond it by looking into it rather than by circumventing it. There is, as mentioned earlier, a mystical component to this broader view, and, in fact, Cărtărescu has been called a "mystic of housing projects."[40] Indeed, he notices more, "other" things; he makes out *all* things and places *in* the one place that he can look at no matter how meager and desolate this looks. But, as his gaze sweeps the dreary projects, the rotting power plants, the run-down historical districts, the dingy side streets, "other" things rise up and with them, inklings and slivers of the All: an imaginary domain where bodies, minds, and their environs suddenly find themselves embedded with much larger aggregates, all-ephic and all-epic, an epos of distinctiveness and particulars. For, Cărtărescu's All is not only "bigger" but truly whole *because* multitudinous, a cornucopia of interlinked tones, nuances, and possibilities of being.

NOTES

1. George Konrád, *Antipolitics: An Essay*, trans. from the Hungarian by Richard E. Allen (Sand Diego: Harcourt Brace Jovanovich, 1984), 179.
2. Mircea Cărtărescu, *Totul* (All), Bucharest, Romania: Cartea Romaneasca, 1985.
3. *Visul* (Bucharest: Cartea Romaneasca, 1989) was republished in complete form in 1993 (Bucharest: Humanitas) and has been translated in a number of languages. For the English version, see *Nostalgia*, trans., with an Afterword, from the Romanian by Julian Semilian, introduction by Andrei Codrescu (New York: New Directions, 2005). Later prose works such as novels like *Travesti* (Disguise) (Bucharest: Humanitas, 1994), the *Orbitor* (Dazzling) 3-volume series (Bucharest: Humanitas, 1996-2007), and the short pieces gathered in the bestseller *De ce iubim femeile* (Why We Love Women) (Bucharest: Humanitas, 2005) detail *Nostalgia*'s description of Bucharest.
4. *Állos* (masculine plural *álloi*) is "another" in Greek. It may designate either another *like* the self (by and large an other of the same sort) or an other *to* this self, in which case its meaning is closer to *héteros*. "The other of two," the latter marks the other's otherness more emphatically. In Latin, *alius* and *alter* enact roughly the same distinction. While unquestionably significant, the difference between *állos* and *héteros* is not instrumental to my argument.
5. Edward W. Soja, *Postmodern Geographies: The Reassertion of Space in Critical Social Theory* (New York: Verso, 1989), 131-137.
6. Jorge Luis Borges, "The Aleph," in *Collected Fictions*, trans. Andrew Hurley (New York: Penguin, 1999), 280.
7. On the Zahir as "an unbearable symbol of the infinite, painful circularity, an[d] obsessive counterpart of the elusive Aleph," see Matei Calinescu's *Rereading* (New Haven, CT: Yale University Press, 1993), 12, 11-16 passim.
8. Soja, *Postmodern Geographies*, 223.
9. Soja, *Thirdspace: Journeys to Los Angeles and Other Real-and-Imagined Places* (Cambridge, MA: Blackwell, 1996), 54-57.

10. Soja, *Postmodern Geographies*, 222-23.

11. Borges, "The Kabbalah," in *Seven Nights*, trans. Eliot Weinberger, introduction by Alasdair Reid (New York: New Directions, 1984), 99. On Borges, the Aleph, the Kabbalah, and Judaic tradition in general, see Jaime Alazraki, *Borges and the Kabbalah and Other Essays on His Fiction and Poetry* (New York: Cambridge University Press, 1988); Edna Aizenberg, *The Aleph Weaver: Biblical, Kabbalistic and Judaic Elements in Borges* (Potomac, MD: Scripta Humanistica, 1984). In Edna Aizenberg, ed., *Borges and His Successors: The Borgesian Impact on Literature and the Arts* (Columbia, MO: University of Missouri Press, 1990), see especially its fifth section, "Hebraism and Poetic Influence," 249-284, which features two lectures by Borges on The Book of Job and Spinoza, respectively. Worth mentioning is also Evelyn Fishburn's article "Reflections on the Jewish Imaginary in the Fictions of Borges," in *Variaciones Borges: Journal of the Jorge Luis Borges Center for Studies and Documentation*, 5 (1998): 145-56.

12. Borges, "The Kabbalah," 99.

13. Konrád, *Antipolitics*, 218.

14. Cărtărescu, "Europa are forma creierului meu" (Europe Is Shaped like My Brain). See the text in his essay collection, *Pururi tînăr, înfăşurat în pixeli* (Forever Young, Wrapped in Pixels) (Bucharest: Humanitas, 2003), 210.

15. Cărtărescu, *Orbitor*, vol. 1, 60.

16. Cărtărescu, *Orbitor*, vol. 1, 278-79.

17. See Aizenberg, *The Aleph Weaver*, vii. Other East European Borgesians, whose work Cărtărescu knows well, include Danilo Kiš (*The Encyclopedia of the Dead*), Milorad Pavić (*Dictionary of the Khazars: A Lexicon Novel*), and, in Romania, the members of the so-called "Tîrgovi□te School" (especially Mircea Horia Simionescu).

18. "Shall I project a world?" famously asks Pynchon's Oedipa Maas in *The Crying of Lot 49* (New York: HarperCollins, 1999), 64. The section's motto is also from *The Crying of Lot 49*, 95.

19. Cărtărescu, *De ce iubim femeile*, 110. In "Pentru D., vingt ans après" (For D., vingt ans après) from the same collection (14-19), a young woman's amazingly elaborate ("architectural") dreams mesmerize the authorial narrator. "Outdreamed" by his character, he admits to have used her oneiric vistas in books such as *Orbitor*.

20. "Eu-rile lui Mircea Cărtărescu" (Mircea Cărtărescu's Selves), interview by Marius Tuca and Mihaela Suciu. *Jurnalul Naţional* (National Daily), June 15, 2005. http://www.hotnews.ro/articol_24568-Eu-rile-lui-Mircea-Cărtărescu.htm.

21. Cărtărescu, "Eu-rile lui Mircea Cărtărescu."

22. Cărtărescu, "Eu-rile lui Mircea Cărtărescu."

23. Cărtărescu, "O vina istorica" (A Historical Guilt), in *Baroane!* (Yo, Your Highness!) (Bucharest: Humanitas, 2005), 211-214.

24. Cărtărescu, *Orbitor*, 214.

25. Cărtărescu, *Orbitor*, 59.

26. See Christian Moraru, *Memorious Discourse: Reprise and Representation in Postmodernism* (Madison, NJ: Fairleigh Dickinson University Press, 2005), chiefly the discussion of Borges's "Funes the Memorious" and "memorious" postmodernism, 21-27, 192-95.

27. Salman Rushdie, *Midnight's Children* (New York: Penguin, 1991), 273.

28. Rushdie, *Midnight's Children*, 4, 121, 143-47, 199, 200, 262, 533, etc.

29. Fredric Jameson, *Postmodernism, or, The Cultural Logic of Late Capitalism* (Durham: Duke University Press, 1991), 285.

30. Jameson, *Postmodernism*, 280.

68   Cosmallogy: Mircea Cărtărescu's Nostalgia

31. Cărtărescu, *Nostalgia*, 289.

32. "Totul" in the Romanian original, for which see *Nostalgia* (Bucharest: Humanitas, 1993), 226. The English translation renders it as "everything"—cf. *Nostalgia* (New York: New Directions, 2005), 225. "The All" strikes me as a somewhat better choice.

33. Maria Todorova, *Imagining the Balkans* (New York: Oxford University Press, 1997), 188.

34. Jean Baudrillard, *Simulations*, trans. Paul Foss, Paul Patton and Philip Beichtman (New York: Semiotext(e), 1983), 1-2.

35. Thomas Pynchon, *The Crying of Lot 49*, 36, 105. The writer refers to Venice as a "counter-city" ("counter-Venezia") in *Against the Day* (New York: Penguin, 2006), 585, 587.

36. Pynchon, *The Crying of Lot 49*, 147.

37. Pynchon, *The Crying of Lot 49*, 104-105.

38. "Bookarest" is the name of the book fair held in Bucharest annually since the mid-1990s.

39. For a discussion of Theophrastus's "concentric interpretation of degrees of kinship and friendship" and his view's place in the history of cosmopolitan thought, see Derek Heater, *World Citizenship and Government: Cosmopolitan Ideas in the History of Western Political Thought* (New York: St. Martin's Press, 1996), 13.

40. "Mircea Cărtărescu is the mystic of housing projects," writes Swiss critic Katharina Döbler in *Neue Zürcher Zeitung* (*Nostalgia*, New Directions edition, back cover).

WORKS CITED

Aizenberg, Edna. *The Aleph Weaver: Biblical, Kabbalistic and Judaic Elements in Borges.* Potomac, MD: Scripta Humanistica, 1984.

_____., ed. *Borges and His Successors: The Borgesian Impact on Literature and the Arts.* Columbia, MO: University of Missouri Press, 1990.

Alazraki, Jaime. *Borges and the Kabbalah and Other Essays on His Fiction and Poetry.* New York: Cambridge University Press, 1988.

Baudrillard, Jean. *Simulations.* Trans. Paul Foss, Paul Patton and Philip Beichtman. New York: Semiotext(e), 1983.

Borges, Jorge Luis. *Seven Nights.* Trans. Eliot Weinberger, introduction by Alasdair Reid. New York: New Directions, 1984.

_____. *Collected Fictions.* Trans. Andrew Hurley. New York: Penguin, 1999.

Fishburn, Evelyn. "Reflections on the Jewish Imaginary in the Fictions of Borges." *Variaciones Borges: Journal of the Jorge Luis Borges Center for Studies and Documentation*, 5 (1998): 145-56.

Heater, Derek. *World Citizenship and Government: Cosmopolitan Ideas in the History of Western Political Thought.* New York: St. Martin's Press, 1996.

Jameson, Fredric. *Postmodernism, or, The Cultural Logic of Late Capitalism.* Durham: Duke University Press, 1991.

Calinescu, Matei. *Rereading.* New Haven, CT: Yale University Press, 1993.

Cărtărescu, Mircea. *Totul* (All). Bucharest, Romania: Cartea Romaneasca, 1985.

_____. *Visul* (The Dream). Bucharest: Cartea Romaneasca, 1989.

_____. *Nostalgia.* Complete edition of *Visul*. Bucharest: Humanitas, 1993.

_____. *Travesti* (Disguise). Bucharest: Humanitas, 1994.

_____. "Realismul poeziei tinere" (Young Poets' Realism). *Competiția continuă. Generația 80 în texte teoretice. O antologie de Gheorghe Crăciun* (The Race Goes On: Theoretical Texts on the 1980s Generation). Pitesti, Romania: Editura Vlasie, 1994, 181-184.

_____. *Orbitor* (Dazzling). 3 Vol. Bucharest: Humanitas, 1996-2007.

_____. *Pururi tînăr, înfășurat în pixeli* (Forever Young, Wrapped in Pixels). Bucharest: Humanitas, 2003.

_____. *De ce iubim femeile* (Why We Love Women). Bucharest: Humanitas, 2005.

_____. "Eu-rile lui Mircea Cărtărescu" (Mircea Cărtărescu's Selves). Interview by Marius Tuca and Mihaela Suciu. *Jurnalul Național* (National Daily), June 15, 2005. http://www.hotnews.ro/articol_24568-Eu-rile-lui-Mircea-Cărtărescu.htm (accessed June 20, 2005).

_____. *Nostalgia.* Trans., with an Afterword, from the Romanian by Julian Semilian. Introduction by Andrei Codrescu. New York: New Directions, 2005.

Konrád, George. *Antipolitics: An Essay.* Trans. from the Hungarian by Richard E. Allen. San Diego: Harcourt Brace Jovanovich, 1984.

Moraru, Christian. *Memorious Discourse: Reprise and Representation in Postmodernism.* Madison, NJ: Fairleigh Dickinson University Press, 2005.

Pynchon, Thomas. *The Crying of Lot 49.* New York: HarperCollins, 1999.

_____. *Against the Day.* New York: Penguin, 2006.

Rushdie, Salman. *Midnight's Children.* New York: Penguin, 1991.

Soja, Edward, W. *Postmodern Geographies: The Reassertion of Space in Critical Social Theory.* New York: Verso, 1989.

_____. *Thirdspace: Journeys to Los Angeles and Other Real-and-Imagined Places.* Cambridge, MA: Blackwell, 1996.

Todorova, Maria. *Imagining the Balkans.* New York: Oxford University Press, 1997.

THE SCREEN OF THE CITY: SOFIA'S TRANSITIONAL URBANSCAPES, 1989–2007

ALEXANDER KIOSSEV

This text summarizes the results of a collective, artistic and research project called "The Visual Seminar."[1] Dedicated to the urban sights of Sofia in the transitional period, the Seminar was initiated because certain groups of Bulgarian intellectuals had the feeling that between 1989 and 2000 Sofia had become "unbearable" for the eye and citizen were obligated to fight the "visual pollution" brought about by the overflow of advertisements and recently built commercial buildings. Today, about 8 years later, the results of this "visual activism" seem rather humble and ambivalent—the project determined only minor changes in Sofia's new, capitalistic appearance, and even the premises of the initial activism were seriously questioned. Yet, the author believes that analytic insights of the Seminar are worthwhile as they offer a strong starting point for discussions of general issues about contemporary cities in transition and about their visual culture. This text is a personal interpretation of the project results; its main idea is informed by visual sociology and urban anthropology[2] and is based on the assumption that social processes and social conflicts in the city do not occur invisibly but have a clear visual coefficient. The problem is that we need to know where to direct our gaze and how to decipher what we see, how to analyze and synthesize urban visual data.

My method views the city space as a "screen" upon which social processes have different projections. The latter are certainly not limited to the direct production of images, advertisements, or even to the visualization typical of "the society of the spectacle," although Sofia, not unlike other East European cities undergoing the transition to market economy, has experienced an incredible boom in this respect. The assumption is that every urban practice—habitation, street behavior, shopping, neighborhood contacts, transport, construction works, signs, advertisements, architecture, and everything else that makes up the multifaceted life of a city—has its own visual potential. The resulting panorama is a conglomerate of heterogeneous images and urbanscapes, which the "screen" of the city tends to represent as a homogeneous visual field for consumption.[3] I will try to analyze the screen-like homogeneity of this heterogeneity, that is, Sofia's image-production in the basic sense of the word, the city-screen itself[4] and the various forms of visual consumption as embodied in the numerous aspects of everyday behaviours, subcultures, political initiatives, inhabiting places and styles, mass urban processes, and institutional conflicts, for all of them make a contribution to Sofia's intricate visual mosaic.

Let us start with a discussion of two different regimes of urban visuality, both of which will be used here as ideal types. The first is the panoptic modern city-machine striving towards rationality, functionality, and transparent, total governmentality. This type transforms the constructive principle[5] into a real structure of the city while using it as its emblem reproduced across an entire spectrum of different urban images from the straight streets and visible infrastructure to the simple geometric and functional architecture, the calculated traffic, and further to the images of progress and the symbols of centralized, political and cultural power concentrated in the city center. In this regime, the politics of invisibility is logically directed at that which eludes central, modernized power; the urban authorities begin to imprison, intern, and drive out of the city everything that cannot be made rational, functional, and normal (the only remaining challenge being those few urban "heterotopias" that reflect, provoke, and even revert this spatial and visual order[6]).

The other regime, that of the postmodern megapolis,[7] stems from the loss of this modern sort of visibility. No longer the city demiurge and all-pervasive, scrutinizing "ray," the abstract, panoptical[8] Eye of power that observes, builds, and governs urban space according to rational principles breaks up into countless eyes, into an extremely diverse and often "irrational" mass of individuals and perspectives: passers-by, private individuals, *flâneurs*, dealers, entrepreneurs, advertisers, tramps, children, ethnic minorities, etc.[9] These scattered subjects are both producers and victims of the city's visual aggression. They are swamped by heterogeneous, fragmentized images; they are overburdened with visual information and tempted by advertisements, scandalized by erotic and shocking images. In short, they live in a "vortex of representations."[10] Thus, the city loses its rational wholeness[11] and its "over-view" type of visibility, blurs its own boundaries, becomes porous, an "overexposed" city[12] open to the global informational and visual flows.[13] In this second regime, the politics of invisibility acquires paradoxical features. Urban space continues to produce traditional, "shady" heterotopias, "shameful" niches, and ghettoes within itself, but it no longer hides them directly, in other words, it does not make them invisible by traditional modern techniques such as internment, imprisonment, segregation, or standardization. Paradoxically, it produces invisibility through excessive visibility. "Deviant" individuals, groups, and places are pushed in the background, "overshadowed," and substituted by their own picturesque simulations constantly produced by the image industry[14]: they are hidden, made imperceptible behind urban phantasms and media clichés about them— sensational news, scandalous rumors—in brief, by a whole image production following the genres of action movies and horror stories.[15]

This politics of "sensational invisibility" also applies to the city's rational infrastructure: the latter is no longer interesting as a perfectly functioning, constructive principle, presenting itself publicly. In a way similar to the image simulation of deviancy, the infrastructure is concealed behind the urban phobias and comes to the fore only in its catastrophic aspect as a threat to the life of the city. Instead of the images of the working urban structure, the late-capitalist image factory prefers to display the spectacle of earthquakes, terrorist attacks, epidemic diseases, and alien invasions, along with the entire spectrum of destruction or malfunctioning of the urban infrastructure,[16] which is another way of saying that the once rational visual regime has now become irrational by displaying fears, claustrophobia, and forbidden passions. The sale and consumption of "trans-rational"[17] images has substituted rational panopticism; the staged visibility of subconscious emotions and pleasure has replaced the ceremonious emblems of demiurgic reason.

1. *Sofia as a Visual Problem*

I have limited the discussion to these two abstract models in order to ask: where between them does the visual production of present-day Sofia take place? I will use the ideal types as coordinate systems through which I will look at the post-totalitarian city and search for differences rather than "deviations" from the standard paradigms. The above ideal types are only cognitive tools instead of the "norms" the Bulgarian capital must necessarily follow. That is to say, the models will be used only as instruments for an analysis of the specificity of Sofia's urbanscape.

Bulgaria's capital underwent a difficult yet rapid transformation between 1989 and 2007. It started as a semi-modern, semi-totalitarian city, went through a short phase (1989-1991/1992) as a carnivalesque stage of the "Velvet Revolution," and landed in a sort of semi-global, semi-"Balkanized" condition. The materials collected and the analyses carried out by the Seminar demonstrate how contemporary Sofia remains a peculiar hybrid of a modern, totalitarian, and postmodern city offering the eye a historically dynamic, "forbidden" mix of different visual regimes. I will describe here what these regimes of visibility/invisibility were, and still are, and how they are connected to the social, political, and economic realities of the city. Media theorists, to begin with, classify images and visual conflicts into several zones: excessive visibility, normal visibility, low visibility, invisibility, and deliberate concealment.[18] The visual regimes of the modern city and of the postmodern megapolis discussed above can relate differently to these zones, thus producing a complex set of visible-invisible effects; the politically active city agents, in turn, can use these regimes consciously, and in fact they sometimes do develop policies in relation to them. We will see, Sofia shows that the zones are shaped by interrelationships of mutual tension and intertwinement and that the various visual regimes too interface and are even capable of "shadowing" each other. Consequently, because they intersect in unexpected ways—for example, at the core of excessive visibility lie blind spots and some phenomena become visible only in comparisons, contrasts, and visual tensions—it is difficult to make hard-and-fast distinctions among such regimes.

2. *Conspicuous Sofia: The Zone of the Screaming Images*

These are series of images by which diverse urban subjects as well as the city in its problematic entirety want to represent themselves, things the potential observer must not miss. They insist on being the focal point of the field of vision, at the center of the city or of its stage; in their conspicuousness, such images make the normal, inconspicuous urban sights difficult to see or even invisible, for, in order to be seen, those sights now require a redirection of attention, a special focus, and a change in viewers' perceptive Gestalt. Yet, these aggressive sets of images transform themselves simultaneously with every historical transformation of the city. In Sofia's case, their dynamics follow the rapid phases of the 1989-2007 transition, moving as they do from a visual regime dominated by the central perspective of totalitarian power to the visions celebrating political liberalism to the regime of limitless market visuality.

In fact, Sofia's urban structure, architecture, and sights were not typically totalitarian even during communism, when the city remained a peculiar historical hybrid. It certainly was not transformed by communism to the extent that Moscow was, for instance; it did not need to be rebuilt after the Second World War, like Warsaw; it was not as horribly cut up by its leaders' megalomaniac visions as Ceaușescu's Bucharest; and it did not have such emblematic "proletarian" streets as Karl Marx Allee in East Berlin. As in the years before communism, the city has always had something Balkanian, familiar, premodern, and, in this sense, anti-totalitarian, about it. Far from the purity of the modern "panopticism" and Benjamin's "visibility of the constructive principle," Sofia has always been a city hard to govern centrally. In the period between the 1878 Liberation and the Second World War, the capital of the newly liberated Bulgaria grew rather chaotically, without a clear urban development plan,[19] keeping its Ottoman neighborhoods as basic urban units, with occasional campaigns of uncoordinated construction.[20] Between 1878 and the Second World War, Sofia proved its modernity less through a centralized, functionally urbanistic rationality than through symbolic de-Orientalization, i.e., through emblematic buildings and other forms of its will to catch up with the civilizational achievements of urbanism.[21] Modern infrastructure was built in a similar way. Historians have shown that, "progressive" as this infrastructure was viewed, it took a long time to build and remained financially problematic. Water, power, and transport facilities were unevenly distributed, insufficiently functional, ill-maintained due to lack of specialists, and, in fact, poorly utilized by the different groups of Sofia residents, some of which were reluctant to change their pre-modern habits.[22] While preserving historical strata dating back to Roman, Byzantine, and Ottoman times, Sofia's relatively narrow streets—for a long time, only those in the central part of the city were paved—eventually filled with buildings in various styles, some designed by foreign architects and others by Bulgarians educated abroad (it was not until 1942 that the first Bulgarian architecture school was created), who favored, in their work, approaches such as National Romanticism, Sofia *Sezession*, pre-war Modernism, or "mature," post-war Modernism. But the "representative" buildings and districts were next door to the spontaneously built, styleless, poor, and chaotic neighborhoods of Yuchbounar and Konyovitsa, and refugee neighborhoods with village-like (rather than town-like) houses complete with yards and gardens (such as those between the Lagera and Pavlovo quarters). Socialism would later build the Stalinist center of the city, the heavy industrial periphery, and the prefab satellite towns Mladost and Lyulin, integrating large rural populations with their premodern mentality into the urban environment.

In the first couple of years after 1989, Sofia, as many other cities in Eastern Europe, was an arena of protest demonstrations and rallies. The latter's slogans called for democracy and a multiparty system while speaking to the kind of protesting public behavior Vaclav Havel called "living in truth" (during the first years of the postcommunist transition, Sofia had even its small "city of truth," erected by protestors living in tents in the front of the Presidency building).[23] Apart from and irres-pective of their specific political goals, the protesters involuntarily produced a sight whose aesthetics and dynamics were designed to shake the totalitarian aura of the city. The Velvet Revolution of 1989 was obli-vious to the complexity of Sofia, a city, as noted earlier, with many historical faces: by way of parodic reversal, the revolution made visible only that layer of the city that had a distinctly communist symbolic meaning. Everything that was associated with communist power and was emanating a feeling of impersonal collectivism, historical pomp, and op-timism was to be subjected to public travesties and parodies. The official architecture of power was objectified in the Stalinist Baroque whose central symmetry and heavy columns dominated the city center (the Largo), in the political aesthetics of the Party House (the Communist Party headquarters)[24] that stood face-to-face with the monument to Lenin (who, in his turn, had his gaze firmly fixed on the future), in the mummy-like aura of the Mausoleum assembling the symbolic order of communism,[25] in the countless statues of communist leader Georgi Dimitrov, his acolytes, and Second World War partisans, in the memo-rial plates, decorations, changeable and unchangeable slogans on bill-boards,[26] in the names of streets and boulevards, and so forth.

The spontaneous, colorful crowds of different people who not only protested but also rejoiced, sang, and celebrated their own boldness, who behaved (walked, jumped, danced, shouted) any way they wanted, staging their own freedom and "lack of restraint" with good-humored, playful irony were in contrast, even in conflict, with the entire system of spatialized symbols of power in communist Sofia. People moved, assembled, and dispersed precisely in such areas emblematic of the communist regime but without conforming to these sites' power perspective. The protesters' behavior placed within ironic quotation marks, as it were, the city squares and tribunes from which the Party eye used to gaze onto the political processions and Party members saluted the "united" proletarian masses. The various hues of the oppositional blue (the color of the newly formed opposition Union of Democratic Forces) and human diversity of every sort and kind drowned the fading red of leftover flags and five-pointed stars. At will, the demonstrators would block traffic, march with lit candles through places that used to be venues of tank and missile parades, surround and symbolically desecrate official public buildings. The new public actions were conducted "in the back" (or, in Bakhtinian terms, against the *dolnica*, the lower body) of the government bastions—the demonstrations had already moved the new, spiritual center of the city behind the Party House and the National Assembly, facing the silhouette of Sofia's Orthodox cathedral.[27]

Thus, the celebrating city made visible its new political life or, more precisely, a contradictory moment in this life: the carnival of the Velvet Revolution. The source, producer, and consumer of images was a paradoxical and theatrical subject: the People-made-up-of-free-individuals (collective and dispersed into single individuals at the same time), who staged and feted itself in its newly won sovereignty. Resorting to the visual, verbal, and spatial codes of the city, the People acted out the Drama of the Two Modernities: the victory of the liberal, non-violent, and individualistic Modernity over the collective and totalitarian one.[28] This political urban spectacle still contained a panoptic moment: the visual production of rallies and demonstrations presupposed a unified urban "stage" and a unified Eye of power that may be attacked, humiliated, and scandalized. That is why this visual regime was hybrid and transient; through scandal and carnival, it made visible for a short while precisely the totalitarian features of otherwise non-totalitarian Sofia.

This public, political, and playful visuality was slowly marginalized and then obliterated completely by another wave of aggressive, conspicuous urban images: the commercial ones. Pictures of lively, civic spontaneity were thus replaced by those of spontaneous consumption, so much so that commodities supplanted the political actors of democracy. Sofia seemed to be turning successfully into a megapolis: fighting for communal places and the public gaze were not protesting and dancing popular masses but a chaotic multitude of private, aggressive advertisements, billboards, logos, signs, banners, avalanches of posters, flyers, specially disguised facades, expensive shop windows, erotic pictures behind which were all sorts of social subjects: firms, holding companies, patriotic circles, small enterprises, Buddhist associations, politicians, global corporations, youth organizations, family cooperatives, individuals, and so on. This was no longer a city where a central power could "engineer" and discipline social space from its panoptic center but where divergent lives and disparate economic initiatives intersected confusingly in a Babel of private perspectives and interests. The "mirror" of "the people," the latter's central, visually governing perspective had broken to pieces; the time of individuals had come. Sofia's variegated stage no longer showed a consistent plot and dramatic unity, but dispersion, conflicting multiplicity and diversity, enacting as it did centrifugal entrepreneurship and commercial aggression.[29] But, as usual, behind this chaos stood difficult-to-see structures.[30] Some of them were unspecific, global, and megapolitan, while others were characteristically Sofian, telling of what was typical to this city—in the postmodern megapolis, global commercial imagery exerts unobstructed power, occupying the conspicuous center of urban visuality; unlike this imagery are several monumental sites and foci developed in Sofia over the last seventeen years.

3. *Globalization and Neighborhoods*

Global was the consumer utopia that served as a framework for the chaotic abundance of commercial images. The sea of advertisements that swamped Sofia was a celebration of a new global lifestyle of oversupply and of happy and unobstructed, universally accessible consumption represented both as a dream and as a norm. The real power of this "dreamed-of norm" in Sofia is borne out by the disappearance of this norm's Other: the glossy, advertising visual layer stages only the heroes and narratives of consumption; absent from it are not only images of misery and poverty but also of labor and production, of industry and technologies, which were so typical to the socialist imagery of socialism just a decade ago. In addition, the new imagery—albeit for seductive rather than disciplining reasons—prefers panoptic places. Commercial pictures came to dominate all possible sites of visibility: the center of the city, the intersections, the spaces along highways, the blind walls visible from a distance, the rooftops, in sum, all places from which the environment could be controlled and manipulated.

If things had not had a specific Sofian color, we could have concluded that this was simply a *sui generis* arrival of globalization in this city. Yet, from the mid-1990s to the present, the advertisements of the big international companies have cropped up successfully alongside the emblems and pictures of the local business of various neighborhood and family enterprises: Luchezar Boyadjiev, a Bulgarian artist and participant in the Seminar, has analyzed the fine spatial hierarchies of this mixing in his project "Hot City Visual." He has found that, as regards advertising, the vertical axis of the urban environment has become the arena for a struggle and spatial redistribution of three different social actors with aesthetics of their own. The first one may be defined as neighborhood aesthetics. It consists of crude, handmade advertisements of small businesses seeking to attract clients from the neighborhood: ugly placards with sloppy lettering, random notices with phone numbers on tear-off strips, photocopied ads, signs written in chalk on the front wall of houses. It dominates the periphery of the city and lies low above the ground, at the eye level of the potential pedestrian-client. Its polar opposite is corporate advertising (Coca-Cola, United Colors of Benetton, Sony, Hugo Boss, etc.), which installs its expensive signs and giant panels on the roofs of the fancy buildings in the city center. It is characterized by global design, gloss, prestige, high professionalism, and spatial domination of the viewers' gazes.

Boyadjiev's key finding, however, involved the middle levels of the spatial hierarchy, where the fledgling Bulgarian businesses (advertising Bulgarian vodka, *rakiya*, sausages, mobile phones, and so forth) displayed its billboards using a strange mixture of global and neighborhood-populist devices complete with strange visual transgressions. Thus, adapting to the habits and preferences of the local public, global aesthetics featured, at a hidden level, a certain degree of Bulgarian "cultural intimacy."

However, it took the sophisticated eye of an artist and critic as Boyadjiev to make out these arrangements; to the untrained eye, these asymmetries and hierarchies remain invisible, undistinguishable in the surrounding chaos. To this eye, the global advertising images simply blend in with the boundless diversity of neighborhood commerce and its squat shops, family businesses, small stores, pavilions, and street kiosks. To put it in spatial terms, for the lay observer, what comes from the "outside" is mixed and confused with what is born "from below"; because of the visual overabundance, the global is submerged into the local. The overall impression is of colorful yet homogeneous and horizontally laid abundance and chaos successfully hiding the big money, of high technology and commercial calculation behind the global corporate ads, as well as of chaotic disfunctionality at the level of local administration, which lends these mixtures an intimate, human touch, making them part of the overabundant and self-generated visuality. Thus, this scopic environment has a powerfully neoliberal message: everything offered to the eye is natural. With a typical, commercial sort of romanticism, it wants to persuade the observer that, even when advertising Coca-Cola or Samsung, what is actually in play is something authentic, not globally managed oversupply or well-calculated advertising strategies, but an immediate, elemental force, a self-generating life that represents and expresses itself.

4. *Weak Municipal Power as Sight*

The breakdown of the previously centralized, ideological, and bureaucratic city government took extreme forms. At times, even the minimum of governmentality needed by any big city was called into question. Along with the many clashes in public and on TV, Sofianites witnessed the municipal authorities' inability to control the city's gradual decline in the midst of one serious municipal crisis after another. The mayoralty, the municipal council, and the chief architect of Sofia largely relinquished their administrative-urbanistic duties. After the first years of postcommunist collective celebrations in the street, city life shifted towards the private sphere, exploded in countless individual, group, and corporate manifestations, and became difficult to oversee and govern while, paradoxically enough, the mayor's media visibility grew constantly, an aspect to which I will return later on.[31]

The weakness of the city's administration had specific causes, some of which were criminal and fall under the jurisdiction of the relevant authorities. But it also had a general, non-specific, structural cause: the huge and chaotic social energy concentrated beyond the loose control of the city's official power. Sofia's space constantly staged the same visible drama of a barely sustained municipal order threatened by merciless pressure from all sorts of private, legal, semi-legal, and criminal structures that subjected the city to manipulations often resulting in sheer plunder. This space was home to a huge number of utterly unscrupulous individual and group-based forms of entrepreneurship along with their struggles, conflicts, and claims. These interests would stop at nothing to reach their goals. Irrespective of the municipal ordinances and regulations, businessmen built whatever they wanted wherever they wanted—for example, they built up the area around Sofia's "ring road," blocking the road's renovation. Likewise, people of various social strata and trades (most often taxi drivers) could decide on a whim to block major intersections and ignite a very visible, citywide traffic crisis.

One of the visible aspects of the crisis of governmentality became apparent in a series of political scandals highly publicized on television. I should add, the visual side of this administrative failure was in no way limited to these incidents. Behind the media theater of the public conflicts, everything the mayor and the municipal council were supposed to look after was left to crumble, abandoned, or sold off, thus shaping Sofia as both a desert- and Babel-like landscape. For more than ten years Sofia's roads, including some of the busiest thoroughfares, were unmaintained and began to look like the moon's surface: strewn with jutting ruts, with cracks, deep potholes, and even with ditches that could swallow a whole car. Still more telling of the breakdown of centralized administration were the repeated crises in various subsystems of urban infrastructure: "the water crisis," "the central heating crisis," and "the garbage crisis," which, under mayors Sofiyanski and Boyko Borissov, broke out regularly and took the form of spectacularly huge, stinking piles of garbage on street corners and pavements. If those crises were temporary, the spectacle of the transport crisis was permanent and conspicuous. The number of cars grew incredibly, exceeding one million in Sofia, a city with one and a half million inhabitants, and began to enact the same scene daily: drivers stuck for hours in the picturesque traffic jams featuring a strange mix of flashy Porsches, dark Mercedes, and silvery BMWs alongside still sputtering Trabants, nondescript Moskviches, and Western-made old wrecks bought for pennies. Thus, the city lived a busy commercial life, a life that was being globalized and taken to a new intensity while its technological infrastructure, deprived of funds, political will, and legal oversight, was falling apart before everybody's eyes. The general consensus was that there was no alternative to capitalism.

Unable to respond appropriately, Sofianites were both authors of these changes and passive observers of the commercial expansion of their city, which, at the same time, was losing the infrastructural and functional backbone that makes a modern city possible.

5. *The Advance of Nature*

Between approximately 1990 and 2000, the absence of strong, local government institutions allowed the city's "Other"—nature, on the one hand, asociality, on the other hand—to threat organized, urban space. From 1990 onwards, grass began to grow in the cracks in the central streets' pavement while gardens and parks turned wild, and, in particular, the lots between blocks of flats in the prefab suburbs were gradually overgrown with weeds and bushes, becoming an impenetrable wasteland. Owing to the malfunctioning of the sanitation services and the sewer system, entire areas were regularly flooded and polluted, and some streets developed perennial puddles brimming with life. Sofianites were witnesses to the biological cycle in which the decay of organic waste gives birth to a new biological mass. "Dust thou art, and unto dust shalt thou return" was the motto of the day as the rusting and natural decay, deterioration, decomposition, disintegration, and dispersal of urban structures, the rotting of timber, the dismantling, theft, and overall disappearance of solid metal constructions, deep underground cable networks, water pipes, heavy rails, and even bronze monuments (whose expensive metal parts were stolen and sold for scrap) were happening before the very eyes of the city's inhabitants.[32] Oddly enough, at times, especially in the first years of the transition, all these looked almost like deliberately staged symbolic acts, as improvised urban performances and installations, what with overflowing garbage cans, incredibly filthy streets, skeletons of abandoned cars breeding their own flora and fauna in their hollow husks, giant pieces of plaster peeling off and crashing near mothers pushing baby carriages, dilapidated buildings crumbling extemporaneously (one of these crushed to death two girls who happened to be driving by in a car when a wall collapsed). One of the biggest nuisance was the packs of stray dogs, which were often aggressive towards the elderly and children, and literally chased away the few remaining, bourgeois-looking, elegant cats that had survived socialism. With their huge number, the dogs were the city's "barking" problem, which gave rise to a whole series of serious political and municipal debates.[33] Artist Krassimir Terziev, a Seminar participant, synthesized the fears of the average Sofianite in a telling video art installation. His work featured a mobile survey of an anonymous, prefab, decrepit, and dirty Sofia neighborhood amidst which there suddenly rose the gigantic silhouettes of stray dogs that looked like prehistoric dinosaurs or Godzillas, heads towering above the concrete apartment buildings in a city where they were the only inhabitants left.

6. *The City-in-Ruins Versus the Vibrant City: Intensification of Space*

The overall decline, rising crime, and the increasing wildness and empti-ness of the centralized urban community was only one side of a more contradictory process. The other side indicated that a new, enterprising, and lively commercial city was being born, a colorful polis of private enterprise that penetrated everywhere in a deep and sometimes quite comic way. This penetration visibly defied the timid attempts at control-ling urban growth by setting up centralized town-planning regulations. Thus, in forms alternately vibrant, cheerful, and unscrupulous, capital-ism was taking over the city space in its entirety.

As a result, around 1992-1993 the old markets suddenly came to life. The unexpected abundance of goods and products that flooded Sofia's marketplaces was truly stunning to a population used to social-ism's meager supplies and abundant shortages. It was as if the socialist shops indiscriminately opened their secret storehouses and poured out all their forbidden riches for everyone to see. Now privately owned, the ordinary neighborhood stores promptly renamed themselves "grocery" and "mini-market" and, accordingly, filled up to the rafters with a variety of native and imported goods most unusual to socialist eyes. All of a sudden, lively commercial areas began to pop up in the most unex-pected places, even where most certainly the previous regime would not have allowed them. You would see, for instance, antiques and souvenirs stalls in front of the St. Alexander Nevsky Cathedral, a new vegetable market by the tramway line in Sofia's narrowest and busiest street, Graf Ignatiev, a flea market by the concrete bed of the Vladaiska River, a book market in Slaveykov Square, new commercial passageways, ar-cades, booths, carts, or wares simply displayed on pieces of cloth on the ground. Thus, capitalism provided a lesson in the intensive use of space while skirting government plans and regulations by utilizing formerly deserted places, niches, holes, and surfaces in all sorts of ways: Sofia's courtyards were transformed into French-style restaurants; old kiosk morphed into taverns; garages and basements were converted into Internet clubs; blank walls became high-demand commercial space; basements opened their neoliberal windows to all sort of trade and retail; post boxes filled with flyers, brochures, and promotional leaflets. After forty years of absence, newspaper vendors reappeared in the streets, and the number of their booths grew exponentially. But the most telling example of this intensification of commercial city life was to be found in the spacious, formerly empty, aesthetically poor, official grand halls and foyers on the ground floors of the National Palace of Culture.[34] After they had been let out—the thirteen-century-old Bulgarian culture could not support the huge building financially—they were filled or, more precisely, glutted with the maze-like tiny shops of a dense flea market where everything was on sale from kitschy souvenirs to Turkish T-shirts, Taiwanese electronics, flip-flops, Swiss watches, and Paulo Coelho paperbacks. Lyudmila Zhivkova's symbolic center of socialist culture— the palace of "national aesthetic education" for the construction of which whole districts of old Sofia were demolished in the 1970s, was taken over peacefully and commercially in a matter of months and in the wholeness of its totalitarian space. From an empty mausoleum of ideologically sacralized culture, it turned into a vending hive; from an urban symbol of centralization, it was remade into a super-intensive, kitschy intersection of multiply branching commercial channels.

7. "Squat Shops" and Hotels: Visual Contrasts in Central Sofia

For a decade, central Sofia showed off the comic contrasts of the city's new entrepreneurship. The first element worth noting here was the aforementioned, ubiquitous mushrooming of stalls, kiosks, pavilions, cafés, grill bars, Afghan and Arab sandwich shops, new Chinese restaurants with paper lanterns, and firms of all sizes. This type of small family business also had its original types such as the ingenious "squat shops" (*klekshop*) in Sofia basements, little shops selling beer, soft drinks, candy bars, and so on out of windows at ground level, which imperceptibly created a whole new, body culture within the culture of shopping. The second element was opposite as the city was visibly taken over also by big money and the concomitant, nouveau-riche pretensions seeking another, either famous designer-made or less known, glamorous visibility: hotels, posh shops, arcades, boutiques, previously unthinkable display windows, pricey restaurants. The new luxury usually concentrated in the upscale shopping streets like Vitosha, Solounska, Stamboliyski, Legè, and Graf Ignatiev, which rapidly filled with Hugo Boss, Max Mara, Bata, Krizia, and other fashion stores. In the center of Sofia, the socialist TzUM Central Department Store was converted into a glitzy yet barely frequented superstore, and the first malls appeared at the end of the period (City Center Sofia in the Lozenets Quarter, Mall of Sofia at Opulchenska Street and Stamboliyski Boulevard; I might add, seven or eight malls are currently under construction). The Stalinist baroque of Hotel Balkan became the Sofia Sheraton redecorated with ornament suggestive of a "commercial" postmodern style of sorts; the socialist Hotel Sofia turned into a Radisson, and, after many twists and turns, a new Hilton finally appeared in Sofia. Also, the number of hotels in the city soared, with luxury hotels alone reaching 144 in 2005 (available statistics tell us that there were just eleven such hotels in communist Sofia). Nobody knows if these hotels, which reportedly are at present about forty percent full, will indeed be ever filled to capacity or if they will eventually be sold as part of some kind of money laundering scheme or will go bankrupt and turn into derelict crystal tombs in the center of Sofia.

But this geography of luxury was not well thought out, especially at the beginning of the transition. Lacking breadth of vision and, probably, enough money, Sofia capitalists did not work with entire districts but with single buildings and separate land lots. Their piecemeal approach ignored contextual urban solutions and had no interest in their projects' vicinities. This yielded some amusing results. For instance, even on Vitosha Boulevard, Sofia's most expensive shopping street, there were squat shops until recently, and to this day, there are street stalls right in front of the super-expensive stores. The new "crystal palaces" of private capital (hotels and business centers), with their dark-mirror glass facades, cropped up (and still do) in the most unlikely urban settings, often in jarring contrast with their surroundings and in total disregard of the city's memory and architectural traditions. The buildings' luxurious silhouettes rose defiantly next to grey old prefab blocks of flats, their mirror glass reflecting rundown apartment buildings with their poor retirees peeping out of the windows. In the text of the city, these new edifices look like absurd quotations of globalization or, better still, like global upstarts who neither know nor particularly care exactly where they are located.

8. Privatization of the Public Domain and the Crisis of Collective Symbols

As specified above, by 1993-1994, Sofia had largely been cleansed of communist public symbols. Simultaneously, it stopped being the public city of the transition. Rallies and demonstrations lost their appeal, meaning, and image. The total 'blueing" of streets and squares—blue was the color of an emerging political coalition—became a thing of the past. The hunger strikes conducted before everybody's eyes and the "tent towns" of truth and protest suddenly began to look unthinkable. The public spaces of socialism were desecrated, abandoned, and at last taken over by commercial symbols and sights. This process was only the surface of something much more far-reaching: the public domain in general was gradually losing its visibility as such, both in its civic and in its official-governmental form. To an important extent, public places, symbols, and emblems were gradually privatized or pushed to the margins by architectural and spatial forms pertaining to private life and the market. Examples of this kind abound. With the exception of certain key political buildings such as the National Assembly and the President's Office, all other symbolic and emblematic buildings and sites of Sofia did not enjoy particular care and maintenance by the municipal or state authorities, and so they gradually fell into ruin, involuntarily staging their own insignificance. For a long time, the roof of the former Palace, now the National Art Gallery, threatened to collapse; the burned-down Party House with its disfigured, five-pointed star symbol remained smoke-stained and smashed for five or six years; the reconstruction of the Central Hali Shopping Centre lasted ten years or so, while that of the Sofia Public Baths has not been completed to date. The overall impression was that of a city which lacked the funds and energy to preserve its traditional architectural landmarks and defining styles, a city which could not and did not want to maintain its "symbolic infrastructure."

Embodied by the symbols of the public, the logic of disintegration was also reproduced by what was happening in the public places of civic life. The expanding market appropriated them, sometimes lawfully and sometimes less so, which has resulted in drawn-out lawsuits over the privatization of various public buildings and land lots. In addition, the city lost about twenty percent of its green areas to various constructions projects, gas stations, and parking lots. The commercial conquest of the public, the civic, and the municipal reached the tiniest urban features: the municipal-owned tramway stops and electric poles were covered with all sorts of private ads and offers, and even the metal bars of traffic signs sprouted additional advertising panels, plates, and signs that actually blocked out the traffic signs themselves.

This is how, both deserted and overpopulated, asocial and overly social, Sofia turned into a city of contrasts. Its public sectors were aging while commercial Sofia was staging its show of youth, unscrupulousness, and vibrancy. In the last ten years, the city has gotten visibly richer and prettier in a peculiarly disorganized kind of way. At least in its central part, Sofia started looking like a European capital even though various objections can be raised against the aesthetics of its beautification. Parallel with the symbolic defeat of panopticism, Sofia became a stage of a neoliberal excess, which, parallel with its extremes and transgressions, brought about uncoordinated renovation of the city in a "molecular" way, at various, unconnected points of the urban space. Typical of this approach were companies that, for the sake of their commercial image, would fix whole buildings whose ground floor they occupied; advertisements that renovated facades and blind walls; private shops that repaired just the doors and windows of the building they were in or only the sidewalk in front of them.

What happened to public buildings, symbols, and places also happened to public figures. The faces and voices of the transition, the heroes of rallies and demonstrations were themselves relegated to history, elbowed aside by the TV and media personalities. The images of the democratic agora were imperceptibly replaced by those of the visual marketplace of sights and faces. In the new context, what was sold on the media market was overall personal charisma rather than principled, left or right political positions. That is why it was not just the constantly visible journalists and media stars who scored visual rating points; so did politicians, who increasingly imitated the media celebrities. They wanted less to represent their electorate than be represented themselves and shown on TV. The difference between political presence, political PR, and television advertising disappeared, and, with it, so did the difference between public and commercial behavior. The visual rating of politicians became much more important than their political messages. More and more, politicians were "watched" on television, not "listened to"; everything that was not visible (on TV) lost meaning, and, quite significantly, the circulation of the dailies decreased drastically. The basic differences between commercial, public, and political visibility were placed under erasure, and the same, market-driven, anonymous mechanisms cut the air time of TV current-affairs programs while increasing that allotted to shows, contests, and commercials. In addition to the large number of game shows, talk shows, and entertainment features that arguably catered more to the eye than the mind, there were shows that parodied public debates, caricaturing this fundamentally civic genre as comic verbal clash (e.g., "Sblusuk" or, "Clash" on bTV).

9. *Visions Outside the Law*

During this time, the criminal underworld was another major player in Sofia's visual refashioning. Not only in its actions but also as representation, crime dominated the city. Even though images of crime and violence were probably less present in people's lives than commercial visuality, these images were no less aggressive and all-pervasive with respect to social space, for they were not limited to the particular urban topography of crime-ridden districts. Every other week saw execution-style killings in the streets of the city, including broad-daylight, gruesome murders, often witnessed by children. It was as if criminals set out to deride the televised statements by the chief of police and the interior minister who were trying to persuade viewers that crime had been brought under control: even as the officials spoke, gangs fought and shot each other in the streets, smashed up discotheques, conducted punitive operations, beat up innocent bystanders, and intimidated witnesses. In other words, this was both goal-oriented as well as symbolic violence[35] that not only occurred in a regime of aggressive, ubiquitous visibility but also deliberately pushed this scopic violence beyond the typical geography of criminality enclosed in specific urban areas.

In this context, it would not be a complete exaggeration to suggest that the underworld advertised itself through direct and overt violence, demeanor, and affluence status symbols. With the exception of the top bosses, who were always invisible, all "midlevel" criminals sought theatrical symbols of their indiscriminate power. They moved around in obscenely expensive limousines, were surrounded by large cohorts of bodyguards, owned and spent time in pricey hotels, restaurants, bars, clubs, and discos in central Sofia, assigned their possessions aggressive names and emblems, and behaved as authoritarian, feudal lords totally outside police control. In fact, the difference between entrepreneurship and criminality was publicly perceived as negligible—moving around in their flashy cars, the symbols of happy consumption and lawlessness merged. Criminals surrounded themselves by the same status tokens as the nouveaux-riches: obligatory designer-made casual dress, expensive sunglasses, mobile phones, which were still rare at the time, and so forth. But unlike the (quasi) legally rich, their proudest symbols were their own, "excessive" bodies, the heavy, overmuscular bodies of ex-athletes[36] with massive gold chains around the thick necks, walking around mutants parading their unthinkably bulging muscles and bellies in the streets of Sofia. This bodily aggressive style of behavior was flouted before the eyes of ordinary people as a sign of prestige, as the only possible model of career and success.

Unpleasant as it may sound, this was actually only the flip side of another visibility—that of sickness, poverty, old age, and hopelessness. As mentioned earlier, the centralized, modern polis had its techniques of pushing such phenomena beyond social visibility. However, in addition to gangsters, thieves, and prostitutes, Sofia had suddenly filled with the homeless, beggars, old people rummaging through garbage cans, with tramps, cripples, abandoned children sniffing glue, and young drug addicts whom the socialist capital had declared nonexistent. The city of the transition was incapable of controlling its outcasts in a modern, panoptic way. Nor did it succeed in hiding them behind their own phobic doubles. To be sure, the human face of Bulgarian poverty was more visible than the imaginal production of phantasms and simulacra. To use Deleuze's expression, Sofia was unable to *impose a form of conduct by distributing things and people in space.* Bulgaria's capital proved to be a city that was incapable of using its most important tool, i.e., a spatial policy of moving people and regulating their social presence and behavior.

Thus, the zone of aggressive visibility and "screaming images" puts forth a multilayered message as a result of the association of several series of discrepant aesthetics, a message of complex meanings in which the global and the neighborly combined with metaphors of commercialism and literal criminality. Very different in their content, these denotations and connotations are quite similar in their aggressive display, which enables them to compete for the viewer's exclusive attention at the expense of everything else. The specific Sofian visual regime must be sought precisely in the spatial juxtapositions, intersections, and hybridizations of these two sets of eye-catching images, the "authentically" commercial and the criminal. This regime could be called *inverted panopticism*. It is not that an invisible power observes everybody; it is that everybody, including those who otherwise, by definition, prefer the underworld's darkness, want to be seen, aggressively pushing their own images in people's faces. Content-wise, this regime has a basic "philosophical" message. Its intertwined images imply that in actuality the market borders on the "dangerous," "manly" life outside the law, that the market and lawlessness are equally worthy, equally without an alternative, equally triumphant and vital, and equally representing attractive lifestyles.[37] It also suggests that capital venture and crime are in fact two sides of the same coin—total freedom, indiscriminate enterprise, ingenuity, and unlimited, incessant boldness—and that in commercialism and lawbreaking alike rules the same Eros, whose images of opulence and ruthlessness watch over the city. As I will show below, this legally ambiguous, aesthetic dominance of the world produced even role models to be imitated by the youth or in political campaigns.

10. *Invisibility of the Visible*

In the previous parts I discussed the changing series of Sofia's conspicuous images and the provocative contrasts they created. This brash imagery pushed other forms of visibility into a zone where they were more difficult to see. On the other hand, many urban images and associated practices did not seek such a brutal effect. They simply coexisted side by side in an incredibly colorful picture leading to absurd, often comic contrasts. In such a regime of marginal, quasi obscured visibility stood the city's various historical layers, juxtaposed to one another or mingled together, indistinguishable to the untrained eye: a mosque next to litter-strewn Roman ruins (located near a glitzy restaurant called Ruini/Ruins) close to the dilapidated public baths built in the Neoromantic national style, a building that, in turn, was placed across the Central Hali (now a supermarket), behind which was the Synagogue, all of them crumbling samples of socialist and pre-socialist architectural modernism. I have already pointed out how the neighborly and the global existed one next to another, just as memorial plates reminding the passer-by of totalitarian times shared the same sites with advertisements of Flirt Vodka and the monument to the national hero Vassil Levski rose opposite a billboard featuring the bare rear of transvestite pop star Azis.

The layperson's eye could mistake the transgressive contrasts of the imaginally obtrusive zone for the ordinary, colorful diversity of "normal" visuality; likewise, people's political and aesthetic nostalgia for "order," which aggravated many a critical observer, could be directed at both indiscriminately. To resists the power of the blatant commercial-criminal images, one needed distance and the critical ability to adapt one's perspective and thus break Sofia's visual codes so as to notice other things behind the immediately noticeable. Of course, one did not take special training to realize that the "demonstrative," public killings pointedly laid bare the weakness of the local government and the lack of an effective police force whose authority, control, and oversight would drive, under normal circumstances, the criminal element back into its dark spaces. However, a particular critical skill was indeed necessary to understand that Sofia's governmentality had lost something else too. For it suffered not only from a loss of functionality but also of Eros and with it, from a loss of image. Symptomatic here were the "visual metaphors," that is to say, the mode of transfer of the dominant visual code onto other realms. To be truly visible, political figures had to disguise themselves in this dominant code, to dress up as daring and vitally necessary heroes of the capital. This became especially obvious during the last mayoral election campaign, late in incumbent Boyko Borissov's term. His political career has been quite amazing: a former fireman, karate champion, and security personnel member of the Bulgarian communist leader Todor Zhivkov, he later became a bodyguard for King Simeon upon the King's return to Sofia in 1996. After that, in 2001, he advanced to the post of chief secretary of the interior ministry in the monarch's government, and then, distancing himself from this government in 2004, he became mayor of Sofia (2005). Today he is a likely candidate to be Bulgaria's next prime minister. His PR team has shrewdly built his image using models that belonged to the sphere of non-institutional, commercially aggressive, legally transgressive, and "daily life" aesthetics. All he does is publicized as ensuing not from the power of his official position but as the personal, risk-taking initiative of a "resourceful" man "like us." As if he were a hero from a Western movie in a world outside the law, he, all alone, defends "justice" against the fierce resistance of bureaucrats and corrupt public figures. His power wants to be seen as that of a business-man and a fighter, not of an administrator. He is, the media would have us believe, a self-enterprising and self-made mayor who does not follow the rules if they do not suit him but nevertheless "gets things done." In sum, the image of the city mayor, personifying the city's political and administrative power, is modeled on the laws of market aggressiveness rather than old-style politics. This indicates that, no longer trusting its traditional emblems involving central administration, procedures, obser-vance of the law, authority, rational principles, control, and so on, the city's political power adopts the reigning images of the visual regime of power.[38] This is why the usual candidate strives to look like a business person, a "cool guy," and shady ex-athlete, all rolled into one. Thus, Sofia's visual regime, too, bears witness to the general retreat of the political under the onslaught of the economic. I might add, both terms are used here in the broadest sense possible. As we have seen, the "economic" encompasses not only the field of commercial exchanges regulated by laws and rules but also all sorts of private initiatives, appro-priations, uses, adjustments, and business gambles barely allowed by law. In other words, this is a conventional term for the overall sphere of unregulated activity, which does not distinguish between businessmen, "resourceful guys," and criminals—no wonder "criminal" and "busi-nessman" have become synonymous in the Bulgarian press.

Otherwise put, similarly to all contemporary megapolises, Sofia made visible not urban order and rationality but its residents' phantasms, which differed from the global projections of growth and success in that they were a hybrid attesting to the totally unrestrained freedom of the "economic," which spilled over into other, usually prohibited, domains. Central here was the problematic message of a certain versatility and multifunctionality, of bold, risky, and legally questionable initiatives, of a "raw" kind of life without limits and regulations in a motley chaos without a city god or master where the "resourceful" type will make it. By virtue of its own phantasmatic logic, this dominant message was associated not only with representations that celebrated the recent, neo-liberal cowboys but also with images that, quite contrary to the usual Western movie, gleefully broke with different variants of order, from outraging commercials that played on porno references and BDSM imagery in a deliberate assault on public decency to advertisements that caused viewers sheer physical revulsion. In short, what the city's new visual regime celebrated was that rules were ridiculous and that, as a result, "everything was permitted."

Approached from another angle, however, this phantasm reveals specific tensions between "indigenous" and "foreign." The global consumer utopia had a "Latin," Western profile. A case in point was the omnipresent dominance of the Latin alphabet as a luxury marker over the "poor" and purely functional Cyrillic. The happy consumers on billboards and in ads overall consumed non-Bulgarian goods, brands, and lifestyles; the luxurious, stylistically sophisticated, material and spatial environment, the expensive cars, fashion outfits, and even the landscape and female beauty in commercials were created by leading international designers and spoke of Mercedes and Armanis, of Rolexes and the Seychelles. Thus, the city staged a true poverty of the imagination while bestowing seductive power on global references and its non-Sofianite, alien fantasies. But these images of global consumption intertwined with Bulgarian and Balkan ones in practice, as they were used. Here, on the terrain of daily praxis, they mixed with the familiar, the all-is-OK, the criminal, and the lawless to become intimate and "authentic." Such hybrids maintained a stable division in the structure of the phantasmal image offered by Sofia: while the commodities, quality, style, and genuine brand marks were on the side of the imaginary West, the various tricks, appropriations, pranks, scandals, and simply practical uses with or without rules were on the local, Balkan, and native side. So, the city played out a semi-visible "self-colonizing" game of sorts in its visual regime: it allowed global and foreign phantasms; in fact, it continuously dreamed of them; but it also dreamed of a nice and familiar local place "outside the law" in which foreign luxury and wealth could be employed in "our own" specific way, in defiance of all standards and regulations.

This central, Western-Eastern phantasmal disconnect the city acted out was of necessity uneasy, officially uncondoned, and full of hidden tensions. This was intrinsically obvious in the very structure of the "domestic-foreign" disjunction, but also in the complex relationships of this split with its urban context, a split reproduced in the contradiction between the spectacle of luxury and the "new-money" construction boom, on one side, and the asocial wilderness of surrounding decay, on the other. The brutal advertising images with which Sofia represented itself were both in harmony and in disharmony with their settings. On the one hand, the squalor, lack of regulation, the "advance of nature," the architectural and urban absurdities were in stark contrast with the imaginary, Western, harmonious, and luxurious lifestyle. On the other hand, the images were perceived as an authentic context of the homegrown, questionable business practices, "creative" uses of foreign goods, and all the rest of local gimmicks. This was, in brief, a visual regime which both supported and renounced its context; there could not be easy and clear relationships in it. This also determined the peculiar modality of relations with "Otherness." Like the "overexposed" megapolises described by Paul Virilio, the city was losing its modern wholeness, penetrated as it was by crisscrossing, global and virtual telecommunications and visual flows of all kinds. Indeed, Sofia dreamed its global dreams as it spilled over into satellite suburbs and villages, as it transformed the dynamic of the center and posh residential suburbs, and received and sent out its Eurocrats, international dealers, and multinational migrant masses. This is how its boundaries became porous and open to Otherness, which entered the city in the form of "global civilization"—yet, in the form of a "non-city" too to the extent that the city screen also projected the crisis of municipal government, abrupt deregulation, and administrative imbalances. In another, drastically different sense, the city experienced Otherness as wild nature, destruction, dirt, chaos, traffic jams, and beyond all these, as a collapse of civic functions and techno-infrastructural functionality, as crime, brutal corporality, violence, and hatred, as well as a whole sequence of urban disasters and crises.

To sum it all up, between 1989 and 2007 Sofia staged itself as a private, neo-capitalistic city dismissive of "rules." The old, centralized socialist city was replaced by a fluid and ambiguous "site" of unregulated, private lives that did not form a communal, civic life. As these private lives were very diverse, their visual emblems, too, moved in various directions, from the pole of entrepreneurship to the pole of crime, from the pole of rich life, vibrancy, and authenticity to that of lawlessness and scandal, and from luxury to poverty. Thus, this motley city ended up building dream worlds simultaneously domestic and foreign, setting up all kinds of polar opposites, and wrestling with a range of serious social problems behind its live and colorful diversity. Is this, I might ask in closing, the transient picture of an urban space moving towards a global megapolis or, to the contrary, is it a typically and purely Sofia-grown hybrid that will stabilize and become one day a permanent, visual and social environment? Time will tell.

Translated by Katerina Popova

NOTES

1. The Visual Seminar consisted of about 30 people. It was funded by the German Kulturstiftung des Bundes and worked closely with its program "relations" department. For three years (2003–2006), the Seminar served as a platform for artists, designers, photographers, architects, and philosophers who tried to intervene in the visual environment of transition-period Sofia. They created individual art projects, performed research, organized public forums, and made recommendations to the Sofia Municipal Council. Some of the results of the Seminar have already been presented in a series of Bulgarian publications, including books.

2. I refer here in particular to studies such as Stuart Ewen's *All Consuming Images: The Politics of Style in Contemporary Culture* (New York: Basic Books, 1988); Chris Jenks's *Visual Culture* (New York: Routledge, 1995); Paul Hockings, ed., *Principles of Visual Anthropology* (New York: Mouton de Gruyter, 1995); and Nicholas Mirzoeff's *An Introduction to Visual Culture* (London: Routledge, 1999).

3. This homogeneity of the vision is peculiar. It does not exclude diversified visual and commercial messages targeting specific customers and audiences. It includes, for instance, signs in Chinese, emblems that can be understood only by bungee jumpers, announcements for preparatory courses for university admission exams, etc. But all of them have one thing in common: they are fighting for visibility as if they stood on a world stage, before a universal public.

4. During the Seminar there were long debates on whether "interface" was perhaps a better metaphor than "screen." The main argument for the former was that "interface" implies activity and interactivity, also suggesting that visual production in the city constitutes an exchange of images and participation by ordinary citizens and many other active agents, as well as, accordingly, an interactive chain where every intervention is followed by a reaction. Still, I insist on my "screen" metaphor because I think that interface-interactivity is operating superficially. In fact, the images circulating in the city are to a large extent produced and controlled by the market, which transforms everything into an environment with a uniform appearance. This is so even when market visuality presupposes and actually features an active response by the consumer. Despite the great heterogeneity of visual practices, it is precisely the eyes of this consumer that perform homogenizing operations. Under the impact of competing images, they produce a secondary homogenizing effect as they see everything as on a screen. However, one has to distinguish between the "implied" consumer (a phantasm of the market itself) and the real users of visual goods. The former is a homogenizing force; the latter could be any number of things and as such is capable of employing market visuality in a myriad of unpredictable ways. Nevertheless, I think that the assumptions about the "creativity" of real consumers are exaggerated, for their ability to perceive and understand images, as well as their visual imagination are governed by the market and by the programmed role of "implied" consumer, that is, the actual ways of consumption are to a certain degree dictated and limited by the market. The truly interactive cases are rare and those effectively creative are even rarer, which is not to say, of course, that they are non-existent. The advertisement strategies put forth more than pure pictures: they give birth to, and control, the very sites of visuality. Metaphorically speaking, genuine creativity and inter-activity are doomed to be isolated, anonymous, and illegal (their best illustrations are the graffiti). In any event, the overarching idea here is my notion of "visual capital," which implies that the market makes everything equivalent by translating all possible heterogeneous phenomena of sociality into the categories of visibility at relevant times (prime time on TV and such) and at relevant places (popular TV channels, forums, billboards, etc.).

5. Architectural modernization is a comprehensive social philosophy in which, to paraphrase Walter Benjamin, "the constructive principle began its domination." Here, geometry, rationality, and functionalism govern not only the architectural environment but also the life of the city's residents. See Benjamin's *Ozareniya* (Illuminations) (Sofia: Critique & Humanism Publishing House, 2000), 162.

6. See Michel Foucault, "On Other Spaces," *Diacritics*, 16.1 (Spring 1986): 22-27.

7. On the cultural geography of the megapolis, see Edward Soja's *Postmodern Geographies: The Reassertion of Space in Critical Social Theory* (London: Verso, 1989).

8. Here I use the Foucauldian term "panopticism" as interpreted by Deleuze, that is, as a spatial, integrative arrangement of the dynamic combination of micro-powers:

> When Foucault defines Panopticism, either he specifically sees it as an optical or luminous arrangement that characterizes prison, or he views it abstractly as a machine that not only affects visible matter in general (a workshop, barracks, school or hospital as much as a prison) but also in general passes through every articulable function. So the abstract formula of Panopticism is no longer "to see without being seen" but to impose a particular conduct on a particular human multiplicity. We need only insist that the multiplicity is reduced and confined to a tight space and that the imposition of a form of conduct is done by distributing in space, laying out and serializing in time, composing in space-time and so on. (Gilles Deleuze, *Foucault*, trans. Sean Hand, Minneapolis, MN: University of Minnesota Press, 1988, 34).

9. See Michel de Certeau's *Izobretyavane na vsekidnevieto* (The Practice of Everyday Life) (Sofia: LIK, 2002), 175–225.

10. Alexander Gelley, "City Texts: Representation, Semiology, Urbanism," in Mark Poster, ed., *Politics, Theory and Contemporary Culture* (New York: Columbia University Press), 1993: 237-260.

11. On the philosophical notion of the city as "rational whole," see Heinz Paetzold, "The Philosophical Notion of the City," in *The City Cultures Reader*, Malcolm Miles, Tim Hall, and Iain Borden, eds. (London: Routledge, 2000), 206.

12. See Paul Virilio, "The Overexposed City," in Neil Leach, ed., *Rethinking Architecture: A Reader in Cultural Theory* (London: Routledge, 1997), 381-390.

13. Appadurai examines the new state of the social imagination as shaped by global media, which inscribe various "possible lives" into real social life. The media mix the real and the imaginary, projecting different "landscapes" onto the urban screens. The term "landscapes" hints at their fluid, unstable character: far from being objective, they are constellations that depend on the perspective and ensue from the position of different heterogeneous actors who produce socially valid images. Such actors can be nation states, multinational communities, subnational groupings, intimate circles, families, neighborhoods, or groups of friends. These constantly project in the social space numerous imagined worlds, which compete with one another and are capable of contesting or even transforming the imagined worlds of the State's official visual policy. The global imagination projects its heterogeneous flows within a local framework. See Arjun Appadurai's *Modernity at Large: Cultural Dimensions of Globalization* (Minneapolis, MN: University of Minnesota Press, 1996).

14. An interesting analysis of the city representation in film from this perspective is offered by James Donald in his study "The City, the Cinema: Modern Spaces," in Chris Jenks, ed., *Visual Culture* (London: Routledge, 1995), 77–95.

15. Here I use suggestions from Jean Baudrillard's "The Precession of Simulacra." In Baudrillard, Disneyland as a localized principle of simulations serves as a cover-up for the

fact that the rest of the world is a Disneyland; in my case, I try to describe the total commercial visualization of phantasmatic Otherness as concealing the real Others.

16. It is another matter whether these phantasms can be said to be specific to the late-capitalist megapolis. They are part of the global, deterritorialized production of images that go around the world through media and migration flows. See Appadurai's *Modernity at Large*.

17. I have in mind images laden with powerful emotions (seduction, temptation, explosive attraction, charm, but also revulsion, fear, and shock). Sofia slang has found an appropriate term (*maniashko* or, "manic") for their effect.

18. Here I follow a model introduced by Klaus Böckmann during his report in the "Interkulturelle Medienpädagogik" section of the conference "Offene Grenzen. Multikulturelle Gesellschaft und die Kommunikationswissenschaft" in Klagenfurt, 15-17 November 1991. He classified images into several very original categories, which I use here in slightly modified form. He spoke of different zones of visibility of the image: (1) the screaming image; (2) the talking image; (3) the silent image; (4) the hiding and "ashamed" image. I think this is an original and useful classification, which takes into account Gestalt psychological factors (focus, zones of attention, relationship between figure and background, etc.) as well as psychoanalytic factors (contents through which the ego manifests itself in consciousness, neutral contents, contents-symptoms, and entirely displaced contents).

19. One of the specialized websites (http://www.gis-sofia.bg/english/cadhistory.html) provides the following information on this issue:

> On the territory of the city of Sofia, cadastral surveying works started more than 100 years ago. The first urban plan of the city dates back to 1879. It was developed under the supervision of Engineer Rowbal and constituted a street planetable photograph [on a] 1:1000 [scale,] supplemented with the more important public and private buildings, [property] borders, and the owners' names. In the course of time the development of the capital city and the public works…determined the need of a more accurate and complete cadastral plan. For this purpose, in 1890 the City Municipal Council [commissioned] the Austrian engineer Wilhelm Bartel to design a complete and accurate cadastre of the capital. Work continued longer than expected[,] and in 1896 Bartel was dismissed without having completed his work on the new cadastral plan development.
>
> In 1930–1932, in relation to the development of a new cadastral plan of Sofia, engineer Adolf Klaya performed basic surveying measurements [including] triangulation and levelling of the city territory. The cadastral plan itself was developed in the period 1935–1952, and up to the year 1962 it was regularly updated. Then its maintenance stopped and it gradually became practically useless in terms of the needs of detailed urban planning….

To this, we may add the failure to implement the so-called Mussmann Plan, a comprehensive urban development project for Sofia designed by a German architect in the 1930s.

20. Konstantin I. Katsarov, *[Shesdeset] 60 godini zhivyana istoriya: [Spomeni]* ([Sixty] 60 Years of Lived History: [Memoirs]). With an Afterword by Svetoslav Kolev. 2nd ed. Sofia: Prozorets, 1993.

21. This consistent urban philosophy is featured even today on the Sofia Municipality website, where the city's history is narrated precisely as civilizational progress showcasing the transformation from "a muddy and dirty village" into "the capital of liberated Bulgaria." According to the authors of the text, this

was a matter of self-affirmation of the entire nation. That is why the entire spiritual and constructive energy of the government and the people was concentrated on achieving this goal. The need of a capital city that would meet the requirements for representativ[eness] of its urban architecture was satisfied by developing vast free spaces, wide boulevards, rich parks, and gardens. Thus, Bulgaria [developed] in its capital city the architectural sites of its dreams.

It is obvious how "representativ[eness]" (as embodied in various "representative buildings that replaced the unsightly structures from the first years after the Liberation") in this narrative has distinct priority over urban rationality and functionality. See http://www.sofia.bg/history.asp?lines=1883&nxt=1&update=all

22. The first project for building a modern water supply system, for example, was completed in 1884–1885 and was financed through a series of large loans. The system, designed for 40,000 people, long supplied water only to some parts of the city and suffered from a shortage of skilled maintenance staff. Its water was often stolen—more than 600 illegal connections to the system were detected over the years—as the population was used to free water supply and was reluctant to pay. The water also posed risks of epidemics. See Svetlana Paunova, "Sotsialno konstrouirane na gradskata infrastruktura" (The Social Construction of Urban Infrastructure), in *Critique & Humanism*, vol. 20, No. 1, 2005, "Obrazi na grada" (Images of the City): 239–258. On the eve of the Balkan Wars (1912-1913), just twenty-two per cent of all buildings were connected to the sewer system. It was not until 1933 that the problem of drinking water supply was finally solved by building a water main from Mt. Rila to Sofia.

23. I have examined the direct, political and public significance of this mass protest elsewhere. Here I will deal only with its visual effects.

24. In a Bulgarian textbook on architecture from the 1950s, the political aesthetics of the Party House is described as follows: the solid, concrete plinth is designed to symbolize the connection with the popular masses; the granite columns, the unshakeable power of the communist party; the tower crowned by the five-pointed star, the communist idea; and the small windows between the columns, the vigilant eyes of the party. When I told this to an architect friend of mine, he first laughed a lot and then said that the symbolism of the building probably went deeper because the columns were actually hollow, the structure being supported by solid steel bars inside the columns. I leave it to the reader to guess what their symbolic meaning would be.

25. On this question, see Vladislav Todorov, *Adamov komplex* (The Adam Complex) (Sofia: IV Publishing House, 1991).

26. By the Lagera tramway stop of Sofia's tram line 5, there was an apartment building on whose flat roof stood a permanent sign which read "Forward to Communism!" and sounded increasingly absurd in the years of socialism's disintegration. The sign disappeared in the early 1990s.

27. It is interesting that the choice of a symbolic place was almost accidental. The demonstrations took place in front of St. Alexander Nevsky Cathedral simply because the earliest ones were held behind the National Assembly, where demonstrators would lie in wait for MPs.

28. One followed the line of the rational panopticism of governmentality intertwined with communist utopianism and brought to an extreme by Soviet totalitarianism: centralization, collectivism, social engineering and forced modernization, bureaucratization of the utopia in a cynical network of apparatchiks and their ideological apparatus, police control, terror, and mass-fear instilled in people and institutions. This had direct, material architec-

tural and urban consequences in cities. It was "spatialized" through the demolition of old bourgeois buildings and sites, through the construction of official, empty town squares with sacralized, Communist Party headquarters, and through the omnipresence of the official, communist visual symbols (tribunes, five-pointed stars, hammers and sickles, red flags, images of the united proletariat and the Party leaders, slogans, etc.) placed at the centers of the power perspectives and ideologically structured space. But this panopticism was also materialized in the architecture of wasteful and polluting heavy industry placed in the immediate proximity of newly built working-class districts, which were actually satellite towns of grey, dismal blocks of flats mixing the urban and rural ways of life in an absurd way. The odd combination of technical rationality, irrational utopianism, and automated bureaucracy gave rise to urban dysfunctionality and spoke to ideology's hold over practical urban functions, with disintegrating infrastructure, overcrowded city transportation, poor-quality construction, communal uniformity of the new concrete ghettoes, blandness of surroundings, environmental threats, etc.

The other modernity was experienced as an agenda of liberal values to which Eastern Europe had no alternative for some time: individual liberties, entrepreneurship, freedom of movement of money and symbols, rule of law, pluralism, separation of powers, and so forth. As the transition did not have enough time to produce this modernity, it only staged it, creating festive performances that represented the civic principle of freedom as opposed to the panoptic, total engineering reason in its ideological mutations. In this sense, the visual layer born of the velvet revolutions—colorful, bright, suggestive of freedom, but temporary—looked like a parodic simulacra compared to the former, impersonal totalitarian spaces.

29. In Sofia there is a successful company named, tellingly, "Agressia" (Aggression).

30. An important characteristic of the chaotically and plural visual regime is that this regime manages to conceal the elements of order within itself. The aggressive visibility of the absence of order makes any moments of order invisible.

31. At least three mayoral "postures" or types changed in succession: the figure of Alexander Yanchoulev (1991–1995), who lacked a clear image, the "smiling-criminal," media image of Stefan Sofiyanski (1995–2005), and that of Boyko Borissov (2005 – present), the macho type, "serious," and "worried" about the city's situation.

32. In 1995 the *24 Chassa* daily published a masterpiece headline: "Electric-Resistant Gypsies Steal 5-Kilometre-Long Power Line."

33. Critics interpreted this debate as a convenient metaphor of the national concerns and urban utopias. The questions were, How do the stray dogs represent us before the foreign tourists' eyes? What is the right approach towards the homeless and the helpless, towards the outcast and the marginal, towards animals, nature, and How are we to deal with the ecological balance of the ideal city? What type of municipal government do we expect: "cynical" and "uncaring" toward people and nature or eco-friendly? Could murder, say, of dogs, be staged in the streets of the city, before children? Will the tough measures against the dogs not turn Sofia once again into a totalitarian city using administrative methods borrowed from concentration camps? On these questions, see Yavor Lilov's study, "Homeless Animals and 'Homelessness' in Bulgaria: Roles and Identities in the Modern Public Debate on the Ideal State," 2004, manuscript, part of the project on "Roles, Identities, and Hybrids," Centre for Advanced Study (CAS), Sofia (forthcoming on the CAS website at www.cas.bg).

34. The pet project of communist dictator Todor Zhivkov's daughter, Lyudmila Zhivkova, built in honor of Bulgaria's 1,300th anniversary in 1981.

35. Since 2000 alone, there have been 155 killings. Words and phrases like "demonstrative," "flagrant," "arrogant," and "with impunity" have become common in Bulgarian

media discourse on crime. That is to say, the public opinion and journalists have become aware of the specific, visible, and defining character of the Bulgarian criminal world, which does not want to remain "in the dark" but shows off its outside-the-law power in broad daylight.

36. Research shows that in the 1970s and 1980s Bulgaria's sports education produced approximately 60,000-70,000 heavy athletes (mostly nationally renowned wrestlers but also boxers, weightlifters, judoists, karatists, rowers, and others) who lived even back then a peculiar, secluded, and excessively hierarchical clan-like life as if in training for future gang wars, wholly dependent on their coaches and developing for them an excessive loyalty bordering on self-sacrifice. In the communist aftermath, the former athletes, who suddenly lost their jobs along with their national athletic prestige, were recruited for their strong physical potential by members of the former secret services and were quickly organized into two private armies that actually outnumbered the diminishing official Bulgarian army. One of these armies was engaged in crime and the other supplied private security guards. It is precisely these paramilitary forces of privatized violence (on which the State had lost its monopoly) that crawled out of the shadows and took over the public stage, thus giving a visual body to physical aggression.

37. Here we can only ask ourselves whether the semi-criminal monopolization of the Bulgarian advertising markets is an expression of commercial or criminal aggression.

38. This did not apply to Bulgaria's capital city only. The image of the scandalous mayor of Velingrad, Fidel Beev, was similarly shaped.

FACING GLOBALIZATION:
LITHUANIAN URBANISM BETWEEN
POSTCOMMUNISM AND POSTMODERNITY

ALMANTAS SAMALAVICIUS

During the last decade Lithuanian society has entered into a new phase of its development, a stage that I have elsewhere termed "high post-communism."[1] I am not going to elaborate here on the features of this liminal state of societal transition that started with the collapse of the Soviet era and continues up to the present moment. But one should keep in mind that this has been a complicated, turbulent, and sometimes contradictory transitory period during which, however, Lithuania has finally established its position among the other countries of the European Union, also making its way into a large number of international and global organizations and networks. In other words, it has finally "normalized" itself after the glorious "singing revolution" and re-mapped its position in post-Soviet space, Europe, and the world. Lithuania was the first of the former colonies of the Soviet Empire to break ties with the union of so-called "socialist republics." Nevertheless, despite many truly significant changes in economy, politics, culture, and social life that have taken place since the country said a firm and resolute farewell to the empire that symbolically crumbled in 1990, post-communist Lithuanian society has experienced many ill-effects of a liminal, transitory stage of development.

This essay does not attempt to present a reflection on each and every aspect of a phenomenon that is categorized by some sociologists[2] as a "liminal state." My contribution focuses on one aspect that exhibits profound social changes: urban discourses and practices, the discussion of which hopefully will add to the understanding of the complex problems of postcommunist Lithuanian society at large. The post-Soviet city, notably Lithuania's capital Vilnius, is here brought under closer scrutiny, in hopes of demonstrating how the present urban body is subjected to changes triggered by the rise of market economy, consumer mentality, and most recently by powerful yet no less ambiguous tendencies of glob-

101

alization, which have serious consequences for a transitory society such as today's Lithuania.

1. Rhetoric of Postcommunist Cityscape

The cityscape of Vilnius is a reflection of many historical and aesthetic layers of the whole urban mass of Lithuania's capital, where visible imprints of different cultural epochs co-exist. Closer study reveals the complicated and sometimes contradictory structure of visual signs narrating the city's centuries-long history—including its rapid transformation and industrialization during the period of Soviet colonization and the present shifts triggered by the new wave of urbanization, concentration of capital, and urban sprawl after the country recovered from the most brutal physical consequences of dependence. "Vilnius is [like] an open book, revealing the history of European art styles from gothic to empire. Vilnius is a real treasure to anyone who is inclined to study art history not with the help of books, but from masterpieces of art itself," wrote Mikalojus Vorobjovas, a renowned Lithuanian architectural historian in 1940, shortly after the country was handed back its historical capital, which had been lost to Poland in the early thirties.[3] Vorobjovas's enthusiasm regarding the architectural heritage was grounded in the physiognomy of Lithuania's historical capital. Despite almost two hundred years of Russia's imperial rule and a brief period of Polish takeover—two periods when it played the modest role of peripheral, provincial city—Vilnius managed to sustain the main features of its urban structure and architectural forms, notably Baroque, with certain surviving ingredients of late Gothic. Few critics, however, would be inclined to share in Vorobjovas's enthusiasm two decades after the period of dependence finally ended in the spectacular year of 1990. It would hardly be an exaggeration to suggest that during the twenty years of independence Lithuania's capital has experienced more profound and far-reaching changes than it did during the period from the third partition of the Polish-Lithuanian Commonwealth (1795) to the fall of the Soviet regime.

The end of Soviet rule in Lithuania was marked by several overlapping tendencies. Immediately after Gorbachev's *perestroika,* which entered Lithuania with a certain delay and gained strength with the help of a vanguard of intellectuals and public figures who set out to create a movement to introduce it to the rather conservative and highly suspicious local Communist party leadership and state *apparatchiks*, a number of new organizations were established. Most of these were set around the ideas of reviving historical consciousness and national dignity through public activism in the fields of heritage protection and ecology. These spheres seemed somewhat detached from mainstream politics and as such provided a legal basis to question many assumptions promoted and guarded by Soviet ideology. The general upheaval of historical consciousness and the huge interest in formerly neglected, unavailable, or forbidden historical texts, written mostly by Lithuanian historians of the pre-Soviet period, as well as other writings that were either banned and taken out of circulation or available only to a limited audience of dissenters (whose number, after the suppression of the postwar armed guerilla movement, was never very high), created a public space where the concept of retrieving a lost or neglected architectural heritage could be openly (and to a certain degree) safely tested and disseminated. No wonder the last several years of the Soviet regime witnessed the rebirth of a large number of communities and associations that put a lot of effort into reviving the public historical consciousness of a formerly atomized crowd, now on its way to becoming a normalized society.

No one could anticipate in those years of public discontent and high expectations that ecological movements and large informal associations that came into being to protect architectural and cultural heritage would fizzle out so fast or, at best, remain tiny and largely ineffective groupings of the most ardent and devoted public activists. And yet this was the logic of eventual social developments in post-Communist Lithuania, where a brief period of political upheaval continued just a few years after independence was finally re-established. Feelings of social solidarity and national dignity so strongly displayed during the period of *Sajūdis* soon gave way to social apathy, indifference, self-defeat, individualism, and the like.

It was during this shift of the emotional pendulum that the cityscape of Lithuania's capital experienced the most fundamental changes, exhibiting an abundance of totally new visual signs, which were characteristic of the rising, mainstream urban culture of a market economy. The arrival of McDonald's, one of the first chain restaurants to be established in the very center of Vilnius, on Gediminas Avenue—which has been and remains the main downtown walking street—marked a new era, one of consumption, even before an average Lithuanian citizen could allow himself or herself to become a regular McDonald's customer. In the symbolic universe of the public values of the early post-Soviet period, the fast-food franchise introduced a disguised message of freedom: finally, Lithuania has arrived into a global area where each and everyone was free to think and act as he or she wanted without being subjected to any outside control. However, in reality this wasn't freedom, but something else; McDonald's came to symbolize the advent of a new era, one of new consumer values, which did not exist during the culture of scarcity of the Soviet period.

The location of Vilnius's first McDonald's restaurant was also highly symbolic. Unlike in other European cities, McDonald's in Vilnius was situated in the most prestigious and expensive central quarters of the city, as if supporting its centrality in a newly born culture of consumption. On the other hand, such a topographical localization of an enterprise that critics like Herbert Gans associates with "lower" culture was an illustration of what the first wave of capital flow meant—at that time, Lithuania had just entered into a stage described by local social critics as a reign of "wild capitalism."

These and other interventions into the vast physical body of Vilnius, which had already been badly maimed during the Soviet era, have largely devastated the city's *genius loci*, the "spirit" of the place. It is worth noting, along these lines, that, according to Isis Brook,

> A place that tells its story, where layers of past history are evident, and preferably not consciously preserved [is one that expresses the spirit of the place]. The presence of configuration of land, houses, ruins and so on, is still working and connected to its past in a meaningful way. There is diachronic integrity...about the place: what is here now makes sense given what was here, [h]as a coherent narrative that connects its past to its present and could guide the future.[4]

2. *Looking Backwards: City as Necropolis*

In 1989, shortly before the fall of the Soviet regime, the Lithuanian prose writer Ričardas Gavelis, who was in his forties at the time, published his visionary novel *The Poker of Vilnius*.[5] He had started to write the book—a postmodern deconstruction of Lithuanian society under Soviet oppression that had never been reconsidered on such a scale—almost a decade earlier. This powerful novel became a national best-seller, selling about a hundred thousand copies in just two editions. This text took many by surprise. Never before had any Lithuanian writer gone that far in destroying the national myths and cultural mythologies, exhibiting as he did a surrealistic image of Soviet realities in which victims were largely no better than their persecutors and the depiction of horrors of totalitarian rule went hand in hand with the reflections on what actually happened to a society that was reduced to a mob and stuck to that prescribed role. The novel was a shock to Lithuanian literary critics, readers, and to other writers alike. The analysis of the essence of Soviet totalitarianism, previously offered by Orwell and Solzhenitsyn, was now provided by a Lithuanian writer who re-examined, among other things, the mental pathologies of the colonized Lithuanian. An openly postmodern novel—and a first of such kind—was structured as four accounts of the same events, viewed through the eyes of several protagonists, one of whom was a dog. It is not unexpected that a novel full of explicit scenes of sexual abuse, pain, and torture caused not only by THEM (the totalitarian power) but also by THEIR victims themselves was taken to task by critics who felt overwhelmed by the abundance of sexual material, a rarity in prose writings over several decades of Soviet regime. The critics could forgive even less the author's attitude toward symbols so dear to the average Lithuanian reader. Gavelis mocked such central items of Lithuanian identity as the Gediminas castle and the Iron Wolf—traditionally the sources of pride during Soviet colonization—as mythologized "true history" opposed to Soviet ideological narratives. In one of the episodes of *The Poker of Vilnius*, the author describes the city through the eyes of one of the novel's main protagonists:

> I listen to the old man Vilnius breathing heavily and wheezing. Cities also fall ill, their diseases are similar to human diseases, they suffer from both high blood pressure and from cancer. Cities also die in horrible agony. But what's even worse is when cities rot alive. When people rummage around in stink rot, thinking that this really is life.

The whole novel is full of similar images of Lithuania's capital. The oppressive, diseased, and destructive atmosphere of social reality is mediated through comparisons between the city and a distorted, aging, decaying, and smelly human body. In the reflections of the main protagonist, Vytautas Vargalys, Vilnius "comes to a stop," "turns to stone"; its "powers of motion" desert it; it is "frozen in paralysis"; it "stinks" or is imagined as "an old depraved exhibitionist," even "a corpse, in whose entrails the worms probably still crawl." For the first time in the history of Lithuanian literature, the city is given this much attention. Vargalys is wandering through the streets of this strange, dying city observing how its body constantly changes. He at times feels, smells, and hears the city as "insipid and soundless" (which causes "chills to travel down [his] spine"), a city in which everything is "decaying and fragmenting." The protagonist calls the city "exhausted" and wasted as if he were speaking of some live but mortally ill organism endowed with consciousness. During the gloomier moments, he describes Vilnius as "a Necropolis of the soul, in which no life remains" or as "an old depraved exhibitionist, who isn't ever trying to cover up his puny blunt phallus." The city's previous inhabitants undergo bizarre, quasi-metaphysical urban metamorphoses, reincarnating in lower life forms or animals. For instance, former city residents like Gediminas Riauba, who initiated the novel's main character into THEIR secrets, turn into dogs or pigeons.

There are, in the novel, more explicit descriptions of sovietized Vilnius, some of them almost devoid of metaphysical character. In the second part of the book, the narrator offers such a description:

> Vilnius is a city of little uniform cement boxes. A city of little uniform clay people. A city of identical tears and identical sperm. If suddenly some giant should turn everything around—the houses, the people, the tears, the sperm, [if he] changed the paces of everything and mixed everything up—absolutely nothing would change.

But the reader also comes across many descriptions of the city and its cultural/historical symbols, which are so dear to the average Lithuanian of the Soviet era. However, these are turned upside down by the author. The great symbols of the past have nothing to do with the city's exhausted and maimed body, deformed and destroyed as this seemed to be by an almost mystical power. That is to say, Gavelis does not reduce his narrative cityscape to the urban realities of the Soviet period. This destructive totalitarian power is presented as an almost supernatural force. He traces the "genealogy" of political evil from the Soviets all the way back to Plato. The Iron Wolf—a mythological being who is supposed to have helped Grand Duke Gediminas to found Vilnius in its present place—is imagined by the main character, Vargalys, as "a mangy dog indifferently moseying along the roadway" in the city more and more resembling a true Necropolis, a city of the dead.

In its various representations, the body of Vilnius does not lack a certain dynamic, although in their moments of discouragement, the novel's characters refer to it as existing in a frozen, lifeless state. Like any living organism, afflicted by illness as it may be, the city changes, mutates, looses its original form, and with it some of its greatness, high culture, spirituality, and authenticity. The main symbol of Vilnius, the legendary tower of Gediminas Castle (the Upper Castle as it is recorded in historical writings), which over the years provided occupied and colonized Lithuanians a feeling of pride in their ancient, especially medieval history (when the Lithuanian Grand Duchy stretched from the Baltic to the Black Sea), in Gavelis's narrative becomes a sign of total helplessness and impotence. All that Vargalys and other characters of the novel see in this glorious symbol of national pride is "a short, blunt, helplessly protruding phallus." Again, Gavelis chooses to interpret the deformations of the city's body as loss of manhood/masculinity. Thus, his city is decaying by changing its sex and becoming feminine. It is also noteworthy that the images of the decomposing body of the city go hand in hand with the personal history of the novel's main hero, who boasts of his huge sexual prowess. But we learn from other characters that he was subjected to physical tortures by THEM (in this case, unmistakably by the KGB). From his own account, we know that during one of the torture sessions, the interrogator injures Vargalys's sexual organ, and yet Vargalys nevertheless keeps bragging about his insatiable sexual appetites and his masculinity overall. Thus one can conclude that the hero creates a whole myth about himself, a cover for a sexual deficiency if not for an actual, physical impotence.

Parallel to distortions of the body of the city are transformations of the bodies of Vilnius's inhabitants. One of the novel's characters, Doctor Kovarskis, shares his observations on a special kind of illness that he terms the "Vilnius syndrome" and goes on to enumerate the symptoms of this fatal illness:

The feeling named love disappears.... Self-respect...pride.... The
language changes. Sometimes I think I could recognize the person
touched by the Vilnius syndrome at once, just from his language.
Vivid words, colors and moods disappear. Tons of clichéd constructions, always the same, meaningless and faceless remain....
Finally, deformation of the body sets in, the joints get contorted,
strange lumps grow in the most unexpected places, the eyes
become blank.

Despite unmistakably metaphysical and allegorical musings,
Gavelis created an accurate and powerful overall picture of Vilnius during the Soviet era. An old city, once famous for its Gothic and Baroque
structures, for its unique harmony between nature and architecture,
gradually lost its former grandeur while being turned into an industrialized wasteland, subjected to faceless urbanisation full of stereotypical
architectural structures that hardly deserve to be called architecture. The
lifeless, gray, and gloomy "physiognomy" of the city as depicted by
Gavelis were the typical features Vilnius acquired during the half century of Soviet domination. The city's "identical boxes" of the so-called
"sleeping quarters" scattered all around Vilnius along with its ugly and
monstrous industrial areas defined the urban "aesthetics" of the period
and thus reflected the struggle of the Communist regime to wipe out
even the faintest traces of individuality in any sphere of life, in urban life
particularly.

3. *The Rise of Consumer Culture and the Decline of Architecture*
Several decades ago, at the height of the Cold War, John Berger insightfully noted that for the majority of East Europeans the "neons of the
cities of capitalism" were the visible signs of freedom and of the "Free
World," something their societies badly lacked.[6] It is no surprise that
immediately after the fall of the Soviet regime and the hasty introduction
of market economy, postcommunist Lithuanians turned to the West,
taking all aspects of contemporary capitalist city life, particularly the
neon lights of advertising, glass architecture, high rise buildings, fancy
cars, designer clothes, busy night life, and so on as unmistakable promises of freedom and "culture of abundance." As soon as the local economy recovered from the local brand of "shock therapy"—which was less
a result of such institutions as the International Monetary Fund or World

Bank and more an outcome of the paralyzing inability of Lithuanian governments to soberly restructure the planned economy into a market economy without painful social consequences—the post-Soviet capital of Lithuania exhibited clearly distinguishable visible signs of the city's capitalist transformation. Immediately after the financial situation of the country was stabilized, local developers, real estate gamblers, and the city's municipal government put all their efforts into the setting up of a new administrative and financial center of the city. The old municipal headquarters in the main central street, Gediminas Avenue, was abandoned and put up for sale, and the municipal government moved to the right bank of the river Neris, where a chain of high-rise buildings, contrasting with the Old Quarters, were being built. Jurga Ivanauskaitė, a renowned Lithuanian writer, who, shortly before her premature death, provided an insightful account of Vilnius' cityscape in a volume dedicated to honor the legacy of Ričardas Gavelis (who died under mysterious circumstances in 2002), observed that

> Each city, in addition to the abstract network of avenues and squares put on paper by cartographers (map-makers), has a metaphysical map, and R.G. (Ričardas Gavelis) was not only one of its main makers, but also a natural part of this drawing. After Ričardas left this world, the Vilnius of *Poker* and *Jazz* (these are separate parts of the so-called Vilnius trilogy by Gavelis) started to deteriorate. The central grocery store and wine restaurant in Totoriu Street no longer exists. The central avenue not only changed its pavement, but also got rid of old trees, turning from a live creature into a stuffed animal with nicely set eyes of the shop windows. The modern glass vibrators that are destroying the sky crowded in on the pure old phallus of Vilnius, and Rulers' Palace took over the cathedral square with their rooms of dead vaginas. Užupis got rid of riff-raff and was taken over by the rich, and Šnipiškes turned to ashes, naively dreaming about the fate of Phoenix...[7]

On the right bank of river Neris and defined by Ivanauskaitė as a "hot spot" for urban changes, Šnipiškės was one of the oldest historical suburbs of Vilnius. Famous for its traditional architecture, it became part of the city's body a couple of centuries ago. Because of its privileged location (it is close to the city center), the area was chosen as the site of the new administrative and shopping center of Vilnius, its "downtown." Such a trend of urbanization was already foreseen in 1989, before the "singing revolution," by architectural theorist and critic Rimantas Buivydas, who argued at the time that

> Only from memories and from a few descriptions can one reconstruct an image of the oldest, Southern part of Šnipiškės. At the very moment the center on the right bank of river Neris that continues to be shaped has not only erased the former structure of buildings, but it has left no trace of the main street of Šnipiškės (eventually renamed Ukmergės) as well as of the net of other larger and smaller streets…. In the seventies, for some unknown reasons, only such [destructive] decisions were possible, and since then, the total destruction in Šnipiškės had gotten under way as a 'groundwork' of sorts, as it was called.[8]

Despite the critical comments and protests by local communities, plans for a future urban center had been drafted long before the independence, and city authorities of the postcommunist period continued the same policy strongly influenced by the demands of market economy and realtors who invested large sums of money into the new municipal and financial heart of Vilnius. The recent, dominating yet dull, high-rise buildings ironically referred to as "Zuokascape" (an allusion to infamous mayor of Vilnius Artūras Zuokas, during whose term the majority of these new structures came into being), have contributed greatly to the significant and almost irreversible changes of cityscape responsible for the loss of many of the city's former qualities. The local, outdated version of "International style" prevailed in the construction of the new urban center as well as of many adjoining parts of the city where developers left their mark. To add to the irony, the public square between the high-rise building of the mayor's office and the newly built trading center "Europe," devoid of any traces of communal character and erected in the vicinity of a large highway, was named the Square of Europe.

As is well known, architectural traditions have been seriously affected by development in some of the world's great metropolises, and during its post-Soviet re-urbanization Vilnius has been no exception. Quite the contrary. The new architectural structures of Vilnius—administrative buildings, trading and shopping centers, and houses alike—continue to be made of the cheapest materials. Their façades are covered by almost impenetrable glass, which suggests isolation and total alienation. The flaws of this glossy and glassy aesthetics have been recently insightfully outlined by Edwin Heathcote, an architectural critic of the *Financial Times*, who noted that

> dim glass slabs became the de facto solution for every plot in every city.... The wholly glass-clad building emerged as the single solution, a one-stop-shop and it sometimes seems the only answer considered. Yet a stroll over London, or any other city, reveals the aesthetic poverty and blandness to which this material's ubiquity has led. The essential assumptions on which the use of glass is based—that it is transparent; that it appears contemporary; that it allows light to penetrate; that it is economical; that it is sustainable—are all deeply flawed. The glass-fronted lobbies of the big corporations do not, as it is often supposed, promote transparency and accessibility. Glass can be opaque and alienating.[9]

This is especially true with respect to architectural structures that continue to be hastily built all over postcommunist Lithuanian towns and are perhaps most visible in the capital. These buildings, which I have termed glassy and glossy, embody a certain symbolism: they speak about the new configuration of economy and power. If Stalinism's large neoclassicist public buildings in Lithuania and other East European cities brought a clear message of Soviet totalitarianism, new architectural structures in Vilnius and other cities spoke to the monetary power poised to complete the destruction of historical cities and their Old Quarters in the name of putatively linear progress. However, as well-known Finnish architect Juhani Pallasmaa has stated, "The mental function of architecture is to enrich, articulate, and strengthen our relations with the world, and, ultimately our awareness of ourselves."[10] What the postcommunist architecture of Vilnius has to say on this highly important issue remains to be seen. The present, chaotic and eclectic character of Vilnius's urban structure and architectural aesthetics represents, perhaps, a contradictory but at the same time natural phase of the city's development during the period of epochal social transition that might be still called postsocialism in spite Lithuania's membership in EU, NATO, and other international bodies.

**4. Instead of Conclusion: The Ambiguous Challenge
of Guggenheim-Hermitage**

Among the most recent attempts to improve city culture of Lithuania's
capital with the help of cultural consumerism as well as to reshape Vilnius into a global city, what I would call the "Guggenheim-Hermitage"
incident is perhaps the most instructive. The idea of building in Vilnius a
branch of the Guggenheim "global museum" was introduced a couple of
years ago and was especially defended and promoted by then mayor
Artūras Zuokas, who personally brought Guggenheim's former director,
Thomas Krens, to Vilnius. Well-known Lithuanian architects, art critics,
curators, and even the general public were critical of this international
venture, and yet the project received not only municipal but also state
support by the government of Gediminas Kirkilas—amusingly enough,
Kirkilas was a former Communist who was heading the Communist
Party of Lithuania's successor, the Labor-Democratic Party—mostly on
the grounds that such a global museum would be instrumental in sustaining cultural tourism and generally in promoting the culture of the
country and re-defining its capital as a cosmopolitan city welcoming
international culture and the arts. The designers of this expensive and
ambitious project claimed that following the example of Guggenheim
Bilbao, the would-be international museum would guarantee economic
success to Lithuania's capital, which, needless to say, was experiencing
chronic financial problems. Consumption of culture was seen as a means
by which to rescue the city's economy. The city rulers envisioned
crowds of visitors queuing up for admission to the Vilnius Guggenheim-
Hermitage, thus bringing huge profits. And so, soon an international
competition was held and the winner, Zaha Hadid, was selected by an international jury to design the museum. However, as emphasized by one
of the project's most sober and balanced critics, Skaidra Trilupaityte, the
unresolved problem was that in order

> to ensure the successful functioning of a global museum in Vilnius,
> it would be necessary to significantly modify the urban environ-
> ment. [Because creative] ideas tend usually to lean towards
> traditional, 'theatrical' architecture, a contest among three world-
> famous architects is being arranged. Today, easily exportable
> 'miracles' work most effectively upon the global and mobile busi-
> ness class and tourists in search of new impressions. Meanwhile,

the quite different cultural expectations of urban citizens are judged
by economic results and evaluated in terms of number of potential
workplaces and benefits to the city's 'peripheries.'... But maybe it
is time to stop the usual whining about the lack of financing experienced by local cultural institutions and to believe in the possibility
of a different future. Perhaps the city's cultural planning should not
be weighed separately from the general situation of the country....[11]

To cut a long story short, the Vilnius Guggenheim-Hermitage project was finally abandoned, possibly due to the recent global financial
crisis as well as to the changes in the strategy of the Guggenheim Foundation, which decided to concentrate on its central museum in New York
(the fact that the Guggenheim-Hermitage alliance had spectac-ularly
failed in Las Vegas did not help either). However, are there any lessons
to be learned from the fate of this aborted undertaking? Can a culture's
economy be miraculously saved by outside sources? Should the citizens
of the postcommunist world not take more responsibility and initiative
themselves in terms of leading a meaningful life and sustaining their
own culture, instead of making their cities into sites of a global tourist
industry that distorts the *genius loci* and replaces it with artifacts produced for global consumption? So far, there has been little discussion
concerning such timely worries. And it can be concluded that thoughtful
considerations are reaching postcommunist space from outside, where
there had been a longer experience of the production and dissemination
of consumer culture. More effectively than in any discussions of Lithuanian critics, the essence of such problems was raised by Steven Miles
and Malcolm Miles, who conclude that "if the aesthetisation of space...
frequently encountered in urban redevelopment" is "driven by cultural or
heritage tourism" and "the identification of new markets," it tends to
translate into "sameness," "so that the local colour, or difference, which
may be the basis of city's tourism promotion, becomes an increasingly
standardized product," in which case such aesthetic transformation "is
self-defeating." Thus, "When so many cities construct niches through
which to market their locally coloured images, the niche may in the end
take prominence over its content."[12] Time will tell whether the challenge
of the Guggenheim-Hermitage debacle will be sufficient to trigger
broader discussions about local art institutions, city culture, forms of
urbanization, and global commodification of culture and so help people

understand that answers to global problems should be sought locally, given that no global solution will ever provide adequately for the preservation of those cultural features and qualities that keep local cultures alive. Meanwhile, it can be suggested, as I am here, that the lack of a sophisticated urban philosophy and architectural criticism, together with the inconsistency of recent urban planning and the apathy of post-Soviet city dwellers, is just another sign that the "transition" period is far from over. In urban planning, design, and research, a whole lot more work needs to be done to return cities like Vilnius to their cultural-historical meanings.

NOTES

1. Almantas Samalavicius, "An amorphous society. Lithuania in the era of high postcommunism." http//www.eurozine.com/pdf/2008-06-11-samalavicius-en.pdf. The essay is also available in Bulgarian, Slovak, and Polish translations.

2. Elemer Hankiss, "Transition or Transitions? The Transformation of Eastern Central Europe, 1989-2007." http//www.eurozine.com/pdf/2007-07-6-hankiss-en.pdf.

3. Mikalojus Vorobjovas, *Vilniaus menas* (Kaunas: Spaudos fondas, 1940), p. 14.

4. Isis Brook, "Can 'Spirit of Place' be a Guide to Ethical Planning?" In Warwick Fox, ed., *Ethics and Built Environment* (London: Routledge, 2000), p. 142.

5. Ričardas Gavelis, *Vilniaus pokeris* (Vilnius: Vaga, 1989). Recently published in English translation as *The Poker of Vilnius* (New York: Rochester University Press, 2009). In this essay, however, I am quoting from the Lithuanian original.

6. John Berger, *Ways of Seeing* (London: BBC and Penguin Books, 1972), p. 131.

7. Nijole Gaveliene, Antanas A. Jonynas, Almantas Samalavicius, eds., *Bliuzas Ricardui Gaveliui* (Vilnius: Tyto alba, 2007), p. 105-106.

8. Rimantas Buivydas, *Architektūra: pozityvai ir negatyvai* (Vilnius: Ex Arte, 2007), pp. 143-144.

9. Edwin Heathcote, "Dereliction of Duty to Glass," *Financial Times*, September 26, 2007.

10. Juhani Pallasmaa, "An Archipelago of Authentic Architecture," in Gregory Caicco, ed., *Architecture, Ethics, and the Personhood of Place* (Hanover and London: University Press of New England, 2007), p. 41.

11. Skaidra Trilupaityte, "Globalus muziejai XXI amziuje," *Kulturos barai,* 2007, Nr. 7, p. 5.

12. Steven Miles and Malcolm Miles, *Consuming Cities* (London: Palgrave Macmillan, 2004), p. 84.

WORKS CITED

Berger, John. *Ways of Seeing*. London: BBC and Penguin Books, 1972.

Brook, Isis. "Can 'Spirit of Place' be a Guide to Ethical Planning?" *Ethics and the Built Environment*. Edited by Warwick Fox. London: Routledge, 2000.

Buivydas, Rimantas. *Architektūra: pozityvai ir negatyvai*. Vilnius: Ex Arte, 2007.

Gaveliene, Nijole, Antanas A. Jonynas, and Almantas Samalavicius, eds. *Bliuzas Ricardui Gaveliui*. Vilnius: Tyto alba, 2007.

Gavelis, Ričardas. *Vilniaus pokeris*. Vilnius: Vaga 1989.

Hankiss, Elemer. "Transition or Transitions? The Transformation of Eastern Central Europe, 1989-2007." *Eurozine*. http://www.eurozine.com/pdf/2007-07-06-hankiss-en.html.

Heathcote, Edwin. "Dereliction of Duty to Glass." *Financial Times*, September 26, 2007.

Miles, Steven, and Malcolm Miles. *Consuming Cities*. London: Palgrave Macmillan, 2004.

Pallasmaa, Juhani. "An Archipelago of Authentic Architecture." *Architecture, Ethics, and the Personhood of Place*, edited by Gregory Caicco. Hanover and London: University Press of New England, 2007.

Samalavicius, Almantas. "An amorphous society. Lithuania in the era of high post-communism." *Eurozine*. http://www.eurozine.com/pdf/2008-06-11-samalavicius-en. pdf.

Trilupaityte, Skaidra. "Globalus muziejai XXI amziuje." *Kulturos barai, 2007*.

Vorobjovas, Mikalojus. *Vilniaus menas*. Kaunas: Spaudos fondas, 1940.

SHAKESPEARE AFTER SHOCK THERAPY: NEOLIBERALISM AND CULTURE IN THE POSTCOMMUNIST CZECH REPUBLIC

MARCELA KOSTIHOVÁ

This essay examines the response of a local site of cultural production—Shakespeare in the postcommunist Czech Republic—to the ideologically, economically, and culturally complex aftermath of the fall of communism in 1989. Specifically, I set out to explore possible implications of the ways in which Czech productions of Shakespeare have reacted to the increasingly pronounced sociopolitical tensions resulting from the "shock-therapy" transitional process implemented after 1989 at the insistent "recommendations" of the West. Together with the increasingly deteriorating façade of postcommunist, West-implemented quasi democracy that has interfered with existing and functional democratic structures, the negative results of this nominally "normalizing" process have led to characteristic evocations of Shakespeare as a tool of resistance against the neocolonial efforts, influences, and practices of the West. Many of these Shakespearean episodes have aimed particularly at resisting the assimilative requirements posited by the West European countries for eventual admission to the European Union (EU), requirements that have sought to shape much of the postcommunist economic, political, and cultural development since the mid-1990s. Positioned this way, Shakespeare productions largely reflect a reimagining of the region's sociopolitical postcommunist self-articulation decoupled from traditional, binary perceptions of contested national identity in order to seek multivalent future possibilities for collective and individual identification. In rejecting the neoimperial neoliberal notions and measures urged by the West, the "Czech Shakespeare" mirrors, I argue, a deepseated commitment of the Czech population to fashioning a collective subjectivity seeking independence from the hegemony suggested by existing Western models.

Under these circumstances, Shakespeare is not the sole litmus text of postcommunist cultural developments. More broadly, evidence of similar postcommunist cultural trends also surface in various contemporary cultural spaces, including literature, film, and music. My focus on Shakespeare provides merely a distinct point of entry that serves to begin a reflection on postcommunist culture against the backdrop of the hegemony of a West-driven global imaginary and of the material consequences of neoimperialism and neoliberalism. Shakespeare proves particularly well-suited to the task of surveying the postcommunist field: his works and persona have been evoked at every major juncture in Czech nation-building since the early nineteenth century. Through the long years of imperial control by various powers from the Austro-Hungarian empire to Hitler's Third Reich to the U.S.S.R., his corpus has not only saturated the Czech literary and theater world, but it has also taken up the cause of imaginary nationhood set up in resistance to the hegemonic imaginary disseminated by the dominant empire du jour. In the allegedly "free" postcommunist era, Shakespeare has again played the role of an instrument of resistance to the cultural, political, and economic hegemony of "globalization" and, more specifically in this case, Western influence.

That Shakespeare could be used as an ideological tool in a socio-political context of nation-building (or nation-bashing) should come as no surprise, considering particularly the by-now well-established and extensive scholarship that has helpfully detailed the widespread use of Shakespeare for political purposes in varied contexts, from British colonial administration to U.S. education, German re-unification, and global popular culture. The political significance of Shakespeare largely relies on the strategic wielding of cultural capital consisting in the repository of transcendental truths about universal humanity that his works presumably reveal. Shortly after the fall of communism in Central and Eastern Europe (CEE), for instance, British critic Terrence Hawkes provided a useful if deliberately extreme summary of the underlying assumptions traditionally made about the "truths" Shakespeare's oeuvre presumably embodies:

1. That human race is permanent, one and indivisible, regardless of place, race, creed and culture. In the end, under the skin, we are all the same and it is to this sameness that Shakespeare speaks.

2. That passage of time, history, makes no difference to this.

3. That, construed aright and analysed with sufficient ingenuity, application, vigour and flexibility, Shakespeare's plays are able to address all people at all times, and everywhere.

4. That to deny any of the above is to reveal serious deficiencies in one's humanity, such as characterize the ravings of the perverse, the envious, and the politically and socially deviant.[1]

This particular account of Shakespeare's universality reveals the ideological hegemony enforced by those who, while claiming to analyze "with sufficient ingenuity...and flexibility" Shakespeare's works, turn a blind eye to his normative model of "permanent...indivisible" human individual and collective identification. As Hawkes suggests, such "universality" conveniently collapses the multivalent complexity of lived material existence into a Shakespearean-endorsed, streamlined narrative. An insistence on universal sameness erases informative and productive categories of difference together with their potential to challenge the status quo, while the limitation of potential interpretive readings of Shakespeare to one correct interpretation, "construed aright," provides "institutional" scholars (who officially oversee the construction of Shakespeare interpretations) with the power to outline the normative boundaries of their audience's response. Even arguments nominally in favor of Shakespeare's interpretive complexity within this context betray a desire for a singular, graspable model of idealized reality that could be mastered, learned, and translated into relevant practice. Finally, Hawkes's fourth category of Shakespearean universality elegantly excludes those who might reject the first three assumptions, hereby affirming the ability of Shakespearean cultural capital to confer hegemonic power on those who would control the interpretation of the Shakespeare canon and the Shakespearean myth overall. In other words, those authorized to define the "truth" or "true meaning" of Shakespeare's works also wield the decidedly political power to categorize dissenting reading and their readers into a variety of categories of otherness.

The aftermath of such categorizations has been particularly well-mapped by postcolonial scholars, who have repeatedly pointed out how the cultural capital in question has been enlisted as a tool of ideological colonial oppression working in concert with the more forceful military, economic, and politically repressive colonial regimes. In this context, Shakespeare has been evoked as an assumed and unassailable paragon of

Western civilization, unmatchable by the cultural achievement of dominated populations. In response, colonial subjects have picked up Shakespeare to argue for their cultural, economic, and political independence by adopting, adapting, or rewriting the Shakespeare canon to prove their cultural equality with the dominant imperial culture. For instance, in their introduction to *Post-colonial Shakespeares*, Ania Loomba and Martin Orkin note that

> Colonial educationists and administrators used this Shakespeare to reinforce cultural and racial hierarchies. Shakespeare was made to perform such ideological work both by interpreting his plays in highly conservative ways...and by construing him as one of the best, if not 'the best,' writers in the whole world. He became, during the colonial period, the quintessence of Englishness and a measure of humanity itself. Thus the meanings of Shakespeare's plays were both derived from and used to establish colonial authority.[2]

On the one hand, Shakespeare has been used by colonial powers to dominate their colonial subjects by creating ideological hierarchies of humanity via interpretations of Shakespeare texts or simply by asserting kinship to, if not ownership of, Shakespeare's genius. On the other hand, as Shakespeare became so central to the ideological contest over the agency of cultural definition, the colonized responded with Shakespearean performances, adaptations, and radical revisions that sought to gain control over this cultural capital as a bid for inclusion and equality within cultural, economic, and political discourse. In other words, the tensions, disagreements, and competitions over Shakespeare quickly moved outside the boundaries of literary discourse into the political sphere, so much so that for postcolonial critics "reinterpreting Shakespeare's plays became...part of the business of reinterpreting and changing our world."[3]

Of late, Shakespeare has asserted its global relevance outside the historical boundaries of the British empire. As in the rest of CEE, Czech Shakespeare has been used as a political tool of anti-colonial nation-building. Coming to prominence during the national revival movements of the mid-nineteenth century, he has been prominently evoked at every major juncture in modern history, whether in the face of the Austro-Hungarian Empire, of the Nazi occupation of the Second World War, or of the Soviet imperialism that followed.[4] Of course, the Czechs have not been directly colonized by the British, the Czech Shakespeare was wielded not as a "master's tool" to dismantle the proverbial master's house, but rather as an independent and universal touchstone of humanity that provided a transcendental template of social organization explicitly subversive to the temporal (and, it was hoped, temporary) domination of whichever imperial power seeking to co-opt Czech lands into its own orbit. As such, Shakespeare became a popular mainstay in Czech theaters. In particular under communism, Shakespeare plays enjoyed great visibility, partially due to the inclusion of the playwright into the central canon of communist-approved literature as one of the classics presumably compatible with socialist realism's broader worldview.[5] Difficult to censor, Shakespeare's works provided a ready symbolic bridge to the forbidden and idealized Western world from across the Iron Curtain.

After 1989, Shakespeare's prominence on Czech stages intensified even further as postcommunist nations were prompted to articulate their independent—and yet assumedly Western—identities that would stake out their presence in the "New Europe." In the absence of ready-made models of cultural identification, Shakespeare was again summoned as a transcendental touchstone of humanity and social organization that was to supply suitable models and ethical correctives to the tumultuous political developments. In all the years for which official statistics are available during the first decade after the Velvet Revolution, Shakespeare seems to have risen to the challenge admirably. In all the categories measured—the number of annual new productions, reruns, overall performances, their venues, paying spectators—Shakespeare led by an enormous margin, accounting for 1/10 of all tickets sold annually.[6] These numbers meant that, as a random sampling of a two-week period in May 2001 showed, in Prague alone, whose population is of a million and half at most, thirteen theaters staged no fewer than thirty-three performances of eleven different Shakespeare plays, not counting two to three daily shows at the Czech replica of the Globe theater.

While, under communism, Shakespeare references were code for opposition to totalitarian ideology, after 1989 they were part of a critique of the emerging sociopolitical realities, a critique grounded in Shakespeare viewed as paragon of universal and transcendental Western values. This unexpected shift in perspective closely paralleled disenchantment with the material conditions of postcommunist society that firmly settled in by the mid-1990s. Much of this disappointment resulted not only from the plummeting living standards in the country—a circumstance that had been predicted by the Czech postcommunist government and that had been accepted as necessary by the Czech populace for the initial stage of the transitional period—but also as more and more Czech experienced first-hand actual life situations in the West. The resistance to Western influences was also compounded by a growing sense of betrayal as the West failed to fulfill its promises to help Eastern countries with the transitional postcommunist process.

As is well known, communism's end prompted Western thinkers to jubilantly proclaim the end of history. But, alongside these proclamations, Western governments also pledged assistance to the Central and East European countries in their attempt to enter another history, that is, to "normalize," reintegrate into a unified Europe, and eventually join their affluent neighbors in the EU powerhouse. However, to general consternation across the East, these pledges turned out to be mostly rhetorical.[7] The assistance that did eventually materialize did not take the expected form of substantial debt relief of debt or financial aid. Instead, Western governments delivered a great proportion of their "aid" as "technical assistance" or "transition industry."[8] In place of grants or loans that postcommunist governments could invest in their states' infrastructures according to locally identified needs, the assistance took up, for the most part, the form of Western "experts"—international financial institutions such as the IMF or World Bank, professional economic consultants, sometimes known as "econolobbyists," and academics—who essentially were to monitor compliance with "shock therapy" policies. Additionally, these experts worked to establish ideologically charged training programs, mostly for inexperienced young graduates so as to ensure long-term adherence to neoliberal economic models.[9] In fact, despite the rhetoric of a "second Marshall Plan" that was supposed to enable a sustainable restructuring of CEE socio-economic systems, the region received what was mockingly called the "Marshall Plan of Advice."[10] What funds were made available to the countries of the former communist bloc consisted in credit distributed predominantly as variable-interest loans. These loans were to sink the receiving nations further in crippling debt, an issue once more urgent at the time of writing, in the context of the global economic crisis (March 2009). The money was not directed, as it should have been, to transitional CEE projects; in many cases, it made an elegant u-turn as consulting fees paid to the "experts."

Not surprisingly, most of the aid to postcommunist countries was given through established neoliberal channels that harnessed loans from international financial institutions to conditions of "structural adjustment," which generally entailed the creation of "free markets" that were supposed to "modernize" the economy and make it more "efficient." Substantively different from the strategically subsidized markets of the West, these "adjustments" were predicated on the removal of trade barriers to Western capital and, most importantly, to the flow of capital and resources outside of the CEE markets. In practice, the required changes have allowed Western investors to treat CEE territories as a new frontier of profit-taking opportunities or, in genteel parlance, as "favorable climate for foreign investment," which in reality meant fewer and lower taxes for Western corporations, pressure on workers' unions to provide a "flexible" (that is, pliable, unorganized, and cheap) workforce, little oversight by host countries in terms of business or ecological practices, and lack of obstructions of capital flow back into investors' pockets. Though claiming generously to assist CEE governments and their citizens—after all, as Katherine Verdery noted, "'shock therapy' represents Western governments as doctors [and] the 'big bang' [of quick economic development] figures them as God"[11]—the Marshall Plan of Advice was designed to benefit primarily the West, whether in the form of financial profits from CEE investments, new markets for Western goods, or increased control over territories of geopolitically strategic significance.

The Czech Republic was among the first CEE countries to protest against the exploitive dimensions of Western aid. As early as 1992, CEE representatives included in the early wave of Western "assistance" began articulating their dissatisfaction regarding policies and agreements that gave short shrift to local economies by "draining [their] domestic markets."[12] CEE governments, it has been noted at the time, had little to no input into how the aid, especially that offered by the U.S., was delivered and distributed; their exclusion from the decision-making process often translated into exclusion from the flow of information altogether.[13]

The outcome of Shock Therapy was radical but not in a way CEE governments had envisioned. These results have been attended to extensively by economists, anthropologists, social and political scientists and, more and more, scholars in the humanities, and yet it bears repeating that, in the region as a whole, living conditions sharply descended below those of the Great Depression. In 1997, well after the "therapy" was promised to deliver its miraculous normalizing results, UNICEF found that "the majority of peoples under transition suffer a deterioration of living standards, unemployment and poverty affecting every third citizen even in the most affluent countries."[14] Lower quality and decreasing availability of social services were paralleled by skyrocketing unemployment, poverty, mortality, suicide rates, alcoholism, violence, and general widening of social inequalities.[15] In an extensive study of "transition economies," Branko Milanovic found that average real wages "dropped by one-fourth between 1987-88 and 1994, while unemployment grew from zero to between 12 and 15 percent of the labor force."[16] Historian Robin Okey cites additional developments such as staggering regional drops in birthrates as an "extreme form of belt-tightening;" spiraling of the middle class into material poverty; youth unemployment; sky-rocketing crime; slashes to health-care funding; a crisis in medication supply; and decrease in cultural consumption and research.[17] Heavy industry and agriculture, the perpetual prime targets for privatization across the region, were crippled by downsizing and relocation of the labor force, reinforcing the binary opposition between agriculture- and industry-dependent regions, on the one hand, and relatively affluent, service-industry oriented, large urban centers such as Prague.

    In this strained economic, political, and cultural ambiance so characteristic of the Czech society of the mid-late 1990s, Shakespeare became a crucial site of cultural production reflecting and refracting ongoing negotiations of postcommunist collective national belonging and individual subjectivities. Shakespearean cachet was widely employed to tackle the tensions surrounding the question of Czech postcommunist national agency, independence, and self-determination. While the postcommunist era brought, it seemed, freedom from historical empires, the Czechs—among the first wave of CEE states applying for EU membership—faced a set of economic, political, and cultural conditions that were to be met prior to admission in the Union. These conditions proved, however, extremely problematic. First of all, they were not negotiable.

Strict EU adherence guidelines were to be followed at every stage of EU enlargement, but these guidelines included economic, political, and cultural conditions that had not been discussed with EU membership applicants. Similarly unprecedented was the insistence on such requirements' implementation, a process inflexibly tied to each state's eligibility. This treatment raised questions about second-class membership that would, by its mere existence, undermine the Union's emphasis on equality among member states.

Economically, the conditions tied into EU admission paralleled many of the "structural adjustments" charted by earlier, neoliberal shock therapy, calling as it did for free markets and unrestricted flow of capital across existing national borders within the soon to expand EU. Yet, as CEE governments were quick to point out, while they were to remove barriers to the movement of Western capital and privatize social services, which de facto translated into cuts in social programs, West European governments insisted on protecting strategic areas of their economies and social services, imposing harsh tariffs on East European goods.[18] Ironically enough, none of the already existing West European members of the EU would meet admission requirements were they expected to meet the same standards.

In the same vein, EU pre-admission stipulations outlined necessary adjustments in candidate-state constitutions or legislation that—under the banner of universal human rights—set up parameters of racial, gender, and sexual identifications for all EU citizens. However egalitarian in wording or well-intended these recommendations might have been, their condescendingly non-negotiable status—and perhaps, more so, their packaging with neoliberal preconditions—resulted in strong objections by Czech and other CEE politicians and overall in widening resistance to the EU and its cultural policies.[19] Similarly to the economic conditions imposed on candidate states but not on the other EU members, these supposedly universal human-rights stipulations did not reflect the actual state of affairs in the EU but were at best aspirational given the human-rights situation in Western Europe itself.[20]

Once their resistance failed to make a difference in the EU forums, Czech legislators had no choice but to begin rearticulating their country's legal code so as to satisfy the EU stipulations. The population too, drawing on generations-old lessons in political make-believe that feigned compliance with ideological tenets and frameworks set by out-

side powers, slipped into familiar patterns of cultural double-conscious-
ness wherein official state policy—aimed at foreign consumption—
diverged sharply from how the people actually felt about such issues.
That is to say, in the same ways in which the Czechs had given the
impression of supporting the totalitarian communist regime while in
actuality recognizing its true nature and, as such, mistrusting and even
subverting it, the Czechs of the postcommunist era learned to tolerate
their elected officials' moves, for the latter would ensure, it was hoped,
the country's economic and political future on the Continent.[21] In sum,
instead of fully accepting the proposed normative changes regarding
gender, sex, race, and other elements of identity and citizenship, the
Czechs have after 1989 developed a collective consciousness strategically subversive of the cultural and legal hegemony embedded in EU-
mandated legislation. In some instances, this opposing undercurrent sur-
faced in the form of strong backlash against central EU concepts and
requirements.

Expressing opposition to outside-imposed views of identity formation,
this alternative, critical consciousness was both reflected and transformed by the avalanche of postcommunist Shakespeare productions.
Trading on Shakespeare's cultural authority and in particular on the
"transcendental" and "universal" humanity immortalized by his works,
Czech directors have used his plays as an antidote of sorts to the EU
rhetoric of forcibly unified economic, political, and cultural values. This
strategy did not target specific economic policies but rather their impact
on the Czech living conditions, including the perceived assault on traditional Czech modalities of identity. Worth mentioning along these lines
is that in 2001, when the Czech parliament debated modifying the laws
to reflect EU norms on gender equality in the public and private spheres,
a flurry of productions of Shakespeare's *Taming of the Shrew* vented, as
it became immediately apparent, widespread skepticism about the government's attempt to enforce the newly forged normative boundaries of
gender roles. Recalling the spectacular failure of the compulsory equality of the sexes mandated decades before by Moscow and communist
ideology broadly, the productions brought the struggle between Shakespeare's main characters to bear on the tensions between publicly

enforced norms of marital relations, on the one hand, and, on the other, on the need for a true, working relationship between two actual human beings with their own lives and individualizing characteristics. On the surface, these productions seemed to condone domestic abuse, incidentally also discussed in the parliament at the time. Yet, from interviews with theater professionals involved in the productions as well as from reviews and debates in the media, one can gather that the performances' directors turned to Shakespeare to highlight the private, interpersonal negotiations that are necessary to mutually satisfactory domestic arrangements while also responding to the public's expectations regarding traditional marital gender roles. In this context, mutual violence in the domestic sphere tested the boundaries of accepted, normative status quo (also present, I might add, in the EU provisions regarding gender, which were discussed by the Czech parliament too). What the productions emphasized, however, spoke to the popular concern about self-determination in terms of setting up normative boundaries of postcommunist, individual and collective subjectivity, independent of external suggestions or demands.[22]

Similarly subversive reflections on the necessity of protecting Czech culture from invasive redefinitions of identity can be found in the representation of homosexual behavior in postcommunist Shakespeare productions. True, popular performance genres such as musicals or vaudevilles have successfully incorporated positive reflections on nonnormative queer identity and behavior, but the treatment of such subjects in Shakespeare has met with public resistance, resentment, and silence. Whereas productions of *The Taming of the Shrew* and other Shakespeare plays have undertaken extensive textual interpretation of nuances in Shakespeare's texts, passages that hint at or explicitly depict intimate same sex behavior have been routinely omitted or glossed over. In the few instances where Czech directors have attempted to reproduce scenes of male homosexual intimacy on stage such as in several recent productions of *The Twelfth Night* or *The Sonnets*, reviews in a range of Czech media deliberately shifted attention to other aspects of each production or simply ignored the productions altogether, opting for silence rather than take the risk of negative publicity.[23] At a time when the EU has mandated legislation of equality of homosexually self-identified citizens in Czech society, such deliberate resistance to homosexuality in Shakespeare—particularly in contrast to the relatively easy public acceptance of representation of male intimacy in popular culture—suggests an orchestrated protection of a perceived ideological core of the Czech nation, that is, of a an identity view to which Shakespeare's play speaks vividly.

While this retrenchment to, some might argue, traditional modes of identity formation and categorization could be easily seen as a form of nationalistic "essentialism," one routinely vilified by proponents and critics of globalization alike, the strategic deployment of Shakespearean cultural capital on the Czech stages hints that a far more complex set of factors are in play. The non-negotiability of the EU admission conditions is, again, one thing to keep in mind. One must also remember that none of the foregoing stipulations have been consistently enforced by older EU member states, whether we are talking about economy or human rights, which, for one thing, betrays a hierarchically conceived double standard that undermines the very EU prerequisites, and, for another, belies the viability of these conditions for postcommunist developments in CEE. The exploitive nature of the neoliberal economic conditions, in particular, renders the requirements about redrawing subjectivity boundaries suspect at best. Simply put, it is quite legitimate, I think, to raise the following question: If the Western neighbors of the Czech Republic seek to benefit materially from the postcommunist transitional process at the expense of sustainable economic and social development of the Czechs themselves, are the aforementioned cultural preconditions similarly aimed at benefiting the West rather than the country on which they are imposed?

To conclude, postcommunist Shakespeare productions suggest that Czech culture sets out to occupy an intellectual and ideological space separate from both externally enforced innovations and reformulations of identitarian issues and representations, on one side, and entrenched traditionalism, on the other side, at equal distance between uncritical assimilation of the cultural models proposed by the EU and their utter refutation. Instead, the provocative, overwhelming presence of Shakespeare in postcommunist Czech theaters seems to attest to an enduring commitment to the process of articulating cultural positions that are not tied to contextual political pressures but are rather based in time-honored models of humanity such as those inscribed in the Shakespearean canon.

NOTES

1. Terrence Hawkes, "Introduction," in *Alternative Shakespeares*, vol. 2, ed. Terrence Hawkes (London: Routledge, 1996): 10. Hawkes is perhaps the most notorious of commentators on the political ramifications of Shakespearean cultural capital. Other relevant texts by him include *Meaning by Shakespeare* (New York: Routledge, 1992), the widely acclaimed *Shakespeare in the Present* (New York: Routledge, 2002), and the essays in the now three-volume series of *Alternative Shakespeares*. I would also like to mention here Michael Bristol's *Big Time Shakespeare* (London and New York: Routledge, 1996); *Shakespeare and National Culture*, edited by John Joughin and John Drakakis (Manchester: Manchester University Press, 1997); Graham Holderness's *Cultural Shakespeare: Essays in Shakespeare Myth* (Hertfordshire: University of Hertfordshire Press, 2002); *Shakespeare Reproduced: The text in history and ideology*, edited by Jean Howard and Marion F. O'Connor (New York and London: Methuen, 1987); and Douglas Lanier's *Shakespeare and Modern Popular Culture* (Oxford: Oxford University Press, 2002).

2. Ania Loomba and Martin Orkin, "Introduction," *Post-Colonial Shakespeares* (London and New York: Routledge, 1998): 1.

3. Ibid., 3. Loomba and Orkin provide one example of the political use of Shakespeare in colonial cultural spaces. In addition to the rest of the essays in their anthology, which includes, for instance, Jonathan Dollimore's relevant article "Shakespeare and Theory," see Thomas Cartelli's *Repositioning Shakespeare: National formations, postcolonial appropriations* (London and New York: Routledge, 1999); Martin Orkin's *Local Shakespeares: Proximations and Power* (London: Routledge, 2005) and "Shifting Shakespeare," in *PMLA*, vol. 118 (January 2003): 134-36; also see Rohan Quince's *Shakespeare in South Africa: Stage Productions During the Apartheid Era* (New York: Peter Lang, 2000).

4. For an excellent historical survey of Shakespeare's impact in the region see Zdeněk Stříbrný's *Shakespeare and Eastern Europe* (Oxford, UK: Oxford University Press, 2000). For a more detailed account of the political use of Shakespeare in the context of communism, see *Shakespeare in the Worlds of Communism and Socialism*, Irena Makaryk and Joseph Price, eds. (Toronto: University of Toronto Press, 2007). For a consideration of Shakespeare in a specific national communist/socialist context, see, for instance, Zdeněk Stříbrný's recent *The Whirligig of Time: Essays on Shakespeare and Czechoslovakia* (Newark, DE: University of Delaware Press, 2007); *Shakespeare in the New Europe*, Michael Hattaway, Boika Sokolova, and Derek Roper, eds. (Sheffield, UK: Sheffield Academic Press, 1994); and Aleksander Shurbanov and Boika Sokolova, *Painting Shakespeare Red* (Cranbury, DE: University of Delaware Press, 2001).

5. Arkady Ostrovsky, "Shakespeare as a Founding Father of Socialist Realism: The Soviet Affair with Shakespeare," in *Shakespeare in the Worlds of Communism and Socialism*, 56-83.

6. The Prague Theater Institute only began keeping comprehensive records and statistics for all Czech stages in 1997, but even these are quite revealing of the firm place Shakespeare has claimed in the Czech theater. In the first season for which we have statistics, 1997-1998, Shakespeare was the most performed dramatic author with 614 performances of his plays countrywide, a figure which was nearly twice as high as the runner-up popular Czech trio of Smoljak/Cimrman/Svěrák, whose plays were staged 322 times. Shakespeare also led in the number of premiers of his plays (nineteen), whereas Chekhov, in the second place, claimed ten. Shakespeare reportedly sold the most tickets, outshining not only all other dramatic authors but also all composers of opera, ballet, musicals, and vaudevilles, with a total of 196,055 people in attendance. His plays were performed in twenty-seven different theaters, whereas Chekhov claimed only fourteen. That year, the most performed

plays were *Romeo and Juliet* and *The Taming of the Shrew*, with 125 and ninety documented performances respectively, both in the top ten performed plays in the season [Ondřej Černý and Vít Vencl, eds. *Divadlo v České Republice 97-98,* (Praha: Divadelní Ústav, 1999): 577-589]. As the data show, Shakespeare's popularity only grew in the subsequent years: in 1998-1999, Shakespeare plays sold 203,347 tickets, a number that rose by another fifty thousand by the following year (263,050). Not only did theaters continue to run successful existing productions, but they also put up a lot of new plays: in 1998-1999, twenty-two new productions were brought out, more than the premieres of the canonical authors in second and third places, Dvořák and Molière (eleven and ten openings respectively), a number that increased to twenty-five by the following year. In the season 1999-2000, Shakespeare began dominating a new genre category, the musical, where an adaptation of *Hamlet* by Janek Ledecký claimed the first place, before all other musicals that year, with a total of 78,807 tickets sold, the most not only for a musical, but also for any privately owned venue. See Černý and Vencl *Divadlo v České Republice 98-99 (*Praha: Divadelní Ústav, 2000): 623-653; *Divadlo v České Republice 99-00* (Praha: Divadelní Ústav, 2001): 642-691). Shakespeare's commanding presence on the Czech stages did not diminish by the end of the 2002-2003 season, the last one for which published statistics were available at the time of writing (Spring 2009), or for the season of 2003-2004, for which the Theater Institute was kind to provide preliminary data for the purposes of this volume; that season saw twenty new Shakespeare productions in addition to thirty-six continuing productions from previous seasons. During the same season, Shakespeare drew 218,421 paying audience members.

7. For a close discussion of this "follow up," see for instance Dmitri Trenin, "Introduction: The Grand Design" in *Ambivalent Neighbors: The EU, NATO, and the Price of Membership*, Anatol Lieven and Dmitri Trenin, eds. (Washington: Carnegie Endowment for International Peace, 2003): 1-14 (particularly p. 1); or Naomi Klein, *The Shock Doctrine: The Rise of Disaster Capitalism* (New York: Metropolis Books, 2007), particularly p. 176 and following.

8. Adam Swain, "Soft Capitalism and Hard Industry: Virtualism, the 'Transition Industry' and the Restructuring of Ukrainian Coal Industry." *Transactions of the Institute of British Geographers*, Vol. 31, No. 2 (June 2006): 208-223, p. 208-210.

9. Janine R. Wedel, *Collision and Collusion: The Strange Case of Western Aid to Eastern Europe, 1989-1998* (New York: St. Martin's Press, 1998), p. 30.

10. Ibid. As historian Robin Okey [*The Demise of Communist East Europe: 1989 in Context* (London: Oxford University Press, 2004)] points out, while the first Marshall Plan equaled 1% of the U.S. gross national product (GNP), the financial commitment to CEE after 1989 equaled only about 0.02% of the GNP of the Western members of the Organization of the Economic Cooperation and Development (OECD). Though in 1949 the Marshall Plan contributed 11.5% of France's GNP, postcommunist Hungary—one of the primary early recipients of Western aid—received only 0.5% of its annual budget; incidentally, the cost of "structural reforms" imposed by the European Union in most CEE countries will swallow about 6% of the GNP of each applicant country (ibid. 181-2). Of the allocated transition funds, only a small proportion consisted of grants (researchers assign between 10-20% to this category) as compared to the 80-90% of the original Marshall Plan.

Beside a disparity in actual amounts of distributed aid, this second "Marshall Plan" was charted along ideological lines fundamentally different from the first. The first Marshall Plan provided aid to war-ravaged Western Europe in hopes that palpable post-war economic development would prevent the spread of communism from the solidifying Eastern bloc (Klein, ibid. 252). In addition, the grant was flexible in application. The eventual, thriving capitalist social-democracies of Western Europe grew from the freedom allowed to individual governments to identify areas of necessary investment with an eye to existing cultural and economic traditions, local understanding of social organization, and sustainable development of the region. In contrast, the aid within the second "Marshal Plan" operated in the absence of the ideological, economic, and political threat that was communism of the post-World War II era and thus was far less generous and more restrictive in terms of its use.

11. Katherine Verdery, *What Was Socialism, and What Comes Next?* (Princeton, NJ: Princeton University Press, 1996): 205.

12. Wedel, ibid., 30.

13. Ibid., 35.

14. Reported by Jacek Moskalewicz in "Alcohol in the countries in transition: the Polish experience and the wider context," *Contemporary Drug Problems*, Vol. 27 (Fall 2000: 561-92): 563.

15. Aleksander Štulhofer and Theo Sandfort, "Introduction: Sexuality and Gender in Times of Transition," in *Sexuality and Gender in Postcommunist Eastern Europe and Russia* (New York: The Haworth Press, 2005): 1-25, p. 2.

16. Branko Milanovic, *Income, Inequality, and Poverty during the Transition from Planned to Market Economy* (Washington: World Bank, 1998): 26.

17. Robin Okey, *The Demise of Communist East Europe: 1989 in Context* (London: Oxford University Press, 2004): 124.

18. This situation has been addressed, for instance, by Heather Grabbe in "Challenges of EU Enlargement," in *Ambivalent Neighbors: The EU, NATO, and the Price of Membership*, Anatol Lieven and Dmitri Trenin, eds. (Washington, DC: Carnegie Endowment for International Peace, 2003): 67-89; Alexander J. Motyl, "Ukraine, Europe, and Russia: Exclusion or Dependence?" in *Ambivalent Neighbors:* 15-43; also see Okey pp. 119, 174-82.

19. Scholars of the postcommunist transition began tracing growing resistance to the values and requirements imposed by the European Union, a resistance also known as "Euroskepticism," which started spreading in the second half of the 1990s. See, for instance, Grabbe, ibid., p. 82, 88; Okey, ibid., p. 120; and Laure Neumayer, "Euroscepticism as a political label," *European Journal of Political Research* 47 (2008): 135-160.

20. For an excellent account of the uneven application of human rights legislation, see Motyl, ibid., p. 18. For a discussion of the political (mis)uses of the rhetoric of universal human rights for Western, neoimperial purposes, see Klein, ibid., p. 118, or David Harvey, *A Brief History of Neoliberalism* (New York: Oxford University Press, 2007), particularly p. 178-79.

21. The flurry of international outrage following Czech President Václav Klaus's remarks to the European Parliament on February 19, 2009, suggests that Czech politicians became less reticent about representing their constituents' wishes once the Czech Republic joined the European Union. In the capacity of assuming the rotating presidency of the EU, Klaus addressed the very issue of forced cultural and economic assimilation, particularly as it was aimed at the EU's Eastern regions. He cautioned EU representatives not to fall into the trap of inflexible cultural practices. The full text of the address can be consulted in the online archives of the Czech daily *Mladá Fronta Dnes* at iDNES.cz: http://zpravy.idnes.cz/, Accessed February 20, 2009.

22. For detailed research of this phenomena see Marcela Kostihová, "Katherina 'Humanized': Abusing the 'Shrew' on Prague Stages," in *World-wide Shakespeares: Local appropriations in film and performance,* Sonia Massai, ed. (New York and London: Routledge, 2005): 72-79.

23. Marcela Kostihová, "Post-communist Nights: Shakespeare, masculinity and Western citizenship" in *Twelfth Night: New Essays.* James Schiffer, ed. Forthcoming from Routledge (2009).

BIBLIOGRAPHY

Abrams, Bradley F. *Struggle for the Soul of the Nation: Czech Culture and the Rise of Communism.* New York: Rowman and Littlefield, 2005.

Baranovsky, Vladimir. "Russian Views on NATO and the EU." *Ambivalent Neighbors: The EU, NATO, and the Price of Membership,* ed. Anatol Lieven and Dmitri Trenin, 269-294. Washington, DC: Carnegie Endowment for International Peace, 2003.

Bate, Jonathan. "Shakespearean Nationhoods." *Shakespeare in the New Europe,* ed. Michael Hattaway, Boika Sokolova, and Derek Roper, 112-129. Sheffield, UK: Sheffield Academic Press, 1994.

Blumenfeld, Odette-Irenne. "Shakespeare in Post-Revolutionary Romania: The Great Directors are Back Home." *Shakespeare in the New Europe,* ed. Michael Hattaway, Boika Sokolova, and Derek Roper, 230-246.

Bobinski, Christopher. "Polish Illusions and Reality." *Ambivalent Neighbors,* ed. Anatol Lieven and Dmitri Trenin, 231-244.

Bristol, Michael D. *Big-time Shakespeare.* London and New York: Routledge, 1996.

_____. "Carnival and the Institution of Theater in Elizabethan England." *ELH* 50 (1983): 637-54.

Cartelli, Thomas. *Repositioning Shakespeare: National formations, postcolonial appropriations.* London and New York: Routledge, 1999.

Černý, Ondřej and Vít Vencl, eds. *Divadlo v České Republice 96-97.* Praha: Divadelní Ústav, 1998.

_____. *Divadlo v České Republice 97-98.* Praha: Divadelní Ústav, 1999.

_____. *Divadlo v České Republice 98-99.* Praha: Divadelní Ústav, 2000.

_____. *Divadlo v České Republice 99-00.* Praha: Divadelní Ústav, 2001.

_____. *Divadlo v České Republice 00-01.* Praha: Divadelní Ústav, 2002.

_____. *Divadlo v České Republice 01-02.* Praha: Divadelní Ústav, 2003.

_____. *Divadlo v České Republice 02-03.* Praha: Divadelní Ústav, 2004.

Černý, Ondřej and Zuzana Jindrová, eds. *Divadlo v České Republice 95-96.* Praha: Divadelní Ústav, 1998.

Chomsky, Noam. *Hegemony or Survival: America's Quest for Global Dominance.* New York: Metropolitan Books, 2003.

_____. *Interventions.* San Francisco: City Lights Books, 2007.

Derrida, Jacques. *Specters of Marx: The State of the Debt, the Work of Mourning, and the New International.* Trans. Peggy Kamuf. New York: Routledge, 1994.

Dollimore, Jonathan: "Shakespeare and Theory." *Post-Colonial Shakespeares,* ed. Ania Loomba and Martin Orkin, 259-276. London and New York: Routledge Press, 1998.

Duggan, Lisa. *The Twilight of Equality? Neoliberalism, Cultural Politics, and the Attack on Democracy.* Boston: Beacon Press, 2003.

Egan, Gabriel. *Shakespeare and Marx.* Oxford: Oxford University Press, 2004.

Fujita, Minoru, and Leonard Pronko, eds. *Shakespeare East and West.* New York: St. Martin's Press, 1996.

Gal, Susan and Gail Kligman. *The Politics of Gender After Socialism.* Princeton: Princeton University Press, 2000.

Giroux, Henry A. *The Terror of Neoliberalism: Authoritarianism and the Eclipse of Democracy.* Boulder: Paradigm, 2004.

Grabbe, Heather. "Challenges of EU Enlargement." *Ambivalent Neighbors,* ed. Anatol Lieven and Dmitri Trenin, 67-89.

Guillory, John. *Cultural Capital: The Problem of Literary Canon Formation.* Chicago: University of Chicago Press, 1994.

Habermas, Jürgen. *The Postnational Constellation: Political Essays.* Edited and translated by Max Pensky. Cambridge, MA: MIT, 2001.

Harvey, David. *A Brief History of Neoliberalism.* New York: Oxford, 2007.

Hattaway, Michael, Boika Sokolova, and Derek Roper, eds. *Shakespeare in the New Europe.* Sheffield, UK: Sheffield Academic Press, 1994.

Havel, Václav, et al. *The Power of the Powerless.* New York: M.E. Sharpe, 1985.

Hawkes, Terrence. "Introduction." *Alternative Shakespeares,* vol. 2, ed. Terrence Hawkes, 1-16. London: Routledge, 1996.

_____. *Meaning by Shakespeare.* New York: Routledge, 1992.

_____. *Shakespeare in the Present.* New York: Routledge, 2002.

Healy, Thomas. "Past and Present Shakespeares." *Shakespeare and National Culture,* ed. John Joughin and John Drakakis, 206-32. Manchester, UK: Manchester University Press, 1997.

Holderness, Graham. *Cultural Shakespeare: Essays in the Shakespeare Myth.* Hertfordshire, UK: University of Hertfordshire Press, 2001.

_____. *Visual Shakespeare: Essays in Film and Television.* Hertfordshire, UK: University of Hertfordshire Press, 2002.

Howard, Jean E., and Marion F. O'Connor. "Introduction." *Shakespeare Reproduced: The Text in History and Ideology,* ed. Jean Howard and Marion F. O'Connor, 1-17. New York and London: Methuen, 1987.

Klein, Naomi. *The Shock Doctrine: The Rise of Disaster Capitalism.* New York: Metropolitan Books, 2007.

Kostihová, Marcela. "Katherina 'Humanized:' Abusing the 'Shrew' on Prague Stages." *World-wide Shakespeares: Local appropriations in film and performance,* ed. Sonia Massai, 72-79. New York and London: Routledge, 2005.

_____. "Post-communist Nights: Shakespeare, Masculinity and Western Citizenship" *Twelfth Night: New Essays,* ed. James Schiffer. Forthcoming from Routledge (2009).

Kott, Jan. *Shakespeare our Contemporary.* New York: Methuen, 1967.

Lanier, Douglas. *Shakespeare and Modern Popular Culture.* Oxford: Oxford University Press, 2002.

Loomba, Ania, and Martin Orkin, eds. *Post-Colonial Shakespeares.* London and New York: Routledge, 1998.

Makaryk, Irena R., and Joseph G. Price, eds. *Shakespeare in the Worlds of Communism and Socialism.* Toronto: University of Toronto Press, 2006.

Milanovic, Branko. *Income, Inequality, and Poverty during the Transition from Planned to Market Economy.* Washington, DC: World Bank, 1998.

Möller-Leimkühler, Anne Maria. "The gender gap in suicide and premature death or: why are men so vulnerable?" *European Archive of Psychiatry and Clinical Neuroscience* 253 (2003): 1-8.

Moskalewicz, Jacek, and Jussi Simpura. "Alcohol supply in developing and transitional societies: The supply of alcoholic beverages in transitional conditions: The case of Central and Eastern Europe." *Addiction* 95 (2000): S505-22.

Moskalewicz, Jacek. "Alcohol in the countries in transition: the Polish experience and the wider context." *Contemporary Drug Problems* 27 (2000): 561-92.

Motyl, Alexander J. "Ukraine, Europe, and Russia: Exclusion or Dependence?" *Ambivalent Neighbors,* ed. Anatol Lieven and Dmitri Trenin: 15-43.

Neumayer, Laure. "Euroscepticism as a political label." *European Journal of Political Research* 47 (2008): 135-160.

Oates-Indruchová, Libora. "The Void of Acceptable Masculinity During Czech State Socialism: The Case of Radek John's *Memento.*" *Men and Masculinities* 8 (2006): 428-450.

Okey, Robin. *The Demise of Communist East Europe: 1989 in Context.* London: Oxford University Press, 2004.

Orkin, Martin. "Shifting Shakespeare." *PMLA* 118 (2003): 134-36.

_____. *Local Shakespeares: Proximations and Power.* London: Routledge, 2005.

Ostrovsky, Arkady. "Shakespeare as a Founding Father of Socialist Realism: The Soviet Affair with Shakespeare." *Shakespeare in the Worlds of Communism and Socialism,* ed. Irena Makaryk and Joseph Price, 56-83. Toronto: University of Toronto Press, 2006.

Otáhal, Milan. *Podíl tvůrčí inteligence na pádu komunismu: Kruh nezávislé inteligence.* Brno: Doplněk, 1999.

Quince, Rohan. *Shakespeare in South Africa: Stage Productions During the Apartheid Era.* New York: Peter Lang, 2000.

Said, Edward W. *Culture and Imperialism.* New York: Vintage, 1994.

Shakespeare, William. *The Norton Shakespeare.* Stephen Greenblatt et al., eds. New York: Norton, 1997; *The Riverside Shakespeare.* 2nd ed. Boston and New York: Houghton Mifflin, 1997.

Shurbanov, Aleksander, and Boika Sokolova. *Painting Shakespeare Red.* Cranbury, DE: University of Delaware Press, 2001.

Simpura, Jussi. "Alcohol in Eastern Europe: market prospects, prevention puzzles." *Addiction* 90 (1995): 467-470.

Stříbrný, Zdeněk, ed. *Charles University on Shakespeare.* Praha: Univerzita Karlova, 1966.

Stříbrný, Zdeněk "Shakespeare Today." *Charles University on Shakespeare,* ed. Zdeněk Stříbrný, 25-37. Praha: Univerzita Karlova, 1966.

_____. *Shakespeare and Eastern Europe.* Oxford: Oxford University Press, 2000.

_____. *The Whirligig of Time: Essays on Shakespeare and Czechoslovakia.* Newark, DE: University of Delaware Press, 2007.

Štulhofer, Aleksander, and Theo Sandfort. "Introduction: Sexuality and Gender in Times of Transition." *Sexuality and Gender in Postcommunist Eastern Europe and Russia,* ed. Aleksander Štulhofer and Theo Sandfort, 1-25. New York: The Haworth Press, 2005.

Swain, Adam. "Soft capitalism and hard industry: virtualism, the 'transition industry' and the restructuring of the Ukrainian coal industry." *Transactions of the Institute of British Geographers* 31 (2006): 208-223.

Trenin, Dmitri. "Introduction: The Grand Redesign." *Ambivalent Neighbors,* ed. Anatol Lieven and Dmitri Trenin, 1-14.

True, Jacqui. *Gender, Globalization, and Postsocialism: The Czech Republic After Communism.* New York: Columbia University Press, 2003.

Verdery, Katherine. *What Was Socialism, and What Comes Next?* Princeton, NJ: Princeton University Press, 1996.

Wallace, William. "Does the EU Have an *Ostpolitik?*" *Ambivalent Neighbors,* ed. Anatol Lieven and Dmitri Trenin, 44-66.

Wedel, Janine R. *Collision and Collusion: The Strange Case of Western Aid to Eastern Europe, 1989-1998.* New York: St. Martin's Press, 1998.

KADARE AFTER COMMUNISM: ALBANIA, THE BALKANS, AND EUROPE IN THE POST-1990 WORK OF ISMAIL KADARE

PETER MORGAN

In the early nineties, the Russian commentator Tatyana Tolstaya remarked on the disorientation of writers released from constraints of censorship and fear in the postcommunist era.[1] The open structures of postcommunism seemed to provide no structure or context for their writing, so used were they to the oblique modes of communication under socialism. The Albanian writer Ismail Kadare has proven the great exception to this rule, bursting through the barrier of 1990 with undimmed creative power and imaginative energy. In contrast to many of his close contemporaries and fellow dissident writers in Eastern Europe, Kadare has remained active at the forefront of his nation's literary intelligentsia.

Unlike most of the other East European socialist dictatorships, Albania remained Stalinist until the fall of the regime in early 1991. During the decades of dictatorship Ismail Kadare (b. 1936) was the only Albanian writer known widely outside his small Balkan nation. He became the alternative voice of Albania to that of the regime with its cultured and clever dictator, Enver Hoxha (1908-1985), himself a would-be writer and Marxist intellectual. Kadare was committed to Albanian language, culture, and national identity, believed in European humanist ideals, and was attracted, to begin with, by the communist model of modernization in his socially and economically backward land. Deeply aware of the need of Albanians to participate in European modernity, he nevertheless came to object profoundly to the new Albania of the communist regime that dominated the country from 1944 until 1991. He remains a towering personality among Albanian public intellectuals and, accompanied by lesser figures such as Fatos Kongoli, Besnik Mustafaj, and others, continues to be a powerful presence in Albanian literary affairs.

Despite his importance as a writer and commentator under the dictatorship, Kadare has received relatively little attention beyond Albania and France, where he became known as a result of the early translation of his novel *The General of the Dead Army* in 1970. Neglect in the English-speaking world was due partly to the inaccessibility of information about the writer and his context during the socialist years. However, suspicions had been aired by Albanian émigrés and others regarding his alleged complicity with the regime. Figures such as the USA-based émigré Arshi Pipa publicized views about Kadare to readers who for the most part did not have a grasp of the Albanian situation. Not understanding the differences among various Eastern communist regimes, Western commentators expected the heroic dissidence they recognized in Czechoslovakia, the GDR, and elsewhere, and many Balkan commentators expressed, apropos of Kadare, views coloured by national and political bias.[2] Since the fall of the Albanian communism, particularly since the discovery and publication of the author's secret government files in 2003, the allegations of collaboration have been shown to be groundless and the Western reception of Kadare's work is now well underway.[3] The writer received the inaugural Man-Booker International prize for literature in 2005, and new translations of his works have been appearing in various presses since the mid-nineties.

1. *Postcommunism in Albania*

In 1989 Kadare was nominated by Nexhmije Hoxha, powerful spouse of the country's long-term dictator Enver Hoxha, for the position of Vice-President of the Albanian Democratic Front. The Front was a long-standing, broad-based organization for cultural, professional, and political groups, chaired until December 1990 by Nexhmije, which had succeeded the National Liberation Front in 1945, and had the nominal function of providing a popular channel for the expression of political views and for mass political education. Its main task was to reinforce the relationship between the party and the people and to popularize and implement the policies of the Albanian Party of Labour. This move was taken by the "reformers" in the regime in the hope of avoiding bloodshed and in order to begin the process of change. At this time, images of intellectuals-turned-political spokesmen, such as Vaclav Havel and various figures from the new political groupings of Eastern Europe, New Forum, Solidarity, Civic Forum, were dominating news broadcasts as they were elected to the positions of political power they had looked forward to for so long. Timothy Garton Ash would coin the term "refolution" for the "mixture of reform and revolution, with more of a revolutionary push from below in Poland and more of pre-emptive reform from above in Hungary."[4] Under the regime, Kadare had little option but to accept the nomination. The Democratic Front, with its newspaper *Bashkimi* (Freedom), seemed to be an appropriate body for the transition to democracy, but ultimately, like the whole structure of the system, it was discredited. In his musings on the figure of Prometheus in *Albanian Spring*, Kadare allows us to intuit the logic of this political decision and to consider for ourselves the level of development of his political insight at this point:

> Prometheus was never the hero of useless sacrifice; on the contrary he is the hero of intelligence and reason. Indeed, it was through reason, not blind obstinacy, that Prometheus won his victory and saved humankind. And mutual concessions between Zeus and Prometheus, tolerance and dialogue, are the essence of his myth.... More faithfully than any other, this myth testifies to the sufferings that humanity has borne—terror, chains, destruction—to reach Olympus (i.e. Parliament) and to send their first deputy to it. Since then, in the halls of Parliament, people have ceased to hear only a single voice, the voice of Zeus.[5]

However, events moved quickly, and the communists were losing strength. In late 1989 and 1990, Kadare stepped forward to make stronger claims for change. Fearing the outbreak of civil war, he sought a meeting with Enver Hoxha's successor, Ramiz Alia, to discuss human rights, the general levels of poverty, Tirana's abandonment of Kosova, and the activities of the *Sigurimi*, Albania's secret police. In *Albanian Spring* he would reproach Alia for his failure to take action.[6] His introduction to the novel *The Knives* by Neshat Tozaj, high-ranking functionary of the Ministry of the Interior, was written in 1989 as an attempt to bring out into the open the workings of the *Sigurimi* for a people for whom all mention of such a topic was taboo.[7] The point of Kadare's text was to emphasize the extent to which the *Sigurimi* had become a form of "mafia," a criminal group whose *raison d'être* was no longer a product of political categories such as class or dogma, but an ethos of shared self-interest linked to the regime. Groups such as this, wrote Kadare, perhaps with an eye on the Romanian situation, where the *Securitate* staged a violent counter-revolution, had become networks in and for themselves, abusing privileges, and abusing the dogma of communism in order to maintain themselves. Tozaj, notes Kadare in one of the earliest Albanian pieces of internal dissidence, "revolts against, and denounces the dubious practices of those who were supposed to be the servants of the people, but who conduct themselves like their masters."[8]

In this article Kadare appealed to the sense of equality entrenched in *Kanun*, the Albanians' ancient code of law, which preceded the French Revolution and the Declaration of the Rights of Man by centuries. Here, as in his literary-intellectual essays, Kadare takes pains to link European traditions of modern democracy to Albanian tradition for a people about to take on political self-determination after decades of political infantilism. This line of argument would become more dominant in his thinking during the nineties, finding expression later in *Albanian Spring*:

> Albania has deep roots in the democratic tradition. She was the only Balkan country that, while in the bosom of the Ottoman Empire, was governed by her own ancient Code, in which certain basic principles, like equality before the law and respect for the individual male, raised to the level of a cult, taught people to live in a kind of democracy—one as primitive as it was tragic. (*Albanian Spring* 39-40.)

In March that year, the editor of *Zëri I Rinisë* (The Voice of Youth) and long-time friend of Kadare, Remzi Lani, interviewed the writer on a range of political topics. Kadare nailed his colours clearly to the wall: "Dogmas must not impede the well-being and the freedoms of democracy," he told the reporter. Kadare reiterated his critique of the *Sigurimi* and divided the education and cultural sectors of the current regime into two groups, one of which was reform-minded, "agile of mind and with a sturdy vision of the future," and the other of which was opposed to change of any sort and must be "booted out of power."[9] In summer 1990 the first open anti-government demonstrations took place. The regime began to make moves designed, at least, to lend a semblance of democracy. At the plenum of the new Central Committee in July 1990, the Democratic Party, the first legal opposition, was allowed. The constitutional ban on foreign capital and credit was revoked in order to lift living standards, and the policy of isolation dating from the chairmanship of the first dictator, Enver Hoxha, was ended as the government indicated its intention of opening diplomatic relations with the two arch-enemies, the U.S.A. and the (soon to be defunct) Soviet Union.

On October 25, 1990, when Eastern Europe was in upheaval and the Albanian regime recognized the extent of its vulnerability, Kadare made a decisive and controversial public gesture in leaving his country in protest at the failure of the government to introduce political change. After his initial (and perhaps politically naïve) hopes for a peaceful transition to democracy and political openness, he realized that compromised figures and factions were staying in power by changing their political colours. The democratic reforms in Albania had not gone far enough, and control remained in the hands of the Tirana ruling class:

> I had told myself that the day the totalitarian state agreed to live with a genuine literature would be the first real sign of reform, of the regime's attempt to humanize itself. Through my work, I've held this dream up to the Albanian people and to thousands of readers around the world. Now I understood that, although there is something authentic in the dream, the illusion was no more than an illusion. To make it a reality there had to be some new impulse, a new dimension. That impulse would be my *absence*. (*Albanian Spring* 58-59.)

There was, however, good reason to suspect that he felt unsafe in the transitional environment where old scores could be settled in a context of upheaval and change. He had never lacked enemies. He was hated by the *Sigurimi,* by factions in the Union of Writers, by Nexhmije Hoxha and her associates, as well as by parties outside Albania and criminal groups with shadowy links to the regime. Rumour had it that a "black list" had been compiled with Kadare at its head.[10] Moreover, he now understood the danger of being drawn into further compromising associations. This was a time when it was essential that he continue to speak with his own voice even, if necessary, from a position outside Albania. He knew that his name could be used as an alibi and an imprimatur in an environment in which democratic government would finally come about.[11]

In December 1990, student protests escalated throughout the country. Multiparty elections took place in March, the following year. The Albanian Party of Labour, now a political party in the multiparty environment, won, due to its control of the media and the ignorance and conservatism of the rural population in particular. Ramiz Alia was installed as the new President. However when Hoxha's massive statue in central Tirana was toppled on February 20, 1991, it was clear that the regime's chances of staying in power were over. It took a further general strike in April, before a transitional "government of national salvation" was set up. The nation was in a state of crisis, with food riots occurring and large numbers of people fleeing the country. At the elections of March 1992, the Democratic Party won a landslide victory, installing Sali Berisha as President. Kadare returned to Albania on May 6, 1992, after the March elections appeared to indicate that the country's political situation had stabilized. Nevertheless, the country continued to suffer food shortages and riots. A massive Italian aid program was undertaken in order to stop the haemorrhaging of economic refugees. The election of Albania to the Council of Europe in 1995 offered hope. Political fragmentation and infighting continued, though, and economic and social chaos dogged the country in the mid-nineties as its population became the victim of international pyramid investment schemes after having bankrupted itself in the communist years.

2. *Kadare in Postcommunism*

When the regime fell in 1991, Kadare, at fifty-five, was a seasoned writer in defiance of the dictatorship. He was not a dissident in the post-totalitarian mode of Havel or Alexander Solzhenitsyn. This was not possible in the Albanian Stalinist environment, which remained resolutely opposed to the changes that occurred in the Soviet Union as a result of the Khrushchev thaw of the mid-fifties. Albanian socialism was Stalinist to the end. In autobiographical works, novels, and literary-historical essays Kadare has challenged the postcommunist silence, producing a body of work in which the recent and the distant past are examined with an eye to the Albanian present and the European future. Since the fall of communism, Kadare has been vociferous in his opposition to various aspects of Albanian life and politics. In the large corpus accumulated after 1991, including novels, stories, essays, and a play, Kadare has continued to document the past and to chart the Albanian present and the European democratic future in the new context. Now the grand old man of Albanian letters, Kadare has nevertheless not endeared himself to many both inside and outside Albania with his trenchant criticisms and his powerfully worded exhortations to his countrymen to reject aspects of their history and to rejoin Europe. Still attacked by the hard-line communists of the "old guard" as well as by the new postcommunists whose corrupt political behaviours he continues to criticize, he appears as undimmed in his tenacity as in his creativity. The key to Kadare's late work is to be found in his Albanian patriotism and in the promise of Europe that had lain dormant for so long during the previous decades. Indeed, no one was more cognizant than Kadare of the opportunity and the necessity of Albania's rejoining Europe in the wake of socialism and dictatorship.

Since the early nineties, Kadare has produced a series of works that lead Albanian literature and culture into new territory after the depredations of the communist era. Using the masks of literature and calling on his impressive reading of European culture, Kadare represents and critiques aspects of the Albanian past and present in order to move his country forward towards membership of the European Union and toward closer alliance with the West in the face of historical and cultural-religious links with Eastern European and Muslim powers. Taking a stand on the Kosova issue, supporting links with neighbouring Greece, criticising political corruption and cronyism in Albania's old and new political parties, and continuing to set the record straight about the communist past in his novels, essays, and drama, Kadare remains the most powerful—if not always the most popular—voice of Albania on the national and international stage.

In self-imposed exile in Paris in late 1990 and 1991, bruised by the events surrounding his departure, and disturbed by the civil unrest in his homeland, Kadare tried to bring the personal and the public aspects of his life into perspective in a series of documentary and autobiographical works. The events leading up to the writer's decision to leave Albania and seek refuge in France are documented in bitter detail in *Albanian Spring: Anatomy of a Tyranny* (1990). Two long autobiographical works followed, *Invitation to the Writer's Studio* (1990) and *The Weight of the Cross* (1991), covering the writer's life from the late fifties until the fall of the regime in 1990. This substantial series of works, along with several book-length interviews with Eric Faye, Alain Bosquet, and Denis Fernàndez-Recatalà, represents a detailed clarification of Kadare's personal history and involvement with the system during the decades of the dictatorship. These texts are an invaluable guide to the inner history of the regime and to the nature of literary creation and imaginative freedom under a dictatorship in a tiny, backward nation, in which all-but-complete political control had been achieved. Over the following years a large number of new stories appeared, in which the writer rehearsed themes that would reappear in his major novels.

3. Coming to Terms with the Past in the Postcommunist Novels

Kadare wrote his novel, *The Pyramid*, over two years between 1988 and 1990 as the edifice of European socialism was crumbling. At this time a pyramid-shaped mausoleum and museum to Enver Hoxha was being finished in central Tirana. However, the political symbolism of this work stretches back to an early poem from the sixties, "The Pyramid of Cheops," in which Kadare uses the pyramid—symbol of dictatorial autocracy—to illuminate the relationships between the pharaoh, his advisers, and bureaucrats. Even in the first part of this novel, written while communism was still in place, Kadare began to explore more openly the workings of absolute political power. Part two of the work was finished in 1990 as the regime was toppling. In the figure of the young Pharaoh in *The Pyramid* (1990), the writer achieved a subtle portrait of the dictator as modernizer and tyrant, whose monument is built solely with the purpose of depleting the energies and imaginations of his people, thereby keeping them under control. This novel can be considered an important transitional work between the Aesopian fiction of the socialist decades and the open essays and novels of the postcommunist period. Over the following years a number of new stories came out, in which the writer rehearsed themes that would reappear in his major novels: "Subterranean Passages," "The Bringer of Dreams," "The Great Wall," "The Church of Saint-Sophia," "The Eagle," The Theft of Royal Sleep, "Men's Beauty Contest in the Accursed Mountains," and "History of the Albanian Writers' Union Reflected in a Woman's Mirror."

Kadare resumed his novelistic output in 1996 with *Spiritus*, a key work for the postcommunist period. With it, the writer's transition from the Aesopian mode is complete. In the frame-narrative, set in the mid-nineties, a foreign delegation is travelling through the lands of Eastern Europe seeking keys to understanding the communist past. They are looking for something other than the usual stories of imprisonment and harassment: "We were looking for something...singular, one of those events or phenomena which have the ability to condense a broad and diffuse truth into something concise. We were convinced that this bane which had covered almost half the globe, could not have failed to have generated signs, hitherto unseen of an eerily prescient nature."[12] At the end, the travellers discover something both banal and true, "that which we had long suspected, namely that the history of communism revealed a universality which was independent of the various lands and peoples it had subdued" (*Spiritus* 10). In the process, however, they experience the communist past as a macabre narrative of surveillance in which little is gained beyond the fulfilment of the dying dictator's fantasies of control of and revenge on a land which has failed to deserve him.

In the provincial Albanian town of B. (Berat, perhaps), the foreign delegation comes across a strange tale which leads them into the maze of surveillance, manipulation, and state-sponsored deceit that characterized Enver Hoxha's final years, as the dictator was going blind from advanced diabetes and beginning to experience paranoid delusions. From the delegation's research into the prohibition of a production of Chekhov's tragi-comedy, *The Seagull*, in the early 1980s, emerge details of a spiritualist group, part of a plot to send a message to NATO via a French delegation after the break with China and at the height of the Albanian global isolation. The main story involves the innovations in communist surveillance through the introduction of bugging devices known as "princesses," which enable dramatically improved efficiency and flexibility in recording seditious conversations. The engineer Shpend Guraziu is killed by a bulldozer only moments after having tried to pass on a message to a visiting French delegation. Around this event is woven a story of intrigue which results in the exhumation, three years later, in October 1984, of Guraziu's body, in order to locate a long-lost bugging device, on which is registered the man's last living moments, enabling the *Sigurimi* to finally locate solid evidence for the plot against the regime. Under the direction of local *Sigurimi* boss Arian Vogli, agents listen to the engineer's last unclear words, a message of despair directed to the French delegation only moments before his death three years earlier. *Spiritus* takes place on several time levels, from 1980, when the spiritualist séances take place and the production of *The Seagull* is prohibited, to 1983, when the State Security police become involved in the search for the origins of the plot against the state, to October 1984, when the details of the plot and its conspirators are presented to the dictator on his last birthday anniversary. The frame narrative is written from the perspective of the mid-nineties' postcommunist present.

The irony of the story inheres in the inverse relationship between the institutions and mechanisms of surveillance on the one hand, and the substance of the surveillance on the other. In fact, there is little evidence that the message was even delivered or that it was of any importance. Nevertheless, over the course of the story, the engineer, Guraziu, his colleagues, the medium, and the other participants in the spiritualist group are arrested, tortured and killed, the actors are harassed and the director dies of a heart attack, an ex-lover of Vogli is tracked in her most intimate moments, a priest is executed, and others are imprisoned. At last, Vogli himself falls victim to his own machinations and is brutally muted and paralysed after his plan to give the dictator the ultimate birthday present misfires.

Communism for Kadare is a system that is opposed to life and is devoted to the suppression of every expression of freedom or spontaneity. The tape recording of the final moments of Guraziu, the speeches by his grave, the muffled sounds of mourning, of earth falling, and then the silence of death give powerful expression to Kadare's most profound theme: the communist regimes' fundamental opposition to life. This is the final, banal truth, the key to communism, discovered by the foreign delegation. It is expressed with a clarity, lucidity of imagination, and immediacy that place *Spiritus* among the best of Kadare's novels. Death and morbidity, symbolized in the figure of the dying and paranoid dictator, are the final truth of this defunct political system. The message to the French is imagined as an appeal to the upper world, of light and life, via a trope which is ubiquitous throughout Kadare's work, namely, the image of communist Albania as an underworld devoid of summer, light, love, imagination, and creativity. Hope lies in the possibility of contact with the spirit world of the dead or across the unbridgeable chasms of death and life and East and West. The tapping of the great collective unconscious of communism in the story's séances goes to the heart of Kadare's lifelong critique of this political system, for which *The Palace of Dreams* (1981) and *The Shadow* (1986) are perhaps the best illustrations.

After the departure of the foreign commission, the séances, the voice from beyond the grave, the plot and the fate of its participants split and take on a life of their own as the stuff of legend and traditional song. Similarly to what happens in *The Great Winter* and *The File on H*, history generates literature. Different versions of the story develop, gradually assuming the epic qualities of brevity and iconicity, focusing on the essentials of existence under Albanian totalitarianism, thus transforming the bugging devices into a plague of black hornets and the recorded message into a voice from beyond the grave. As in *The File on H*, where the anthropologist's tape recorder appears as a motif in the rhapsodist's song, so in *Spiritus* the ancient Albanian art of epic song transforms history into literature and reality into images, providing a perspective from the *longue durée* of history.

Where the Aesopian techniques of writing "between the lines" rendered early novels such as *The General* and *The Monster* (1965) difficult and opaque to later readers, *Spiritus* is released of the need for such writing strategies and so communicates very directly the truth, the satire, and the tragedy of Albania's communist past. Indeed, one of Kadare's writing strategies since the demise of the dictatorship has been the use of Kafkaesque black humor to critically deconstruct the memory of the regime. Coming to terms with the new postcommunist writing environment in works such as his only play to date, *Bad Season on Olympus* (1996), Kadare begins the process of ironic revisiting of themes from his earlier work, in this case the relationship between Zeus and Prometheus as a comic allegory of the complex dynamic of the dictator and the writer. The recollections are preserved in these works, but the machinations of power and the structures of intimidation and fear are pilloried. This represents a classic Central European application of literary irony and satire in order to achieve the transition from one historical era to another, a technique comparable to Hermann Broch's "nicht mehr und noch nicht" ("no longer and not yet") in *The Death of Vergil* or to Kafka's macabre humor in *The Metamorphosis* or *The Trial*.

Like other East European writers, such as the (East) German Wolfgang Hilbig in *"I,"* or the Hungarian Peter Esterházy in *Improved Edition*, Kadare goes over the events of the past from different angles to reveal the hidden core of communist dictatorship. *The Life, Game, and Death of Lul Mazrek* (2002) was inspired by a bizarre episode from the past decades. The Greek island of Corfu lies just opposite the resort town of Saranda in the south of Albania and was a popular if closely guarded point of attempted escape. In order to dissuade potential refugees from swimming the distance, the regime paraded the bloodied bodies of escapees along the beachfront—the bodies, as it turned out, of live soldiers, bloodied and wrapped in sheets for effect. The dead were left to sink to the bottom of the Adriatic after being shot. A famous case occurred during the eighties when three siblings tried this means of fleeing the country, only one of whom survived. The imagery of life and death and of crossing over from the realm of death to that of life is ubiquitous in Kadare's work, and so in *Spring Flowers, Spring Frost* (2000) Kadare returns to the world of Albanian tradition and folklore (familiar to his readers from earlier texts such as the 1978 book *Broken April*) in order to explore the interrelationships of past and present in the postcommunist environment.

The ancient Greek legends of the House of Tantalus, in particular the Iphigenia story, provided Kadare with images to match the excesses of ruthlessness of the families and clans at the center of power in Tirana. In the 1986 novel, *Agamemnon's Daughter*, Kadare's implied reference is to the Shehu family. He continued his fascination with the bizarre and criminal episodes of the dictatorship at its height in the late seventies and early eighties, with *The Successor* (2003), a sequel to *Agamemnon's Daughter* based on the mysterious death of Hoxha's long-time second-in-command, Mehmet Shehu. The betrayal of a daughter by her father and the chain of violence and crimes that follows in the house of Agamemnon reveal the ultimate inseparability of the political and the private realms. This account of the perversions of power becomes another version of the story of the sacrifice of Albania by her leaders:

> The three-portaled door of the Atreids became in my eyes the sym-
> bolic dwelling of every communist leader. These same residences
> existed in every country of the East. But that of the Albanian Prime
> Minister, Mehmet Shehu, where on the night of 17th December
> 1981 the terrible murder was perpetrated...was perhaps the closest
> to the palace of Agamemnon.[13]

On April 26, 1980, Mehmet Shehu was relieved of duties as Minister of Defense and succeeded by Kadri Hazbiu, ex-Minister of the Interior and husband of the sister of Shehu's wife. On December 17, 1981, Shehu was found shot dead in his home in suspicious circumstances. The bullet wound was such that it was unlikely to have been caused through suicide, although the regime immediately cast it as such. Shehu's newly renovated home was situated only several hundred metres from the Hoxha residence and close to the Central Committee headquarters in the enclosed and heavily guarded *"Blloc"* in central Tirana. Rumour abounded in the capital and around the world as various figures were implicated, including the Minister of the Interior, Kadri Hazbiu, the wife of the dictator, Nexhmije, and Enver Hoxha himself.

Shehu was one of the original partisans who marched with Hoxha through the streets of Tirana after the German withdrawal. He established a reputation as a ruthless, hard-line Stalinist in the regime. On the day of his death Hoxha made a public announcement that Shehu had committed suicide after having been exposed as an enemy counter-agent. One of Shehu's sons committed suicide; his widow, Fiqret was removed from her post as secretary in charge of ideology on the Central Committee and imprisoned and interrogated along with Shehu's other sons. An earlier scandal over the planned marriage of Shehu's second son to the daughter of a "class enemy" had damaged Shehu's position the year before. A period of renewed political terror, dubbed by Bashim Shehu the "autumn of fear," descended over the country as Mehmet Shehu's "accomplices" were named and purged.[14] Kadare suspected that the aging and paranoid dictator had become suspicious of his long-time comrade and wanted to remove him, as he had done with so many powerful figures over the past four decades. On the basis of his knowledge of members of the family, in particular Shehu's third son, Bashkim, and his wife, Kadare surmised that fate was sealed by Yugoslav blackmail of Hoxha over matters dating back to the forties.[15] I might note, Shehu was a fierce enemy of the Yugoslavs. After the 1981 massacres of Kosovar Albanians, the Yugoslavs tried to blackmail Hoxha into silence by publishing part of a denunciation of Hoxha by Nako Spiru to the Comintern. Realizing that Hoxha would have to protest the situation in 1981, the Yugoslavs demanded in turn that Hoxha purge Shehu for treason.

At the time, Kadare was worried that he too would become a target in the wave of repressions that were sure to follow as Shehu's "accomplices" in the alleged plot to assassinate the dictator were identified and brought to justice. The Central Committee was in the process of reviewing *The Concert,* in which Kadare had portrayed Mao Tse-tung as a shadowy and sinister tyrant responsible for the aeroplane crash in late 1971 that would kill his second-in-command, Lin Biao, and his family on their flight to Hong Kong after the failed assassination attempt on the leader. The death of Lin Biao had taken place only eight years before the manuscript of *The Concert* was completed in 1979, and less than two years before the death of Mehmet Shehu. It was all far too close for comfort.

In November 1982, the Soviet General Secretary Leonid Brezhnev died after a period of senescence, and the last of the old guard, Andropov and Chernenko, would follow in quick succession. The ascent of Gorbachev would herald a new era, which would end Soviet communism. This was the era of the passing of the partisan generation, and it heralded a critical period of transition. Enver Hoxha was obsessed with purging Albania of impure elements before his own demise. Adil Çarçani succeeded Shehu as Premier and Hoxha's new protégé, Ramiz Alia, replaced Haxhi Lleshi as chief ideologist and President. The next generation of Albanian leaders, Hekuran Isai, the new Minister of the Interior, Haxhi Lleshi, Adil Çarçani, and other members of the Central Committee were desperately seeking preferment. The one remaining powerful member of the old guard was Kadri Hazbiu. Hazbiu had replaced Mehmet Shehu as Minister of the Interior (the most dangerous of ministries in those early days of "division of power") in 1954 when Hoxha resigned as Prime Minister and was succeeded by Mehmet Shehu, the former Minister of the Interior.

Kadare refashions the ancient Greek legend of the Atreids to suggest the ways in which the political crimes of the parents come back to haunt the sons and daughters of the former communist rulers. He suggests in this novel that the killing of Shehu can only be imputed to "Comrade Clytemnestra," Shehu's wife, the ex-partisan Fiqret,[16] and that this recognition contributed to the trauma and bitterness of the Shehu children, of whom only Bashkim survived. The novel is structured as a detective story, tracing the likely and possible murder suspects after Shehu's body is discovered in the bedroom of his locked and guarded house. The existence of a secret tunnel, connecting the Shehu house to that of the Hoxhas only several hundred metres away, suggests complicity of the dictator or his hawkish wife. Half blind and yet all-seeing, the dictator does not carry out his acts of justice and revenge but directs and stage-manages events.

In works such as *Spiritus* and *The Successor*, the writer focuses on the machinations of the communist state, on the Party, its committees, factions and personalities and, above all, the overarching presence of the dictator, Enver Hoxha. This focus is not, however, an avoidance of the political reality of dictatorship, but rather represents Kadare's attempt to penetrate beyond the surface of the East European regimes to identify the underlying malaise. In the evocations of the ageing, blind, hate-filled Enver Hoxha in *The Shadow* (a novel finished in 1986 and subsequently smuggled out of Albania as a manuscript) and in the postcommunist books such as *Spiritus* and *The Successor*, Kadare identifies the dictator as the symbol of death, the morbid, dark core of the Albanian communist system. This figure is no longer a realistic presence, any more than Hoxha himself was in the day-to-day running of the state. He is a shadowy incarnation of human evil, the symbol of that which is part of the human nature, and which, at certain points in history, has predominated. In Kadare's mythology, Albania under Hoxha is an underworld in which life, not death, darkness and blindness, not light and vision, evil, not good, reign. The spirit of negation exists only because it is reflected and regenerated at all levels, from the Politburo, the Central Committee, and the Party bosses down to the foundations of Albanian society. There are few innocents in Kadare's world—perhaps the children, the sacrificed girls, and the young lovers of *Chronicle in Stone* (1971), or the Italian deserter in *The General*. But ultimately everyone is drawn into participating in, and hence responsibility for, the existence of the regime.

In his epigraph to *The Successor*, Kadare notes that "any resemblance between the story and real people and events is inevitable." The figure of the Minister of the Interior, Kadri Hazbiu, appears thinly veiled as Adrian Hasobeu in the novel. With Mehmet Shehu out of the way, Hazbiu was the last of the high-ranking ex-partisans and members of the Stalinist Old Guard after Enver and Nexhmije Hoxha. The other major player, Hysni Kapo, had died under mysterious circumstances in 1979. Hazbiu, like Nexhmije, hated Kadare and took part in the attack on *The Palace of Dreams* in 1982. However, Nexhmije was quick to turn on her old ally. After Shehu was dispatched, Hazbiu's turn came promptly as a result of yet another conspiracy in this "most sinister phase" of Albania's communism.[17] In 1982, a band of agents landed on the Albanian coast intending to foment a coup. Forewarned, the regime captured and executed the agents and began the search for collaborators. The coup, the conspiracy, and the subsequent purges in autumn 1983 involved the Minister of Foreign Affairs, the Minister of Health, and various high-ranking officials, along with the prize, Hazbiu, who "committed suicide" late, but nevertheless according to plan.[18] In passages reminiscent of the bizarre dream-world of *The Shadow*, Kadare imagines the supreme leader's revenge fantasies of betrayal and destruction, which would transform Tirana into a nightmare city as he planned Hazbiu's suicide after the long years of political intimacy.

In 2008, two new novels appeared, *The Accident* and *The Last Dinner,* both hailed in Albania and elsewhere as masterpieces. In *The Accident* Kadare moves into new territory, exploring postcommunist mentality in the story of a mysterious car accident that kills two lovers, a story organized as a detective novel and leading deep into the trauma-tized psyche of survivors of the dictatorship. The narrative does not focus on the upper levels of the Party, but is rather set in the post-communist period, thus marking a move away from the historical perspective to one focusing on the present and the opening up of Albania to Europe and the European Union. In late 2008, the author commented in a personal interview that his current manuscript, which deals with the myth of Orpheus and the return from the underworld (one of his tropes of life after communism), will be his last novel. Whether that is so remains to be seen.

4. *Kadare, France, and Europe*

Kadare's earliest links to France came about as a result of the 1970 pub-lication of *The General*. Having been educated in the post-war era with Russian as his second language, he did not speak French at the time. As he points out in *The Weight of the Cross*, he was born into a Southeast European Marxist environment and had no contact with the West until he was well into his twenties. For this reason, when they took place, these contacts necessarily involved a great deal of intellectual and emo-tional adaptation and learning. The writer first considered requesting asylum in France in the autumn of 1983, when the terror reached new heights for him personally, after the difficulties associated with the pub-lication of *The Palace of Dreams*, and when the forces were already re-grouping for the transition of power after the death of Enver Hoxha. By this time he had good friends and supporters among French publishing and intellectual circles.

A recent commentator has referred to Kadare as the "darling of the French intellectuals," but nothing could be farther from the truth.[19] A dissident intellectual from the only Maoist state in Europe was unlikely to be feted by the French intellectuals of the seventies and eighties. As Kadare remarked in the interview,[20] he represented an uncomfortable reality for the Western Maoist left: a writer who experienced a hardline Stalinist regime with close links to Maoism from the inside, and who could not be brought into line with the fantasies of dictatorship and social purification entertained by the French intellectuals in the safety of Paris. This stigma has remained: as late as 1992 Kadare was publicly castigated by the intellectual media-star, Bernard-Henri Lévy, on French national television for failing to respond appropriately to the crisis in his home country, an event for which Lévy later apologised to the author. Kadare's friends and supporters were primarily among the moderate left, such as Claude Durand of the French publishing house Fayard, and in cinema and theatre circles. Michel Piccoli had directed and acted (with Marcello Mastroianni) in a film version of *The General* in 1983. The important literary journalist and television arts commentator, Bernard Pivot, and academics and writers like Robert Escarpit and Alain Bosquet were also among Kadare's powerful supporters in the West. The experience of France, documented in *Invitation to the Writer's Studio,* was an education in the ways of a West European country for a Balkan writer whose only foreign experiences had been in Soviet Moscow and whose cultural background was determined primarily by Albania's Ottoman and Muslim past.

After Kadare's defection in 1990, Paris offered an asylum in which the author could engage with the immediate and the remote history of Albania from the perspective of the European Union and of French post-enlightenment democracy. In this new location he critically re-evaluated his earlier views on questions of cultural identity, politics, and modernization, as he reconsidered his own complex role in post-war Albanian society. Like many previous intellectuals in exile, Kadare began to develop new perspectives on his native culture, on France, and on his own identity as a national writer and public figure. He encountered the ambivalent heritage of French Enlightenment in relation to questions of national and ethnic identity, that is, on the one hand, the cosmopolitanism of the revolutionary tradition, and on the other, the powerful sense of ethno-national identity which pervades French civilization. The axis Paris-Tirana is central to the works of the 1990s in particular. Indeed, these works carry the imprint of France as Kadare's second home. While his Albanian patriotism hearkens back to Herderian and 19th-century Central European notions of language and culture, the French model of modernity, individualism, and existential authenticity provides a challenging and stimulating counter-example to the Balkan, specifically Albanian, sense of identity in his work.

The broadening of the European Union after 1992, specifically the move to plan for the inclusion of countries from the former communist Eastern Europe, strengthened Kadare's resolve to work towards the restitution of Albania's European cultural heritage. No longer hindered by his early belief in communism as a modernizing force or by the later resentment at the failure of Europe to have acted to save Albania from Soviet socialism, Kadare set about establishing Albania's European credentials and his own European voice in a range of important literary-cultural essays. In the late eighties, drawing on his emotional and spiritual foresight and sensing that nothing would again be as it was in intellectual and cultural life, Kadare had set about creating the environment for a renewed and more profound re-orientation of Albania towards Europe. The detailed study of the common roots and the shared themes of Albanian and Greek culture contributed to the writer's vision of a new and committed rapprochement with Europe.

Taking Greece and, implicitly, the idea of Europe as his model, he devoted several long essays to the topic of his nation's European roots. In 1971, expressing his growing sense of alienation from the version of Albanian history propagated by the communists, he had written a controversial study of his nation's traditional epics, *The Autobiography of the People in Verse*. Subsequently he used his study of the ancient Greek tragedian Aeschylus to suggest underlying similarities between Greek and Albanian ethno-cultural developments in *Aeschylus or the Great Loser* (1985/1995).

As we have seen, Kadare's links to Greece and to Greek history and culture are long-standing and complex. Born and raised in southern Gjirokastra, a town close to the Greek border, he became aware early on of the links between Albania and Greece. As a child, he witnessed the

Greek encroachments onto Albanian territory in the wake of the Italian campaigns in Albania and northern Greece. Later, as a young adult in Moscow, he was befriended by an older Greek refugee from the Civil War, to whose intelligence, insight, and wisdom he gives testimony in *The Twilight of the Steppe Gods* (1976). Thus, the Greek myths and legends made for a source of political and literary reference for Kadare from early on, in particular the figure of Prometheus, around whom Kadare would weave an evolving set of metaphors of opposition, similarity, and rapprochement between power and creativity. Concluding his long-standing Prometheus trilogy in the mid-nineties, the satiric comedy set in a postcommunist "Olympus" (*Bad Season on Olympus*, 1996) uses the myth of the bringer of fire and light to describe the interrelationships between the dictator (Zeus), the writer and intellectual (Prometheus) and the world of mortals. Zeus's punishment of Prometheus was the dominant metaphor for the fate of the writer under dictatorship. However, in the new, postcommunist context Kadare rewrites Aeschylus's lost third play of the trilogy so as to reinstate Prometheus to his position among the gods. The battle between the tyrant and the rebel is about power and knowledge. Kadare toys with the image of a Prometheus "unbound" and sharing power as the deputy and successor of Zeus, a role the author himself played briefly in the hope of bringing about a smooth transition from dictatorship to democracy in the newly-formed Democratic Front of 1989.

For Kadare, Greece is one of history's winners. Greece suffered Ottoman occupation but nevertheless managed to achieve European integration and internal political, social, cultural, and economic stability well before its Balkan neighbours. Albania's southern neighbour was saved, ultimately, through the link to Rome and thereby to post-imperial Christendom. While Greece also suffered centuries of relative isolation from West European culture between the 14th and the 19th centuries, the link with Byzantium and with Christianity remained. Benefiting from Western Europe's love affair with antiquity and classical culture after the 18th century, Greece was re-integrated into Europe and represents for the writer an image of prosperous democracy and of what Albania could become as a Balkan member of the European Union. Kadare is sympathetic to the needs of his countrymen and strongly aware of the strength and the economic, political, and cultural support of Greece in the rebuilding of Albania since the collapse of the socialist regime.

Despite his alertness to issues of national sovereignty and self-determination, Kadare is one of his country's strongest supporters of mutual peaceful relations with Greece, as well as with the other surrounding Balkan states. In his long essay on the first great playwright of ancient Greece, *Aeschylus or the Great Loser* (1985/1995), Kadare found the inspiration to understand the deep, cultural-civilizational links between Greece and Albania, creating through them a powerful argument for Albania as an early form of European culture and for its country's sense of belonging to the West despite five centuries of Ottoman subjugation. Kadare's reading of ancient history and literature may be questionable in his literary and cultural essays, amounting in places more to an allegory of the national culture than as an accurate philological and historical study. However, in its intuition of the passing of an era, and in its anticipation of the writer's need to prepare the ground for the nation's cultural and political future developments, *Aeschylus or the Great Loser* is imaginative and courageous.

Kadare's works do not speak only to his interest in literary history. Conscious of his obligations to both the nation and to humanity and bridging the millennia-old break between Illyro-Albanian culture and the new age in which rapprochement with Europe might again be possible, Kadare himself is Aeschylus, the national writer who, against the odds of history, has also survived for succeeding generations. Intact throughout the years of the dictatorship, the writer's gratitude to the European tradition takes the form of a willing identification with the great writer of the Greek transition from oral to written culture. Like Milan Kundera, Czeslaw Milosz, and other members of the Central and East European literary intelligentsia, Kadare's sense of socio-political exclusion from Europe heightened his appreciation of the values of European literature and civilization.[21] Unlike the countries of these Central-East Europe writers, however, Kadare's Albania did not have direct access to the European heritage of the Renaissance and Enlightenment. Therefore, he is forced to dig much deeper into history to find the European origins of the Albanians. True, the bond with the Greeks was broken a long time in the past, but the shared original "Greco-Illyrian" culture was the foundation stone of Europe.

In contrast with Greece, Albanian history is one of loss, beginning in the period of the Norman conquests, after which the movements towards Albanian proto-national identity failed in the context of the fragmentation of Byzantium and the incursions of the first Ottoman forces into the Balkans in the second half of the 14th century. After the collapse of the Ottoman empire some five hundred years later, Albanian independence flickered briefly after national liberation in 1913 to shrink gradually with the failed democracy of Fan Noli and then with the dependency on fascist Italy under the monarchy of King Zog, to end with the Italian occupation in 1939. Communism released the country from war but plunged it into renewed isolation and backwardness, especially after the break with Moscow in 1961. The period since 1990 has been for Kadare one in which his country's independence—political, economic and cultural—has been threatened by various forces. While encouraging the development of capitalism, he, like his countrymen, realized just how unprepared they were when the pyramid schemes of the mid-nineties resulted in almost complete social breakdown and civic unrest. A resurgent Islam, funded by Saudi Arabian interests, represented for him a reversion to the religion and culture of the Ottomans via a rigid and backward Sunni orthodoxy completely at odds with his own orientation towards secular and democratic Europe.

In his introduction to the work of the Albanian poet Migjeni, "The Explosion of Migjeni into Albanian Literature" (1990), Kadare reflects on the problems of the Albanian writer, paying homage to his predecessor, Migjeni, who sacrificed his life as a cosmopolitan intellectual in order to live in and write about provincial Albania. Migjeni represents for Kadare the writer as voice of the nation and victim of a history of arrested cultural development. This too, apparently, has been his fate as a postcommunist writer who after 1990 embarks on the long process of transition by seeking to retrace his and his nation's path to modernity amid the conflicting demands of individual, ethnic, and state identity. To chart this trajectory, he uses both the essay genre and the novel, that essentially European form with its origins in the Homeric epic, which speaks of "the relativity and ambiguity of things human" and, incompatible with the "one single Truth" of the totalitarian universe, managed to survive the Hoxha era. [22]

In the wake of his increasing disillusionment with the directions of Albanian political and social life in the early years of the 21st century,

Kadare again turned his attention to the ties between Albania and Europe. In a series of essays, this line of approach has been radically restated, free now of political restraint and deeply aware of the dangers that his small country has faced historically in times of change. He carries on his analysis of profound Albanian-European cultural connections with new force in *Dante, the Inescapable, or A Brief History of Albania with Dante Alighieri* (2004) and in *Hamlet, the Impossible Prince* (2006). To Kadare, Cervantes, Dante, and Shakespeare constitute the three most powerful European cultural influences. Each of these book-length essays contributes explicitly towards the project of re-integrating Albanian culture into Europe, with the agenda of committing Albania to the future of the European Union. Dante, for instance, represents the European Christian cosmos at the time when the Balkans were about to be taken over by the Ottomans following the weakening of Byzantine Christianity. No other writer, Kadare observes, focuses more forcefully on the human conscience, or more exactly, on its sufferings.[23] In his essay, he argues that the Italian poet is deeply appreciated in Albanian culture as marking the historical and cultural point of separation of Albania and Europe for the five hundred years of the Ottoman occupation. Dante embodies the level of European development attained by the Albanians, after which Ottoman culture all but expunged their European consciousness. Likewise, the rediscovery of Dante at the time of the Albanian renaissance and liberation corresponds to the Albanians' rediscovery of Europe and of what was lost in the meantime. Using the translations and commentaries of learned Albanians such as Ernest Koliqi, Albanians began again where they had left off some six hundred years earlier. Linked though he was to Italian fascism, Koliqi nonetheless enabled the reconnection of Albanian culture with Europe. In his implicit comparisons of his own spiritual and literary universe with that of Dante, Kadare implies that one of his tasks as a national author has been to bridge the gap, to try to help his native land to rebecome part of Europe. The powerful influence of Dante in Albanian letters and the deep structures of commonality born of Dante's importance in Albanian cultural history render the poet particularly significant in Kadare's pantheon of literary heroes.

For Kadare, Albania is an originally European Christian culture occupied and colonized by an eastern, Islamic empire over a period of five hundred years. No country has been more deeply affected by the fault lines of civilizations in conflict than Albania, which experienced marginalization at the end of Europe's ancient classical period and again at the time of Rome's fall, as the borders of the Empire shrank. With the weakening of Byzantium in the late 14th century, Albania was again the point of conflict as Turkish mercenaries began to plunder the country. After the Ottoman collapse in the early 20th century and through the two world wars, the country came under the influence of vastly different political-civilizational powers. For Kadare, in the new millennium it is imperative that Albania both retain its autonomy *and* become reintegrated into Europe in order to put an end to the dangerous and indeterminate postcommunist limbo in which regressive political, social, and cultural forces threaten to regain power. In his essays Kadare constructs an idiosyncratic but brilliant reading of Albania's European identity, a literary-historical mythology of the Greek-Illyrian roots of European civilization and hence of his nation's deep connections with European culture and civilization despite the depredations of the intervening millennia. With an eye to the European Union, Kadare recently reiterated his opinion that Albania must be reintegrated into Europe in his essay, "The European Identity of the Albanians" (2006). Having been excluded twice already, in the late 14th century, when the Ottoman armies began the invasion of the western Balkans and again in 1944 with the advent of the communist regime, it would be a catastrophe, he writes, if Albania were kept out of Europe a third time.[24]

Kadare's single-minded critique of Ottoman culture and his argument on behalf of his nation's European roots have led to an acrimonious debate about Ottoman influence, Orientalism, national history, and Albanian identity. A group of younger intellectuals have challenged the romantic nationalism of Kadare's presentation of Albanian national history. In reaction to the writer's highly charged and negative accounts of Ottoman occupation and colonization, they have offered more sympathetic readings of the Albanian-Ottoman symbiosis. In these readings, Kadare's work is criticized for its "Occidentalism," for its alleged subservience to Western political and cultural imperialism in the wake of the collapse of the Eastern empire of the Ottomans. This controversy, influenced by the work of Edward Said and postcolonial theory, represents the main debate on national identity, although, particularly as a result of the support received for Kosovar autonomy in 2007, few Albanians would consider strengthening ties with Turkey or the Middle East at the cost of Albania's strong relations with Europe and the USA.

While openly hostile to historical revisionism, Kadare's response to this debate is also based in a carefully worked-out, pragmatic view of his nation's future, a view that takes into account both the immediate history of communism and the *longue durée* of Ottoman assimilation. While Ottoman influences are still clearly visible in terms of Albanian religion and culture, food, music, dress, and everyday life, Kadare's argument is primarily focused on political and historical issues and involves a detailed and incisive critique of the failure of Ottoman imperialism to have established the basis for forward-looking, modernizing political, social, and economic institutions in his country. The Ottomans performed, I might add, an allegorical role in the works produced under the dictatorship, where they served as a cipher for the communist regime. In that context, Kadare's romantic nationalism was a form of defiance of the regime's instrumentalization of Albanian customs, history, and identity.[25] Far from "Occidentalist," Kadare's views on the Ottoman occupation are actually comparable to current, postcolonial critiques of French and British imperialism.

Civilizational analysis has become an important tool in the comparative study of social and cultural entities.[26] Albania is a striking case of an ethno-cultural and national entity that has been caught between three major civilizational-historical structures: Byzantium, the Ottoman Empire, and Soviet communism. The Albanian roots are Christian and European, but the schism between the Eastern and Western church brought about Albania's peripheralization on Europe's cultural and political map as the country was drawn into the Byzantine sphere until the 14th century, when it was invaded by the Turks. Modernization came to Albania in the particularly severe communist version of Enver Hoxha in 1945 and lasted until 1990. From his earliest writings, Kadare put forth alternative models of development for his native land, in which he highlighted the failure of Ottoman feudalism and communist modernization to either create Albanian citizens or to implant ideas of modern individual identity and individual rights. These models, in particular that of the modern individual, are adopted from his intellectual home, France, via ideas of identity authenticity in post-war existentialist novelists and philosophers.

Closely related to the issue of the national self and rapprochement to Europe has been the fate of the predominantly Albanian enclave of Kosova, which was an autonomous federal territory in the former Yugoslavia and, despite Kosovar Albanians' wish for independence in the referendum of 1991, was incorporated into the Serbian state after the break-up of Yugoslavia.[27] As Marshall Tito's grip weakened at the end of the seventies, and particularly after his death in May 1980, Kadare recognized the signs of increasing ethnic unrest in the Yugoslav territory. By the late eighties Kosova would become a major post-Yugoslav problem as the emerging Serb state reclaimed sovereignty over the largely ethnic Albanian region. Kadare had long been critical of the arrangements regarding the primarily Albanian territory, which were settled in secret after World War II by Enver Hoxha and Tito. Kadare has been an advocate of Kosovar and Albanian rights, obliquely under communism and explicitly and outspokenly since 1990.

In an echo to the unrest in the late seventies and again in the wake of Slobodan Milosevic's mobilization of Serb nationalism in the late 1980s, Kadare wrote several fictional works whose theme is Kosova, using his typically Aesopian literary strategies in order to broach topics that could not be openly addressed (*Dorentine*, 1979; *The Marriage Procession Turned to Ice*, 1981; *The File on H.*, 1982). The subject also emerges in his greatest novel, *The Palace of Dreams* (1982). After communism, the situation deteriorated into violence and civil war. Kadare intervened in the national debate through the stories collected under the title *Three Elegies for Kosovo* (1998) and through a documentary essay, *"This mourning was necessary to our self-rediscovery": Journal of the War in Kosovo* (1999). Kadare's contributions to the debate about Kosova are among his most outspoken and controversial in the postcommunist context; in fact, his Serbian detractors have levelled charges of chauvinism against him. Kadare's advocacy of Kosovar independence is certainly tinged with bitterness at the developments in Serbia since the late eighties, but, particularly if one takes into account the Balkan configuration, he cannot be accused of one-eyed nationalism or sabre-rattling. Indeed, Kadare has consistently appreciated the open, enlightened, and forward-looking aspects of Serb culture, and worth mentioning here is especially his praise of great Serb, Serbo-Croatian, and Yugoslav writers such as Ivo Andrić and Danilo Kiš. Kadare's work must be seen in the framework of the history of the regime's curious position vis-à-vis Kosova and of the increasingly unstable situation as the East European regimes began to fall after 1988. Kadare's engagement in the controversies about Kosova has been driven by his Albanian patriotism rather than by belligerence or nationalism, and he has consistently worked towards peaceful solutions. Rather than imposing power-driven solutions in the form of military might or global influence, these solutions acknowledge the realities of ethnic and cultural identification.

Kadare continues to write, to speak as a witness of socialist dictatorship, and to represent his country at home, in Europe, and the world. He is regularly anthologized in his nation's educational texts and is generally recognized to be a master stylist in his native tongue. Over the past two decades of postcommunist freedom, Kadare has explored and revealed the history of the "captive mind" (Milosz) under the Albanian dictatorship, has attacked political corruption and the remnants of communist cronyism in his own country, and has promoted the reintegration of Albania into cultural and socio-political Europe. His literary and essayistic output is prodigious, and his contributions to the global recognition of his small nation have been immense. With his help, the world has begun to appreciate Albania's potential in the postcommunist era, and the country now looks forward to a possible inclusion into the European Union and to playing a part in global affairs.

5. Annex: Chronology

1990   Mid-year: First anti-government demonstrations. July 11: Central Committee plenum results in superficial changes to the regime. December: Student protests escalate; multiparty elections scheduled for early 1991; the Albanian Democratic Party, the first legal opposition, is founded. **Kadare**: revises *November of a Capital* to remove pro-Hoxha material. October 25: leaves Albania and requests political asylum in France. **Kadare**: *Invitation to the Writer's Studio, Albanian Spring, Conversations with Eric Faye*, "Subterranean Passages," "Before the Bath."

1991   February: Hoxha's statue is toppled. April: General strike and fall of the regime. Government "of national salvation" established. Albanian Party of Labour renamed Socialist Party of Albania. Food riots and exodus of refugees to Italy and Greece. June: 10th Congress of the PLA. **Kadare**: *The Weight of the Cross*, "The Bringer of Dreams," "Cousin of Angels."

1992   March 22: Victory of the Albanian Democratic Party. April 9: Sali Berisha becomes first post-war democratically elected president. "Operation Pelican," Italian humanitarian aid program. May 6: **Kadare** returns to Albania after the election.

1993   Ramiz Alia, Fatos Nano tried and convicted to prison sentences; Pope John Paul II visits in April. Fayard *Œuvres* edition commences in Albanian and French. **Kadare**: "The Great Wall."

1994   *Dialogue with Alain Bosquet*, "The Church of Saint-Sophia."

1995   Albania is elected 36th member of the Council of Europe. Privatization and lowering of foreign debt. **Kadare**: "The Eagle," "The Theft of Royal Sleep."

1996   May 26: Third postcommunist parliamentary elections: Democratic Party gains control; USA gives $100 million aid. **Kadare**: becomes member of the Académie Française. *Spiritus, Bad Season on Olympus*, "Men's Beauty Contest in the Accursed Mountains."

1997   February: Collapse of the pyramid investment schemes; state of emergency, social dissolution, vigilante groups, and criminal gangs. Resignation of Democratic Party and national reconciliation government established. **Kadare**: *Time of Silver.*

1998   Imprisonment of corrupt members of Berisha's government on charges of crimes against humanity during 1997 unrest. November 28: first postcommunist constitution signed into law. Outbreaks of violence between Kosova Liberation Army and Serbian police and army. **Kadare**: *Three Elegies for Kosovo.*

1999   War in Kosova; arrival of NATO troops in Kosova. Albanian Kosovar refugees stream into Albania. Dispersal of criminal gangs. **Kadare**: *Journal of the War in Kosovo, Barbaric Times: From Albania to Kosovo. Conversations with Denis Fernandez-Recatalà*, "Art as sin."

2000   Albanian economy stabilized through European and US aid. President Rexhep Meidani travels to Kosova, stresses the importance of a Europe of regions versus a "Greater Albania." **Kadare**: "Knight of the Falcon," "History of the Albanian Writers' Union Reflected in a Woman's Mirror," *Spring Flowers, Spring Frost.*

2001   Ethnic conflict between Albania and Macedonia. June and July: Socialist Party gains an absolute majority in fourth democratic general elections.

2002   **Kadare**: *Life, Game, and Death of Lul Mazrek.*

2003   **Kadare:** *The Successor, The Four Intepreters: Conversations with Denis Fernandez-Recatalà.*

2004   **Kadare:** *A Climate of Madness.*

2005   Shaban Sinani publishes *The Kadare File.* **Kadare:** receives the inaugural International Man-Booker prize for Literature. *Dante, the Inescapable, or Brief History of Albania with Dante Alighieri.*

2006   **Kadare:** *Hamlet, the Impossible Prince,* "The European Identity of the Albanians."

2008   **Kadare:** *The Accident, The Last Dinner.*

NOTES

1. Tatyana Tolstaya, "Is There Hope for Pushkin's Children?" *Wilson Quarterly* 16/1 (1992): 121.

2. In the late eighties, the refugee Albanian-American Arshi Pipa set the tone for later critics by referring to the author's relationship with Enver Hoxha as a "gentlemen's agreement" marking a "memorable stage in the history of the unholy alliance between dictatorial power and literary talent." Pipa coined the pejorative term "double game" for Kadare's literary strategies. See Arshi Pipa, "Subversion vs. Conformism: The Kadare Phenomenon," *Telos* 71 (1987-88): 77. In a television interview in 1991, moderator Bernard Rapp introduced Kadare to French audiences as a potential Nobel prize winner. See Bernard Rapp, *Caractères: Engagement = Caractères* no. 25, interview with Ismail Kadare et al., Antenne 2, 1991. The suggestion unleashed decades of pent-up suspicion of the author. In 1993, Hans Joachim Hoppe identified Kadare as "an active part of the totalitarian system." See Hans-Joachim Hoppe, "Ismail Kadaré: ein regimetreuer Dissident?" *Osteuropa* 43 (1993): 988-91. In postcommunist Albania, members of the younger generation of intellectuals such as Fatos Labonja view Kadare as one of the "grey wolves" of the communist intelligentsia, who "dipped their paws in flour before entering the house of democracy." See Fatos T. Lubonja, "Albanian Culture and Pilot Fish," Lubonja, Fatos T., and John Hodgson, eds., *Përpjekja/ Endeavour: Writing from Albania's Critical Quarterly,* trans. John Hodgson (Tirana: Botime Përpjekja, 1997): 37. The critique of Kadare was given wide coverage by Noel Malcolm in an influential article in the *New York Review of Books* in 1997. Since the fall of Albanian communism in 1990, wrote Malcolm, Kadare has come under attack for having been "a beneficiary and active supporter" of Enver Hoxha's Stalinist regime. Malcolm criticized Kadare for the "plaintive and insistent" tone of the postcommunist works, suggesting that the writer's revisions are motivated by a "sense of unwilled complicity" in the Albanian dictatorship and finding in them worrying "omissions and mystifications." Malcolm recognizes Kadare's literary merit in works such as the great 1981 novel *The Palace of Dreams* but concludes his piece reiterating that Kadare remained "an employee of the Palace of Nightmares that was Enver Hoxha's Albania." See Noel. Malcolm, "In the Palace of Nightmares," *The New York Review of Books* 44/17 (November 1997): 21-24. However, Malcolm's review was written before Maks Velo's discovery of the "Red Pashas" manuscript or Shaban Sinani's publication of the regime's files on Kadare, and is colored by his objection to the tone of Kadare's "self-promoting" and "defensive" autobiographical works of the nineties.

3. Cf. Peter Morgan, "Introduction," *Ismail Kadare: The Writer and the Dictatorship 1957-1990* (Oxford, UK: Legenda, 2009).

4. Timothy Garton Ash, *In Europe's Name: Germany and the Divided Continent* (London: Vintage, 1993), 344.

5. Ismail Kadare, *Albanian Spring: The Anatomy of Tyranny*, trans. Emile Capouya (London: Saqi Books, 1995), 132. All further page references in brackets are to this edition.

6. Kadare gives details of this meeting in *Albanian Spring*, 26-34. Cf. Elizabeth Champseix and Jean-Paul Champseix, *L'Albanie ou la logique du désespoir* (Paris: Editions la Découverte, 1992), 214.

7. Ismail Kadare, Preface to Neshat Tozaj, *Les Couteaux* (Paris: Denoël, 1989), 9-15. Tozaj's novel was originally published in *Drita*, 15 October 1989.

8. Kadare, "Preface to *Les Couteaux*," 12.

9. Quoted in Edwin E. Jacques, *The Albanians: An Ethnic History from Prehistoric Times to the Present* (Jefferson, N.C.: McFarland & Co., 1995), 598-99.

10. Champseix and Champseix, 214.

11. See Kadare's letter to the President of the People's Socialist Republic of Albania, 23 October, 1990, in *Albanian Spring*, 108-09.

12. Ismail Kadare, *Spiritus, roman avec chaos, révélation, vestiges,* trans. Jusuf Vrioni (Paris: Fayard, 1996), 10. References in brackets after quotations are to this edition; translations by Peter Morgan.

13. Ismail Kadare, *Dialogue avec Alain Bosquet,* trans. Jusuf Vrioni (Paris: Fayard, 1995), 143.

14. Jacques, 512.

15. Cf. Ismail Kadare, *Invitation à l'atélier de l'écrivain, suivi de Le poids de la croix* (Paris: Fayard, 1991), 418; Bashkim Shehu, *L'Automne de la peur* (Paris: Fayard, 1993), 25.

16. Ismail Kadare, *Le Successeur,* trans. Tedi Papavrami (Paris: Fayard, 2003), 160.

17. Kadare, *Albanian Spring*, 7.

18. Kadare, *Dialogue avec Alain Bosquet*, 72-73; Kadare, *Invitation*, 485.

19. Murray Waldren, *The Australian*, Review Section, 16/17 June 2005, 15.

20. With Peter Morgan, November 6, 2004.

21. Milan Kundera, "The Tragedy of Central Europe," *New York Review of Books,* 26 (April 1984): 33-39.

22. Milan Kundera, *The Art of the Novel* (London: Faber and Faber, 1986), 13-14.

23. Ismail Kadare, *Dante, l'incontournable, ou Brève histoire de l'Albanie avec Dante Alighieri,* trans. Tedi Papavrami (Paris: Fayard, 2006), 7.

24. Kadare, *Dialogue avec Alain Bosquet*, 202.

25. Cf. Peter Morgan, "Sacrifice, modernité et perte dans *Le pont aux trois arches* de Kadaré," *Colloque Kadaré,* Véronique Gély and Arianne Eissen, eds. (Paris, 2009, in press.)

26. Cf. Samuel P. Huntington, *The Clash of Civilisations and the Remaking of the World Order* (London: Simon & Schuster, 1997); Johann P. Arnason, *Civilizations in Dispute: Historical Questions, Theoretical Traditions* (Leiden: Brill, 2003); S(amuel) N. Eisenstadt, *Tradition, Change, and Modernity* (Malabar, Florida: Robert E. Krieger Publishing Company, 1983), "The Breakdown of Communist Regimes and the Vicissitudes of Modernity," *Daedalus* 121 (1992): 21-41, "Multiple Modernities," *Daedalus* 129 (2000): 1-29.

27. While English usage has standardized the name as "Kosovo," I use the Albanian term, "Kosova," in this article.

WORKS CITED
A. WORKS BY ISMAIL KADARE

Kadare, Ismail. "L'Irruption de Migjeni dans la littérature albanaise." Migjeni, *Chroniques d'une ville du Nord et autres proses*. Trans. Jusuf Vrioni. Paris: Fayard, 1990. 9-121.
_____. "La Vérité des souterrains." Interview with Stéphane Courtois. *Le Dossier Kadaré*. Ed. Shaban Sinani. Trans. Tedi Papavrami. Paris: Odile Jacob, 2006. 141-205.
_____. "Statement on going into exile, and interview." *East European Reporter* 4 (1990): 45.
_____. *Albanian Spring: The Anatomy of Tyranny*. Trans. from the French by Emile Capouya. London: Saqi Books, 1995.
_____. *Autobiographie du peuple en vers*. Trans. Edmond Tupja and Pashuk Matia. Tirana: Editions '8 Nëntori,' 1981.
_____. *Dante, l'incontournable, ou Brève histoire de l'Albanie avec Dante Alighieri*. Trans. Tedi Papavrami. Paris: Fayard, 2006.
_____. *Dialogue avec Alain Bosquet*. Trans. Jusuf Vrioni. Paris: Fayard, 1995.
_____. *Entretiens avec Eric Faye*. Paris: José Corti, 1991.
_____. *Eschyle ou le grand perdant*. Trans. Jusuf Vrioni and Alexandre Zotos. Paris: Fayard, 1995.
_____. *Froides fleurs d'avril*. Paris: Fayard, 2000.
_____. *Hamlet, ou le prince impossible*. Trans. Artan Kotro. Paris: Fayard, 2007.
_____. *Il a fallu ce deuil pour se retrouver: Journal de la guerre du Kosovo*. Paris: Fayard, 2000.
_____. *Invitation à l'atélier de l'écrivain, suivi de Le poids de la croix*. Paris: Fayard, 1991.
_____. *L'Accident*. Paris: Fayard, 2008.
_____. *La Fille d'Agamemnon*. Trans. Tedi Papavrami. Paris: Fayard, 2003.
_____. *Le Successeur*. Trans. Tedi Papavrami. Paris: Fayard, 2003.
_____. *Les quatre interprètes*. Interviews with Denis Fernàndez-Recatalà. Paris: Editions Stock, 2003.
_____. *Mauvaise saison sur l'Olympe: Tragédie de Prométhée d'un groupe de divinités en quatorze tableaux*. Trans. Jusuf Vrioni. Paris: Fayard, 1998.
_____. *Œuvres*. Ed. Eric Faye. 12 vols. Paris: Fayard, 1993-2004.
_____. Preface to: Neshat Tozaj, *Les Couteaux*. Paris: Denoël, 1989. 9-15.
_____. *Printemps albanais: Chronique, lettres, réflexions*. Trans. Michel Métais. Paris: Fayard, 1991.
_____. *Spiritus, roman avec chaos, révélation, vestiges*. Trans. Jusuf Vrioni. Paris: Fayard, 1996.
_____. *Spring Flowers, Spring Frost*. Trans. from the French of Jusuf Vrioni by David Bellos. London: Harvill, 2002.
_____. *Temps barbares: De l'Albanie au Kosovo*. Interviews with Denis Fernandez-Récatala. Paris: L'Archipel, 1999.
_____. *The Pyramid*. Trans. from the French of Jusuf Vrioni by David Bellos in consultation with the author. New York: Vintage, 1998.
_____. *The Successor*. Trans. from the French of Tedi Papavrami by David Bellos. Edinburgh: Cannongate, 2006.
_____. *Trois chantes funèbres pour le Kosovo*. Trans. Jusuf Vrioni. Paris: Fayard, 1998.
_____. *Vie, jeu et mort de Lul Mazrek*. Paris: Fayard, 2002.

B. OTHER WORKS CITED

Arnason, Johann P. *Civilizations in Dispute: Historical Questions, Theoretical Traditions.* Leiden: Brill, 2003.

Ash, Timothy Garton. *In Europe's Name: Germany and the Divided Continent.* London: Vintage, 1993.

Champseix, Elizabeth, and Jean-Paul Champseix. *L'Albanie ou la logique du désespoir.* Paris: Editions la Découverte, 1992.

Eisenstadt, S(amuel) N. "Multiple Modernities." *Daedalus* 129 (2000): 1-29.

Eisenstadt, S(amuel) N. "The Breakdown of Communist Regimes and the Vicissitudes of Modernity." *Daedalus* 121 (1992): 21-41.

Eisenstadt, S(amuel) N. *Tradition, Change, and Modernity.* Malabar, Florida: Robert E. Krieger Publishing Company, 1983.

Hoppe, Hans-Joachim. "Ismail Kadaré: ein regimetreuer Dissident?" *Osteuropa* 43 (1993): 988-91.

Huntington, Samuel P. The Clash of Civilisations and the Remaking of the World Order. London: Simon & Schuster, 1997.

Jacques, Edwin E. *The Albanians: An Ethnic History from Prehistoric Times to the Present.* Jefferson, NC: McFarland & Co., 1995.

Kundera, Milan. "The Tragedy of Central Europe." *New York Review of Books,* 26 (1984.): 33-39.

Kundera, Milan. *The Art of the Novel.* London: Faber and Faber, 1986.

Lubonja, Fatos T., and John Hodgson, eds., *Perpjekja/Endeavour: Writing From Albania's Critical Quarterly.* Tirana: Botime Përpjekja.

Lubonja, Fatos. "Albanian Culture and Pilot Fish." Lubonja, Fatos T., and John Hodgson, eds. *Përpjekja/Endeavour: Writing from Albania's Critical Quarterly.* Trans. John Hodgson. Tirana: Botime Përpjekja, 1997. 33-40.

Malcolm, Noel. "In the Palace of Nightmares." *The New York Review of Books* 44/17 (November 1997): 21-24.

Morgan, Peter. "Sacrifice, modernité et perte dans *Le pont aux trois arches* de Kadaré." Véronique Gély and Arianne Eissen, eds. *Colloque Kadaré.* Paris, 2009. In press.

_____. *Ismail Kadare: The Writer and the Dictatorship 1957-1990.* Oxford: Legenda, 2009.

Pipa, Arshi. "Subversion vs. Conformism: The Kadare Phenomenon." *Telos* 71 (1987-88): 47-77.

Rapp, Bernard. *Caractères: Engagement = Caractères* no. 25. Interview with Ismail Kadare et al., Antenne 2, 1991.

Shehu, Bashkin. *L'Automne de la peur.* Paris: Fayard 1993.

Sinani, Shaban. *Le Dossier Kadaré, suivi de La Vérité des souterrains, Ismaïl Kadaré avec Stéphane Courtois.* Trans. Tedi Papavrami. Paris: Odile Jacob. 2006.

Tolstaya, Tatyana. "Is There Hope for Pushkin's Children?" *Wilson Quarterly* 16/1 (1992): 121.

POSTCOMMUNIST SPECTACLE:
GERMANY, COMMODITY, COMEDY

JENNIFER RUTH HOSEK

1. *Voicing Remains and Remedies:*
An Archaeology of a Landscape
As the reader will discover, the essays in this volume attest to common-
alities and specificities among East and Central European postcommunist cultures. The German case is unique by virtue of what has become a
dominant mythology of the union of the former GDR and FRG:
reunification of two parts of a national whole that "belong together."[1]
Allegories of this merger tend to normalize it in other ways as well, for
instance, as the cathartic embrace of an estranged family[2] or as a heterosexual marriage, with the West as strong male provider.[3] My contribution will sketch post-1990 German *Wende* narratives in public discourse,
literature, and film, particularly in relation to the question of how
Western interpretations became generally accepted. Then it will analyze
the blockbuster comedic melodrama *Good Bye, Lenin!* (2003) as an
exemplar of mainstream narratives that further reunification on Western
terms even when they appear non-partisan. It will show how, in postcommunist globalization, choice as socio-political practice dissolves
under the spell of postmodern spectacle.

Debates on basic questions such as the appropriate term for the
merger of 1990 express, shape, and highlight the disparate perspectives
involved. The construction of a provisional binary is illuminating here,
through it risks oversimplification. According to *reunification* narratives
of history, the GDR (East Germany) was not more than a failed experi-
ment, terminology that resonates with the well-known 1957 campaign
slogan of conservative FRG (West German) Chancellor Adenauer: "no
experiments." This allusive rhetorical constellation casts West Germany's market-driven social welfare state oriented towards NATO,
Europe, and the USA as successfully participating in Western democratization. Conversely, East Germany is seen as having diverged from this
course and represents a sort of prodigal son in the wilderness, its participation in a larger constellation that was the Soviet Union and the Soviet

Alliance notwithstanding. This "outlier" model of the GDR is comple-
mented by a related assessment that situates the GDR as a continuation
of Nazi fascism permuted into Stalinist authoritarianism.

In contrast, *unification* narratives suggest that Weimar Germany is
neither repeatable nor normative. They emphasize geographical borders
and contend that a symbolic return to Weimar suggests dubious claims
on territories that have been organized as independent polities since
World War II. In resisting the conception of one German past, present,
and future, unification narratives tend to shore up the notion of the GDR
as a sovereign, functioning nation. By extension, they tend to support the
right of former GDR citizens to shape their government rather than
assuming that they should accept or welcome all the governmental,
societal, and economic structures of the Federal Republic of Germany.[4]
Unification implies negotiation.

In this contested discursive landscape, popular identification with
consumer identities further hampered—and continues to hamper—
political negotiations in the 1990s and 2000s. Voices calling for stake-
holder arbitration were drowned out, largely by Western German politicians and business leaders and by Western media but also by the
demands of many in the East German populace who expressed desire for
consumer goods more vigorously than they struggled to maintain
broadly-supported aspects of their societal structure. Mass identification
as consumers had been increasing since at least the 1960s, when, responding to financial necessity and citizen demand, the GDR government began to expend significant resources in the production, marketing,
and distribution of consumer goods.[5] This program included instituting
shops that carried Western products, a means of recapturing the hard
currency flowing into East German households through various channels. That GDR citizens increasingly considered themselves consumers
rather than producers was part of a widespread trend in post-war Europe
and North America. This shift in identification primarily shored up
capitalist societal models in which individual identities are shaped by
commodities. Moreover, because some Western goods were superior to
Eastern products, the West German system that produced them often
seemed superior, especially if the fact that their accessibility was strati-
fied along class lines was not considered. Finally, individual identification as consumer encouraged individualistic modes of labor that centered
on optimizing purchasing power.

This move from a focus on production to a focus on consumption set the stage in East and West Germany alike for support of a quick merger under the pre-existing West German system, a merger which, according to Chancellor Kohl, would bring material benefits to all Germans. This focus was underscored through the much-feted 100 West German Mark "welcome money" (*Begrüßungsgeld*) handed out to East Germans and by the policy of exchanging East German currency 2:1.[6] Many East Germans had substantial savings, which initially positioned them as middle-class consumers even as they were being laid off as producers. The merger was in part organized around enabling the increased consumption of Western, globally marketed, and globally available mass-produced commodities.

At the same time, infrastructure and other resources were being redistributed transnationally. While the merger became a rush for consumer goods on the part of the average Eastern German, it became a takeover of Eastern production on the part of Western German firms.[7] Some Eastern Germans continued to identify as producers and with their workplaces.[8] Yet, they were little able to control the terms under which the new government took over firms and factories and sold them to Western German and multinational companies.[9] Whether or not these enterprises were antiquated, the transfer of local infrastructure into Western hands ignored the GDR economic system under which all workers had owned it. Unlike in some other state socialist countries, former citizens received no payout from the sales of the infrastructure they had built up over 40 years.[10] One reason for the success of these redistribution programs was the strength of the intact West German system. Another was the alienation of many Eastern Germans from the structures of power in the GDR and the FRG at the governmental and institutional levels.

Many public intellectuals in East and West Germany were more vocal in regards to politics and policy, arguing that the terms of a new German state should be negotiated. Activist groups, intellectuals, and artists, many of whom had been involved in attempts to reform the GDR, tried to influence the terms of the merger. However, beset by financial concerns, distanced from the halls of power, and speaking a language that established politicians seldom wanted to hear, their efforts made little impact.[11] Consumer issues played a role here as well. For one, many of these intellectuals had lived lives of privilege in the GDR; their call to put political convictions first was criticized by some in East and West as hypocritical. Relatedly, their material advantage had been enabled by a privileged relationship to the government and the Party, a relationship that many in the West in particular considered suspect. Criticism of Eastern intellectuals became more pronounced with the merger. As in all state socialist systems, art was an important vehicle of critique. In the GDR many citizens engaged as active consumers in this alternative public sphere.[12] Although West scholars took some note of the influence of the state and state funding in the production of GDR art prior to 1990, they focused on the societal commentary in such production. The merger brought the relationships between artists, the government, and police regulatory agencies into the public eye. Narratives about collaboration were generally told from distinctly Western, idealized understandings of the proper function of artistic work in which patronage systems other than those of the market delegitimize artistic production.

The practice of informational collaboration was particularly unacceptable to an educated West mainstream accustomed to societal structures that engender the possibility of artistic voice and expect the artists themselves to provide the means of amplification. Thus, for many, the revelation that members of the avant-garde Berlin Prenzlauer Berg group worked as civilian informants for the secret police discredited their artistic work. Yet, the exemplary contest took place not over the admission by well-known and well-respected writer Christa Wolf that she had briefly worked as an informant but over her publication of the autobiographical short story "Was bleibt?" (What Remains?), in which the protagonist describes being observed by secret agents. Wolf was lambasted for opportunism. Anna Kuhn has pointed out that the sex of this critically minded writer made her particularly vulnerable and that her political position was a sticking point.[13] Wolf stood in for GDR intellectuals who were critical of both the GDR and the FRG. As in daily and political life, the most unsettling and unacceptable stories were those that called both systems into question.[14] These are the tales seldom told, stories that continue to be elided in the globalized world of commodity and spectacle. Wolf was both an East German Cassandra and an Eastern German Medea calling for a Third Way. It is perhaps unsurprising that academics and critics do not typically classify her novels *Cassandra* (1983) and *Medea* (1993) as Wende novels.[15]

The ideological and market forces sketched above influence the production and dissemination of all artistic commentaries on the GDR's end and the aftermath. Famously, scholars and reviewers have never identified *the* Wende text, that is, the work that adequately captures the "turn" from Germanies to Germany. This continuing search, which functions as publicity for German artistic production in the competitive national and global marketplace, also speaks to the multiplicity of *Wende* experiences. Striking is that so few works by Eastern Germans, who might be understood as resident experts, are profiled in such discussions. Two literary texts are most often mentioned. Narrated retrospectively by a picaresque antihero, Thomas Brussig's satirical epic *Helden wie wir* (Heroes like us) (1995) presents a darkly humorous picture of the GDR. To be sure, this book struck a chord with many Eastern German readers. Yet, its popularity is explained by its resonance with Western mainstream interpretations of East and West German culture, for instance that the East German system depicted is reminiscent of Nazi Germany. Ingo Schulz's *Simple Storys* (1998) offers what seem more light-hearted sketches of everyday challenges for Eastern citizens in the larger FRG. Scholars such as Jill Twark argue that Schulz's work critiques the global through the local and the West as well as the East. Yet, they also point out that these gentle intimations are little noted in popular reception, which often focuses on what is seen as personal and provincial.[16] In these texts, consumer culture plays a major role in the formation of identity while a potential Third Way is more lightly traced.[17] Less well known are Wende texts by women, such as Kerstin Hensel, whose dark novella *Tanz am Kanal* (Dance by the Canal) (1994) disarmingly criticizes East and West alike.[18] In contrast, novels by younger-generation Eastern Germans such as Jana Hensel's *Zonenkinder* (Children of the Zone) (2002) and Jakob Hein's *Mein erstes T-Shirt* (My First T-shirt) (2001) articulate individual GDR childhood experiences, often as expressed through the presence of certain consumer goods.[19] It is telling that it is great Western German Günter Grass's *Ein weites Feld* (Too Far Afield) (1995) that is most often criticized and praised for its commentaries on the Wende. The practice of Western voices articulating the history of the merger to a mainstream public is even more pronounced in the capital-driven realm of filmmaking.

The recent smash hit *Das Leben der Anderen* (The Lives of Others) (2006) by Western German Florian Henckel von Donnersmarck exemplifies a shift in narratives about the merger. It is only recently, as Germany's unified history lengthens and government agendas shift to "normalization" within the European Union, NATO, and the United Nations, that serious GDR critique has a role to play in influencing and articulating public opinion.[20] *Das Leben der Anderen* may be, in Tony Kaes's well-known phrase, a "return of a repressed desire" of Westerners to disparage the GDR, an impulse that many well-situated Western intellectuals and artists resisted through the fragile beginnings of unification and expressed only once the general public accepted the merger.[21] Such narratives also articulate neoliberal affinities: contemporary hardhitting critique of state socialism undermines interest in on-the-ground, organized struggle against contemporary sociopolitical systems.[22] In the majority of these fictional works, left-leaning sentiments remain largely personal and avoid engagement with structural questions; in this melodrama, for instance, such sentiments are most overtly depicted by the Stasi protagonist's personal discovery of Brecht's writings.

2. Giving Voice

Literary and filmic narratives by both Eastern and Western creators have been largely characterized by humor. Why does cultural production on the Wende so often try to be funny? Twark presents some reasons in her work on Eastern German literature of the 1990s. Drawing on Kant, she reminds that laughter is understood as tension released due to an unexpected turn of events. Drawing on Freud, she submits that laughter is enabled by the lowering of inhibitions. Humor certainly helped artists and audiences come to terms with the difficulties that change brought and helped express unexpected events and resultant disorientations. Satirical humor in particular draws on a GDR tradition developed under censorship and this practice experienced a flowering post-1990. Twark also points to the Bakhtinian carnavalesque: humor can further temporary inversions of power dynamics and create distinctions and distance. Through it, (former) GDR citizens could gain at least symbolic leverage against the power of the GDR or the new FRG systems.

    In assessing post-1990 film, I differentiate between critical humor, which tends to unsettle the situations depicted, and affirmative humor, which seeks to entertain and tends to shore up diegetic logics.[23] Many Eastern German Wende films are satirical and serious. Reinhild

Steingröver has demonstrated that criticism of the GDR drove the last DEFA films of the very early 1990s.[24] Examples include Jörg Foth's Brechtian *Letztes aus der DaDaeR* (Latest from the Da-Da-R) (1990); Herwig Kipping's *Das Land hinter dem Regenbogen* (The Land beyond the Rainbow) (1991) with its biting critique of Stalinism; Helke Misselwitz's *Herzsprung* (1992), a film about small town racism; Roland Gräf's *Der Tangospieler* (The Tango Player) (1991); Andreas Dresen's unification tale *Stilles Land* (Silent Country) (1992); and established filmmaker Heiner Carow's East-West love story *Verfehlung* (The Mistake) (1991). The relative lack of success of these films has many causes, including insufficient access to Western funding and distribution. Significantly, they are also politically thorny. Leonie Naughton has shown that Eastern German Wende films often problematize unification and reinscribe divisions between Eastern and Western Germans.[25] I propose that these films were also unattractive to distributors because their message hampered unification by depicting a GDR that was too problematic and unattractive to be worth the effort of bringing into the FRG fold.[26]

In contrast, the initial embrace of affirmative humor in mainstream Wende films had everything to do with furthering societal acceptance of unification. Successful mainstream post-1990 comedies cast the GDR both as quaintly interesting and as unoriginal enough to be superfluous in a near future. Such comedies placated Westerners unhappily paying "solidarity" taxes and instantiated conveniently nebulous and mild attitudes of superiority/inferiority. Consider *Sonnenallee* (1999) written by Eastern German Thomas Brussig and the only mainstream hit directed by an Eastern German, Leander Haußmann. In it, East Berlin life for the young protagonists primarily involves creating simulacra of the West—e.g., homemade drug cocktails—or in importing the "real thing" such as bootlegged vinyl rock and roll albums. Consider the ridiculous, enlarged penis featured in the filmic version of the bawdy *Helden wie wir* (Heroes like us) (1999), whose screenplay was co-authored by Brussig but that was directed by the Western German Sebastian Peterson.

The comedic melodrama *Good Bye, Lenin!* exemplifies affirmative humor that furthers reunification.[27] I have proposed elsewhere that the cultural capital of the exotic in allegorical works can encourage viewers to engage with topics that they would not turn to otherwise.[28] If the perpetual assertion of comedic value as a selling point for popular film is any indication, humor functions similarly. The promise of comedy or light entertainment seduces a public who might be unwilling to consider a particular issue more seriously, for instance because of perceived threats to personal and national identity. In *Good Bye, Lenin!*, humor functions variously to shore up reunification logic. Comedy helps to cast the merger in terms of consumerism and consumer choice. It encourages audiences to seriously entertain idealistic notions about the GDR that they might otherwise dismiss entirely. And, at the same time, it furthers the ways in which consumer choice takes the place of political choice in the film and helps to foreclose serious consideration of either.

3. *Good Bye, Lenin!*

The poignant comedy *Good Bye, Lenin!* by Western German director Wolfgang Becker was a hit in and beyond Eastern and Western Germany. Such international success remains unusual for films set in Germany and/or made by German directors. They are considered too local for the globalized media landscape and therefore as too difficult for non-German audiences to appreciate.[29] While a strictly "national" cinema concept is more anachronistic than ever in a world of multinational media conglomerates,[30] public perception and publicity strategies create lived experiences of film as nationally specific, with the attendant results in the market. As a film marked as German, then, what accounts for *Good Bye, Lenin!*'s popularity outside as well as inside of the larger FRG? Becker famously states that it is "a very human story, a story that can be understood by everybody,"[31] and indeed, we do have familiar oedipal triangles packaged into a family narrative of humorously presented ordinary lives. Yet, there is more to it than this, and that surplus is how the film treats the shift to German postcommunism. *Good Bye, Lenin!*'s popularity is due in part to its treatment of a topic of global interest—the predicament of postcommunist transition—told in a Westernized language that is broadly comprehensible because it takes up the problematic of globalization embodied in mass-produced, mass-distributed, mass-consumed commodity. While the film speaks to the negotiations of tensions between the local and the global, between the past and the future, it does it in a way that, for all its aesthetically postmodern sensibilities, describes an inexorable trajectory into a market-based future.

Although numerous viewers would agree that this mainstream cinematic text forefronts anxieties concerning capitalist globalization in a postcommunist state, the change that *Good Bye, Lenin!* underwrites is not what most commentators have taken it to be. Critics generally find that the film furthers (re)unification through its even-handed treatment of both the capitalist West and the socialist East.[32] Many analyses point to the importance of consumer culture in the film, but almost none recognize how consumerism furthers a Western reunification agenda. An exception is Roger Cook, who argues that the narrative focus on East German consumer culture and what he sees as an escapist East German *Nischengesellschaft* (society of private niche-oriented living) furthers precisely that against which these life practices promise respite: neo-liberal globalization.[33] While I question Cook's point on filmic *Nischengesellschaften*, I agree with his argument that the film has a pro-Western capitalist market bias and approach the narrative from a related perspective.[34] In what follows, I will demonstrate how *Good Bye, Lenin!*'s humorous focus on consumer choice downplays and finally undercuts political choice. It is primarily in this manner that the film normalizes the inexorability of reunification on Western terms, even as it validates some aspects of East German experience.

Good Bye, Lenin! offers intriguing domestic and consumer perspectives on GDR life. The family-focused narrative revolves around teen-aged Alex, who attempts to hide the political changes of the Wende from his invalid mother, Christiane Kerner, whose heart attack and subsequent collapse also allegorize the fall of the GDR. With varyingly enthusiastic support from his sister Ariane, her West German boyfriend Rainer, his West Berlin colleague Denis, and his Russian girlfriend Laura, Alex re-creates East Germany within the domestic space of the Kerner apartment, to which he and Ariane return Christiane to shield her from recent events. Much of the story revolves around attempts to recreate this past through continuing to supply Christiane with the consumer goods that were available in the GDR. Alex's inexorable acceptance of the new Germany quietly accompanies this plotline. For Cook and Dominic Boyer both Western and Eastern viewers are invited to engage positively with the characters by establishing experiential correspondences, for instance around notions of family.[35] However, in regards to consumer identification, Cook in particular finds that the narrative strengthens a Western position because GDR consumer products are understood by viewers as inferior to Western products and because the representation of these GDR goods fits into Western logics of market consumerism.

Insofar as this tale fetishizes commodity, it is a filmic narration of the spectacle. For Debord and a host of other theorists, modern society evidences the transformation of social relations into commodity relations. Being is defined by having. Relationships between people are defined by relationships with products. In such situations, history fades in a spectacle of commodity relations and people are confined to life in the moment without critical perspectives. For Alex as for Christiane, the life of commodity is the life of a lie, yet it is their true life: "in a world that really has been turned on its head, truth is a moment of falsehood."[36] Debord might be correct that the culture industry pervaded both East and West societal systems. However, Cook's point concerning the specific commodification in *Good Bye, Lenin!* suggests that here it is the Western spectacle of the commodity that obviates any critique. The protagonists and the viewers are focussed on the brand marketing of the GDR products. Otherwise articulated, Western-style brand orientation reorganizes the East German commodity landscape, in which the ubiquity of the few brands available had encouraged a kind of social cohesion through them, rather than a differentiation based on them. In this way the narrative redefines commodity as consumerism goes West.

4. *Selling Consumerism*

In *Good Bye, Lenin!*, the merger becomes a comedic and overtly depoliticized tale of Western and Eastern consumerism. The humor relies in part on audience recognition of common unification tropes; political referents are not made explicit. For instance, Alex first traverses the border wearing a Palestinian scarf (*Pali-Tuch*). The potential for this cloth to be read as an emblem of political solidarity is overshadowed by the popular dubbing of East/ern Germans as the "Palestinians of Germany." This punning connection is underscored by the appearance of the scarf exclusively at Alex's first crossing of the "Jordan (river)," a slang term for the border. Moreover, Alex's first experience of the capitalist West is more that of consumer than citizen. He partakes of the freedom to enter an adult video shop, joining a crowd gawking at a screen above the video bins. The fare is a woman in a garishly lit bedroom stage set manipulating whipped cream around her silicon-enhanced breasts for the benefit of the camera. What is depicted as an unerotic and unimaginative consumer product functions as an ironic commentary both on the offerings of the West and their Eastern consumption. Although diverse Western groups criticize pornography as a sign of decadence or oppression, for a time after the Wall was dismantled, commercialized sex came to symbolize Western freedoms because the state censored this commodity in the GDR. Here as elsewhere in its depiction of consumer culture, the film emphasizes the humor of these situations, focusing viewers specifically on the empty ironies of consumer desire in West and East.

The humor-consumerism connection finds its *sine qua non* in the East German gherkin. Western goods are humorously derided in their own right. The worn shock absorbers of the ostensibly high-quality BMWs sold in the nearby parking lot and the enormous bra billboard behind Christiane as she stands in the street are certainly recognizable across audiences as amusing commentary on Western goods and their marketing. Western viewers in particular may liken Ikea products to the mass-produced Eastern window fixtures and furniture that Ariane rejects. Yet the pickle taste is the litmus test that demonstrates that Western goods are equal or superior to Eastern ones. It reveals a little noted hierarchy in *Good Bye, Lenin!*'s ironic treatment of consumerism. Christiane's taste for the Spreewald brand produced locally is satisfied by a globalized product, Moscow-brand pickles from Holland that Alex has disguised in a falsely labelled jar. Jennifer Kapczynski calls the East German packaging "quite literally, an empty symbol," and invokes Paul Cooke's phraseology "all form and no content."[37] More than this, in the gherkin scene, any putative superiority of East German goods is revealed to be chimerical.[38] There is a double irony in this humorous shell game in which West successfully replaces East through false advertisement. Even socialist consumer sensibilities are met by marketing—i.e., the label—rather than by the product itself. Such a promotional strategy, of course, counters typical East marketing that focussed on the qualities of the saleable. The depiction of the successful takeover of the East through Western consumer products suggests that the latter better fulfills demand. The superior survive in the Wende, which is depicted first and foremost as a shift in consumer goods.

Thus, the film represents the GDR as an inferior consumer world through substitutability and lack. The amusing tale of the Spreewald gherkin refutes the notion that Eastern products are irreplaceable and this claim to matchlessness is important. Martin Blum argues that the post-unification popularity of GDR brand goods resists the political system of the larger FRG.[39] He cites the success of Vita-Cola in 1994 in the Eastern states in direct competition with Coca Cola, a Western product that had great cultural capital in the Democratic Republic. Not only are Eastern goods substitutable in the film, but *Good Bye, Lenin!* forecloses the possibility of resistance to such substitution. Kept in a protective state of political immaturity by Alex, Christiane is unaware of societal changes throughout the comedy and therefore cannot act as a citizen-consumer in her gherkin selection, or make choices about more significant substitutions made for her.

The "successful" gherkin hunt in the larger Germany resonates both with post-Wende plenitude and supply-side deficits in the GDR. In another example of such lacks, Alex blames consumer shortfalls for his mother's collapse on a sweltering October day. The heat of October may connote political events among viewers; the film represents Alex's statement denotatively. Moreover, because Christiane represents the GDR,[40] Alex's explanation hints that scarcity led to national collapse. In a related example, the Western satellite TV company for which Alex works penetrates Eastern Berlin, creating and supplying a market as it goes. In this case, the national demand for live satellite coverage of the international soccer world championship ironically represents what could be demand for transnational connections as demand for international entertainment. Moreover, as the closure of the GDR firm in which Alex works implies, the Western economy is producing its consumers through the production of unemployed laborers who desire to fill their time inexpensively. The Vietnamese/Asian inhabitants of the large apartment complexes in which Alex and Dennis sell recall another demographic left without employment post-GDR. Yet they and their Eastern German neighbours are presented solely humorously, drawing on stereotypes of unrefined Easterners. Indeed, because Alex and Dennis may be selling on the weekend, the employment status of their customers is not even clear. These humorous, deprecating representations of Eastern German relationships to consumer products overtly depoliticize these relationships while focussing viewers on them.

5. *Persuading with Gravity*

Good Bye, Lenin!'s wit also functions to make the challenges of many Easterners interesting to a broad audience. The voiceover is important here. Generally speaking, it expresses Alex's contemporary—viewing time—perspective and narrates the filmic events with hindsight. Comedic effect arises through the juxtaposition of the descriptions of the events and their visual unfolding. This effect is furthered in that the voiceover employs speech patterns and terminology of official GDR parlance. It conjures GDR documentary such as *Aktuelle Kamera*, newsreels in which events taking place on screen often appear more complex than their voiceover interpretation. In *Good Bye, Lenin!*, it is funny when stories unfolding according to the motivations of the individual characters are discordantly and flatly described through official Eastern logics quickly becoming antiquated and official Western paradigms fast becoming normative.[41] The voiceover narrates many light-hearted events but also comments on scenes showing negative results of unification such as unemployment and identity crisis. The humorous disjunction between the visual and the aural depictions increases the palatability of these serious topics.[42]

Good Bye, Lenin! also takes a specific further step in exploiting humor to promote acceptance of certain largely unachieved GDR ideals: it gets serious. Humor research demonstrates that the use of humor in communications increases the probability that audiences will process a given message expansively and uncritically. However, the employment of humor also decreases the possibility that they will take a given message seriously. Such discounting is especially probable if audiences hold attitudes that differ from those of the message. Yet they seemingly discount less if, after its communication in humorous terms, a message is invested with more authority through a "restoration of gravity." In such a case, the so-called sleeper effect may also have an impact. In sum, when humorously communicated messages are reiterated with a sense of gravity, they can impact the attitudes of even sceptical audiences, especially when the passage of time allows further rumination on the issue.[43]

Good Bye, Lenin! uses precisely this technique to validate these GDR ideals to potentially sceptical audiences through Alex's final voiceover interpretation of his mother's East Germany. As described above, the voiceover generally functions humorously. The scattering of Frau Kerner's ashes into the night sky, however, introduces a restoration of seriousness that continues throughout the next sequence. Narrating over slightly yellowed scenes of calm, sunny cobblestone city streets, a home movie style video of a family beach outing, and the melancholic theme song, Alex's voiceover describes the GDR utopia that his mother (and he) loved: "The land that my mother left was a land in which she had believed. And that we allowed to survive until her last seconds. A land that had never existed in that way in reality. A land that in my recollection will always be bound up with my mother."[44] Here, the primary filmic message is brought home through a shift to gravity; this sequence takes seriously the GDR ideals so closely woven into so many German identities. As I will show later, *Good Bye, Lenin!* honors these ideals of cooperation and equity in an ever-expanding community of citizens even more explicitly in the speech of the Sigmund Jähn look-alike. Yet, it always consigns them to the realm of the personal, often through humor.

6. Mythologies of Choice

When it depicts choice as something other than consumer selection, *Good Bye, Lenin!* presents it as individual practice, deemphasizing constraints and granting immense scope to individual agency. Humor furthers this representation. Alex's humorous voiceover comments on a scene depicting Ariane as a fast-food employee. The voiceover casts the situation as a personal migration from theories of Marxist economics to market-based practices: "[Mother missed] how Ariane chucked her major in economic theory…and had her first practical experiences with the circulation of money."[45] As elsewhere in the film, the voiceover helps listeners to "get the joke." Here, getting the joke means recognizing the incongruity between the abstract and technical description of "circulation of money" (*Geldzirculation*) on one side, and Ariane's mundane duties at Burger King, on the other. Such labor is seldom described in these terms, which are generally reserved for the functioning of monetary systems or the work of elites. Audiences who identify this incongruity experience the scene as humorous and maintain their insider status in the cultural-linguistic game of the teller, the knowing narrator Alex.[46]

In this rare scene that overtly thematizes individual options within the new economy, viewers might notice uncomfortably that Ariane's participation in this economy is as a service worker. However, the narrative structure furthers unexamined acceptance of Alex's classification of career change as her choice. For one, the film does not depict her departure from the university and entrance into the fast-food sector. For another, the Burger King sequence emphasizes the second part of the voiceover utterance by means of the joke. Humor elides the critical potential of the scene. Later, the characterization of Ariane's choice as choice is underscored again through a restoration of gravity. As the siblings prepare the apartment for Christiane's return, Alex discounts Ariane's opinions by reminding her that she had wanted to withdraw life support from their mother. As evidence of the necessity of hiding the Wende from Christiane to protect her life, he shouts: "What do you want to tell her, Ariane? That you chucked your studies because you now sell hamburgers? [E]njoy your meal, and thank you for choosing Burger King."[47] The usually articulate Ariane's only riposte is to push Alex and stalk out, actions which suggest that she has no alternative understanding of her new circumstances. Both scenes mock the hollowness of individual consumer choice; even more significant is that humor, followed by a return to gravity, represents Ariane as at liberty to choose her occupation.

While Hollywood-style melodramatic comedies tend to stress individualization, it is nevertheless striking the degree to which these scenes elide societal strictures that make Ariane's choice no choice at all. With the fall of the Wall, degrees in economics from Eastern German universities had little value. Indeed, degree holders were suspect and made unlikely career candidates. This single mother's employment at Burger King should be understood in relation to socio-economic pressures in the new political economy. Indeed, the above sequence ends with a snapshot of Ariane as employee of the month, lightly embraced by her boss Rainer. Alex's humorous voiceover of this sequence notwithstanding, the images suggest to informed viewers that her romance with her Western German superior might have been strategically chosen as career advancement. Yet such readings necessitate specific knowledge, to which the film does not gesture. When read against the grain in historical context, scenes such as these can connote the shaping of the personal by the political. However, when context is erased, whether extra-diegetically through the globalized viewing context or diegetically through humor, the few sequences that touch on choice as something other than consumer selection nevertheless cast it according to market logics, that is, as free and individual.

7. Foreclosing Political Choice: Retrospective as Inevitability

Good Bye, Lenin! largely forecloses choice that is not consumer choice. Alex's voiceover furthers comedic effects and certain serious messages, but it does a lot more as well. Its retrospective viewpoint precludes alternatives to Western-led reunification and therefore to political choice. Older, wiser, and more experienced than the characters within the story proper, its explanation has authority. Through its narration from a point beyond official reunification, this voiceover sets the terms: political choices have already been made in international politics as well as individually through Alex's move into the larger Germany. Expressed slightly differently, humor conveyed by the voiceover furthers the elimination of Third Way alternatives in German socio-political futures.

It might be objected that political alternatives are expressed through the Sigmund Jähn look-alike. Certainly the news scene articulates GDR ideals, yet the terms of their representation delegitimize them. Jähn is the adult hero that a younger Alex would like to have become. As state president in Alex's fictional newscast, Jähn represents Alex's self-insertion into official politics. This might be read as an act of political participation from below by a younger citizen finding his place in the contemporary governmental structure. Yet, Alex's symbolic political participation here is no more based on democratic principles than were GDR political structures. Thus, this metaphorical representation of political choice turns out to be a potentially authoritarian fantasy. Alex's talk about a socialism without borders with less competition and more parity and social cohesion presented through Jähn in these scenes does resonate with Third Way alternatives for a reformed GDR or a larger FRG and functions as an index of the ideals that he, his mother, and indeed the narrative itself support. But while, historically speaking, grassroots democratic organizations such as the *Runder Tisch* struggled for such a Third Way, in the film this alternative is delimited by at once personal fantasy and dissimulation. As a political choice, it is not seriously entertained, and its representation calls the validity of the attempt into question. Never democratic societal choices, these ideals are presented as stateless dreams held within past memories and future hopes.

The filmic structure validates certain GDR ideals while confining them within the personal realm. This recognition explains the jarring pragmatism of the voiceover statement as family and friends meet on the roof for Christiane's memorial service. Alex's voiceover—in this

instance with a gravity that brings the message home to the viewer—
recalls that the decision to shoot his mother's ashes into the cosmos was
forbidden by East and West alike. The rejection of these sanctions by the
mourners defies official constraints, but this resistance has only personal
significance. Within the new political reality, the socialist ideals that
Alex's mother represented have become private affairs. They are toler-
ated within the pluralistic structures of the new system if they swirl as
personal utopias in the heavens over the "Berlin Republic." Separated
from real-existing political structures, they will have limited impact on
choice.[48]

In *Good Bye, Lenin!* the merger takes place through commodity,
not politics. Its humor pokes fun at consumerism and depicts consumer
options as personal. Although the narrative alludes to the political
choices involved in the change from real-existing socialism to real-
existing capitalism, ironic humor in conjunction with a narrative structure of retrospective voiceover forecloses earnest consideration of
options such as an organized negotiation of both West and East structures. Instead, in this coming-of-age comedy, Alex's move into a Western socio-political system is inevitable. *Good Bye, Lenin!*'s wit brings its
filmic messages to international audiences, furthers the reverent place-
ment of never fully practiced GDR ideals into the personal realm, and
peddles individualized Western paths to disaffected younger generations
and any others who may seem to have a choice to make in a postcommunist reality. This blockbuster comedic melodrama is exemplary of
popular narrations of the Wende and post-1990 Germany. It resonates
with global audiences whose identities as Westerners are furthered by
reunification narratives told from Western perspectives by Westerners in
manners that emphasize the benefits and success of the end of state
socialism in Eastern Germany. The dominance of these voices tend to
drown out those of Eastern avant-gardes whose more Brechtian aesthetics and critiques of both unified Germany and the GDR compete poorly
in the now differently globalized art and entertainment industry.[49]

NOTES

1. In the words of former Chancellor Willi Brandt as he stood with other politicians at the newly opened Brandenburg Gate in 1989, "Now that which belongs together should grow together" (*"Nun muß zusammenwachsen, was zusammengehört"*).

2. Jennifer Ruth Hosek, "Buena Vista Deutschland: Gendering Germany in Wenders, Gaulke and Eggert," *German Politics and Society* 25, no. 1 (2007).

3. Cheryl Dueck, "Gendered Germanies: The Fetters of a Metaphorical Marriage," *German Life and Letters* 54, no. 4 (2001); Belinda Carstens-Wickham, "Gender in Cartoons of German Unification," *Journal of Women's History* 10, no. 1 (1998).

4. The many excellent studies on the Wende on which I draw in this article include: Ruth A. Starkman, *Transformations of the New Germany*, 1st ed. (New York: Palgrave Macmillan, 2006); Osman Durrani, Colin H. Good, and Kevin Hilliard, *The New Germany: Literature and Society after Unification* (Sheffield, England: Sheffield Academic Press, 1995); Stuart Taberner and Paul Cooke, eds., *German Culture, Politics, and Literature into the Twenty-First Century: Beyond Normalization* (Rochester, NY: Camden House, 2006); Brigitte Young, *Triumph of the Fatherland: German Unification and the Marginalization of Women* (Ann Arbor, MI: University of Michigan Press, 1999); Stephen Brockmann, *Literature and German reunification, Cambridge Studies in German* (Cambridge, U.K.: Cambridge University Press, 1999); Carol Anne Costabile-Heming, Rachel J. Halverson, and Kristie A. Foell, *Textual Responses to German Unification: Processing Historical and Social Change in Literature and Film* (Berlin: W. de Gruyter, 2001); Wolfgang Jäger and Ingeborg Villinger, eds., *Die Intellektuellen und die deutsche Einheit* (Freiburg/Breisgau: Rombach, 1997); Paul Cooke, *Representing East Germany since Unification: From Colonization to Nostalgia* (Oxford; New York: Berg, 2005); Anne Fuchs and Mary Cosgrove, *Germany's Memory Contests and the Management of the Past* (Rochester, NY: Camden House, 2006).

5. E.g., Ina Merkel and Neue Gesellschaft für Bildende Kunst e. V, eds., *Wunderwirtschaft. DDR - Konsumkultur in den 60er Jahren* (Köln: Böhlau, 1996); Ina Merkel, *Utopie und Bedürfnis: Die Geschichte der Konsumkultur in der DDR* (Köln: Böhlau, 1999); Krisztina Fehérváry, "Goods and States: The Political Logic of State-Socialist Material Culture," *Comparative Studies in Society and History* 51, no. 02 (2009); Gernot Schneider, *Wirtschaftswunder DDR: Anspruch und Realität* (Köln: Bund-Verlag, 1988).

6. Thomas Lange and J. R. Shackleton, eds., *The political economy of German unification* (Providence, RI: Berghahn, 1997).

7. K. H. Domdey, "Privatization in the New Bundesländer: A Critical Assessment of the Treuhand," in *The Political Economy of German Unification*, ed. Thomas Lange and J. R. Shackleton. Cp. Thomas Lange and J. R. Shackleton, "The Treuhand: A Positive Account," in *The Political Economy of German Unification*, ed. Thomas Lange and J. R. Shackleton.

8. Daphne Berdahl touches on the dialectic of consumption and production in her analysis of the role of Eastern German commodities for Eastern German identities. See Daphne Berdahl, "'(N)Ostalgie' for the Present: Memory, Longing, and East German Things," *Ethnos: Journal of Anthropology* 64, no. 2 (1999).

9. Olaf Baale, *Abbau Ost* (München: dtv, 2008).

10. Wolfgang Dümcke and Fritz Vilmar, *Kolonialisierung der DDR: Kritische Analysen und Alternativen des Einigungsprozesses*, 3rd ed. (Münster: Agenda, 1996).

11. Karoline Von Oppen, *The Role of the Writer and the Press in the Unification of Germany, 1989-1990* (New York: Peter Lang, 2000).

12. E.g., John C. Torpey, *Intellectuals, Socialism, and Dissent: The East German Opposition and Its Legacy* (Minneapolis, MN: University of Minnesota Press, 1995).

13. Anna Kuhn, "'Eine Königin köpfen ist effektiver als einen König köpfen': The Gender Politics of the Christa Wolf Controversy," in *Women and the Wende: Social Effects and Cultural Reflections of the German Unification Process*, ed. Elizabeth Boa and Janet Wharton (Amsterdam: Rodopi, 1994).

14. Von Oppen.

15. Thomas Anz, ed., *Es geht nicht um Christa Wolf: Der Literaturstreit im vereinten Deutschland* (München: Edition Spangenberg, 1991); Markus Joch, "'Es geht um Christa Wolf?' Die Logik des deutsch-deutschen Literaturstreits," in *Nachbilder der Wende*, ed. Inge Stephan and Alexandra Take (Köln: Böhlau, 2008); Kuhn, Bernd Wittek, *Der Literaturstreit im sich vereinigenden Deutschland* (Marburg: Tectum, 1997).

16. Jill E. Twark, *Humor, Satire, and Identity: Eastern German Literature in the 1990s* (Berlin–New York: Walter de Gruyter, 2007). See also Paul Cooke, "Beyond a *Trotzidentität?* Storytelling and the Postcolonial Voice in Ingo Schulze's *Simple Storys*," *Forum for Modern Language Studies* 39, no. 3 (2003).

17. Horst Dieter Schlosser, "Ostidentität mit Westmarken? Die 'dritte Sprache' in Ingo Schulzes *Simple Storys*," in *An der Jahrhundertwende. Schlaglichter auf die deutsche Literatur*, ed. Christine Cosentine, Wolfgang Ertl, and Wolfgang Müller (Frankfurt/M: Lang, 2003).

18. Jennifer Ruth Hosek, "Dancing the (Un)State(d): Narrative Ambiguity in Kerstin Hensel's *Tanz am Kanal*," in *Kerstin Hensel*, ed. Beth Linklater and Birgit Dahlke (Swansea: University Wales Press, 2002).

19. Paul Cooke, "'GDR' Literature in the Berlin Republic," in *Contemporary German Fiction Writings in the Berlin Republic*, ed. Stuart Taberner (Cambridge: Cambridge University Press, 2007). Cooke also questions whether differences between Hein's work and that of West "pop" authors are significant (69).

20. This relationship between politics and culture finds a parallel in academic research. Since unification, studies analyzing the GDR as a dictatorship have received a disproportionate amount of funding relative to other types of GDR research. Commissioned under the Social Democrat-Green coalition and contested by the Christian Democratic Party, the Sabrow Commission report has systematically explored this phenomenon and offered remedies. Thomas Hofmann, "Bloß kein Erinnerungskombinat (1)," *Freitag*, 23 März 2007, Thomas Hofmann, "Die Opfer der Sieger (2)," *Freitag*, 30 März 2007. The Sabrow Commission report can be found at the *Stiftung zur Aufarbeitung der SED-Diktatur* website: www.stiftung-aufarbeitung.de. A book on the Sabrow Commission and debates surrounding it has recently been published. See Günther R. Mittler, Review of: Sabrow, Martin; Eckert, Rainer; Flacke, Monika et al. (eds.), *Wohin treibt die DDR-Erinnerung? Dokumentation einer Debatte*. Göttingen: Vandenhoeck and Ruprecht, 2007. In: H-Soz-u-Kult, 21.02.2008, <http://hsozkult.geschichte.hu-berlin.de/rezensionen/2008-1-148>.

21. Anton Kaes, *From 'Hitler' to 'Heimat': The Return of History as Film* (Cambridge, MA: Harvard University Press, 1989). In contrast to my reading, some critics and scholars protest that the film presents the GDR in a too positive light. See Inge Stephan and Alexandra Tacke, "Einleitung," in *Nachbilder der Wende*, ed. Inge Stephan and Alexandra Tacke (Köln: Böhlau, 2009).

22. I remain unconvinced by the suggestion that *Das Leben der Anderen* gestures towards a general critique of contemporary systems of oppression and surveillance such as

"Homeland Security." While some viewers might find parallels, the text itself does not explicitly further them.

23. I base this working distinction on current categorization debates, see, e.g., Gillian Pye, "Comedy Theory and the Postmodern," *Humor: International Journal of Humor Research* 19, no. 1 (2006).

24. "Filming the End of the Cold War," in *A Fearsome Heritage: Diverse Legacies of the Cold War*, ed. John Schofield and Wayne Cocroft (Walnut Creek, CA: Left Coast Press, 2007).

25. *That Was the Wild East: Film Culture, Unification, and the "New" Germany* (Ann Arbor, MI: University of Michigan Press, 2002).

26. The DEFA Film Library has recently made many of these films more accessible with their tour entitled Wendeflicks, which will hopefully be followed by the release of these films on DVD. http://www.umass.edu/defa/

27. My work on Cuban readings of *Good Bye, Lenin!* first illuminated the significances of choice for me. See Jennifer Ruth Hosek, "Leveraging Cuban Perspectives on Choice in the Film *Good Bye Lenin!*," in *German Studies Association Conference* (San Diego, CA: 2007). Blum recognizes consumer choice as political, but only in that, for him, choosing East over West products resists Western hegemony. Cuban reception emphasizes how non-consumer choices become *de facto* impossible in a market-driven economy.

28. Hosek, "Buena Vista Deutschland: Gendering Germany in Wenders, Gaulke and Eggert."

29. Randall Halle, "German Film, European Film: Transnational Production, Distribution and Reception," *Screen* 47, no. 2 (2006).

30. Randall Halle, *German Film after Germany: Toward a Transnational Aesthetic* (Urbana-Champaign: University of Illinois Press, 2008). *Good Bye, Lenin!* also defies easy categorization as a German film, having been underwritten by the publicly funded, artistically, and pedagogically-oriented ARTE. Arguing that ARTE does not seek to participate directly in "globalized media structures," Halle calls this production firm a "unified states of Europe" that seeks to promote "a transcultural dialogue based on an assertion of a primary commonality throughout Europe's regions" (183-4).

31. Quoted in Roger Cook, "Good Bye, Lenin! Free-Market Nostalgia for Socialist Consumerism," *Seminar* 43, no. 2 (2007). 2

32. E.g., Seán Allan, "*Ostagie*, fantasy and the normalization of east-west relations in post-unification comedy," in *German Cinema since Unification*, ed. David Clarke (London: Continuum, 2006). For an interesting problematization in relation to East European cinema post-1990, see Dina Iordanova, "East of Eden: *Good bye, Lenin!* is the nearest cinema has come to exploring former East Germans' disappointment with reunification," in *Sight and Sound* 13, no. 8 (2003).

33. Cook article; see note 31.

34. I thank Gabriele Müller and James Skidmore for bringing Cook's article to my attention after I had written the first version of this text.

35. Cook article; Dominic Boyer, "Ostalgie and the Politics of the Future in Eastern Germany," *Public Culture* 18, no. 2 (2006).

36. Guy Debord, *Society of the Spectacle*, trans. Donald Nicholson-Smith (New York: Zone Books, 1994). Thesis 9. "Dans le monde réellement renversé, le vrai est un moment du faux." *La société du spectacle* (Paris: Buchet-Chastel, 1967).

37. "Negotiating Nostalgia: The GDR Past in *Berlin is in Germany* and *Good Bye, Lenin!*," *The Germanic Review* 82.1 (Winter 2007), no. 78(23), 5; Cooke, *Representing East Germany since Unification: From Colonization to Nostalgia,* 134 (quoted in Kapczynski).

38. In actual consumer practice, this attitude was expressed by the contemporary popularity of specialty shops for Eastern German goods. See Mathias Wedel, "Jetzt seid ihr alle Spreewaldgurken," *Freitag,* 29 August 2003.

39. Martin Blum, "Club Cola and Co.: Ostalgie, Material Culture, and Identity," in *Transformation of the New Germany,* ed. Ruth Starkman (New York: Palgrave, 2006), 133, 145.

40. Joseph F. Jozwiak and Elisabeth Mermann, "'The Wall in Our Minds?' Colonization, Integration, and Nostalgia," *The Journal of Popular Culture* 39, no. 5 (2006), 7. Cp. Elizabeth Boa, "Telling It How It Wasn't: Familial Allegories of Wish-Fulfillment in Postunification Germany," in *Germany's Memory Contests and the Management of the Past,* ed. Anne Fuchs and Mary Cosgrove (Rochester, NY: Camden House, 2006), 78-82.

41. Cf. Henri Bergson, *Le rire* (Paris: F. Alcan, 1900).

42. Robin L. Nabi, Emily Moyer-Gusé, and Sahara Byrne, "All Joking Aside: A Serious Investigation into the Persuasive Effect of Funny Social Issue Messages," *Communication Monographs* 74, no. 1 (2007). See also Janet Holmes and Meredith Marra, "Over the edge? Subversive humor between colleagues and friends," in *Humor: International Journal of Humor Research* 15, no. 1 (2002).

43. Nabi, Moyer-Gusé, and Byrne.

44. "Das Land, das meine Mutter verließ, war ein Land, an das sie geglaubt hatte. Und das wir zu bis zur ihren letzten Sekunden überleben ließen. Ein Land, das es in Wirklichkeit nie so gegeben hat. Ein Land, das in meiner Erinnerung immer mit meiner Mutter verbunden sein wird" (translation mine).

45. "[Mutter verpasste] wie Ariane ihr Studium in der Wirtschaftstheorie schmiss...und ihre ersten praktischen Erfahrungen mit der Geldzirkulation machte."

46. Cf. Pye. pp. 57-59

47. "Was willst du ihr denn sagen, Ariane, dass du dein Studium geschmissen hast, weil du jetzt Hamburger verkaufst? Guten Appetit, und vielen Dank, dass Sie sich für Burger King entschieden haben."

48. Cook and Cooke read this scene differently. See Cook's article; Cooke, *Representing East Germany since Unification: From Colonization to Nostalgia.*

49. I would like to thank students in my winter 2008 Berlin course who thought about this film with me in the context of Queen's initiative to bring faculty research into the undergraduate classroom: Julian Elce, Tamara Nadolny, Susanne Miller, Patrick Faller, Emily Kulms, Angelika Le Beau, and Mark McNair, as well as Professors Gabriele Mueller and James Skidmore. A much different version of this article was presented at the Cinema and Social Change conference at University of Waterloo in May 2008. Thanks to Stefan Seum, as always.

BIBLIOGRAPHY

Allan, Seán. "*Ostagie,* fantasy and the normalization of east-west relations in post-unification comedy." In *German Cinema since Unification,* edited by David Clarke, 105-26. London: Continuum, 2006.

Anz, Thomas, ed. *Es geht nicht um Christa Wolf: Der Literaturstreit im vereinten Deutschland.* München: Edition Spangenberg, 1991.

Baale, Olaf. *Abbau Ost.* München: dtv, 2008.

Berdahl, Daphne. "'(N)Ostalgie' for the Present: Memory, Longing, and East German Things." *Ethnos: Journal of Anthropology* 64, no. 2 (1999): 192-211.

Bergson, Henri. *Le rire.* Paris: F. Alcan, 1900.

Boa, Elizabeth. "Telling It How It Wasn't: Familial Allegories of Wish-Fulfillment in Post-unification Germany." In *Germany's Memory Contests and the Management of the Past,* edited by Anne Fuchs and Mary Cosgrove, 67-86. Rochester, New York: Camden House, 2006.

Boyer, Dominic. "Ostalgie and the Politics of the Future in Eastern Germany." *Public Culture* 18, no. 2 (2006): 361-81.

Brockmann, Stephen. *Literature and German Reunification.* Cambridge, U.K.: Cambridge University Press, 1999.

Carstens-Wickham, Belinda. "Gender in Cartoons of German Unification." *Journal of Women's History* 10, no. 1 (1998): 127-56.

Cook, Roger. "*Good Bye, Lenin!* Free-Market Nostalgia for Socialist Consumerism." *Seminar* 43, no. 2 (2007): 206-19.

Cooke, Paul. "Beyond a *Trotzidentität?* Storytelling and the Postcolonial Voice in Ingo Schulze's *Simple Storys.*" *Forum for Modern Language Studies* 39, no. 3 (2003): 290-305.

_____. "'GDR' Literature in the Berlin Republic." In *Contemporary German Fiction Writings in the Berlin Republic,* edited by Stuart Taberner, 56-71. Cambridge: Cambridge University Press, 2007.

Costabile-Heming, Carol Anne, Rachel J. Halverson, and Kristie A. Foell. *Textual Responses to German Unification: Processing Historical and Social Change in Literature and Film.* Berlin: W. de Gruyter, 2001.

Debord, Guy. *Society of the Spectacle.* Translated by Donald Nicholson-Smith. New York: Zone Books, 1994.

Domdey, K. H. "Privatization in the New Bundesländer: A Critical Assessment of the Treuhand." In *The Political Economy of German Unification,* edited by Thomas Lange and J. R. Shackleton, 44-55. Providence, RI: Berghahn, 1997.

Dueck, Cheryl. "Gendered Germanies: The Fetters of a Metaphorical Marriage." *German Life and Letters* 54, no. 4 (2001): 366-76.

Dümcke, Wolfgang, and Fritz Vilmar. *Kolonialisierung der DDR: Kritische Analysen und Alternativen des Einigungsprozesses.* 3rd ed. Münster: Agenda, 1996.

Durrani, Osman, Colin H. Good, and Kevin Hilliard. *The New Germany: Literature and Society after Unification.* Sheffield, England: Sheffield Academic Press, 1995.

Fehérváry, Krisztina "Goods and States: The Political Logic of State-Socialist Material Culture." *Comparative Studies in Society and History* 51, no. 02 (2009): 426-59.

Fuchs, Anne, and Mary Cosgrove. *Germany's Memory Contests and the Management of the Past*. Rochester, New York: Camden House, 2006.

Halle, Randall. *German Film after Germany: Toward a Transnational Aesthetic*. Urbana-Champaign, IL: University of Illinois Press, 2008.

_____. "German Film, European Film: Transnational Production, Distribution and Reception." *Screen* 47, no. 2 (2006): 251-66.

Holmes, Janet, and Meredith Marra. "Over the edge? Subversive humor between colleagues and friends." *Humor: International Journal of Humor Research* 15, no. 1 (2002): 65-87.

Hosek, Jennifer Ruth. "Buena Vista Deutschland: Gendering Germany in Wenders, Gaulke and Eggert." *German Politics and Society* 25, no. 1 (2007): 46-69.

_____. "Dancing the (Un)State(d): Narrative Ambiguity in Kerstin Hensel's *Tanz am Kanal*." In *Kerstin Hensel*, edited by Beth Linklater and Birgit Dahlke, 107-19. Swansea: University Wales Press, 2002.

Hosek, Jennifer Ruth. "Leveraging Cuban Perspectives on Choice in the Film *Good Bye Lenin!*" In *German Studies Association Conference*. San Diego, CA, 2007.

Iordanova, Dina. "East of Eden: *Good bye, Lenin!* is the nearest cinema has come to exploring former East Germans' disappointment with reunification." *Sight and Sound* 13, no. 8 (2003): 26-9.

Jäger, Wolfgang, and Ingeborg Villinger, eds. *Die Intellektuellen und die deutsche Einheit*. Freiburg/Breisgau: Rombach, 1997.

Joch, Markus. "'Es geht um Christa Wolf?' Die Logik des deutsch-deutschen Literaturstreits." In *Nachbilder der Wende*, edited by Inge Stephan and Alexandra Take, 17-32. Köln: Böhlau, 2008.

Jozwiak, Joseph F., and Elisabeth Mermann. "'The Wall in Our Minds?' Colonization, Integration, and Nostalgia." *The Journal of Popular Culture* 39, no. 5 (2006): 780-95.

Kaes, Anton. *From 'Hitler' to 'Heimat': The Return of History as Film*. Cambridge, MA: Harvard University Press, 1989.

Kapczynski, Jennifer. "Negotiating Nostalgia: The GDR Past in *Berlin is in Germany* and *Good Bye, Lenin!*" *The Germanic Review* 82.1 (Winter 2007), no. 78(23) 1-14.

Kuhn, Anna. "'Eine Königin köpfen ist effektiver als einen König köpfen': The Gender Politics of the Christa Wolf Controversy." In *Women and the Wende: Social Effects and Cultural Reflections of the German Unification Process*, edited by Elizabeth Boa and Janet Wharton, 200-15. Amsterdam: Rodopi, 1994.

Lange, Thomas, and J. R. Shackleton, eds. *The Political Economy of German Unification*. Providence, RI: Berghahn, 1997.

Lange, Thomas, and J. R. Shackleton. "The Treuhand: A Positive Account." In Lange and Shackleton, eds..

Merkel, Ina. *Utopie und Bedürfnis: Die Geschichte der Konsumkultur in der DDR*. Köln: Böhlau, 1999.

Merkel, Ina, and Neue Gesellschaft für Bildende Kunst e. V, eds. *Wunderwirtschaft. DDR - Konsumkultur in den 60er Jahren*. Köln: Böhlau, 1996.

Nabi, Robin L., Emily Moyer-Gusé, and Sahara Byrne. "All Joking Aside: A Serious Investigation into the Persuasive Effect of Funny Social Issue Messages." *Communication Monographs* 74, no. 1 (2007): 29-54.

Naughton, Leonie. *That Was the Wild East: Film Culture, Unification, and the "New" Germany*. Ann Arbor, MI: University of Michigan Press, 2002.

Pye, Gillian. "Comedy Theory and the Postmodern." *Humor: International Journal of Humor Research* 19, no. 1 (2006): 53-70.

Schlosser, Horst Dieter. "Ostidentität mit Westmarken? Die 'dritte Sprache' in Ingo Schulzes *Simple Storys*." In *An der Jahrhundertwende. Schlaglichter auf die deutsche Literatur*, edited by Christine Cosentine, Wolfgang Ertl and Wolfgang Müller, 56-68. Frankfurt/M: Lang, 2003.

Schneider, Gernot. *Wirtschaftswunder DDR: Anspruch und Realität*. Köln: Bund-Verlag, 1988.

Starkman, Ruth A. *Transformations of the New Germany*. 1st ed. New York: Palgrave Macmillan, 2006.

Steingröver, Reinhild. "Filming the End of the Cold War." In *A Fearsome Heritage: Diverse Legacies of the Cold War*, edited by John Schofield and Wayne Cocroft, 253-72. Walnut Creek, CA: Left Coast Press, 2007.

Stephan, Inge, and Alexandra Tacke. "Einleitung." In *Nachbilder der Wende*, edited by Inge Stephan and Alexandra Tacke, 7-15. Köln: Böhlau, 2009.

Taberner, Stuart, and Paul Cooke, eds. *German Culture, Politics, and Literature into the Twenty-First Century: Beyond Normalization*. Rochester, NY: Camden House, 2006.

Torpey, John C. *Intellectuals, Socialism, and Dissent: The East German Opposition and Its Legacy*. Minneapolis, MN: University of Minnesota Press, 1995.

Twark, Jill E. *Humor, Satire, and Identity: Eastern German Literature in the 1990s*. Berlin. New York: Walter de Gruyter, 2007.

Von Oppen, Karoline. *The Role of the Writer and the Press in the Unification of Germany, 1989-1990*. New York: Peter Lang, 2000.

Wedel, Mathias. "Jetzt seid ihr alle Spreewaldgurken." *Freitag*, 29 August 2003, 1.

Wittek, Bernd. *Der Literaturstreit im sich vereinigenden Deutschland*. Marburg: Tectum, 1997.

Young, Brigitte. *Triumph of the Fatherland: German Unification and the Marginalization of Women*. Ann Arbor, MI: University of Michigan Press, 1999.

THE ANXIETY OF FREEDOM: CONTEMPORARY SLOVENIAN LITERATURE AND THE GLOBALIZING/POSTMODERN WORLD

MATEVŽ KOS

1. *The End vs. the Beginning of History*

This essay proposes that key to understanding the anatomy of contemporary Slovenian literature and culture, particularly in the context of the debates on postcommunism, postmodernism, and the (post)modern "global world," are the 1980s. Clearly, the discussion of these thematic clusters must develop at least at two related levels, literary-aesthetic and cultural-historical given that the 1980s were a period when Slovenia witnessed a number of parallel social, ideological, and cultural-artistic processes and phenomena, which intertwined with, crossed, or even opposed each other. A similar situation prevailed in the rest of Central and Eastern Europe, including the other republics in the former federal Yugoslavia, of which the Socialist Republic of Slovenia was part. All these processes were linked to the antagonisms existing at the time, especially to the epoch-making end of socialism/communism and the subsequent world domination of "liberal capitalism." Another name for this watershed event, to borrow Francis Fukuyama's famous late 1980s phrase, is "the end of history" (Fukuyama 1992). The historic event symbolizing this "end" and heralding a new union of "Old" and "New" Europe is, of course, the fall of the Berlin Wall in 1989.

In a letter to Miss Harkness in 1888, Friedrich Engels stated that Balzac's novels tell us more about the French society of the first half of the nineteenth century than do historians, economists, or even statisticians of the time. By analogy, the East and Central European literature of the late twentieth and perhaps even the early twenty-first centuries might be expected to provide a "cultural-historical" or even "political-economic" document of the recent social metamorphoses and contradictions, be it with regard to postcommunism, liberal democracy, globalization, multiculturalism, or universal human rights. This analogy, however, is problematic because the prevailing literature of our era has long ceased to be realistic, that is, interested in an "accurate portrayal of typical characters under typical circumstances," to quote Engels's definition from the above-mentioned letter. Rather, this literature bears witness to what Hans Bertens, in his book on the "idea of postmodernism," terms "a crisis in representation: a deeply felt loss of faith in our ability to represent the real, in the widest sense. No matter whether they are aesthetic, epistemological, moral, or political in nature, the representations that we used to rely on can no longer be taken for granted" (Bertens 1995: 11). The literary-historical labels applied to literature representative of "a crisis in representation" are, at least where Slovenian literature is concerned, modernism, postmodernism, and, in the last decade or two, "literature after postmodernism." Largely going beyond traditional *mimesis*, this kind of writing is informed by the experience of the avant-garde (both historical and recent) as well as of various experiments, which have radically expanded the fields of literariness and of metaliterary discourse, thus confronting the art of interpretation with new challenges.

But this is not all. What Fukuyama calls "the end of history" in a universal sense, in the particular case of Slovenia is a "beginning of history" as well. It was only in 1991 that Slovenia, which had been for centuries subsumed into the Austrian Empire (or the Austro-Hungarian monarchy), from 1918 to 1941 into the Kingdom of Yugoslavia, and from 1945 to 1991 into the Socialist Yugoslavia as one of its federal republics, became an independent, internationally recognized state, going on to join NATO, the European Union, and finally the Eurozone as the first of the new member states.[1]

2. *Forward to the Past*

Slovenia's historical lack of state sovereignty and corresponding institutions resulted in a glorification of culture in the nineteenth century, the era of growing national awareness and the "Spring of Nations"—a process characteristic of other Central European nations as well. Since language is the corner-stone and primary medium of national life, particular significance was attached to literature. The special status of Slovenian literature within the national mythology has been described by philosophers and cultural sociologists in such phrases as "the governorship of Slovenian culture" or "the Slovenian cultural syndrome." This critical, detached understanding of literature as a national and moral institution, that is, of the relationship between Slovenian society and culture (literature included), could not be achieved before Slovenian society and culture had gone through a process of modernization and before the postwar totalitarian system of Slovenian/Yugoslav communism had relaxed enough to grant the arts, humanities, and, over time, even social criticism relative autonomy. In the nineteenth century, Slovenian literature was a crucial form of the nation's self-awareness. With the romantic poet France Prešeren (the key figure of the Slovenian literary canon and the founder of Slovenian literature proper), with the "Modern" (fin-de-siècle) writers active between 1898 and 1918 (Ivan Cankar and Josip Murn among others), and finally with the historical avant-garde around 1920 (Srečko Kosovel, Anton Podbevšek), the development of Slovenian literature as an autonomous art form rose to international standards. On the other hand, due to its specific, national and social role, the country's literature was continually subjected to the pressures of various rival ideologies. In the late nineteenth century, these were mainly Catholic and Liberal, both essentially conservative on aesthetic issues and often seeking in Slovenian literature primarily a confirmation of the national spirit, of a historical vitalism inherent in a stateless nation. These pressures and attempts at literature's instrumentalization were more or less successfully resisted by writers until the battle for the autonomy of art was won.

After World War II and the establishment of the communist regime, which abolished all competition, either political or ideological, Slovenian literature gained a new dimension. Even though its social "commitment" in a communist sense was quasi negligible, literature could not help performing an important emancipating "function" since literary texts remained one of the few media of *freedom* and ideological independence in an era of total ideologization. In the 1950s, after the break with the Soviet Union in 1948 and the abandonment of the officially prescribed "poetics" of socialist realism in art, the totalitarian structure began to relax and thus ideological volunteerism abated. The political and ideological initiative was taken over by a less aggressive and more pragmatic orientation of the ruling Communist Party. This approach allowed more or less everything that posed no threat to the foundations of the single-party Power, and basic tolerance towards the autonomy of art was among such "friendly" governmental gestures. While the literature of 1950–1970, especially prose and drama, had inclined towards existentialism and modernism in both content and form, it now began to address suppressed, "undesirable" themes. Thus, a segment of literary writing gained, albeit indirectly, a political dimension of opposition, dissidence, or quasi dissidence until the 1980s, when particular significance came to be attached to memoirs and testimonies of documentary value, that is, to non-fictional books which spoke to the reader directly and no longer "metaphorically." By the late 1980s, however, the government's critics no longer needed to hide behind literary discourse: the critical stance gradually secured a place in alternative mass media, at public meetings, and finally in an organized political opposition, which went on to win the first free elections in 1990.

In terms of style, the status of literature in 1950–1990 was at least partly reminiscent of the nineteenth-century situation, except that the national emancipation function and impact were replaced by a particular type of reading practiced by the public. What was sought and found in the great texts of postwar Slovenian literature such as the poetry of the "dark modernist" Dane Zajc, the existentialist plays by Dominik Smole, or the modernist novels by Lojze Kovačič, Vitomil Zupan, and other authors, were all-embracing metaphors expressing criticism of the communist system and the Party state. This is particularly true of the texts that addressed such taboo themes as the 1941-1945 civil war, postwar killings, the prison camp of Goli Otok, where the opponents of Tito's regime were interned, show trials, etc. In the oppressive, suffocating social atmosphere of the postwar decades, the novels, stories, plays, and poems of Slovenian authors were often laden with various "added," politically subversive meanings. Indeed, literature under non-democratic conditions such as those in the Slovenia of the post-World War II years might be described as a symbolic manifestation, as an *economy of freedom.*

In the 1960s and especially the 1970s, this orientation was mostly abandoned by the younger modernists such as the poets Tomaž Šalamun and Niko Grafenauer and the prose writer Rudi Šeligo, by the ultramodernists, and the neo-avant-garde. The Sartrean *philosophy of freedom,* as well as the social commitment and critical attitude of the first postwar, "critical" generation largely gave way to "intratextuality" and to a freedom that was, above all, freedom *in* language—language *qua* "the house of being," as the relatively numerous Slovenian followers of Martin Heidegger would repeat after their teacher.

This intratextuality was promoted by literary critics, who drew, among other resources, on the then popular French (post)structuralism, especially on Roland Barthes. But this critical philosophy's second and parallel aspect became visible in 1968, the year of student protests, which in Slovenia occurred with a three-year delay. In contrast to the cities of Western Europe, Slovenian (and Yugoslav) students never doubted, generally speaking, the nature of the social system in which they lived. i.e., the system of socialist self-government, based on "the accomplishments of socialist revolution." Student upheavals elsewhere in Europe, especially in Paris, displayed a markedly left-wing, revolutionary, anti-capitalist orientation. In other words, they were attacking the institutions of a "bourgeois" society. The legendary graffito on the Sorbonne in Paris—"Let's Be Realists, Let's Demand the Impossible!"—is just that: a call for the destruction of the ruling system. The students bodied forth the *realism* of this demand as a critique of ideology where ideology was understood from the Marxist perspective, that is, as a perverted, false consciousness of a perverted, false world. The demand for the impossible resulted from an insight into the social relations of domination, into the nuts and bolts of political reality.

The situation in Slovenia and elsewhere in the former Yugoslavia was fundamentally different because the student movement was, like its Western counterpart, essentially left-wing, anti-capitalist, and often revolutionary. Thus, it participated in the very idea that was, at least formally, backed by the Slovenian communists, who held all levers of power in the single-party state. This power, however, was not questioned by Slovenian students, let alone recognized as totalitarian, for the contrast between totalitarianism and Western democracy was, from the left-wing perspective, usually perceived as artificial. (Along these lines, it is no coincidence that the word "totalitarianism" continues to apply to fascism and occasionally Stalinism but much less to communism overall.) Therefore, the demands of Slovenian and Yugoslav students were not set *against* the system but contained *within* it, urging that the declarations of the Communist Party congresses should be transferred from paper to reality and calling for the abolition of bureaucratic privileges, the return of revolutionary spontaneity, a more people-centered character of the people's government, etc. These slogans, accompanied by revolutionary symbols and iconography, were fairly loud and need here no particular "ideological" explanation. What is historically more important is that the student movement gradually died down. Some of its leading participants in Slovenia and Europe decided to take a "long walk" through institutional responsibilities. The most radical faction in the West, which considered such cohabitation with the *existing conditions* as high treason, went underground and started a serious rebellion against the system, engaging in terrorist attacks on the financial, political, and jurisdictional "pillars of society." It was this atmosphere that contributed to the formation of the German Red Army Faction (founded 1968) or the Italian Red Brigades (founded 1969).

For the reasons outlined above, the student movement in Slovenia was incapable of similar radical measures or of any serious questioning of the legitimacy of the communist government. Most importantly, the only revolution that might have been endorsed, for example, by writers at the time would have been only a "revolution of the spirit." It would have been an aesthetic, spiritual metamorphosis, a change of one's *stance*, of one's *attitude*, rather than *direct action* that would seek to change radically the existing circumstances, least of all in the way of an anti-communist, liberal-democratic, "bourgeois" promotion of a multi-party system, private property and initiative, and the like. This means that the aesthetic revolution was, and is, practically the only kind of "revolution" possible and still permitted within the clearly drawn boundaries of a socialist society, even under a "socialism with a human face." The boundaries are, of course, drawn and enforced by the levers of domination, by the distribution of political power, and by control of political antagonisms.[2]

This "passivity" helps explain the interest of the Slovenian post-Beatnik generation in Oriental thought and forms of religion such as Buddhism and Confucianism. The writers' interest in Far-Eastern cultures spoke to an attempt to gain an insight into different life practices, which might provide an alternative to the state of the Western world, to the dictates of capital logic and of the consumerism displayed by an apolitical, politically inert, or ideologically indoctrinated middle-class that was rapidly growing in Slovenia and was leading a fairly prosperous life, traveling freely outside the country, and so on. At the same time, this glance beyond Europe was part of an effort to step out of Europocentrism, logocentrism, subjectivism, of the notion of man as the center and measure of the universe, an intention which, from the 1970s on, has yielded a significant body of work in Slovenian literature, especially in poetry. A major author illustrating this philosophical and reflective direction is the poet Milan Dekleva, since the 1990s one of the most prominent Slovenian poets, who is also important for the debate on postmodernism in contemporary Slovenian literature (see M. Kos 2007).

3. The Crisis of Modernism: Postmodernism and Its Aftermath

Slovenian modernism (Tomaž Šalamun, Veno Taufer, Dane Zajc, Niko Grafenauer, Franci Zagoričnik, Lojze Kovačič, Rudi Šeligo, Dušan Jovanovič, and others) peaked around 1970, reaching its extreme forms in the mid-1970s with ultramodernism, contemporaneously with the new avant-garde. After 1975, when (ultra)modernism and the neo-avant-garde had exhausted their thematic and formal possibilities, there followed sundry attempts at overcoming the crisis of modernism through the revival of the more traditional narrative models (especially by drawing on the tradition of neorealism), through the first magic realist and new age works, and through the return to a moderate, non-radical modernism or (in poetry) to postsymbolism and neodecadence (cf. J. Kos 2001: 376–380). It is no coincidence that 1975 is perceived by some Slovenian literary historians as the beginning of Slovenian postmodernism.

Unique to the first Slovenian discussions of this phenomenon was that, in contrast to other world trends and movements, postmodernism was being discovered in poetry rather than prose (cf. M. Kos 1996: 87–173). The initial disagreement on what constitutes the "essence" of postmodernism not only persisted but grew ever more pronounced, as a cursory survey of the most prominent theories on the subject goes to show. Such theories and views were instrumental to Slovenian debates as well. Leading writers would refer to a wide range of critical concepts and philosophical paradigms (by Lyotard, Habermas, Jameson, Baudrillard, authors of pioneer texts that would set the course for the major conversations around postmodernity) or to thinkers who focused on literary postmodernism (such as C. Olson, L. B. Meyer, J. Barth, I. Howe, L. Fiedler, W. Spanos, and I. Hassan in the 1960s and 1970s, and later D. Lodge, M. Calinescu, D. Fokkema, B. McHale, L. Hutcheon, B. K. Marshall, and many others in the following decades). What links all these theories, which are often in disagreement or even diametrical opposition, is precisely their regular focus on prose texts. According to

Douwe Fokkema's introduction to *Approaching Postmodernism*, a volume of proceedings published more than twenty years ago and one of the first international comparative attempts to explain postmodernism, the literary genre best suited to postmodernist poetics is prose, followed by drama, while poetry comes in last (Fokkema, Bertens 1986: IX). A similar picture emerges from the second, no less representative international volume, *Exploring Postmodernism*. The only discussion of postmodernism in poetry comes from Marjorie Perloff, who notes that the literary criticism of the late twentieth century no longer has poetry at the center of critical discourse (Calinescu, Fokkema 1987: 95).

The status of poetry as the privileged genre of postmodernism may well be a distinctive Slovenian feature. I might note, the 1980s and even the early 1990s hardly produced a poetry collection not linked by critics to postmodernism directly or indirectly. The reading of practically all 1980s Slovenian poetry as postmodernist partly results from the crisis of radical modernism in the mid-1970s. Modernism had dominated Slovenian literature for several decades after World War II while poetry has been, at least symbolically, the privileged national genre ever since the poet France Prešeren, "the father of the nation," hence the surviving stereotype of the Slovenians as a "nation of poets," a stereotype founded, as pointed out earlier, on the fact that literature happened to be the vehicle of Slovenian national identity. Not surprisingly, this interpretation and function of older, premodernist Slovenian literature is now widely known as the "Prešeren structure," a notion articulated by Dušan Pirjevec, one of Slovenia's leading, late twentieth-century literary theorists and philosophers (see Pirjevec 1978).

From the present time's more distant perspective, the enthusiasm about postmodernism in poetry was probably exaggerated. An author who indisputably established the "model" of postmodernism in this genre is the poet Milan Jesih with his collections *Soneti* (1989, Sonnets) and *Soneti drugi* (1993, Sonnets the Second). Jesih's sonnets, unfortunately rendered untranslatable by their virtuoso manipulation of language registers, fit postmodernism in terms of style and literary history as well as from a more global, comparative perspective. Style-wise and historically, one of the postmodern characteristics is genre syncretism, a dialogic quality or "return to tradition" on the premise that literature can only "return" to tradition in the postmodern manner after having first departed from it, or, if it has experienced modernism and avant-garde, after having questioned it radically. Globally speaking now, postmodernism zeroes in on the singular position of the subject and his/her view of the world by emphasizing fictitiousness, decenteredness, ambiguity, simulation, the "pluralism of truths," and "ontological doubt" (see M. Kos 1996: 15–32). Yet at the same time, Jesih's poetry problematizes the coherence of the poetic "I"—indeed, one of his discreetly ironical sonnets even introduces a "character" named "the poetic subject"—thus bearing out the observation made in James McCorkle's *The Inscription of Postmodernism in Poetry*, according to which "central to postmodern poetics" is "the critique of the privileged and entitled 'I'" (Bertens, Fokkema 1997: 46).

Beside the initial focus on poetry (cf. Hribar 1984), another feature of the burgeoning Slovenian debate on postmodernism in the 1980s was the speed at which postmodernism made its way into the mainstream, including university discourse and academic discussion. This may be an additional reason for the relatively early loss of postmodernism's subversive quality. As an undergraduate student of comparative literature and philosophy at the University of Ljubljana in the late 1980s, I attended lectures on postmodernism and the postmodern era and wrote papers on Borges, Calvino, Eco, Fowles, Barnes, American metafiction, and so on while most literary magazines were publishing translated texts on the theory and practice of postmodernism not only in literature but also in other fields. Indeed, postmodernist poetics was what the youngest literary generation, born around 1960, identified itself with at the time. In terms of the generation gap, also worth mentioning here, postmodernism helped define the young writers in opposition to the literature of the older, modernist writers.

According to the recent studies of Tomo Virk, the leading Slovenian expert on postmodern prose, two consecutive forms of postmodern writing may be identified in Slovenia (as well as, for example, in Serbia, Russia, or Croatia). They are termed "political" and "metafictional-deconstructionist" postmodernism respectively:

> While Western postmodernism first appeared in its 'metafictional' or 'deconstructionist' variant and only later in the 'political' one, some Slavic countries (similarly to Latin America), especially those where postmodernism flourished, witnessed the opposite chronological sequence (Virk 2006: 185).

Following Virk's argument, the key authors of Slovenian political postmodernism in the early 1980s were Drago Jančar and Dimitrij Rupel, both belonging to the then middle generation. Jančar, nowadays considered the most important living prose writer in Slovenia, limited his postmodern narrative techniques to select novellas (his intertextual references, for example, are to Bulgakov and Borges), while his primary interest was the issue of totalitarianism. In the 1980s, this approach had an indisputable political charge. Rupel, the Slovenian Foreign Minister from 1990 until recently, published two novels in the early 1980s, *Maks* (1983) and *Povabljeni pozabljeni* (1985, Those Invited and Forgotten). Both are written in a playful, metafictional and intertextual manner, but this "intratextual" form conveys clear political "messages" of social criticism.

The shift from political postmodernism to an emphatically meta-fictional and autoreferential type occurred in the late 1980s, with authors who were born mostly around 1960. These include Andrej Blatnik with the novel *Plamenice in solze* (1987, Torches and Tears) and with a collection of short fiction, *Biografije brezimnih* (1989, Biographies of the Nameless), Branko Gradišnik with his short stories *Mistifikcije* (1987, Mystifictions), Igor Bratož with the short-story collection *Pozlata pozabe* (1988, The Gilt of Oblivion), and Aleksa Šušulić with the book *Kdo mori bajke in druge zgodbe* (1989, Who Is Killing Fables and Other Stories). All these works abound in references not only to literature, but, especially in Blatnik's case, also to film and popular culture and are strongly influenced by American metafiction and Borges while "programmatically renouncing any reference to extratextual reality" (Virk 2006: 186). The same period, of course, saw a number of other, different prose writers, who continued as heirs to the modernist poetics, worked in the tradition of neorealism, or tried their hand at genre literature. Thus, the period since the 1980s may well be described as one of heterogeneity, syncretism, and plurality, with no predominating literary orientation.

In the 1990s, most authors of Slovenian postmodern metafiction either stopped writing or adopted a different style, which can hardly be a coincidence. These metamorphoses are most evident in the case of Andrej Blatnik, formerly a leading figure of Slovenian postmodernism. Blatnik's work is symptomatic of a transition from metafiction to a "minimalism" close to the literature of Raymond Carver, who gained considerable popularity among the younger Slovenian authors at that time.[3] However, when compared to Carver's, Blatnik's prose—especially in his book of stories *Menjave kož* (1990, Skinswaps) and *Zakon želje* (2000, Law of Desire)—is more intellectual and contains no obvious references to the social standing of the protagonists. Finally, Blatnik's most recent novel, *Spremeni me* (2008, Change Me), introduces into his writing and contemporary Slovenian prose in general a new thematic emphasis. The novel is set in the near future of a globalized consumer's world ruled by multinational corporations, where individuality and genuine human relations are dying out. Blatnik's novel tells the story of a middle-aged advertising agent who has all sorts of problems with himself, his wife, and the world around him. Contentwise, there is a noticeable dimension of social criticism to this book, while the narrative devices are for the most part the minimalist techniques of Blatnik's short fiction.

A similarly (for lack of better words) anti-globalist and anti-corporate orientation rooted in a humanist and individualist philosophy emerges in contemporary Slovenian drama. An example are the works of Matjaž Zupančič, one of the most prolific Slovenian playwrights of the middle generation. His latest plays, *Hodnik* (2003, The Corridor) and *Razred* (2006, The Classroom), both winners of the award for the best Slovenian dramatic text, problematize the world of reality shows and global capitalism. While drawing on the drama of the absurd, they nevertheless display a trenchant socially critical attitude. *Razred* ends, in fact, with the Internationale, if somewhat ambiguously, not necessarily as an appeal to class mobilization—apparently, in a world of global supply and demand, the "international proletariat" has been more or less integrated into the consumer society, becoming a mass without old-fashion, Marxist "class consciousness."

Poetry, at least in the context of Slovenian literature, has been less open to such socially critical attitudes. The post-1990s Slovenian poetry reveals a gradual departure from the poetics of Slovenian postmodernism, whose paradigm was set up around 1990 by Milan Jesih and his two books of sonnets. The poetry of younger authors born in the 1960s and especially in the 1970s has lately been dubbed "urban poetry" or, following the American example (especially the so-called New York poetry school), "the poetry of open form." Features of an "urban poetry of open form" had already emerged in the 1960s and 1970s, for instance, in the early work of Tomaž Šalamun, the contemporary Slovenian poet who is best-known abroad and most frequently translated, as well as in some Slovenian (neo)avant-garde writers from the same period. Over the last decade, this direction has come to the fore in the authors of "young Slovenian poetry" such as Uroš Zupan, Primož Čučnik, Tone Škrjanec, and Gregor Podlogar (cf. M. Kos 2007: 245–272). Not surprisingly, many of them have been strongly influenced by North American poets, particularly by Frank O'Hara and his poetological principles, which have received their clearest expression in his "personist manifesto." In Slovenian literature, the impact of O'Hara and the "Polish O'Harists" (the latter have influenced P. Čučnik in particular) obtains mainly in the problematizing of the elevated language of poetry and the Orphean pathos, as well as in the predilection for street humor and "pure" and "dirty" language. The blend of high and low poetic idioms admittedly belongs with the other features of postmodern poetics, but since an important segment of younger Slovenian poetry is marked by the rehabilitation of the poetic "I" and by the so-called new "intimism," this literature arguably falls outside the "classic" postmodernism of the 1980s. Insofar as it does "return" to modernism, its voice is moderate instead of radical, with no sharp edges. Rather than shock, surprise, or de(con)struct the audience's perception of the world, it seeks to establish a human contact. Finally, other distinctive traits of younger Slovenian poetry and literature in general include an a-metaphysical quality, that is, a farewell to metaphysical visions, wanderings, and quests, the abandonment of broader, supraindividual historical reflection, and a shift to the sphere of tangible, "everyday" experiences permitted by this literary practice.

4. *Back to the Future*

Crucially determining for the social status of Slovenian literature in the 1980s—the era of the so-called "Slovenian Spring"—was the important role played by writers, most of whom gathered around the Slovenian Writers' Association and the *Nova Revija* monthly, in asserting national independence and breaking with socialism. Needless to say, the general public of the time was more interested in real history than in literary fiction. The 1980s, especially in their second half, had witnessed two parallel processes in Slovenia, both fueled by the general crisis of socialist economy and by increasing international tensions in multiethnic

Yugoslavia: a turn away from official socialist ideology, on the one hand, and a struggle for national independence, more specifically, for an independent Slovenian state, on the other. Owing to the parallelism of the two developments, the rejection of the old order in 1989–1991 (the referendum on national independence, the first democratic elections, the war for independence, the passing of a new constitution, etc.) was more equivocal than in the other East and Central European countries: it was blurred, masked, and in some respects not fully articulated because the independence process by and large called for political unity and absence of internal conflict. What Slovenia experienced was not a "democratic revolution," that is, a violent removal of the illegitimate single-party government, but a "gentle transition" to a different social order, which in essence meant a gradual withdrawal of the Communist Party from its previous positions of leadership and control. Thus, the democratic, post-communist elections of the 1990s brought two successive presidential mandates to the former Party leader, Milan Kučan, while the propor-tional election system resulted in predominantly coalition governments forced to seek national and ideological consensus. By becoming a full member of European and Euro-Atlantic institutions and associations, Slovenia became part of the globalized world and more or less free flow of people, ideas, and, not least, capital. And so, after 2000, Slovenia, too, seemed to have experienced what Fukuyama had termed, back in the late 1980s, "the end of history."

In democratic Slovenia, the freedom of literature and the arts in general is no longer threatened by the ideological or repressive state apparatus as it was in the decades after World War II. Rather, the threat is posed by the market: if the Slovenians were to stop subsidizing the culture and arts of their two-million people nation, the production of original, as well as translated, non-commercial literature and humanities scholarship might be endangered since the average print run of such works in Slovenia amounts to a few hundred copies. It follows that political freedom, in particular the freedom of association, writing, and thinking, which had been the goal of many Slovenian writers and intel-lectuals in the postwar decades, does not necessarily stimulate literature itself, its penetration and imaginative power. What suggests itself is then a provocative thesis: the political freedom brought by liberal democracy is less *liberating* than the lack of this freedom. This is partly because, when it was not a trivial ideological instrument, a degradation of the aesthetic, literature under non-democratic, totalitarian conditions was in fact, in and of itself, a manifestation of freedom. While Slovenia preserves the representative and symbolic value of literature, the age of mass media and, in particular, digital media has brought about a worldwide marginalization of literature's role and influence in society. To be sure, marginality can also be a form of freedom, one demanding great creative courage and confidence. But there is a flip side to this form in the context of an awareness of unlimited freedom and its universal availability, namely, the anxiety of freedom.

5. *Postscript*

In light of the current financial and economic crisis, which has suddenly become the *reality* of our globalized world, the brave new world arising from "the end of history" is faced with serious trials and dilemmas. One of them is laid out in the question: Will the global difficulties give rise to an attempt at a global solution, thus laying the foundations of a new *world order*? Or will they prompt a return to the pre-globalized, divided world of individual nationalisms, protectionist politics, and various antagonisms, including ideological ones, which had seemingly been transcended?

In March 2009, an international seminar "On the idea of Communism" took place in London. The seminar was organized by the Slovenian philosopher Slavoj Žižek, and the list of participants included such famous names as Alain Badiou, Terry Eagleton, Michael Hardt, Toni Negri, Jacques Ranciere, Gianni Vattimo, and, of course, Žižek himself. Despite their common sympathy with the idea (ideal?) of communism, these theorists cannot be reduced to a common denominator. The event itself, however, is proof that, for an important and influential part of the European left-wing intelligentsia, the idea of communism does not belong to a story about *the passing of an illusion*, as it was considered in the 1990s, for instance, by the historian François Furet, the author of a comprehensive work "about the idea of communism in the twentieth century" (Furet 1995). In an interview for the central Slovenian newspaper immediately following the conference, the French philosopher Alain Badiou said, enigmatically and elusively, that the communist idea was for him nowadays "a possibility of the possibility of the possibility of an event." To the interviewer's explicit question where he saw the idea of communism at work today, he gave the abstract reply that it was all about the anticipation of an event as a possibility of "a new political truth arriving" (*Delo*, 21 March 2009). The thrust of Badiou's thought, however, could be reformulated. How shall the idea of communism be kept alive in today's postmodern world, after the fall of the Berlin Wall? The answer might be vaguely postmodern: in an age of "capitalism without work," the idea of communism is not kept alive through an organized movement of the (still) employed and unemployed "working class." Rather, it survives in the limelight, on the stage where philosophers at an international conference propose the reconsideration of "a new content for the concept of 'communism'."

The question remains, of course, *how* to give *a new content* to a concept so burdened with its historical heritage, with the fate of Marx's utopian *Kingdom of Freedom*, which disintegrated in the *Kingdom of Necessity* of real socialism. In this context, and as a comment on the London conference, we may turn to the observation made ten years ago by the German sociologist Ulrich Beck: "The neo-Marxist picture of the capitalist world-system no longer has any utopian energy, any systematic political hope or fantasy. For its analysis cannot find any place for a political subject. In the long run, is it not inevitable that such a cosmopolitan neo-Marxism will join in the great lament at the irrevocable sinking of the *Titanic*?" (Beck 2000: 98)

Destiny is pleased by repetitions, variants and symmetries, says a well-known maxim by J. L. Borges, the great precursor of postmodern prose. Borges's idea of destiny being pleased by repetitions can probably be applied to the debate "on the idea of communism." Tragedy or farce: that is the question. And, perhaps with the added incentive of dramatic social instability and of the individual's position in a chaotic global "world society," there is no reason why these dilemmas and illusions, old and new, should not be tackled by the postmodern era's future world literature, including Slovenian.

NOTES

1. The path to Slovenian statehood was not simple, for Slovenia's assertion of independence was linked to the collapse of Yugoslavia, including the so-called "Ten-Day War for an Independent Slovenia," which was fought in the summer of 1991 between the Slovenian Territorial Defence Forces and the Yugoslav People's Army. This conflict heralded the long and bloody war which raged in two former Yugoslav republics, Croatia and Bosnia, and in the autonomous region of Kosovo, a war whose aftermath is being brought to a close by the International Criminal Tribunal for the former Yugoslavia in the Hague.

2. A telling example is the case of postwar Slovenian literary magazines banned for political reasons, from _Beseda_ (1951–1957) and _Revija 57_ (1957–1958) to _Perspektive_ (1960–1964). An even more graphic illustration is the fate of Jože Pučnik (1932–2003), a contributor to these magazines and the best-known dissident and political prisoner in Slovenia. When Pučnik, a philosopher and sociologist, began to criticize publicly the nature and actual structure of the government, all "tolerance" was over: one of the texts which led to his imprisonment was significantly entitled _Naša družbena stvarnost in naše iluzije_ (Our Social Reality and Our Illusions). This was in 1958, more than a decade before the idealistic student movement. In the late 1980s and early 1990s, Pučnik, having returned from his long exile in Germany, headed the democratic opposition and became one of the most important leaders of the movement for Slovenian independence and democracy.

3. The first book-size Slovenian translation of Carver's prose was published in 1991. The accompanying study was written by Aleš Debeljak, who had helped to promote Slovenian debates on postmodernism in the 1980s, authored the first Slovenian book on postmodernism (Debeljak 1989), and edited the influential anthology _Ameriška metafikcija_ (1988, American Metafiction).

BIBLIOGRAPHY

Beck, Ulrich. _What Is Globalization?_ Trans. Patrick Camiller. Cambridge, UK: Polity Press, 1997.

Bertens, Hans. _The Idea of the Postmodern: A History._ London and New York: Routledge, 1995.

Bertens, Hans, and Douwe Fokkema (eds.). _International Postmodernism: Theory and Literary Practice._ Amsterdam, Philadelphia: John Benjamins Publishing Company, 1997.

Calinescu, Matei, and Douwe Fokkema (eds.). _Exploring Postmodernism._ Amsterdam, Philadelphia: John Benjamins Publishing Company, 1987.

Debeljak, Aleš. _Postmoderna sfinga: kontinuiteta modernosti v postmodernosti._ Klagenfurt, Salzburg: Wieser Verlag, 1989.

Fokkema, Douwe, and Hans Bertens (eds.). _Approaching Postmodernism._ Amsterdam, Philadelphia: John Benjamins Publishing Company, 1986.

Furet, François. _Le passé d'une illusion: Essai sur l'idée communiste au XXe siècle._ Paris: Édition Robert Laffont, 1995.

Fukuyama, Francis. _The End of History and the Last Man._ New York: The Free Press, 1992.

Hribar, Tine. _Sodobna slovenska poezija._ Maribor: Založba Obzorja, 1984.

Juvan, Marko. "Iz 80. v 90. leta: slovenska literatura, postmodernizem, postkomunizem in nacionalna država." _Jezik in slovstvo_ 40.1–2 (1995): 29–33.

Kos, Janko. *Primerjalna zgodovina slovenske literature*. Ljubljana: Mladinska knjiga, 2001.

Kos, Matevž. *Prevzetnost in pristranost: Literarni spisi*. Ljubljana: LUD Literatura, 1996.

_____. "The Poetry of Milan Dekleva." *Milan Dekleva: Blind Spot of Time*. Ljubljana: Slovene Writers' Association, 2007. 113–159.

_____. *Fragmenti o celoti: Poskusi s slovenskim pesništvom*. Ljubljana: LUD Literatura, 2007.

Pirjevec, Dušan. *Vprašanje o poeziji. Vprašanje naroda*. Maribor: Založba Obzorja, 1978.

Virk, Tomo. *Strah pred naivnostjo. Poetika postmodernistične proze*. Ljubljana: LUD Literatura, 2000.

Virk, Tomo. "'Politični' (prozni) postmodernizem v nekaterih slovanskih literaturah." *Literatura in globalizacija*. Ed. Miha Javornik. Ljubljana: Znanstvenoraziskovalni inštitut Filozofske fakultete, 2006. 183–190.

LATE COMMUNIST AND POSTCOMMUNIST AVANT-GARDE AESTHETICS: INTERROGATIONS OF COMMUNITY

NATAŠA KOVAČEVIĆ

1. *Introduction*

In narratives that celebrate the European Union and North America as democratic, multicultural communities bringing economic prosperity to all, Eastern Europe is emerging as a democratic apprentice gradually waking up from the nightmare that was communism. Obscured in these narratives is the multiplicity of lifestyles and the proliferation of creative, playful avant-garde aesthetics that interrogated socio-political narratives of the late-communist period, frequently extending into postcommunism. In what follows, I will explore how this aesthetics blurred the boundaries between "serious" ideologies of everyday practices of post/communism, on the one hand, and these practices' "creative" reworkings via art, performance, and the media, on the other. Specifically, comparing Situationist-type interventions of Slovenian artist collective Neue Slowenische Kunst and Russian artist collective Necrorealists, I will highlight the role held in their works by techniques and features such as reliance on absurd humor and political taboo, estrangement of "common-sense" reality, and conflation of everyday life and performance.

These artists' strategies include an investment in an absurdly excessive "overidentification" with and a *detournement* of both communist and capitalist rhetoric, and a collapsing of their differences to create a utopian opening toward another politics and another type of global community. In the performative wor(l)ds of NSK and Necrorealists, art demands fanaticism: art becomes both the fanatical, total art of living (with an original philosophical outlook, rhetoric, style of dress, and/or habits) and the exposure of the fanaticism of ordinary, everyday life in late communism and postcommunism. The intervention of this avant-garde aesthetics in the last twenty years makes for an uneasy relationship to NATO, the EU, and the social effects of global neoliberal capitalism, ultimately questioning Eastern Europe's internalization of its status as an "other" on the outskirts of "legitimate" Europe.

Addressing both local and global issues as they occupy universally taboo spaces, NSK and Necrorealists do not fit into either dissident or mainstream positions. They do not aim to gain acceptance by artistic or political establishments, which is a radical stance since so many discussions of postcommunist art have focused precisely on measuring the liberal spirit of the newly democratic states based on their readiness to "accept" previously controversial artwork. As Boris Groys suggests, postcommunist artistic practices are for the most part characterized by an extension of the communist paradise in which "everything is accepted that had previously been excluded," so these practices represent "a utopian radicalization of the Communist demand for the total inclusion."[1] Instead, these artist collectives operate on the margins of artistic practice by inhabiting politics (NSK) or biology (Necrorealists) *as* a space of art to interrogate existing models of society and community, both locally and globally. While NSK replicate and expose the limits of the state and any transcendental signifiers used as immanent, grounding concepts for the community the state claims to represent, Necrorealists query the biopolitical erasure of singular deaths in contemporary models of statehood, ultimately pointing to the possibility of a community that is not based on an assumed organic, immanent identity.

2. *Neue Slowenische Kunst (NSK)*

Neue Slowenische Kunst, to begin with, is an "organized cultural and political movement and school"[2] established in 1984 in Slovenia (then part of socialist Yugoslavia) to unite the music group Laibach, fine arts and painter collective IRWIN, and Scipion Nasice Sisters Theater into a single organization. Later, other "departments" were added, such as the design and promotion sector called New Collectivism, the self-explanatory Department of Pure and Applied Philosophy, and Cosmokinetic Theater Red Pilot. In a characteristically performative and playful fashion, NSK has mocked bureaucratic structures as it put its own art into boxes, providing a detailed yet absurd map of the "Principle of Organization and Action" of its own sectors and sub-sectors, all of which are informed by a ubiquitous transcendental signifier "Immanent, Consistent Spirit." Perhaps the most prominent and internationally pop-

ular portion of this collective has been Laibach, a music group that both
put NSK on the map in Yugoslavia in the 1980s and inspired a veritable
cult following around the world for the next twenty years. Frequently,
Laibach concerts paved the way for other NSK actions and exhibitions,
so in this essay I will focus mostly on Laibach's role in highlighting
NSK's critique of Europe, NATO, and global capitalism, as I connect
this to the NSK project of a "State in Time."

As critics such as Alexei Monroe, Slavoj Žižek,[3] Aleš Erjavec, and
Marina Gržinić have noted, Laibach (and NSK more broadly) rely on an
overidentification with dominant political and cultural discourses that
effects its own manipulation of signs rather than assuming an oppositional or marginalized position in society, itself vulnerable to manipulation: "All art is subject to political manipulation...except that which
speaks the language of this same manipulation."[4] In this respect, the
many textual NSK documents such as interviews, website postings, stat-
utes, and philosophical statements persistently flaunt this manipulation
and performativity of language, at once satisfying the public hunger for
testimony from NSK about what they "really" mean—and the very word
testimony implies a level of seriousness or truthfulness to each statement—and undermining this possibility of separating language as a
mask from "real" thought presumably "behind" it. In their first, 1983
public appearance on a Slovenian cultural and political TV show called
"TV Tednik" ("TV Weekly"), Laibach wore military uniforms, and,
addressing the question about the suicide of their first singer Tomaž
Hostnik, opened with a quote from Hitler: "Art is noble mission that
demands fanaticism, and Laibach is an organism whose goals, life, and
means are higher—in their power and duration—than the goals, lives,
and means of its individual members."[5] This announces one of the subjects of their manipulation, Nazi-Kunst, but other subjects are "industrial
production...totalitarianism, bruitism...and, of course, disco."[5] Such a
methodology, also described as the principle of "monumental retro-
garde," freely combines avant-garde symbols of Russian Futurism or
Suprematism, Socialist Realism, Western pop music, industrialism, and
Slovenian nationalist mythology.

As Alexei Monroe asserts, "Laibach's use of language is terroristic
in that it is explicitly designed as a disorienting, alienating device as
violent as its sounds and images."[6] By forming an assemblage of artistic
and political elements which preclude the "pinpointing" of their "real"

attitudes, art and politics collapse into each other, not so much signaling that Russian Futurism is "the same as" Nazi-Kunst, but highlighting their collusion in what Laibach describe as a goal of their concerts:

> terror as therapy and as a principle of social organization...the effective disciplining of the revolted and alienated audience; awakening the feeling of total belonging and commitment to the Higher Order...by obscuring the intellect, the consumer is reduced to a state of humble remorse, which is a state of *collective aphasia*, which in turn is the principle of social organization.[7]

Laibach necessarily recreate a totalitarian rally atmosphere at their concerts to make visible, and therefore strange, what Guy Debord identifies as "the society of the spectacle."[8] At the same time, Laibach themselves are spectacular, because they operate on the aforementioned "principle of social organization," and as Jean-Luc Nancy says, "There is no society without the spectacle because society is the spectacle of itself."[9] Therefore to Nancy, in order for a society to exist, it must project itself in some spectacular form, so the Situationist question of doing away with the spectacle altogether becomes replaced with the question about whether it is possible to think society as a different type of community, that is, as a spectacle that is *not* alienated.

Refuting the conventionally understood distance between art and politics, NSK have become a spectral image of society, haunting the "real" society on which they parasitically subsist. Like a megalomaniacal political leader, Laibach, especially, have inspired and fed a cult following while echoing Stalin's dictum about writers: "We, LAIBACH, are the engineers of human souls."[10] Rather than occupying a dissident, self-consciously marginalized position vis-à-vis either socialist Yugoslavia or capitalist Slovenia (or the global market for that matter), NSK have effectively built themselves as their own institution with their own artistic support network, and later—and logically—transformed themselves into a "State in Time." Insisting on their Slovene "origins" during their performances in Yugoslavia could have made them globally marginalized because of the relative obscurity of Slovenia in relation to the more famous Yugoslavia. However, they made Slovenia globally relevant by their controversial use of German and English language to speak of national issues, their use of Slovenian (quasi)historical national imagery to comment on the shared European legacies of Nazism and communism, and their insistence on blurring the political boundaries between the "democratic" West and the "communist" East. Insofar as they remain *parallel*, rather than *oppositional* to, the state, NSK are indifferent to whether the state accepts, praises, bans, or ignores them: all these positions would reinforce the distance between art and politics. They limit themselves neither to politicizing their art nor to aestheticizing political positions: for NSK, politics *is* a space of art, a space they freely inhabit.

The political space NSK have always inhabited has been that of taboo, and this habitation has secured them an unfriendly, nightmarish, and distanced relationship with the official state. In the 1980s' socialist, multicultural Yugoslavia, NSK were recreating the taboo Slovenian national and historical symbols in their theatrical performances and music videos and on their canvases, but the almost mantric, ad-nauseam repetition of ambiguous symbols—themselves ambiguously national—stripped those symbols of any predetermined ideological meaning they might have, even if the audience had managed to discern some sort of solid meaning in the first place. The ubiquitous deer antlers, Malevich-type black crosses, Alpine skiing, and folk costumes both are and are not "essentially" Slovene; as Aleš Erjavec argues, foregrounding the objects in such a way points to their "literal meaning...which at that time, as representations, still existed essentially as ideological symbolic entities."[11] It is not clear, however, what the symbolism is precisely, but the case can be made that it operates indirectly, by analogy, rather than mimetically, as Erjavec's statement would suggest.

Thus, as spectral supplement of the budding Slovene nationalism, NSK make visible the collective spectacle of nationalist desire (which gets them in trouble with the pro-Yugoslav sentiment). However, they also interrogate "pure" Slovene identity by insisting on its traumatic relationship with the Austro-Hungarian Empire and the Slovenian history of collaboration with both Austrian and German authorities in the Balkans. Laibach, for instance, have claimed that "It is impossible to imagine Cervantes or Leonardo as Russians, Voltaire and Verdi as Germans, Dostoevsky and Wagner as Italians or LAIBACH as Yugoslavs."[12] But even as they claim they are inextricably linked with Slovene identity, they justify this by an ambiguous statement that itself seems to interrogate the modern nationalist question of the responsibility of artists to "their" nation:

> Every artist comes from the depths of his nation, from the dark, subterranean workshop of the national psyche, and through his creation illuminates its basic, typical features, the essence of spirit and character.[13]

Outraging Slovene nationalists and Yugoslav socialists alike, this illumination of national features arrived in the guise of Nazi-Kunst symbols transposed onto Slovenian folkloric elements and socialist mythology. Because this is possibly the most famous and well-analyzed part of NSK's intervention, I will not dwell on it here.[14] What is more interesting in this period is NSK's successful attempt to make themselves relevant not only locally, but also globally. Crossing back and forth between Eastern and Western blocs was arguably easier for a group of Yugoslav origin due to socialist Yugoslavia's exceptional status as a non-aligned state lodged between the two ideological entities.[15] Undermining Cold War boundaries, not only did Laibach remind Slovenes of their unexamined, traumatic relationship with Germany, but they also pointed out to their audience, at a 1998 Vienna concert, that Austrians "are Germans,"[16] thus challenging Austrian revisionist history that claimed that Austria was occupied by, rather than openly collaborated with, Germany in World War II. Additionally, Laibach refused to align themselves with Orientalist hierarchies between Germans and Slovenians, asserting that "the contemporary Germans are an inferior sort of Slovenes."[17]

Long before the Berlin Wall's fall, Laibach foresaw the new course of European politics, which would become clearer in the 1990s with the establishment and expansion of the European Union in a close economic and political alliance with the United States. Because of the shared terror and "collective aphasia" of consumers as a "principle of social organization," Europe in the 1980s was equally "occupied" in the East as well as in the West, but its future—the "United States of Europe"—was an even more dystopian vision of American spectacular consumerism. Worth noting along these lines is that Laibach conducted the first "Occupied Europe Tour" in 1983-85 and printed Ronald Reagan's 1985 speech on the back cover of the tour album: "It is my fervent wish that in the next century there will be one Europe, a free Europe, *a United States of Europe.*"[18] The realization of this wish would indeed arrive, first through the expansion of the military machine NATO, and then through a gradual, conditional acceptance of most of the former communist states into the neoliberal capitalist project that is the EU, which itself increasingly resembles the United States of Europe. In the midst of the Balkan wars of the 1990s, Laibach deflected Europe's fixation on this area as the "sore spot" of European politics by launching a second "Occupied Europe" tour, this time adding NATO to the title to imply that Europe was everywhere under occupation, just as it once had been by German Nazi troops. One of the tracks on the tour album is "Geburt einer Nation," invoking the American white supremacist film *Birth of a Nation*. Significantly, Laibach held two concerts in Sarajevo just as the Dayton peace agreement was being signed; stating provocatively that the concert showed that NATO would come to Bosnia one way or another, they again anticipated future political developments.[19] Bosnia's entry into the new type of "democracy" was appropriately exposed through the manipulation of Nazi-Kunst: "Nazi-fascism under the disguise of democracy is the *rule of financial capital itself*."[20]

Just as in the 1980s NSK made visible the repressed Germanic shadows of Slovene national identity, so in the 1990s they further distanced themselves from the newly independent Slovene state to avoid being categorized as a Slovene artist collective. Furthermore, they re-emphasized the weakening connections among former Yugoslav states, as well as among former communist countries, which were rushing to "rejoin" Western Europe and deny their communist pasts in the process. As Alexei Monroe states, "No Laibach action is free of paradox, and it is significant that together with the other NSK groups, it maintains active links with former Yugoslavia and Eastern Europe."[21] In the face of Yugoslavia's disappearance, NSK created their own deterritorialized "State in Time" in 1992, which, according to Gordan Paunović "still seems like the perfect solution to the Yugoslav problem"[22] This utopian qualification is indeed justifiable: by creating a "State in Time" rather than space, NSK implicitly provide a mooring site for all those displaced Yugoslavs who have become extra-territorial by not being able to align themselves with a clear, post-Yugoslav national identity, a non-territory of sorts that would appeal to all anti-nationalists, refugees, and offspring from mixed marriages. But the "State in Time" is also a global state, interrogating and overflowing the traditional understanding of borders everywhere: practicing a policy of absolute non-discrimination, NSK freely issue passports to anyone who applies and open embassies and consulates wherever they are invited, inhabiting such eclectic, "apolitical" spaces as the National Theater in Sarajevo, an apartment kitchen in Umag, or a hotel room in Florence. On the NSK website, this project is described as "a utopian state without a concrete territory, but with several thousands of citizens plus formal national symbols such as a flag, stamps, emblems and a passport that everyone is free to obtain."[23]

Literally entering the symbolic space of political exchange, NSK state paraphernalia do more than parallel and haunt the "real" states; they rival them through the issuing of travel documents that have in some cases been taken seriously and helped, for instance, besieged Sarajevans escape from the city.[24] In a related attempt to highlight the parasitic relationship between artistic and political praxis, IRWIN launched its "NSK Garda" project, for which they hired the army personnel of whatever country they were visiting to guard the NSK flag while wearing armbands with the black Malevich cross. In a characteristic gesture that manipulates collective nationalist desires, they staged these *tableaux vivant* in countries that either recently gained independence, and thus had an official army (Georgia), or desired independence but already had paramilitary units (Kosovo and Montenegro). While "NSK Garda" makes visible perhaps the most problematic and least utopian element of each new state—the army, inherently built on violence and murder—it also confuses alliances and loyalties to the state by dressing up soldiers in "foreign" state paraphernalia that effectively makes them defend someone else's flag, thus becoming, as IRWIN jokes, "General Malevich's army."[25]

Therefore, according to this utopian reading of the NSK "State in Time," at stake is a staging of the impossibility of an organic, enclosed state community by repeating the territorial project of the state but hinting at what lies "beyond" the borders: an open community that is both defined by flexible citizenship and utterly absurd and impossible because it *still* depends on the "emptiness" of the sign of citizenship. The NSK overidentification strategy reassembles the signs of the state, which themselves act as manifestations of exclusion: as long as we are operating in terms of citizenship, this citizenship will have defining content; as long as there are embassies, they will be defined in terms of what is outside; as long as there is a State, it has the potential to become a "Higher Order," or an "Immanent, Consistent Spirit" to which the citizens subject themselves much like the audience subject themselves to the rhythm of Laibach performances. Thus, we arrive at a much more ambivalent reading of these performances: it is legitimate to ask, for instance, how can one possibly view as utopian the highly publicized issuing of NSK diplomatic passport to the controversial Croatian and Kosovo Liberation Army General Agim Čeku? Would NSK, whose art both haunts and symbolizes the proliferation of postcommunist disintegrations, endorse Kosovo's project of yet another drawing of clear national boundaries? Or would they hand the passport to Čeku so as to performatively "remind" him of his duty to be a tolerant diplomat, while reveling in Čeku's acceptance speech full of utopian political clichés about multicultural coexistence and Kosovo as a hopeful new state?[26]

Possibly the clearest warning against understanding the state as a utopian concept *per se* arrived at the moment NSK set up their "embassy" in Sarajevo during the "Occupied Europe NATO tour" in 1995. Dressed in a military uniform, NSK's Peter Mlakar, delivered a lecture on the "Apocalypse of Europe and Possible Deliverance" that critiqued the New World Order and Europe's racist attitude to the Balkans. While the audience's shaken self-confidence in the face of a fratricidal war would be affirmed by statements that "the truth of Europe is evil itself" and that "here European political history traumatically purged itself of its symptoms," its message was complicated by allusions to Bosnians' own pretensions to theological and political legitimacy and to the ways in which a state justifies the wiping out of its enemies by embracing questionable self-victimization:

> Death to criminals, that's OK. But it's only in forgiveness that you process criminals into sausages, [it's] only by forgiving the greatest evil that you will be forgiven and freed. Then the defeated will truly be defeated, God will stand on your side, and the winner will bear your name. I myself guarantee you that.[27]

The last sentence echoes Slobodan Milošević's promise, made on the eve of Yugoslavia's dissolution, to protect Kosovo Serbs against Albanians.

Ultimately, the NSK "State in Time" remains dependent on the logic of the spectacle that it otherwise sets out to derail in a Situationist fashion. This project, however, cannot think the community outside of the subverted alienated spectacle even as it interrogates its guiding discourses through overidentification. NSK state reenacts what Jacques Derrida calls the hauntology that makes any *res publica*, any modern state, possible. This reenactment employs the news media, tele-technologies, internet communication, and so forth, which are all inhabited by the phenomenality of the political and thus invested with the specters of the nation, history, and community.[28] The project points to the bankruptcy and deathly mythology of the state, but, at end of the day, does not offer any alternatives.

3. Necrorealists

Necrorealists are a loosely connected group of performance artists, filmmakers, and painters who emerged from the St. Petersburg underground culture of the 1970s and 1980s. While they are currently mostly associated with Evgenii Yufit's necro-cinema, in the 1970s they were primarily a group of friends whose lifestyle, interests, and everyday life practices were only later articulated as an aesthetics of "Necrorealism." Even categorizing them as an artistic "group" or "aesthetics" is perhaps philosophically inadequate. Early Necrorealist interventions were highly spontaneous, without a predetermined goal or program, and, like the Situationist practice of *dérive*, focused on making everyday reality strange by creating bizarre and unusual situations in the city. Alexei Yurchak characterizes their "public spectacles" as a "refusal of clear-cut boundaries between reality and performance, common sense and absurdity."[29] During some of these interventions, Necrorealists rode on packed subway cars and read aloud medical textbooks about death and decomposition, both fascinating and revolting their "audiences"; they staged massive brawls, managing to involve unsuspecting passers-by, using mannequins that they would "beat up" or throw from buildings; they dressed up as zombies and simulated homosexual intercourse outside a commuter train, while their comrades staged a fight in the background.[30] Frequently, such interventions were carried out spontaneously and in an improvisational manner; the unpredictable participation of other city-dwellers made them even more open-ended and multidirectional.

This difficulty to pinpoint what Necrorealism is "all about" or to define with any certainty their artistic program is derives from their work itself—one could say it is one of its built-in features—and this makes them similar to NSK. Much like in the latter's case, it is hard to determine the Necrorealists' position vis-à-vis the state or other artistic groups. For instance, in the 1980s, they were occasionally arrested for their Situationist interventions, but it was impossible to extract a straightforward testimony from them about their goals, as well as to charge them for beating up a mannequin. Evgenii Yufit reminisces, "I remember the sergeant's face: he was at a loss.... What could he do next? Take us to the police station? But then what would he write in his report? That he arrested several people for carrying a dummy?"[31] Like NSK, Necrorealists do not assume a self-consciously dissident position that would make them vulnerable to repression and marginalization; rather, they confuse authority by freely taking over entire cities and operating in experimental spaces that cannot be either sanctioned or placed off limits by existing legal codes.

Necrorealist writings and interviews are equally performative and evasive, bringing into question the very possibility of truthful testimony and consistency. Asked about the politics of his films, Yufit replies:

> There are disasters, airline disasters, for example, to which everyone is susceptible, even political figures. In this context, politics definitely falls within the sphere of my interests. Although in such cases the process of identification is very complicated. The remains are scattered across three square kilometers. It is a very complex disaster.... A corpse is a corpse.... Its metamorphoses interest me.[32]

Equally frustrating for critics and journalists looking for a clear definition of the group's objectives is the anecdote about how Necrorealists selected their name. As Victor Mazin claims, it is impossible to recall when or how this came about, but Yufit is reported to have "pronounced this word in the presence of a great number of men. It was immediately forgotten. It was repeated over and over: necro-realism. Repetition gave birth to the name. The name gave birth to the phenomenon."[33]

In a sense, then, Necrorealists reserve their right to incomprehensibility just like the NSK. Yufit's insistence that he is only interested in politics insofar as he can study corpses of political figures who died in an airline disaster does not mean that he is not political. Rather, Necrorealism interrogates the concept of the political itself while not occupying a recognizable, mainstream or dissident political position, and, as we will see, controversially inhabiting biopolitics as a space of art. The very anecdote about their "naming," which brings them into "being" according to the logic of the artistic market, where groups must succumb to a politics of proper names in order to be endowed with a clear "identity," points to a philosophical insistence on a free assemblage and repetition of signs, which in effect empties them of an essential meaning. That *repetition gave birth to a name* is indeed apposite as it highlights an ad-absurdum rehashing of a sign that underscores its performative rather than symbolic or metaphoric value. Whether the anecdote itself is "true" or not is irrelevant: there is nothing "behind" the surface of the various Necrorealists masks, even though their endlessly repeated acts of simulated zombification or sex predictably have led commentators to believe that the artists are "deranged," "gay," and so forth.

Indeed, Necrorealists have productively confused both local and foreign critics, who have time and again proven unable to explain this phenomenon through any of the available discourses and approaches that either aligned the artists with anti-communist dissidence and Western-influenced exploration of homosexuality or diagnosed them as pathological and, even worse, as apolitical by taking Yufit at his word, as it were. Olesya Turkina writes that the first Western critics who attended to Necrorealism understood it as a particular spin on "socialist realism" and accordingly interpreted it as a parody of the official Soviet style.[34] For Alexander Borovsky, Necrorealist images of death and zombies reflect the late Soviet era of political stagnation and biological decline of old Party cronies.[35] In both lines of argument, Necrorealism is given a constructive, oppositional, critical role, and is seen as directly reflexive of the political situation, which it interrogates. In this account, Necro-realism would be politicized art. This is the reading of Necrorealism along Western wishful-thinking lines that identify and praise anti-communist dissident aesthetic forms in Eastern Europe.

On the other hand, according to Thomas Campbell, Necrorealists have been seen as sadistic "necrophiliacs" and "sodomizers" both during the Soviet and post-Soviet era, but their grating insistence on homo-sexuality as spectacle has been even more controversial in the post-communist period, when Russian conservative, nationalistic, hyper-masculine discourses took center stage and Western critics interpreted Necrorealist "gayness" as a democratic endorsement of sexual non-discrimination.[36] However, this angle too is debatable, at least in part. A case in point is José Alaniz and Seth Graham's essay "Early Necro-cinema in Context." The critics read in the gruesome and violent homosexual scenes in Necrorealist films a "re-enactment of homophobic fantasy (or dread) meant as a riposte to Soviet archetypes of manhood" and lament that the films do not take their critique to the point of "affirming a more positive, consensual model of homosexual sex."[37] The very terrorizing of audiences with homophobic spectacles and decomposing bodies would seem to rule out any notion of consensual gay sex.

This type of interpretation, however, belies Western critics' tendency to narcissistically read into postcommunist art their own liberal politics, implying that it is the artist's duty to promote such politics in a didactic fashion. In other words, these commentators understand Necrorealism as an aestheticization of politics.

Like NSK, Necrorealist art, especially the films, terrorize its audiences by making everything—the body, language, community, relationships, sexuality—strange, un-identified as well as un-identifiable. Both early, technologically unsophisticated and later, technologically advanced Necrorealist films directed by Evgenii Yufit dwell on bodily decomposition, zombification, Sadean torture, suicide, sodomy, and excrement, all of these presented in an impressionist, non-narrative way so as to suggest a surrealist insistence on probing and exposing subconscious fears.[38] Ellen E. Berry and Anesa Miller-Pogacar's apt characterization of Yufit's films as showcases of "hilarious horror, flatline numbness, overt refusal of meaning, and punk acts of viciousness for [the sake of] fun" underscores the difficulty of assigning Necrorealist cinema a straightforward meaning with reference to political events and concerns.[39] Rather, these films open up the space of political meaninglessness, more exactly, of a lack of political meaning "as is," by representing the muttering, growlingly incoherent language of metamorphosis (human into zombie, human into animal, human into tree, and so on). Labeled as idiots and nonsensical punks, then, Necrorealists strategically differ from NSK, who are ultra-intellectual and, as I have shown, "overidentify" with various assemblages of existing political signs and narratives. For Yufit, Necrorealists are "packs of dogs" roaming the country.[40]

I suggest that we read such packs of dogs and their movements as Deleuzian becoming-animal moments that interrogate the traditional politics of identity, individuality, humanist subjectivity,[41] and with them the inherited understanding of community. Not only do Necrorealist films occupy taboo spaces in terms of representing what the state itself represses, such as bodily waste, gory violence, or homosexuality, but, as Yurchak argues, these films also bring to life, as it were, "the lifestyle and selves that the system could not represent at all…something inexplicable, uncanny, and beyond representation."[43] The films operate in the hinterland between the living and the dead, organic and inorganic, and animal and human, which casts frequent homosexual frolics *and* rapes—e.g., *The Cruel Masculine Disease* (1982)—as, paradoxically, more familiar instances of an "impossible" socially reproductive desire. This becomes particularly apparent in scenes of human-tree intercourse: a man fellating a wooden stick in a forest in *Urine-Crazy Body Snatchers* (1985), man-tree copulation, and attempts at producing anthropo-vegetal hybrids in *Silver Heads* (1998).

Longer, non-narrative, and structurally intricate, Yufit's 1990s films display a fairly constant and clear preoccupation with crossbreeding, biopolitics, and eugenics. Like *Silver Heads*, *Killed by Lightning* (2002) and *Bipedalism* (2005) feature scientific projects obsessed with creating new species. Both movies ultimately mock humanist eugenics because they either produce uncontrollable ape-man hybrids in their attempts to recreate the alleged natural disaster that shocked simians into standing upright (*Bipedalism*) or conclude that homosexuals, criminals, and sadomasochists are a super-species (*Killed by Lightning*).[42] The scientist from *Killed by Lighting* challenges humans' self-proclaimed exceptionalism by stating that

> evolution doesn't exist. A stone and a human are units of one chain…. Reproduction is probably only pathology, a mistake unprogrammed by nature. A man can suddenly be transformed into a different, absolutely new creature in the space of one human life. He can become the forefather of a stone, and a stone or a bird can be transformed into the forefather of a man.

Despite such narrative allegories of biopolitics as a state prerogative, Necrorealist films appropriate the biological itself—and, with it, the biopolitical—as a space of art in a similar way that NSK inhabit politics in their artistic praxis. In this respect, Necrorealist films are not aesthetic in the usual, spectacular way where a film would record "lives" of its "subjects" in the form of bildungsromans or where it would make comments on what happens in "society," thus reflecting back to the audience what Jean-Luc Nancy calls the spectacle *that is* society. Rather, Necro-realist films employ a more radically *different* gesture in that they focus on bodies who die numbly, have compulsive, meaningless homosexual intercourse, or end up suspended between life and death in a grey area that cannot be appropriated by society of either the living or the dead. Perhaps we could glimpse in these desiring bodies what Jacques Derrida describes as a specter in *Specters of Marx*: a certain "thing" without identity or substance, neither platonic image or simulacrum nor body but a certain corporeality, a becoming-body. A specter is something we have to learn to speak to, even if that means being as "mad" as Hamlet who speaks to the ghost of his father.[43]

Fascinated by biology textbooks which stage dead bodies as spectacles made safely distant, impersonal, and uniformly "scientific," Necrorealist movies reverse the biopolitical appropriation of death as an object of study, reviving instead humans as zombies or slowly dying bodies about to become cadavers whose protracted agonies viewers are witnessing as they watch the films but which prove ultimately meaningless and cannot be co-opted into the available biopolitical narratives of the state, whether communist or capitalist. For instance, *Fortitude* (1988), *Knights of Heaven* (1989), and *The Wooden Room* (1995) feature either immobile but live bodies or decomposing corpses, often submerged in water, and hauntingly interfering with any collective actions that might take place around them. This disturbing gesture possibly explains why Necrorealist films are just as controversial in postcommunist Russia as they were under the communists, and why they remain so locally and globally alike: they interrogate the very concept of community underlying most existing states.

According to Jean-Luc Nancy, regardless of political differences between various countries, we have only known a single model of community: one that presupposes an "immanent unity, intimacy, and autonomy." From this perspective, "community is not only intimate communication between its members, but also its organic communion with its own essence."[44] In this type of community, the death of the other is not a singular event, but always absorbed into the destiny of the community, sublated into "the life of the infinite."[45] But since the other's death is always singular—it can only take place before me as a witness but I cannot truly experience it—Nancy proposes that a true, inorganic community (a community without communion) opens up in this realization of the "impossibility of community" where "death loses the sense-less meaning that it ought to have."[46] A community opens up precisely at the moment where an "I" witnesses someone else's death and realizes that there is an excess of singularity in this event that cannot be made into a common or shared experience of an organic community. For Nancy this re-visioning of community has implications for questioning the traditional concept of the subject, which, he argues, underwrites most states we have known, communist, capitalist, as well as Fascist.

I suggest, then, that we read Necrorealist cinema as a mock-spectacular staging of death which exposes how both communist and capitalist models of statehood think of death as a spectacle that they can appropriate and translate into stable meaning, into "the life of the infinite." Necrorealist cadavers and zombies are nameless and subject-less; this focus on physical bodies, on mere, literalized life deprived of an objectifying, scientific meaning, highlights the aspects of death that cannot be explained away rationally and thus integrated into a commu-nity narrative and the status quo the latter underwrites. Unlike NSK, who reinforce the alienation of the society-as-spectacle in order to expose it, Necrorealists undermine the very logic of the spectacle that has taken over the place of community: they expose the community's limits and margins, which casts them as seemingly antisocial and pathological be-cause they do not offer any type of spectacular mirror that could reflect the community back to itself. At the same time, the viewers' disturbing exposure to the other's uncanny, bodily experience of pain and death renders the desensitizing biopolitical spectacle strange again, and thus, as Nancy would argue, points to the space where a community without community, a groundless ground, appears.

4. *Conclusion*

If, as argued throughout this essay, NSK and Necrorealists interrogate in fundamental ways the concept of the political itself and the globally shared grounding model of community, then their interventions hint at the lack of *radical* political change in Eastern Europe in the post-1989 period. In NSK performances, the intensifying sway of financial capital-ism becomes the full-circle realization of "Nazi-fascism" and the fore-closure of a utopian horizon, which may explain why, in their parasitic relationship to the state, NSK can only restage the alienated spectacle of society. In Necrorealist cinema, a growing preoccupation with rampant, technologically eugenicist dystopia and other absurdist genetic modifications certainly resonates with global anxieties about surviving a progress-driven humanist project that has all but destroyed the environment.

While I recognize in Necrorealists a possible conceptual gesture toward a different type of community and politics, perhaps the most hopeful aspect of both artist collectives is the absence of an enemy, of a political scapegoat that has, as Jacques Derrida points out, characterized every traditional "politics of friendship."⁴⁷ It is impossible to identify, with any certainty, a particular group that NSK performances and Necrorealist cinema target as their opponent. Rather than positing an oppressive state establishment or any other identifiable entity as a target, their spectacles involve exposing our shared contributions to the perpetuation of the "Immanent, Consistent Spirit," the myth of a closed-off state and organic community that leads us to war.

NOTES

1. Boris Groys, *Art Power* (Cambridge, MA: MIT Press, 2008), 170.
2. NSK, *Neue Slowenische Kunst* (Los Angeles, CA: AMOK Books, 1991), 53.
3. An interview with Žižek is featured in Daniel Landin and Chris Bohn's film *Laibach: A Film from Slovenia & Occupied Europe NATO Tour 1994-95.*
4. *Neue Slowenische Kunst*, 18.
5. The full text of the interview can be accessed on the NSK State website at http://www.nskstate.com/laibach/interviews/first-tv-app-83.php (accessed February 28, 2009). The Hitler quote is from Boris Groys, *Art Power*, 133.
6. Alexei Monroe, *The Interrogation Machine: Laibach and NSK* (Cambridge: MIT Press, 2005), 66.
7. *Neue Slowenische Kunst*, 44.
8. For Debord, the spectacle is "not a collection of images: rather, it is a social relationship between people that is mediated by images." *The Society of the Spectacle* (New York: Zone Books, 1995), 12.
9. Jean-Luc Nancy, *Being Singular Plural* (Stanford: Stanford University Press, 2000), 67.
10. *Neue Slowenische Kunst*, 50.
11. Aleš Erjavec, "Neue Slowenische Kunst – New Slovenian Art: Slovenia, Yugoslavia, Self-Management and the 1980s," in *Postmodernism and the Postsocialist Condition: Politicized Art under Late Socialism,* ed. Aleš Erjavec (Berkeley, CA: University of California Press, 2003), 147.
12. *Neue Slowenische Kunst*, 44.
13. *Ibid.*

14. Alexei Monroe's *Interrogation Machine* dwells on this subject in depth. Also see *Laibach: A Film from Slovenia & Occupied Europe NATO Tour 1994-95.*

15. Predictably, Laibach take advantage of Tito's speech about Yugoslavia's exceptionalism, appropriating his words and signing the speech "Josip Broz TITO – LAIBACH 1958-1985": "It should be clear to *everyone* that we cannot be no one's appendages of nobody's politics, that we have our own point of view," *Neue Slowenische Kunst,* 63.

16. Quoted in *The Interrogation Machine,* 145.

17. *Neue Slowenische Kunst,* 54.

18. *Ibid.,* 37.

19. *Laibach: A Film from Slovenia & Occupied Europe NATO Tour 1994-95.*

20. *Neue Slowenische Kunst,* 57.

21. *The Interrogation Machine,* 176.

22. Gordan Paunović, "Laibach's Homecoming," *The Wire,* December 1998.

23. The full text of the statement can be accessed at http://www.nskstate.com (accessed March 5, 2009).

24. In the last several years, Nigerians have increasingly begun applying for NSK passports, hoping to use them in lieu of "real" passports. Although crossing borders with an NSK passport is in most cases unsuccessful (and both NSK and the Slovene government issued warnings on official websites against using these documents for travel), this tendency shows that an artifact has become a relatively viable document. Commenting on this development, NSK wonder: "How can light be thrown on such a close encounter between two mutually exclusive worlds: the complex, highly sophisticated, and abstract sphere of contemporary art, and the politically, culturally, and economically profoundly destabilized Third World, where bare survival is frequently an issue and whence people decide to emigrate en masse to find a better life? (With Europe the coveted destination, the media report on worse shipwreck disasters every year and the growing numbers of casualties as people set off on expensive and dangerous illegal crossings.)" One of their responses has been to interview Nigerians, and citizens of other countries, about reasons for applying for an NSK passport. The full text of the discussion can be accessed on NSK State website at http://www.nskstate.com/irwin/exhibitions/NSK-Passport-Holders.php (accessed March 3, 2009).

25. IRWIN, "NSK Garda," *Dictionary of War,* Multitude e.V. and Unfriendly Takeover Frankfurt/Munich/ Graz/Berlin June 2006–February 2007. http://dictionaryofwar. org/concepts/NSK_GARDA (accessed February 28, 2009)

26. The acceptance speech is broadcast in IRWIN's "NSK Garda" presentation, available at http://dictionaryofwar.org/concepts/NSK_GARDA (accessed February 28, 2009).

27. *Laibach: A Film from Slovenia & Occupied Europe NATO Tour 1994-95*

28. Jacques Derrida, *Specters of Marx: The State of the Debt, the Work of Mourning and the New International* (New York: Routledge Classics, 2006), 63.

29. Alexei Yurchak, *Everything Was Forever, Until It Was No More: The Last Soviet Generation* (Princeton, NJ: Princeton University Press, 2006), 244.

30. For more information on these interventions, see Yurchak's *Everything was Forever, Until It Was No More* and his recent article "Necro-Utopia: The Politics of Indistinction and the Aesthetics of the Non-Soviet," *Current Anthropology* 49, no. 2 (April 2008): 199-224. Also see Thomas Campbell, "Homosexuality as Device: Necrorealism and Neoacademism," *Ante Projects* no. 5, http://www.anteprojects.com/FILES/Ante5_Campbell. pdf (accessed March 5, 2009).

31. Quoted in "Necro-Utopia: The Politics of Indistinction and the Aesthetics of the Non-Soviet," 204.

32. Victor Mazin, "Cabinet of Necrorealism: Iufit and," in *Necrorealism: Contexts, History, Interpretations*, ed. Seth Graham (Pittsburgh, PA: Russian Film Symposium, 2001), 47.

33. "Cabinet of Necrorealism: Iufit and," 32.

34. Olesya Turkina, "Freedom and the West: Shifting Meaning in Post-Soviet Culture," *Apexart*, Conference in Rio de Janeiro July 2001. http://www.apexart.org/conference/Turkina.htm (accessed February 28, 2009).

35. Quoted in Vladimir Perts and Andrey Fomenko, "Kunstkammer," International Contemporary Art Network, http://www.c3.hu/ican.artnet.org/ican/text6491.html?id_text=79 (accessed February 10, 2009).

36. For more information, see Thomas Campbell, "Homosexuality as Device: Necrorealism and Neoacademism," and Thomas Campbell, "The Bioaesthetics of Evgenii Iufit," *KinoKultura*, http://www.kinokultura.com/2006/11-campbell.shtml (accessed March 6, 2009).

37. José Alaniz and Seth Graham, "Early Necrocinema in Context," in *Necrorealism: Contexts, History, Interpretations*, ed. Seth Graham, 14.

38. Yufit says that he is inspired by Surrealism, and that his films are a philosophical rather than biological exploration of death. For more information see Arthouse, "Evgenii Yufit." http://www.arthouse.ru/attachment.asp?id=634 (accessed March 17, 2009).

39. Ellen E. Berry and Anesa Miller-Pogacar, "A Shock Therapy of the Social Consciousness: The Nature and Cultural Function of Russian Necrorealism," *Cultural Critique* 34 (Autumn 1996), 200.

40. "Cabinet of Necrorealism: Iufit and," 39-40.

41. Gilles Deleuze and Felix Guattari describe the concept of becoming-animal as a process of killing all symbolism, metaphor and signification in favor of metamorphosis; to become animal is "to find a world of pure intensities where all forms come undone, as do all the significations, signifiers and signifieds, to the benefit of an unformed matter of deterritorialized flux, of nonsignifying signs." See *Kafka: Toward a Minor Literature* (Minneapolis: University of Minnesota Press, 1986), 13.

42. For more information on this theme in Yufit's films, see Thomas Campbell's "The Bioaesthetics of Evgenii Iufit."

43. *Specters of Marx,* 5-6.

44. Jean-Luc Nancy, *The Inoperative Community* (Minneapolis, MN: University of Minnesota Press: 1991), 9.

45. *Ibid.,* 13.

46. *Ibid.,* 15, 14.

47. Derrida offers a historical analysis of key political theorists to argue that politics has traditionally revolved around the friend-enemy binary. See Jacques Derrida, *The Politics of Friendship* (New York: Verso, 2005).

BIBLIOGRAPHY

Alaniz, José, and Seth Graham. "Early Necrocinema in Context." In *Necrorealism: Contexts, History, Interpretations*, edited by Seth Graham, 5-28. Pittsburgh, PA: Russian Film Symposium, 2001.

Arthouse. "Evgenii Yufit." http://www.arthouse.ru/attachment.asp?id=634.

Berry, Ellen E., and Anesa Miller-Pogacar. "A Shock Therapy of the Social Consciousness: The Nature and Cultural Function of Russian Necrorealism." *Cultural Critique* 34 (Autumn 1996): 185-203.

Campbell, Thomas. "The Bioaesthetics of Evgenii Iufit." *KinoKultura.* http://www.kinokultura.com/2006/11-campbell.shtml.

_____. "Homosexuality as Device: Necrorealism and Neoacademism." *Ante Projects* no. 5. http://www.anteprojects.com/FILES/Ante5_Campbell.pdf.

Debord, Guy. *The Society of the Spectacle.* New York: Zone Books, 1995.

Deleuze, Gilles, and Felix Guattari. *Kafka: Toward a Minor Literature.* Minneapolis, MN: University Minnesota Press, 1986.

Derrida, Jacques. *The Politics of Friendship.* New York: Verso, 2005.

_____. *Specters of Marx: The State of the Debt, the Work of Mourning and the New International.* New York: Routledge Classics, 2006.

Erjavec, Aleš. "Neue Slowenische Kunst – New Slovenian Art: Slovenia, Yugoslavia, Self-Management and the 1980s." In *Postmodernism and the Postsocialist Condition: Politicized Art under Late Socialism,* edited by Aleš Erjavec, 135-75. Berkeley, CA: University of California Press, 2003.

Groys, Boris. *Art Power.* Cambridge, MA: MIT Press, 2008.

Gržinić, Marina. "Neue Slowenische Kunst." *In Impossible Histories: Historical Avant-gardes, Neo-avant-gardes, and Post-avant-gardes in Yugoslavia, 1918-1991,* edited by Dubravka Đurić and Miško Šuvaković, 246-70. Cambridge, MA: MIT Press, 2003.

IRWIN. "NSK Garda." *Dictionary of War.* Multitude e.V. and Unfriendly Takeover Frankfurt/Munich/Graz/Berlin June 2006 – February 2007. http://dictionaryofwar.org/concepts/NSK_ GARDA.

Mazin, Victor. "Cabinet of Necrorealism: Iufit and." In *Necrorealism: Contexts, History, Interpretations,* edited by Seth Graham, 28-53. Pittsburgh: Russian Film Symposium, 2001.

Monroe, Alexei. *The Interrogation Machine: Laibach and NSK.* Cambridge, MA: MIT Press, 2005.

Nancy, Jean-Luc. *Being Singular Plural.* Stanford, CA: Stanford University Press, 2000.

_____. *The Inoperative Community.* Minneapolis: University of Minnesota Press, 1991.

NSK. *Neue Slowenische Kunst.* Los Angeles, CA: AMOK Books, 1991.

Paunović, Gordan. "Laibach's Homecoming." *The Wire,* December 1998.

Perts, Vladimir, and Andrey Fomenko. "Kunstkammer." International Contemporary Art Network. http://www.c3.hu/ican.artnet.org/ican/text6491.html?id_text=79.

The State of NSK. http://www.nskstate.com/index.php.

Turkina, Olesya. "Freedom and the West: Shifting Meaning in Post-Soviet Culture." *Apex-art.* Conference in Rio de Janeiro July 2001. http://www.apexart.org/conference/Turkina.htm.

Yurchak, Alexei. *Everything Was Forever, Until It Was No More: The Last Soviet Generation.* Princeton, NJ: Princeton University Press, 2006.

_____. "Necro-Utopia: The Politics of Indistinction and the Aesthetics of the Non-Soviet." *Current Anthropology* 49, no. 2 (April 2008): 199-224.

GLOBAL MEDIA AND NATIONAL VALUE: POSTSOCIALIST NEGOTIATIONS

ANIKÓ IMRE

1. Media Convergence and Nationalism

For those of us who have vivid memories of socialism, the transformations of the past two decades seem nothing short of seismic. Global economic, political, and cultural flows have not left a single corner of the former Soviet empire unaffected. The transformation of regional and national media cultures has been especially influential. It brought about the partial privatization and globalization of formerly state-owned television industries, the transnationalization of film production, the increasing digitalization of social exchange, an undeniable decline in the culture of reading, and the proliferation of audiovisual entertainment. The region's accelerated transition towards an information-processing, entertainment-saturated, consumerist culture has undermined the nation-state's hegemony over media and educational institutions and engendered new, more accessible, deterritorialized, mobile, and arguably more democratic forms of communication.

While these changes are occurring in ways specific to regional and national transitions, they are also part of larger-scale transformations that have been happening over a longer period of time in late-capitalist Western countries. The logic that propels media globalization has been recently described in terms of "convergence," most influentially by Henry Jenkins. In his book *Convergence Culture*, he offers his model of global convergence culture to be a shared platform between pessimistic accounts that decry the frightening global concentration of media ownership and celebratory accounts of emerging fan and consumer agency. Jenkins calls convergence an open-ended process that, at least in the U.S. and other global media centers, is being negotiated between, on one side, top-down corporate forces, who are looking to accelerate the flow of media content across delivery platforms to expand revenue and markets, and, on the other side, bottom-up, consumer-driven forces, which facilitate consumer interaction, inspire participation, and, presumably, empower the struggle for shared control over media content (Jenkins 2006).

Jenkins acknowledges that the rate of convergence is uneven within a given culture and even across cultures. Convergence privileges those individuals, communities, and nations who have the luxury of time and money to play. It is reasonable to conceptualize this unevenness in terms of the speed or degree of convergence, as Jenkins suggests. However, from a postsocialist point of view, we are dealing with more than a time lag, which creates a quantitative difference between have and have not nations, but which the have nots will eventually overcome. Instead of assuming such an inevitable and linear development, I think that a more subtle geopolitical map of convergence will reveal important qualitative divergences among and within different regions and nations. In postsocialist Eastern Europe, as in other globally marginal areas, the two-way negotiation between corporations and consumers is much more directly interrupted by the nation-state and mediated by more powerful discourses and representations of nationalism than is the case in the U.S. and even Western Europe.

This picture is complicated by the fact that media convergence in its specific postsocialist neoliberal forms is happening in the context of the region's staggered accession to the European Union. This means constant negotiations among at least four players: the nation-state, eager to represent the ongoing accession to the EU as a national project and part of historical destiny; the EU itself, invested in maintaining the appearance of European unity in diversity and downplaying the imperial division between core and peripheral member states; transnational media corporations, who are eager to turn Eastern and Southern Europe into a vast consumer market; and emerging grassroots groups, often seeking transnational affiliations to develop democratic media spaces. As John Downey puts it, the postsocialist media landscape is perhaps best seen as a patchwork of alliances and competition for legitimacy among these agents (Downey 1998, 49).

Some other regional tendencies are also evident. The gap between the perspectives, skills, and values of the generations who grew up under socialism and those for whom socialism is an inherited memory is exceptionally large. This gap poses particular challenges and causes great anxiety for political and cultural elites invested in guiding and controlling the next generation of national citizens, whose subjectivities are being shaped by radically new experiences. Within individual post-socialist nation-states, we are witnessing an intense negotiation over what qualifies as proper knowledges and values for the future of the nation. These negotiations are accompanied by a transition of power from intellectual and political elites to a much more dispersed set of constituencies. Converging media forms and technologies serve as both crucial platforms for and subjects of discussion over the decline of print-based national cultures, which have been thoroughly bound to national values represented by literature, particularly poetry.

However, converging media forms and technologies are also differentiated in the course of these negotiations according to their potential to serve as tools for building a democratic, national postsocialist public sphere. The national public sphere has an unspoken racialized, gendered, and sexualized dimension (Morley 2000, 105-126). I am interested in how this unspoken dimension is activated in the process of valuing various converging media forms and technologies. While all electronic media are viewed as possible threats to postsocialist national cultures, the Internet and new media technologies are assigned a higher, or at least more ambivalent value than television. Global television programming such as reality shows are associated with foreign, feminized, and even racially "contaminated" entertainment, which is perceived as posing a threat to postsocialist cultures. In the following, I take a closer look at how anxieties about the encroachment of global entertainment media and its new technologies on national culture clash and combine with euphoria over the democratizing potential of new technologies, European mobility, and transnational exchange in the course of negotiations over national value.

2. *The National Value of the Internet and New Media Technologies*
"Catching up with Europe"—a goal shared by postsocialist nations— has been understood to involve not only a political transformation that brings about democracy but also a way to become part of a powerful economic network, which would provide protection from threatening transnational processes of globalization. Uncontested and accelerated technological development has been seen by postsocialist states as one of the winning tickets to joining Europe. Therefore, many policy makers, educators, and scholars (especially in the sciences) celebrate modernist

progress represented by information and communication technology. There are also critical voices, who distrust the Internet and other new media as tools of American imperialism and worry that the visually-oriented, entertainment-focused, non-linear kind of learning that these media encourage undermines the values of language-based rationality, literature, and history on which national culture has hinged from the start. Such critics have adopted the tone of alarm Neil Postman raised in the U.S. in the 1980s to lament that children are rapidly being trans-formed from readers into "vidiots" (Domokos 2004; Horvath 2000, pp. 92-93). The unprecedented degree of visual information that has largely replaced the centrally censored media culture of communism is often represented in Hungarian education and culture journals, for instance, as a threat to children's skills and identities, as the "child's disease" of our time. In this scheme, the (American) audiovisual overload overwhelms kids' (supposedly uncontaminated, pure) imagination and renders the new generations forever immature and childish—in implied opposition to the mature, rational citizen of a European nation.

The commitment to modern European technological progress and the insistence on high cultural, print-based values regarded as part of the European heritage converge in the desire to save and strengthen national cultures. Both approaches favor the same narrow pool of agents—white men of some national power. Both oversimplify the complexity of the Internet's and new media technologies' effects on populations that are much more heterogeneous than the narrow confines of the nationalist approach would allow.

In fact, the Internet introduces a new, transnational playing field that is much less bound by territorial divisions. On the one hand, its pen-etration has brought new freedoms and opportunities for civic activism and artistic expression; on the other hand, it has undeniably enhanced class divides and the extent of corporate takeover. The European Union's role in wiring the new and prospective member states is crucial in this regard. The European Commission's 1997 Green Paper envisions a Europe-wide "information society" devoted to promoting civic dis-course and democratic participation (Horvath 2000, 78). This directive, as John Horvath notes, rests on the problematic assumption that civic discourse did not exist under communism, when media was entirely dominated by propaganda. This was far from true. It is evident, however, that promoting technological "progress" in the East is accompanied by a certain Western missionary fervor and rests on an unconditional faith in consumerist democracy (Horvath 2000, p. 85).

There are some other obstacles to a politically progressive utilization of the Internet and new media technologies. One is the enduring and increasing economic differences within the region, which have created "fast" and "slow" lanes of technological development (86). The speed of technologization depends to a great extent on the attention of investors such as George Soros and his Open Society Institute, which has singlehandedly re-written the technological map of the region. Internet service providers often follow outdated business practices, which are hindered by state-run telecommunication firms (92-93). Another obstacle is an enduring "island mentality," a general fear of engaging in Internet-based civic activism out of a historically internalized caution, which sees change as risky and shies away from experimentation and play (97). In "fast-lane" postsocialist countries such as Hungary, Poland, the Czech Republic, Slovenia, or the Baltic states, the Internet has greatly contributed to breaking down artificially erected walls between practical and theoretical knowledge, the humanities and the sciences, teaching and research, and institutional and non-institutional learning (Nyíri 1997). Increasing broadband access has helped to undermine the long-held division between high and low culture while also prioritizing new cognitive competencies, selection and problem-solving skills. At the same time, the rapid colonization of virtually virginal postsocialist media and information technology markets by transnational corporations should make one very cautious about the democratizing potential of the Internet and other interactive digital technologies. For the most part, the corporate transformation of the postsocialist media landscape has been welcomed by nation-states aspiring to share in the economic and ideological profits and has been wrapped in EU-phoria over an expanding European audiovisual sphere that can stand up to competition with U.S.-based and Asian media and communication industries.

Moreover, despite increasing technological access, nationalistic mechanisms of cultural gatekeeping restrict political uses of the Internet by a wide array of constituencies. Such a mechanism works to determine public national value for the media and divide the select few capable of and entitled to creating such value from the rest, who are relegated to the position of grateful national audiences or, worse, unworthy consumers. As I elaborate in relation to the globalization of the television industry, the principles of selection are motivated by, and naturalize, Eurocentric nationalisms, which work through unspoken but no less violent mechanisms of homophobia, misogyny, racism, ethnocentrism, and xenophobia.

3. Global Television and National Culture

In Western Europe, television emerged after World War II in the service of national cultures and under the control of nation-states. National broadcasters have carried an uncontested public service broadcasting (PSB) remit or followed a mixed PSB-commercial model until recently. Programming has privileged a liberal, romantic-modernist quality associated with balanced news and high art, driven by the author-director's creative vision (Nelson 2007, 39). Such high-minded, pedagogical beginnings, best exemplified by John Reith's ambitions to bring high culture to the masses, were redirected somewhat as early as 1955, when the BBC adopted a more popular programming strategy similar to those of commercial channels (Nelson 2007, 40).

The global deregulation and convergence of the television industry, which began in the 1980s, gradually undermined both public service broadcasters' status as carriers of national values and the very national character of broadcasting. The emergence of satellite and cable delivery radically increased the number of channels available and opened the way to transnational and niche programming. Technological innovation and improved production features such as high resolution, a dynamic and rapid editing style, and digital post-production allowed a cinematic look and attracted film directors to television (Nelson 2007, 43; Meinhof 1999, 71). These changes have favored large, mostly U.S.-based companies and disadvantaged smaller, national broadcasters. The current highly competitive, increasingly commercial global environment has also released a need for distinctive programming (Meinhof 1999, 49). Within the European Union, "quality" and "value" have become key terms in projections about the future of broadcasting. The growing tension between a cherished but increasingly obsolete national public service broadcasting culture and the new qualities introduced by global popular programming, often targeting specific micro-audiences, is most evident in the recent debates about redefining European cultural values and quality.

The decisive policy document of these debates, the Television Without Frontiers directive, points towards a globally competitive European audiovisual area integrated primarily on commercial ground and curtails the legacy of nation-based PSB, which requires protectionist policies. Two kinds of future projections vie in contemporary Europe: an optimistic one, which welcomes the increase in programming choice and points to the continuing market for high-quality production; and a pessimistic one, which sees ever more cheap programming of dubious quality flooding European cultures. The latter view is deeply rooted in the cultural pessimism of the Frankfurt school and of Matthew Arnold, F. R. Leavis, and Richard Hoggart—a legacy that links television with "bad" culture (Meinhof 1999, 121).

The future of a public national interest tied to European high art and culture, widely seen to be threatened within Western Europe by market principles, is the most volatile in postsocialist Eastern Europe. Nation-states in this region are joining the European struggle between commercial and state-regulated television systems after having followed a very different path of development. Under Soviet-style socialism, television was controlled by, and directly served the political goals of, communist parties. After the collapse of the Soviet empire, regimes all over the region set out to build democratic public spheres, where PSB in the Western European tradition would play a central role in ensuring a pluralism of voices and an effort to support national languages and cultures (Vadic 2004; Stetka 2002). Such an ambition was invariably undermined, however, by cash-strapped economies in need of commercial investment by transnational media corporations and by the resurgence of right-wing nationalisms driving party leadership, often in ways that border on direct censorship and control. The economic and the political mutually and inseparably infuse each other in the postsocialist media regimes (Sparks and Reading 1994), resulting in what has been variously called a system of national corporatism (Vadic 2004), paternalist commercialism, or political capitalism (Splichal 2000).

In the struggle over media power between the state, markets, and EU directives, certain issues are always viewed as more urgent while others remain off the agenda. Research on television and the media in general has tended to concentrate on questions of the national public sphere and media regulation. Whereas this approach is understandably important, it carries two, mutually related problems. First, it takes for

granted the continued authority and primacy of the nation-state in negotiation with corporations and the European Union. While policy-oriented
approaches do occasionally evoke a civil society made up of a composite
of different voices as an ideal, they do so in an abstract, top-down, normative fashion, keeping these identities ultimately contained within and
subordinated to the interests of their respective nation-states and national
communities. Second, such an inquiry renders less relevant and even
suppresses alternative questions, especially those that concern programming content, audience engagement, and issues of ideology, which may
undermine the national framework. As a result, the transformations that
new, popular programming, accessed via rapidly changing technologies,
are effecting in people's everyday interactions, memories, and identities
remain disconnected from the scholarly analyses and debates waged on
the supposedly shared platform of an idealized, abstract, and homo-
geneously national public.

This disconnect is inseparable from the crisis of authority that postsocialist intellectuals are experiencing. While intellectuals have been
traditionally privileged and expected to speak for an allegedly unified
national public, now that public is being fragmented into groups and is
directly addressed by ratings-driven media, most evidently in reality
shows (Jenei 2006). The globalization of the media, television in particular, threatens the centralized, normative judgments about cultural value
that intellectuals have traditionally been empowered to issue from a
position somewhere outside of ideology, charged with an educational
mission to propagate good taste. Now the criteria for establishing what is
good taste are being challenged by what is pleasurable, understood in
terms of the viewer appeal of *Big Brother*, telenovelas, and *24*.
Dismissing these shows as signs of harmful American commercialism—
following and augmenting a West European pattern—does not prevent
audiences from choosing to watch them, even if these preferences are
not publicly condoned.

Much of East European media criticism—which employs standards
derived from festival-worthy art films—is obsessively devoted to ridi-
culing talk shows, reality shows, and all those who produce and participate in them. Speaking about Hungarian society, but in a manner
generalizable across post-Soviet cultures, Hungarian media sociologist
Lajos Császi calls the top-down intellectual tradition of judgment
exercised by teachers, politicians, and cultural experts profoundly pater-

nalistic (Jenei 2006). As in the case of the Internet and digital interactive technologies, this nationalistic gatekeeping isolates local cultures from practices and theories of global television. A number of media scholars have recently proposed that the globalization and commercialization of television has rendered the hierarchical separation between national citizenship and televisual entertainment untenable. New kinds of citizenship are forming around TV watching, creating a "fan democracy" (van Zoonen 2004) of television viewers, or "normal citizens" (Ellis 1982), whose activities take place in the sphere of "democratainment" (Hartley 2004). John Hartley argues that television citizenship challenges the boundaries of traditional political theory, which typically sees citizenship as something prior to, separate from, and eroded by media consumption (Hartley 2004). Liesbet van Zoonen goes even further when she claims that the interactive consumption afforded by public voting on programs such as the British-inspired *Pop Idol* and the Dutch-originated *Big Brother* can be seen as civic processes taking place in the public space, where entertainment and politics are inseparable (van Zoonen 2004, 40). Interactive formats have mobilized audiences to participate, intervene, judge, and vote—even if the stakes of these negotiations remain unavoidably trivial. Fandom is creating communities that behave like ideal, consensus-building political constituencies, with a range of investments in their causes. Furthermore, despite political scientists' insistence on the rational decision-making involved in civic activities, in both politics and fandom it is the participants' emotional investment and the development of affective intelligence that drives activity (Van Zoonen 2004). Nick Couldry also urges us to break with the model of the passive media consumer holed up in an individual, virtual bubble, and reconnect otherwise isolated areas of consumption and citizenship (Couldry 2004, pp. 21-23). He sets out to investigate hybrid objects of research, which cross the "real digital divide" between the languages of markets and politics. This division hides the participatory production practices of consumers, which generate and sustain new spaces of public connection. Moving away from large-scale models of network activity toward local resistance, Couldry is interested in subnational or other local networks that initiate public interaction related to consumption and which should be studied in international comparative research (27). Similar to Hartley, he wants to foreground the continuities between new, global and older, state-centered forms of citizenship (28).

This point is particularly relevant in Europe's postsocialist countries, where nation-states have remained active negotiators over media ownership and where media citizenship is channeled through powerful, affective ties to national languages and cultures. Studies of postsocialist media, politics, and identities are very much mired in the traditional frameworks, which position citizenship as prior to and necessarily damaged by media relations (Hartley 2004, p. 524). Van Zoonen's proposition that emotional involvement is the link between participation in public politics and television fandom should also help redirect attention from top-down, elite cultural forms and controls to the affective activities of ordinary citizens in TV land in an era of what George E. Marcus calls "affective citizenship" (Marcus 2002).

However, due the limited financial capacities of both state and small commercial production and distribution companies in the region, which force them into package deals with large transnational corporations, postsocialist television is inundated with (primarily American) imports. The local production consists of reality formats and newly transplanted varieties of established genres such as soap operas. Television programming as a whole, therefore, has a derivative, awkward quality. State-controlled channels only contribute to this alienation, for their programming is widely—and correctly—perceived to serve the political agendas of ruling parties. Therefore, the idea and practice of television fandom is something rather foreign in Eastern Europe. The postsocialist situation underscores the relevance of Daniel Dayan's question: Under what conditions could TV audiences actually become publics (Dayan 2001)? In the last section, I ponder this question via a brief case study of the national reception of a particularly controversial recent TV series, the Hungarian *Győzike Show* (RTL Klub, 2005-).

4. *What Can We Learn about National Culture from Global Television Trash?*

The *Győzike Show* is set in Hungary and revolves around Roma pop singer Győző Gáspár and his family. The series has been a massive audience success and, at the same time, an object of wide criticism and ridicule. Its reception teems with contradictions that raise important issues about television's national significance. The absence of critical attempts to understand the contradictions embedded in the *Győzike Show* and the responses to it is symptomatic: While those who are well-versed in the (English) language of television and cultural theory have no access to or little interest in the complexities of a Roma celebrity docu-soap, those who speak the local languages are eager to distance themselves from a doubly demonized association with, on the one hand, forms of commercial television generally deemed unhealthy for national culture and, on the other, with ethnic minorities deemed parasitic with respect to the national body.

Native cultural critics generally despise commercial television for its affective appeal, its perceived reduction of a print-based national culture to audiovisual infotainment, its derivative, "foreign" practices and forms, and its overall "feminizing" effect on its audiences. Romany Studies scholars tend to be similarly dismissive of television. They operate with a somewhat anachronistic and idealized image of the Gypsy unaffected by contemporary popular culture and tend to turn their ethnographic eye, instead, towards the authentic, folk Gypsy. However, native critics, along with the often overtly racist and not so silent moral majority, have targeted the "savage" in the Gypsy image conjured up by the show, whereas Romany Studies scholars have, for the most part, quietly ignored the show because of the supposedly "tarnishing" impact the program makes on the "noble" Roma image.

The recent rise of Roma celebrities across the region does not fit into either images of the "cultural" Roma or of those of the poor, struggling Roma. A wealthy Roma family who do not keep to strict Roma traditions to star in a reality show in Hungary may seem like an unlikely success story. Figures from the RTL group's Annual Report 2005 show that *Győzike* featured nine times in the top 20 most popular programmes in Hungary in 2005[1], with an audience share average rating of 46.1% amongst adults 18-49 years of age.[2] *Győzike* airs on Hungary's most successful commercial channel, RTL Klub. It is based on the U.S. program *The Osbournes* (MTV, 2002-2004), which followed rock star Ozzy Osbourne and his family in their everyday lives. The weekly 90-minute primetime reality show, which airs at 9 pm on Monday nights, began in February 2005, promising a series that would contain 8 episodes focusing on the family's everyday life. Three years later, in June 2008, the show finished its eighth season, with stories about the family appearing consistently on the front pages of the tabloid press throughout the show's airing.

The Hungarian public and the media's reaction to the show has been a love/hate relationship—or, rather, a love-to-hate relationship. Győzike and his wife Bea were voted favourite TV personalities in 2008 by the readers of the Hungarian celebrity gossip magazine *Hot*. At the same time, in a wider survey of 15-69-year-olds, the stars were voted the least liked celebrities in Hungary.[3] Győzike's prominent media presence has brought, according to Roma activist and media presenter János Daróczi, "severe disadvantage to the Hungarian Roma" through their bad example: "I must send a message to everybody: we, the Roma, are not like that" (quoted in Kürti 2008, 16).

The reason for the show's extreme reception has less to do with its inherent aesthetic value than with its potential to set off profound anxieties about what constitutes national culture. The show threatens long-held distinctions between high (normative) and popular culture, the national majority and the Roma, native/state and commercial/global/ American culture. I analyze here two distinct kinds of audience responses, as a way to comment on the role global popular television formats play in ethnic and national identifications in contemporary Hungary and, by extension, the broader postsocialist region: the first are online audience reactions in the form of blogs, discussion lists, and other informal and anonymous commentary. The second are reviews and reflections published in print newspapers, magazines, and journals that speak on behalf of the "value norms" in Hungarian culture.

5. *"Fan" Reactions*

"They are not humans…. They stink up the whole country. Why don't they get the hell out of here at last? I'd like to drown all the black kids and sterilize all the women to stop them from reproducing. They are like cockroaches. Even their names are disgusting…. I wish they were all eaten by cancer, from the smallest newborn to the oldest stinking Gypsy. Death to them!!!!!!!!"[4]

This is a typical selection from the last six months of postings on the fan forum of the show's official website. There are about 2,500 posts altogether. For a series that is so eagerly and universally watched, it has hardly any fans, or at least very few who would defend it in public. Even the self-identified Roma posters tend to dismiss it as a program about "show Roma," who give the entire minority a bad name. The degree of hatred and fear revealed by the posts, replicated by thousands of other reactions in various other discussions, is rightly shocking to Western liberal ears. The comments almost parodically reproduce patterns of ethnonationalism successfully erased from the Western vocabulary of politically correct talk about minorities: the Roma are lazy and repugnant parasites who shun work and drain collective resources. Their excessive procreation contaminates the pristine national body and threatens the survival of the rightful majority. These discourses are routinely encouraged by state and local politicians' suggestions and policies, which are often just barely more subtle in their racism than the quotations above.

It is remarkable that a commercial television show's fan forum provides the space for such venting of frustrations redirected against the Roma over the shared anxieties about globalization, whose main threat is seen to regard the survival of national culture. Whereas some have claimed that fan communities may become spaces of mobilization for political expression, and even alternative, affective public spheres in media and communication studies, such arguments always face one very substantial objection, namely, that the mobilization built around fandom hardly ever transgresses the boundaries of a television series, cast, or auteur. The outpouring of opinions around the *Győzike Show*, ironically, does the opposite: commentators tend to ignore what actually happens on the show and focus on its status as a social text, on its significance for the national community. These online responses constitute precisely the kinds of televisual, mediated, affective public spaces suppressed in the Habermasian (ideal of) the national and rational public sphere.

Even though they could be dismissed as ignorant and racist rants, most such reflections nevertheless issue commentary on larger issues of race, gender, and the uneasy relations between national and global identities. They manifest what Appadurai calls the predatory identities unleashed by globalization. He defines predatory identities as those whose social construction and mobilization depend on extinguishing other, similar social identities, which are seen as threats to the very existence of the first "we" (Appadurai 2006, 51). As he writes, "predatory identities emerge, periodically, out of pairs of identities, sometimes sets that are larger than two, which have long histories of close contact, mixture, and some degree of mutual stereotyping. Occasional violence may or may not be parts of these histories, but some degree of contrastive identification is always involved. One of these pairs or sets of identities often turns predatory by mobilizing an understanding of itself as a threatened majority" (51).

Appadurai's argument aptly explains the excessive resentment towards celebrity TV Roma in terms of the narcissism of minor differences. He takes up this Freudian concept to argue that globalization induces a deep anxiety about the national project and turns nationalistic identities predatory. Minorities' mixed status, languages, and ambiguity in relation to national citizenship, their movement across borders, and their financial transactions all blur the boundaries of the nation and render minorities flash points where social tensions about globalization are released. When minorities are wealthy, they evoke the threat of elite globalization. When they are poor, they are seen as symbols of failed forms of development and welfare. Ideas of nation and peoplehood tend to rely on ethnic purity and suppress memories and experiences of plurality; instead, ethnic minorities obscure the boundaries of national peoplehood and inadvertently foreground the failure of many countries to achieve economic sovereignty under the compromised circumstances of neoliberal globalization, which puts considerable strain on states to serve as trustees of the interests of territorially defined majorities (2006, 44-5).

Győzike and his family evoke both the poor, welfare-bound ghost of the enemy within and the threat of a wealthy transnational network. This dual menace is exacerbated when they appear on commercial TV and become identified as creatures of an emasculating media regime of entertainment seen as the enemy of national culture, feminizing and racializing at once. As a celebrity television Roma in a nation-state where national political and economic sovereignty has remained an unfulfilled promise, Győzike is a glaring reminder of the problematic nature of the classical national project.

6. *Critical Responses*

The *Győzike Show* must be the only television program in the world where the press reviews section on the program's own website, normally a vehicle of promotion, consists entirely of negative echoes. Reflections in national critical journals, radio, television, and online publications, which constitute a normative public sphere, are invariably outraged about the show's "quality" and "values." However, while "fan" responses by ordinary viewers target the ethnic minority with which Győzike and his family are identified, professional commentators tend to tone down the racist edge of their criticism and focus instead on the show itself as the flagship of an alarming downward trend in national culture in general and television in particular.

While the worries about commercializing the public sphere are legitimate and the lifestyle and emotional intelligence models displayed on the show are hardly wholesome by any standards, a number of assumptions remain unreflected in this hierarchical assessment—assumptions that bound together official criticism and fan responses much more intimately than it seems. In fact, the explicit anti-Roma racism of predatory identities and the worry about the decline of print-based, rational national culture headed by a literate, national elite are two sides of the same coin. In their shared, nationalistic anxiety over hybridity and mixing, they are more similar than their differences in terms of style and critical objectivity regarding the issues at stake would lead us to believe. Racist bloggers tend to equate Győzike with real Gypsies and personalize their attacks through their own "experiences" with the Roma. "Intellectual" critics, who would certainly resent charges of latent racism or discrimination against minorities, tend to interpret, abstract, and judge, while eliding their own personal investment and masquerading as rightful embodiments of collective norms. Their indignation and dismissal shift away from the protagonists and the minority they represent onto the medium and the genre. However, the threat of cultural heterogeneity and "miscegenation" allegedly presented by the suspect transnational ethnic minority and the threat of transnational television genres converge in the perception that they both target national culture, whether national culture is seen in terms of ethnonationally homogeneous family ties or of Eurocentric cultural values.[5]

The focus on the "doomed" state of national culture serves to increase the distance between "the masses," mesmerized by "bad" TV, and the shrinking number of those blessed with absolute aesthetic and moral sense. It also relieves intellectuals of the responsibility to build pedagogical bridges between "high" and "popular" cultural forms. One critic acknowledges this blatantly: "With the appearance of commercial

television, it has become clear what the Hungarian television viewer
needs." And, "you cannot expect quality from commercial television
stations. I don't even think that a critic who writes for intellectual
journals should write about the horrific programs of commercial television.... The interests of those who read criticism—or those who read at
all—and the interests of TV viewers don't coincide.... I'd like to believe
that we are not quite the way we think of ourselves based on all this:
indifferent, poor and subsequently cynical; and shockingly tasteless. I'd
like to believe [this]" (Kolozsi 2005).

The outrage over—along with the fascination with—the *Győzike
Show* stems from the sense of profound change that such a thing as a
Roma celebrity docusoap signals. This transformation involves inter-
secting shifts in normative class, racial, gendered, and national identities
within a globalizing and Europeanizing environment. In class terms,
Győzike is a threat to traditional notions of national culture because it
represents the emergence of an inherently heterogeneous, middle-class
cultural and economic concept. *Győzike* sets off especially intense
anxieties because the show poses a threat to the implicit racial and gendered parameters of intellectual exceptionalism. Two central, unspoken
components of this exceptionalism are whiteness and masculinity. The
liberal sympathy that public intellectuals have long displayed for Hungary's single visible racial minority has at once solidified and occluded
the racialized aspect of this one-directional, hierarchical relationship. No
wonder *Győzike* is often unfavorably compared with "proper" ways of
representing Gypsies such as nostalgic documentaries about victimized,
poor Roma (Örkeny 2005; Bori 2005). The implication is that the true
Roma is a victim whose social position is fixed, unchangeable, and can
only be sympathetically revealed through the hard work of those who are
able to see, understand, and show. This attitude is not essentially different from the racism of those who openly charge Gypsies with backwardness and unwillingness to "assimilate." Gypsies are tolerable on reality
shows as long as they are passive victims for whose exploitation the
medium alone can be blamed (Kolozsi 2005; Schubert 2007; Fáy 2001;
Varró 2005; Darab 2008).

Győzike and East European reality shows generally always remind
their viewers of the inferior and precarious status of their nations. Such
implicit comparisons are repeatedly performed in critical responses. A
Roma man appearing on a "debased" media's most infantile and

melodrama-prone kind of programming, Győzike himself embodies the most embarrassing version of East European national identity. There is no saving grace here. The figures of gendering and infantilization in which anxieties about *Győzike* are often expressed are coupled with worries about the nation's image. Veronika Koncz, for example, is in disbelief watching "this man," especially in the first season finale's trip to Turkey, an outpost of Europe and a country even farther from full European legitimation than Hungary. She hopes that Turkey will not make the same mistake Hungary made when joining the EU as it brought with it the baggage of shame *Győzike* represents. "There's still hope" for Istanbul, she writes (Koncz 2005).

But the intellectual distancing from anxieties over the national image is belied by the show's popularity, which, in all likelihood, derives precisely from its ability to externalize national anxieties. The reality show format is an especially apt way to perform traumatic citizenship. In a culture where public emotional expression has been suppressed by decades, if not centuries, of collective trauma, and where, especially during socialism, the familial was a hidden and private fortress, Győzike and his family also provide a collective outlet with their unrestrained expressions of anger and sentimentality. In fact, the show's popularity probably resides in its familiarity as much as in its shock value. The protagonists' interactions, daily troubles, and arguments constitute a widespread pattern of intimacy within the context of the national family.

Furthermore, if reality shows are meant to teach and set up norms for "proper," responsible neoliberal class conduct, Győzike's unapologetic celebration of irresponsibility evokes a mix of anxiety and celebration. In fact, the show associates irresponsibility with respectability. This respectability does not require the kind of cultural capital derived from Eurocentric national values. Győzike does not need education, does not need to control his emotions, and does not even need to speak proper Hungarian to be successful and therefore respectable. He embodies the entrepreneurial individual who makes the most of wild, postsocialist neoliberal conditions but who also continues to stand for the collective.

Within the confusing circumstances of the postsocialist transition where no reliable predictions can be made about the region's future, the *Győzike Show* provides an ambivalent template for the changing nation. Whereas in the West the middle-class viewers addressed by reality shows easily distance themselves from the abject spectacle of trauma-tized individuals in need of televisual sympathy, charity, and assistance, in East European national cultures the distance between viewer and spectacle is reduced and occluded. It can only be re-crystallized in racial terms by foregrounding Győzike's Roma difference, a difference constructed and performed on the show for commercial purposes. In turn, however, such efforts at distancing are undermined by Győzike's economic success.

7. Conclusion

The advent of converging global media forms and technologies has profoundly altered hierarchies of cultural and cognitive authority in the postsocialist region. Nation-states and intellectual elites are losing the power to determine national cultural value to economically profitable transnational media forms such as Internet sites and television formats, whose appeal to consumers is more direct and renders intellectual and political mediation secondary. These changes would seem to push in the direction of a democratic and pluralistic cultural opening. However, instead of entering the happy cosmopedia of fan democracies, citizens of the New Europe are experiencing a selective process of media globalization. Rather than helping to build a sense of civic responsibility on the ruins of socialist apathy towards politics, this transformation may even discourage political participation. There is no automatic equivalent of the active, politically conscious democratic consumer in the political wasteland left over by socialism, which European integration aims further to depoliticize and tame into a market for media entertainment and tourism. In addition, subtle forms of exclusion and control remain embedded in otherwise useful critiques of media globalization issued by postsocialist intellectuals. The refusal of trash, the rejection of American cultural imperialism, the call for state or EU monitoring of media content, and the unexamined preference for a literary, high culture are often grounded in restrictive and reactionary forms of nationalism, Eurocentrism, and cultural imperialism. While of a different kind, this attitude tends to be no less uncritical than the equation of technological innovation with progress.

NOTES

1. RTL Group Annual Report 2005, available via RTL Group web page, http://www.rtlgroup.com/files/AR2005_RTLGroup_COMPLETE.pdf [accessed 16/02/ 2007].
2. RTL Group audited results year ended 31 December 2005. Document available via RTL Group web page http://www.rtlgroup.com/files/Full_Audited_Results_Doc_ 15032006doc.pdf [accessed 16/02/2007].
3. See the magazine: *Hot Top 100 Sztár: A száz legfontosabb magyar híresség* (2008/1).
4. http://forum.sg.hu/forum.php3?azonosito=gyozike.
5. A well-respected cultural critic, for instance, talks about "parasite media" in his regular columns in the high-brow Hungarian literary and cultural journal *Élet és irodalom*. The primary example of parasite media happens to be the *Győzike Show*. See Péter György, "A hír." *Élet és irodalom* 49.22, June 3, 2005. (http://www.es.hu/pd/display.asp?channel= MUBIRALAT0522&article=2005-0605-2241-12PHRS).

BIBLIOGRAPHY

Appadurai, Arjun. 2006. *Fear of Small Numbers: An Essay on the Geography of Anger.* Durham and London: Duke University Press.

Bori, Erzsebet. 2005. "Cigányutak. Roma Dokumentumfilm." *Filmvilág* 2005: 6. http://www.filmvilag.hu/xista_frame.php?cikk_id=8270.

Couldry, Nick. 2004. "The Productive 'Consumer' and the 'Dispersed Citizen.'" *International Journal of Cultural Studies* 7(1): 21-32.

Darab Zsuzsa. 2008. "Pop, Tabu, Satöbbi: A Hét főbün a televízióban." *Filmvilág* 2008: 2 http://www.filmvilag.hu/xista_frame.php?cikk_id=9262.

Dayan, Daniel. 2001. "The Peculiar Publics of Television." *Media, Culture and Society* 23(6): 743-67.

Downey, John. 1998. "Full of Eastern Promise? Central and Eastern European Media After 1989." in *Electronic Empires: Global Media and Local Resistance*, ed. Daya Kishan Thussu, 47-62. London: Arnold.

Fáy, András. 2001. Mónika, avagy a buta ország. *Élet és Irodalom* 45(23) http://www.es. hu/index.php?view=doc;3445.

Hartley, John. 2004. "Democratainment." In *The Television Studies Reader*, ed. Robert C. Allen and Annette Hill, pp. 524-533. London: Routledge.

Horvath, John. 2000. "Alone in the Crowd: The Politics of Cybernetic Isolation." In *Culture and Technology in the New Europe*, ed. Laura Engel, pp. 77-103. Stamford, CT: Ablex Publishing.

Jenei, Ágnes. 2006. "Neotelevízió: válság vagy megújulás?" (interview with Lajos Császi and István Síklaki). *Médiakutató*, Spring 2006. http://www.mediakutato.hu/cikk/ 2006_01_tavasz/03_neotelevizio/01.html.

Jenkins, Henry. 2006. *Convergence Culture: Where Old and New Media Collide.* New York and London: New York University Press.

Kolozsi, László. 2005. "Smink nelkul: kultura a kepernyon." *Filmvilág* 2005:5. http://www. filmvilag.hu/xista_frame.php?cikk_id=8258

Koncz, Veronika. 2005. "Lapszél: Európa, országimázs, Győzike." *Uj Ember* 61(25) http://ujember.katolikus.hu/Archivum/2005.06.19/0305.html

250 *Global Media and National Value*

Kürti, László. 2008. "Media Wars: Cultural Dialogue and Conflict in Hungarian Popular Broadcasting." SUSDIV paper, 8 January 2008, from the Fondazione Eni Enrico Mattei Series Index. http://www.feem.it/Feem/Pub/Publications/EURODIVpapers/default.htm

Marcus, George E. 2002. *The Sentimental Citizen: Emotion in Democratic Politics.* University Park, PA: The Pennsylvania State University Press.

Meinhof, Ulrike. 1999. *Worlds in Common? Television Discourse in a Changing Europe.* Routledge, London.

Morley, David. 2000. *Home Territories: Media, Mobility and Identity.* London: Routledge.

Nelson, Robin. 2007. "Quality TV Drama: Estimations and Influences Through Time and Space." In *Quality Television: Contemporary American Television and Beyond,* eds. Janet McCabe and Kim Akass, pp. 38-51. London: I. B. Tauris.

Nyíri, László. 1997. "A számítógép hatása az iskolára." ("The Influence of Computers on Schools."). *Educatio* no. 4 (1997). www.neumann-haz.hu/tei/education/educatio/1997tel/studies/hu.prt.

Örkeny, Antal. 2005. "Cigány film vagy romafilm? A Dallastól a Nyóckerig." *Filmvilág* 2005: 6. http://www.filmvilag.hu/xista_frame.php?cikk_id=8271.

Schubert, Gusztáv. 2007. "Mauni-ka. Hetperces sztárok." *Filmvilág* 2007:3. http://www.filmvilag.hu/xista_frame.php?cikk_id=8916.

Sparks, Colin, and Anna Reading. 1994. "Understanding Media Change in East-Central Europe." *Media, Culture and Society* 16(2): 243-270.

Splichal, Slavko. 2000. "Reproducing Political Capitalism in the Media of East-Central Europe." *Media Research* 6(1): 5-19.

Stetka, Václav. 2002. "The Czech Nation in front of the Screen: Defining the Public Sphere through National Broadcasting." Paper presented at The Contours of Legitimacy in Central Europe conference, European Studies Centre, St. Antony's College. Oxford, 24-26 May 2002. http://users.ox.ac.uk/~oaces/conference/papers/ Vaclav_Stetka.pdf.

Vađić, Maja. 2004. "Television Broadcasting in Eastern Europe: How Much Has Changed After the 1989 Revolutions?" *Media Research* 10 (1): 23-37. http://209.85.173.132/search?q=cache:Tfvv8qErmXkJ:hrcak.srce.hr/file/36249+television+broadcasting+in+eastern+europe&hl=en&ct=clnk&cd=5&gl=us&client=safari.

Varr, Szilvia. 2005. "Romák a képernyön. Sötét hírek." *Filmvilág* 2005: 6. http://www.filmvilag.hu/xista_frame.php?cikk_id=8272.

Zoonen, Liesbet van. 2004. "Imagining the Fan Democracy." *European Journal of Communication* 19 (1): 39-52.

LOVE GAME:
EAST EUROPEAN ATHLETES AND
THE CULTURE OF GLOBAL CELEBRITY

PHYLLIS WHITMAN HUNTER

I believe great people have no nationality.
Only little people fight over borders.
— Vasif Iruizou, 2005[1]

Sport may be the quintessence of nationalism on many occasions, but
it is also one of the most effective means yet devised of uniting the
global village.
— *Guardian* [Manchester, U.K.], 1994[2]

In 2005, when the winning Croatian Davis Cup tennis team returned
home to Zagreb, a huge crowd welcomed them. The light rain and dark
clouds did little to dampen the enthusiasm of the tens of thousands
gathered in the main square of the city. Confetti and flares brightened the
grey skies. Schools closed and business came to a standstill as the nation
celebrated its achievement. Team captain Niki Pilic summed up the
nationalistic fervor: "What's important is the feeling in my own people
we won it. This is for us an historic moment."[3] Croatia's winning of the
Davis Cup, the highest national team prize in tennis, symbolized the
improbable emergence of a gifted generation of world-class athletes in
certain regions of Eastern Europe (in tennis, a generation is more like ten
rather than twenty-five years). Rising like a phoenix not from the
burning nest of its forbearer but from the burning ruins of the towns and
cities of the former Yugoslavia have come a number of players who
have astonished the tennis world in the last decade.[4]

Sports are certainly a part of the globalizing process—a powerful
means of forming a sense of connection across geographic and cultural
divides. Sports contests and the athletes that participate in them form a
common component in the global imaginary, although one often
dismissed by academics and politicians as banal, trivial, or mere enter-

tainment. Yet some of us remember how the unmatched cultural anthropologist Clifford Geertz used a sport—Balinese cockfighting (a dubious
sport perhaps)—to peel back layer after layer and reveal that sport and
the betting on its outcomes as the very center of cultural negotiations
about power and masculinity on Bali.[5] I suspect the same could be done
for many of our favorite sports today; not only are athletic competitions
central to constructions of power and gender, but in some cases such as
auto racing and bullfighting they become a matter of life and death.

Sports developed as an arena for nationalistic contestation in the
Victorian era according to Eric Hobsbawm's study of the "invention of
tradition." As Hobsbawm argued, the last three decades of the nineteenth
century marked "a decisive transformation in the spread of old, the
invention of new, and the institutionalization of most sports on a national
and even international stage."[6] The evidence of sports as an expression
of and a shaping force in nationalistic sentiment is clear even in the
present day. One sports scholar cites the very British example that in
preparing for the 1991 Rugby World Cup Tournament, the players in the
dressing room listened to a recording of Sir Laurence Olivier reciting
Shakespeare's Agincourt speech in *Henry V*, reminding the players that
they were playing for God, country, and St. George.[7] As sporting events
have become available to millions simultaneously across the world
through the medium of television and on-line streaming to computers, an
alternative vision of sports has emerged. World Cup football matches
(soccer to Americans) and the Olympic Games are now watched on TV
by millions of people across the world. The FIFA 2006 World Cup was
broadcast to 214 countries and territories. The final match between Italy
and France had an estimated global audience of 715 million viewers.[8]

This worldwide presence offers a new potential for sports. Inspired
by a cosmopolitan global vision of humanity, it holds out the ideal of
human beings coming together on the playing field as well as in the
imagined community of spectators to celebrate the honorable mastery of
skill, teamwork, and fair-play. The Olympics have long been an expression of this ideal, of this global imaginary. Momentarily one world, we
are mesmerized by the performances of extraordinary athletes. As we
celebrate each national achievement through compulsive medal counting, the opening and closing ceremonies of the Games—the segments
with by far the largest television viewing audience—enact, if only for a

few hours, the hope of a shared humanity as a product of a global sporting event. Even the United Nations has taken note. In a speech to The Global Forum for Sports and Environment in Lahore, Pakistan, a U.N. official acknowledged that "there is growing realization within the United Nations that sports and the sports industry have a major role to play in promoting the U.N. goals of a common future of peace, dignity and prosperity."[9]

Since 1989, sports figures from Communist bloc countries have entered this global arena on the same civic footing as athletes from Western and, more recently, African and Asian countries. Prior to the end of Communism, talented tennis athletes born behind the Iron Curtain such as Martina Navratilova, Ivan Lendl, and Monica Seles had to relocate to the West to reach the highest levels of the sport. Navratilova and Lendl, both born in the former Czechoslovakia, and Seles, born of Hungarian parents living in what is now Serbia, moved to the U.S. to train, gained American citizenship, and represented their adopted country during the culmination of their professional tennis careers. Facilities and weather may differ from one nation and region to another, but birthplace no longer inhibits a talented athlete. Certainly the current example of three of the world's top ten tennis players emerging from the war-torn former Yugoslavia demonstrates that.[10] Their careers as both local heroes and worldwide celebrities offer a glimpse of the problematic dual nature of the postmodern global imaginary at work.

The example of the homecoming celebration for the Croatian Davis Cup Team demonstrates the intensity of local identification with prominent sports figures. Leading the players in their triumphant return was Goran Ivanisevic—no stranger to the adulation of Croatian fans. The celebration for the Davis Cup team in Zagreb was dwarfed by his earlier homecoming in 2001 after his surprise win of the men's singles title at the Wimbledon Championship—the most esteemed title in all of tennis. In his hometown of Split a crowd estimated at 150,000 "roared" as the private plane carrying Ivanisevic from England circled the city center. One fan threw himself on the car bearing the tennis star proclaiming "You are the symbol of this town." As the hero made his way to a makeshift stage, he was flanked by bodyguards and by "Goran for President" signs. In return, Ivanisevic shouted to the crowd: "There are only 300,000 of us [in Split], but man, we are crazier than anyone else," and then to prove it, proceeded to strip to his skivvies as he tossed his clothes to the crowd.[11]

The Croatian adulation for Ivanisevic after his win at Wimbledon linked citizens of the young nation to the worldwide stage of global sports through the person of their flamboyant tennis star. Ivanisevic began his pro tennis career in 1988 playing for Yugoslavia, but most of his victories came in the 1990s as a player for the newly independent nation of Croatia. In 1992, playing both singles and doubles, he garnered two bronze medals for Croatia in its first Olympic outing. He attained his highest ranking, number 2 in the world, in 1994. After reaching the finals of Wimbledon in 1992, 1994, and 1998, he was sidelined with a serious shoulder injury for most of 1999 and 2000 as his world ranking fell to 125th. Granted a wildcard to the 2001 Wimbledon tournament based on his previous record, he surprised everyone with a string of upsets that led him to the finals against popular Aussie Patrick Rafter. During his career, Ivanisevic modeled himself after his tennis idol John McEnroe in more ways than one. Like McEnroe, he was known for temper tantrums and broken racquets. His win at Wimbledon, the first ever by a wildcard entrant, was his last title on the pro circuit. It came at a time when his fledgling country had been racked by the decision to turn over two former leaders to the United Nations War Crimes Tribunal in the Hague.[12] For Croats and for the world, Ivanisevic's win functioned as symbol of ethnic pride and as a sign for the rebirth of Eastern Europe after the fall of communism.

Since 2006, three young talented tennis players from Serbia—a country with little in the way of a tennis tradition and caught in the struggle to recover from war and ethnic cleansing—have vaulted into the top ranks of professional tennis. All three grew up in Belgrade during the difficult aftermath of communism's collapse and Yugoslavia's disintegration. Novak Djokovic, who won numerous European tournaments as a teenager, first came onto the international scene as a professional player in 2005, and at the end of that year he placed 78th in the ATP world rankings. By the end of the following year he ranked 16th. In 2007, he began winning Master's tournaments. To claim the title in Estoril, Portugal, he defeated Andy Roddick, the top U.S. player, Rafael Nadal (then world number 2), and the incomparable Roger Federer, often considered the best player ever in the game of tennis. By the end of

2007, Djokovic reached number 3 in the world, where he remains through March of 2009.[13] This marks an astounding climb through the ranks for a player from a newly independent country just emerging from civil war.

Ana Ivanovic, also from Belgrade, was spotted at fifteen by an Israeli businessman who was so impressed by her commitment to becoming number 1 in the world that he offered to finance her career (to the equivalent of $10,000 to $20,000 per month), which allowed her to train in Basel, Switzerland.[14] She joined the women's pro circuit in 2003 and gained a spot in the top twenty in 2005, her breakout year. In 2007, she advanced into the top ten and earned over $2,000,000 in prize money. After winning her first Grand Slam tournament in Paris in spring of 2008, she became number 1 in Women's Tennis Association's singles world rankings, the eighteenth woman to reach the top spot since rankings began in 1975.[15] Her fellow countrywoman, Jelena Jankovic took a somewhat different route to tennis proficiency when, at twelve, she and her mother moved to the United States so she could train at a top tennis academy in Florida. She emerged on the international scene earlier than her two compatriots by wining the Junior Australian and U.S. Open titles in 2001 and was the number 1 female junior player in the world that year. That same year Nick Bollettieri, her well-known coach in Florida, predicted that "Jelena is a girl that will dominate the world's scene of tennis." After moving to the senior ranks, she climbed steadily, winning WTA tournaments. In 2008-2009, she gained the number 1 ranking in women's tennis, which she held for several months.[16] Like Ivanovic, Jankovic is an attractive young woman who has celebrity status in the Serbian press, although her world-wide fame cannot equal Ivanovic's.

All three Serbian stars claim that their mettle and determination was honed in the frightening years of the 1990s when the former Yugoslavia, held together by the autocratic rule of Tito, disintegrated after his death and the collapse of the regime. The unraveling of an artificial polity cobbled together in the wake of World War II resulted in brutal fighting and ethnic cleansing between Serbs, Coats, and Muslims.[17] It was amidst this fighting that Djokovic, Jankovic, and Ivanovic came of age. Djokovic learned to keep his composure on the tennis court as NATO forces bombed Serbia in 1999 in an attempt to remove President Slobodan Milosevic from power. As sirens howled and bombs exploded in the distance, Djokovic continued to practice on the court. It was this experience that made him the fierce competitor he is today. Tennis "saved us" believes Djokovic's mother. "If we didn't have tennis, we would have spent the days scared, always looking to the sky, wondering when the bombs would come." His father observed, "Novak was very scared then, but he never showed it.... Now he is scared of nothing."[18]

Ivanovic echoed similar experiences. She recalls practicing in an abandoned Belgrade swimming pool because no tennis courts survived. Practices were scheduled in the mornings before the bombings began. The family tried to keep up the illusion of a normal life, refusing to go to the basement during air raids. The other female Serbian tennis phenom, Jankovic, was living in Bradenton, Florida with her mother, training at Bollettieri's Tennis Academy while her father and brothers remained in Belgrade. She watched the destruction on CNN's daily news broadcasts and cried with American friends. This shared experience of surviving the crucible of war has, according to Ivanovic, made them "all very good fighters" with a "tough mentality." "I think that's what we probably have in common."[19]

These three players represent the fierce emerging nationalism of Serbia—perhaps one could even consider them an invented tradition in the making. But they are also global figures, perpetual nomads. From everywhere, as it were, they represent another aspect of the global imaginary—they may be idolized in their homeland, but they rarely spend time there; they are no longer "of" any place in particular. Although surrounded by luxury trappings that any of us would envy, these world-class tennis players are what one scholar refers to as "elite labour migrants." Part of a working cosmopolitan elite, they travel almost constantly, live in glamorous locations, represent high-style consumer goods, and are global celebrities.[20] Their lives are remarkably detached from their ethnic origins.[21]

The ATP (Association of Tennis Professionals) pro tour has 67 official tournaments with locations around the world from Chennai, India and Doha, Quatar to St. Petersburg, Russia and Tokyo, Japan. In a nod to the upsurge of players from Eastern Europe, the ATP has recently added tournaments in Croatia (two, Zagreb and Umag), Romania, Poland, and Serbia to its schedule. Each tournament typically runs for 5 to 8 days plus travel time. While no single player participates in all tournaments, the travel and peripatetic lifestyle is extremely demanding, particularly when practice time is limited and top-level performance is expected. Players and commentators have remarked on the brutal schedule. Jankovic, for instance, noted that "in other sports they play a few months and they take off, you know, a few months where they can recover their body and prepare." In tennis, she said, "We play almost, I think, nine or 10 months per year, which is very hard on our bodies. And we have to compete at the highest level. We always have to be ready." Her comments came after the top three women players exited the 2008 Wimbledon championship early due to injury or fatigue. A leading Russian female player, Svetlana Kuznetsova, echoed Jankovic's concerns. "No one has time to get used to grass after the French Open," she said. "Everyone needs rest—the season is too long. It's because of this that everyone is out."[22] Since rankings depend on winning or placing well in tournaments, and matches are arranged so that the top-ranked competitors do not meet until the final stages of play, the pressure is on. On the other hand, prize money is substantial and lucrative endorsements go to the players with the best records (and an aura of personality). Therefore, although the biggest tennis stars have some level of control over their own schedule, the structure of the profession, personal ambition to succeed at the highest level, financial considerations, and pressure from tournament organizers, sponsors, and agents combine to produce a very demanding schedule of worldwide travel and appearances.

Ivanovic keeps a diary on her website that chronicles some of her travels. After spending two weeks in Spain, where she purchased a vacation home on Mallorca, she started 2009 by training for three weeks in Australia for the first grand slam of the season, the Australian Open in Melbourne. After an early exit there she rested for a few days and then returned to her hometown of Belgrade for a match in the women's version of Davis Cup, the Fed Cup, the first ever held in Serbia. While there she visited her childhood training venue at the 11 April Sports Center where she was filmed for an HBO special and later attended a state dinner for the Japanese ambassador to Serbia. Then she was off to a WTA tournament in Dubai, where the top players stayed at the Burj Al-Arab Hotel, the world's only seven-star hotel, which sits like a sail reaching out over the water in the harbor. From Dubai she traveled to New York for an exhibition match against Serena Williams at Madison Square Garden, where she enjoyed the city covered in snow more than in her previous visits during the heat and humidity of the U.S. Open in

August. In New York, Ivanovic, Jankovic, and America's top women players, the Williams sisters, conquered the city in a media blitz. Alongside WTA Tour Chairman & CEO Larry Scott, Jankovic went on Fox Business' television program "Money For Breakfast," and Venus Williams and Scott met with several editors of the *New York Times*. Then the four women players had meetings with high-end lifestyle magazines. Ivanovic, Jankovic, and the Williams sisters then attended a luncheon at the Sony Club in New York City, hosted by Sony Ericsson, the [WTA] Tour, and the Luxury Marketing Council, an exclusive, collaborative organization of top CEOs and marketing executives who represent major luxury goods and services companies.[23] The travel, exotic locations, and high-profile appearances that are now part of the professional tour contribute to the aura of celebrity surrounding the athletes.

After appearances in New York, Ivanovic flew to the desert for some warm weather training in Las Vegas, taking time out to visit the strip, grab a roller coaster ride at New York, New York casino, and take in a show at the Bellagio. Then she traveled to Indian Wells, California for a WTA/ATP tournament which she loves because " the crowds are great...even for practice" and "you have the breathtaking views of the mountains and the fresh desert air." "I find it very relaxing," she declared. She hoped, of course, to defend the title she won last year at Indian Wells. During this busy period, she spent no time at "home" in her principal residence in Basel, Switzerland. This series of events both athletic and promotional, spread across four continents, comprised Ivanovic's schedule for the first two and one-half months of the 2009 season. As a peripatetic wanderer and worker in the playgrounds of the rich, she fit the definition of an "elite" laborer and migrant, a citizen of nowhere and everywhere.[24]

Djokovic's schedule was almost as full. In January of 2009, after playing two lead-up tourneys and attempting unsuccessfully to defend his 2008 title at the Australian Open, he headed to a tournament in Marseilles, France and then played in and won an ATP tournament in Dubai. Djokovic then made a quick stop in Belgrade to view the site of the upcoming Serbian Open, the first ever ATP event to be held in Serbia, which will be played in a new sports center. After Belgrade, he played Davis Cup matches for Serbia against the host team in Benidorm, Spain and then jetted off to California for the Indian Wells tournament, where he lost to American Andy Roddick in the quarterfinals. Following Indian Wells, he plans to compete at back-to-back events in Miami, Monte Carlo (where he currently lives), and Rome, where he will be the defending champion once again. This comprises his schedule for the first four months of 2009.

These high-pressure calendars are typical of top-flight tennis pros and of professional athletes in many sports—a product of the globalization of sport. The migration of sports talent is part of what Arjun Appadurai characterizes as the "new global cultural economy."[25] Further, he argues that "the transformation of everyday subjectivities through electronic mediation and the work of the imagination is not only a cultural fact. It is deeply connected to politics, through the new ways in which individual attachments, interests, and aspirations increasingly crosscut those of the nation-state."[26] The Serbian and Croatian sports figures profiled above sit right at the center of that problematic intersection. Products of newly formed nation-states but enmeshed in a career of worldwide travel and performance, they are celebrated both as ethnic heroes and global stars. One scholar of sports after the Cold War views these top athletes as "virtually stateless and part of a world jet-setting circuit." He complains, in fact, that the athletes are "elite performers, many of whom have no patriotic loyalty to their country of birth."[27] But in the case of the Serbian and Croatian tennis stars at least, the reality is much more complicated. They are negotiating many competing claims in fashioning their lives. They move to enviable places like Monte Carlo, Florida, Mallorca, in part because they require the infrastructure—warm weather, courts, coaches, trainers, nutritionists, psychologists, agents, easy travel access, lower taxes—most of which are not available in their home towns. They have to respond not only to the exhausting competition schedule, and their zealous, nationalistic fans at home but also to the demands of an aggressive sports marketing industry and media, which transmute their winning athleticism into global stardom.

Through celebrity, the workings of the global imaginary and its nationalistic components are instantiated in a worldwide flow of production, distribution, and consumption of goods and people. In terms of industry, sports/entertainment is big business. The London Stock Exchange lists a "Global Sports Fund" that invest in the top 250 sports and leisure businesses.[28] In the United States, what is termed "the sports business industry" is twice the size of the automobile industry and seven times larger than the movie business.[29] The industry has created a planetary commodity chain of production and consumption.[30] Marketers guiding the leading sporting goods firms have managed to construct "a convincing world of symbols, ideas, and values" that harness individual desire to the possession of everything from athletic footwear to the latest tennis racquet model. Nike's "Just do it" slogan provides an excellent example, inspiring each potential consumer that he or she can also accomplish inspiring feats of athleticism if properly equipped with Nike brands. Along with Reebok and Adidas, Nike has also managed to transform what was originally a specialized athletic shoe into what is now considered a kind of all-purpose footwear.[31]

As Eastern European athletes begin to make an impact in the world of global sports, the region is also entering the global marketplace for sports-related goods. In 2005, Eastern Europe led the world with the fastest growing rate of consumption of sports drinks.[32] Worldwide sales of sports equipment, apparel, and footwear inspired by celebrity sports figures, increased to $278.4 Billion USD (€ 185.6 Billion) in 2007, according to leading economic research company The NPD Group, Inc.[33] Again, Central and Eastern Europe comprised the fastest growing market, with sales up 20% from the previous year. These numbers indicate that Eastern Europe is now a significant participant in the global marketplace as well as the global sports arena.

And the Serbian tennis stars play an important role in that participation. Both Djokovic and Ivanovic are sponsored by (that is to say, for large sums of money they endorse the products of) Adidas, a German firm with international clout in sports clothing and footwear. The firm has designed for Ivanovic a dress called the "Adilibria Dress Ana." The dress, inspired by her "bombastic and unique style," offers, we are told, technological advances that will pamper the wearer with "allover ClimaCool® ventilation" and provides "devastating tennis court performances." The dress is available to all aspiring players (as well as to couch potato poseurs) for $70.00. Women consumers can each imagine themselves as the powerful and alluring Ivanovic dominating their sphere of influence.[34]

Considered one of, if not the, most beautiful women players in the game, Ivanovic also represents the luxury watch brand of Rolex. For the sports audience, Rolex plays up its connection to and sponsorship of sports events. Their Sports and Culture web page opens with a dramatic photograph of an America's Cup yacht in action. A "testimony" by Ivanovic, placed among a long list of notable sports figures and musicians, includes a glamour shot of her dressed in black wearing an Oyster Perpetual Datejust model.[35] Rolex is one of the sponsors for several tennis events including Davis Cup and Wimbledon. Ivanovic is also sponsored by Yonex, a relatively new Japanese producer of sports clothing and equipment for tennis, badminton, and golf that early on sponsored Billie Jean King and Martina Navratilova, both former top world tennis players. In 2004, Yonex agreed to become the official racquet of the Asian Tennis Federation—also a relatively new federation and a testimony to the global growth of sports.[36] Ivanovic's endorsements illustrate perfectly the global reach of international sports and the businesses that support it.

Djokovic also represents Adidas, which has thus captured the two leading East European tennis stars, an important move in its global competition with Nike, the foremost manufacturer of athletic footwear. As is well known, Djokovic has made a name for himself by doing clever impersonations of many of the leading tennis players. He repeated some of his spot-on renditions on the Tonight Show with Jay Leno in March of 2008, adding more luster to his celebrity status. As a result of his comedic skill he has earned the nickname "Djoker."[37]

Product endorsements have consequences. In addition to the photo shoots and public appearances that must be sandwiched into a busy schedule, sponsorships can vitally affect the players' ability to perform. In the case of Ivanovic, her ability to draw on her coaches' advice prior to one of the most critical matches of her career was blocked by her contract with Adidas. The firm has a tennis development team comprised of trainers, including the highly regarded Gil Reyes (former trainer of Andre Agassi and considered to be a key element in Agassi's impressive comeback), and coaches including Sven Groeneveld, who worked on behalf of Adidas as Ivanovic's primary coach. She has, in fact, praised the Adidas team: "Having Sven and Adidas in my corner as advisors has been very important to my progress. Together with my trainer, management and family, I feel that I have found the right team structure to get me to the next step, which is winning Grand Slams and reaching No. 1." However, as Ivanovic prepared for the French Open finals match—her second Grand Slam final—she was unable to draw on Groeneveld's advice because her opponent, Dinara Safina, was also an Adidas player coached by the development team. Nonetheless, she accomplished both of her stated goals by winning the match and the tournament title, which propelled her to number 1 in the Women's rankings.[38]

As for Djokovic, he has had to deal with an even more difficult situation imposed by the imbrication of sports and capital that characterizes the culture of globalization. His racquet endorsement contract with Wilson, a leading sports equipment manufacturer headquartered in the United States, was due to expire in December 2008.[39] This set the stage for a competition to sign the newest entrant into tennis's top three. New reports claimed that his clothing sponsor Adidas "plans to launch a tennis racket next year and wants star endorser Novak Djokovic to swing with it."[40] But, in the meantime, he chose to sign with Wilson's major competitor, Head, yet found it difficult to adjust to the new racquet.[41] He blamed the racquet for an unexpected first-round loss in the opening tournament of the year. The early adjustment period did not go well, even though Djokovic acknowledged that "they try to make the racket as best as possible, you know, to my wishes." He insisted that "They did a good job. They're really trying. So even though the racket is the same practically, it takes time mentally to be able to get used to something new."[42] However, he was not successful in defending his Australian Open title with his new racquet either. Whether he will overcome a history of difficult racquet transitions remains to be seen. Other players who have switched racquets in mid-career have found it tough going. In two recent instances, players signed "blockbuster deals" to switch racquets and then promptly (but surreptitiously) returned to their old rackets emblazoning the new logos on them—until the media got wise. How a player, his agent, and his support group are able to negotiate among competing powers in the global sports enterprise can impinge dramatically on a player's performances, endangering the very skill that supports the celebrity and produces profits for player and company alike. Thus an individual decision is never just that in the complicated terrain of postmodern sports, where a single choice may have far-reaching ramifications.

We might wish to view the new East European tennis stars as exemplars of global cosmopolitanism. Citizens of the world they are indeed, growing up and beginning their training during the wars of ethnic cleansing, then moving to Spain, Switzerland, Monte Carlo, or the United States to complete their coming of age. They have achieved the dual feat of moving to the highest levels in the professional ranks while rising to the position of heroes in their home countries. Playing their way around the globe from Shanghai, Melbourne, Dubai, to Paris, London, and New York, their global reach is made possible by the fall of the Berlin Wall and the explosion of tennis into a worldwide enterprise. No longer a preserve of Euro-American elites, the game and its venues have expanded as quickly as have the purses to be earned. Ivanovic has earned over six million dollars in prize money through 2008 while Djokovic has garnered over eleven million in winnings. Each has earned multiples of that in endorsement contracts.

But what position do these East European tennis celebrities occupy? Are they representatives of a postmodern, material global imaginary? Do they epitomize a rising above the ethnic and nationalist confrontations that characterized the twentieth century, or are they harbingers of increasing nationalism in the face of, or as another face of, the global? The intense adulation these young phenoms receive from their hometown and home-country crowds ranging from the general populace to the highest officials—the President of Serbia attended Ivanovic's twenty-first birthday party as a mark of honor to her—indicates a potential dark side to the celebrity of global sports figures. Does the appearance of internationally recognized Croatian and Serbia stars like Ivanisevic and Djokovic betoken a "post-postmodern" global citizenship and a return to modernist nationalism? This dual, seemingly contradictory move is addressed by the term "glocal," which points to the intensification of local—we might even say tribal—identification as an outcome of globalization.

Along these lines, the East European example is once again telling. Starting gradually after World War II, significant numbers of Croatians and of their ethnic rivals, Serbians, emigrated to Australia. By 1986, there were over 250,000 people in Australia who were born or had parents who were born in Yugoslavia. The Croatians and Serbians focused their patriotism and identity around soccer (football) clubs formed in the suburbs of Sidney, Melbourne, and Adelaide—between 1945 and 1984, over fifty Croatian soccer clubs formed in Australia.[43] Isolated from the Anglo and native Australians by language and religion, the immigrants found each other as well as jobs and housing often through local ethnic soccer clubs. Croatian priests also worked through the sports clubs to reach out to single young men liable to go adrift in their unfamiliar surroundings. As the President of the Melbourne Croatia Club put it, "in a time when the place of the Croatian community was yet to be established in Europe, the tournaments and soccer clubs provided the Croatian people a chance to unite with a common purpose."[44]

Other European immigrants down under, including Italians and Hungarians, set up national or ethnic soccer clubs. For many years the clubs established by various immigrant groups were not accepted into the mainstream Australian leagues. Thus, while they formed a means of positive identification with others of like-minded culture and values, they may have contributed to an isolation from Australians more generally, hence limiting integration into the broader society and perhaps even creating "an embattled siege mentality among Croatians in Australia."[45] This way, sports enhanced ethnic identification and created an imaginary link with the homeland.

Recent events in Australia suggest the presence of both integrative and divisive tendencies in the globalization of sports and demonstrate the protean power of celebrity in a global age. In 2007, Croats and Serbs, invigorated by the rise of top ranked tennis players from each country, reenacted their destructive ethnic rivalry in their Australian homeland. On the first day of the Australian Open Tennis Tournament, Serbian and Croatian fans, many bedecked in their national flags, held a bitter pitched battle on the grounds of Melbourne Park as up-and-coming Croatian player Mario Ancic contested his first match. The Serbs were reportedly shouting "Die Croatians, die." It took forty policemen to quell the disturbance and over 150 fans were ejected. Serbian Cultural Club president Thomas Banjanin claimed Croatian supporters had been flaunting their colours and said it was disappointing that the bitter history between the two groups had flared at a sporting event. "I think Croats are always overdoing things, they are always mixing politics with sport," Mr. Banjanin said. The Croatians saw it differently of course. Tom Starcevic, Croatian Community Association secretary and editor of Melbourne's *Croatian Herald* explained, "National pride is one thing but this is unacceptable," and he added: "I wasn't there but from what I've seen and heard the Serbs were quite provocative." Some local observers traced the violence back to the clashes between Croat and Serb soccer fans in the earlier days of immigration from Eastern Europe.[46] In 2009, savvy Serbian player Janko Tipsarevic, considered "one of the more rounded and intelligent characters in tennis," warned Australian Open officials in advance of his match with rising Croatian newcomer Marin Cilic, a protégé of Ivanisevic's and currently ranked 19th on the men's tour, that fans might get disruptive. Tipsarevic asked that the match be moved to Court 2 (usually reserved for the most well-known players), where the security is much tighter than on the outer courts. This may have avoided a repeat of the 2007 riot. Even within the stadium, fans of the two new nations wearing national colors and seated in opposite corners, "chanted slogans and shouted obscenities in their own languages—which, fortunately, were completely unintelligible to the majority of spectators." The players, in contrast, supported each other with friendly comments and concluded with a warm handshake at the end of the match. The police were able to keep order even as the rival groups marched out of the venue shouting slogans and songs at each other.[47] Tipsarevic thoughtfully explained the intensity of the Australian tennis fans. "Normally the problem is with people who live abroad," said Tipsarevic. "And especially in Australia because it's so far away from their homeland. It's stupid to say these people love Serbia more, but they do feel nostalgic for it – and sometimes they cheer too much."[48]

This incident illustrates perfectly the dual nature of sports and its stars under globalization. As the "great people" of global sports, the leading professional tennis players profiled here are truly global celebrities, living a nomadic life in the playgrounds of the rich yet also working hard to prepare for and perform amazing feats of athleticism. As celebrities, they are positioned between the demands of their sport, the expectations of the global capitalism that underwrites and profits from their careers, and the local and worldwide fans that claim intense identification with their heroes and heroines. As we imagine moving toward a more inclusive and cosmopolitan identity in the wake of global interaction, the riots in Australia and moments like those remind us of the dual nature—the love-hate rivalries—that are reenacted on the field of play and in the limelight.

The young Serbian and Croatian tennis superstars illustrate phenomena, both material and immaterial, that move goods and people in ever faster worldwide circulation. The processes formed by a global commerce in personality swirl around a star, sweeping up family, fans, and promoters into a storm of finance and fantasy. Local identity functions as a pivot point for postmodern circulation, a specific, limited, focused unit larger than the nuclear family but comprehensible as a stand-in for family and kin. These young heroes of the former Yugoslavia link their hometowns to the global stage; in turn, memories of dictatorship, war, and constraint serve to ground the newly emerging celebrities in their East European past. Thus, the Croatian and Serbian tennis stars occupy a dual position, one that serves to forward both ethnic attachments and dreams of a global humanity. Only time will tell which impulse will triumph in this game of love.

NOTES

1. Vasif Iruizou quoted in Rachel Louise Snyder, *Fugitive Denim: A Moving Story of People and Pants in the Borderless World of Global Trade* (New York: W. W. Norton & Co., 2008), 60. Snyder interviewed Iruizou in fall of 2005 in Bilasuvar, Azerbaijan. He was in charge of the region's only cotton gin owned by an Azerbaijan company, which was called MKT. Iruizou and his family were wealthy, but the local economy, based on oil and cotton, seemed impoverished. When Snyder went back six months later to talk with Iruizou, she could not find him. According to others, he had been "admitted to a sanatorium beyond the borders of his country for undisclosed reasons...completely unreachable to anyone." Snyder, *Fugitive Denim*, 69.

2. *Guardian* [Manchester, U.K.], July 6, 1994, 23, quoted by Joseph Maguire, *Global Sport: Identities, Societies, Civilizations* (London: Polity Press, 1999), 2.

3. Quoted Dec 5, 2005 in Goranonline http://www.goranonline.com/news/gi_news. html. Accessed February 23, 2009.

4. I am indebted to the invaluable research assistance of Kim Rueger in preparing this article.

5. Clifford Geertz, "Deep Play: Notes on a Balinese Cockfight," *Daedalus* 101, No. 1 (Winter 1972), pp. 1-37.

6. Eric Hobsbawm and Terence Ranger, *The Invention of Tradition* (Cambridge, UK: Cambridge University Press, 1983), 298.

7. Joseph Maguire, *Global Sport*, 177.

8. The "overall cumulative audience" in Asia reached over 8 billion viewers. Fédération Internationale de Football Association, Zurich, Switzerland. http://www.fifa.com/mm/ document/fifafacts/ffprojects/ip-401_06e_tv_2658.pdf. Accessed March 15, 2009.

9. Eric Falt, Director of Communications, UNEP, in a speech to The Global Forum for Sports and Environment, Lahore, Pakistan, Nov 24-26, 2004. http://www.unep.org/Documents.Multilingual/Default.asp?DocumentID=413&ArticleID=4671&l=en. Accessed March 15, 2009.

10. Men and women are ranked separately in tennis.

11. "Tennis: No Place Like Home for Ivanisevic," *New York Times*, July 11, 2002; "Zagreb's joy at Ivanisevic victory," BBC Sport Online, July 9, 2001, and "Goren comes home to hero's welcome," BBC Sport Online, July 11, 2001. http://news.bbc.co.uk/sport2/hi/in_depth/2001/wimbledon_2001/photo_galleries/1433040.stm. Accessed February 24, 2009.

12. "Sports of the Times: Extra Day Turns Into Special Day," *New York Times*, July 10, 2001; Ivanisevic's win was recalled recently in the *Croatian Times* when he predicted in the summer of 2008 that a young Croatian player, Mario Ancic, affectionately known as 'Baby Goran,' might be in line to repeat the 2001 victory. *Croatian Times* (English), June 8, 2008, http://www.croatiantimes.com/index.php?id=193. Accessed April 1, 2009.

13. Novak Djokovic's website. http://www.novakdjokovic.rs/index.php?jezik=2. Accessed February 20, 2009.

14. Christopher Clarey, *International Herald Tribune*, June 8, 2008.

15. Due to illnesses and injury she has dropped to no. 7 in the WTA rankings as of March 2009. "Career in Review," Ana Ivanovic website. http://www.anaivanovic.com/. Accessed February 3, 2009.

16. Jelena Jankovic official website. http://www.jj-jelenajankovic.com/eng/bio.html. Accessed March 24, 2009.

17. On the disintegration of Yugoslavia and the rise of ethnic conflict see, James Wilkinson and H. Stuart Hughes, *Contemporary Europe: A History*, 9th ed. (Upper Saddle River, NJ: Prentice Hall, 1998), 606-609, 618-622.

18. Srdjan Djokovic quoted by Juliet Macur, "From Chaos, Serbia's Star Players Draw Strength," *New York Times*, June 3, 2007.

19. *Time* World edition on-line Sept 4, 2007; Ana Ivanovic quoted in Macur, "From Chaos."

20. The tennis world's first postmodern celebrity was Anna Kournikova, known for her athleticism and sex appeal. She left her Russian homeland at 14 to train at Bollettieri's academy. The official website of Anna Kournikova, http://www.kournikova.com/about/bio. Accessed April 1, 2009. On the connections between sport, corporate sponsors, and media in the making of Kournikova's career as a global celebrity, see Chapter 6: "Cultures of Sport Stardom: David Beckham and Anna Kournikova," in Barry Smart, *The Sport Star: Modern Sport and the Cultural Economy of Sporting Celebrity* (London: Sage Publications, Ltd, 2005), 144-190.

21. Maguire, *Global Sport*, 99.

22. Richard Jago, *The Guardian* [Manchester, U.K.], Jul 1, 2008.

23. WTA website, March 6, 2009, http://www.sonyericssonwtatour.com/3/newsroom/stories/?ContentID=3049. Accessed March 24 2009.

24. "Diary," Ivanovic website. http://www.anaivanovic.com/. Accessed March 22, 2009.

25. Arjun Appadurai, "Disjuncture and Difference in the Global Cultural Economy," *Theory, Culture, & Society* 7, quoted in Maguire, *Global Sport*, 98.

26. Arjun Appadurai, *Modernity at Large: Cultural Dimensions of Globalization* (Minneapolis, MN: University of Minnesota Press, 1996), 10.

27. James Riordan, "Sport after the Cold War: Implications for Russia and Eastern Europe," in *East Plays West: Sport and the Cold War*, eds. Stephen Wagg and David L. Andrews (London: Routledge, 2007), 281, 285.

28. Maguire, *Global Sport*, 60.

29. Street and Smith's *Sports Business Journal,* March 2009.

30. On the commodity chain, see M. Korzeniewicz, "Commodity chains and market-ing strategies: Nike and the global athletic footwear industry," in G. Gereffi and M. Korzeniewicz, eds. *Commodity Chains and Global Capitalism* (Westport, CT: Greenwood Press, 1994), 247.

31. Maguire, *Global Sport*, 130-32.

32. Overall growth was driven by new brands, brand and flavour extensions and novel product concepts as well as greater focus on the role of exercise in health and well-being. "Eastern Europe Leads Global Sports Drink Growth," *Food Navigator*, February 21, 2006, unpaginated.

33. The NPD Group, Inc., Port Washington, NY, July 25, 2008.

34. See the Adidas website. http://catalogue.adidas.com/catalogue/com/product/E15799/ADILIBRIA-DRESS-ANA. Accessed March 21, 2009.

35. Rolex website. http://www.rolex.com/en/index.jsp#/en/xml/world-of-rolex/sports-culture/testimonees/tennis-ana-ivanovic. Accessed March 21, 2009.

36. Yonex website. http://www.yonex.com/company/history.html. Accessed March 21, 2009.

37. Novak Djokovic blog, March 14, 2008. http://djokovic-tennis.blogspot.com/2008/03/jay-leno-hosts-novak-djokovic.html. Accessed March 24, 2009.

38. *Tennis Week*, March 13, 2009. http://www.tennisweek.com/news/fullstory.sps?inewsid=6628950. Accessed March 24, 2009; Adidas Press Release, June 9, 2008, http://www.press.adidas.com/DesktopDefault.aspx/tabid-11/16_read-9155/. Accessed March 24, 2009.

39. Wilson, headquartered in Chicago, is a leader in equipment for tennis, golf, base-ball, and (American) football. In business for over a century they are number one in world-wide sales in racquet sports, baseball, and American football products. Amerisports web site, n.d. http://www.amersports.com/brands/wilson/. Accessed March 24, 2009.

40. Street and Smith's *Sports Business Journal*, Sept 8, 2008, 3.

41. Head came to the fore as an important sports manufacturer with their production of the first metal ski. They are now leading producers in racquet sports, skiing, and diving equipment. They go head to head with Wilson in tennis racquets. Head corporate website, n.d., http://www.head.com/corporate/ Accessed March 24, 2009.

42. Reuters New Agency, January 14, 2009. http://www.reuters.com/article/sports News/idUSTRE50D16320090114.

43. Roy Hay, "Croatia: Community, Conflict and Culture: The Role of Soccer Clubs in Migrant Identity," in *Sporting Nationalisms: Identity, Ethnicity, Immigration and Assimi-lation*, eds. Mike Cronin and David Mayall (London: Frank Cass, 1998), 54-55, 61 and Table 1: Croatian Soccer Clubs in Australia, 63-64.

44. And(j)elko Cimera, *19th Annual Croatian Soccer Tournament Programme*, (Mel-bourne: Melbourne Croatia Soccer Club, 1993), 7 quoted in Hay, "Croatia: Community, Conflict and Culture," 58.

45. Hay, "Croatia: Community, Conflict and Culture," 57, 61.

46. Jessica Halloran, *Sidney Morning Herald*, January 15, 2007; *The Age*, January 15, 2007, http://www.theage.com.au/news/National/Tennis-Open-marred-by-ethnic-violence/2007/01/15/1168709659874.html. Accessed March 23, 2009.

47. Simon Briggs, *Telegraph* [U.K.], Jan 21, 2009; *Miami Herald*, March 23, 2009.

48. Janko Tipsarevic quoted by Simon Briggs, *Telegraph* [U.K.], January 21, 2009.

BIBLIOGRAPHY

Appadurai, Arjun. *Modernity at Large: Cultural Dimensions of Globalization.* Minneapolis, MN: University of Minnesota Press, 1996.

Cronin, Mike, and David Mayall. *Sporting Nationalisms: Identity, Ethnicity, Immigration and Assimilation.* London: Frank Cass, 1998.

Geertz, Clifford. "Deep Play: Notes on a Balinese Cockfight," *Daedalus,* Vol. 101, No. 1 (Winter 1972): 1-37.

Gereffi G. and M. Korzeniewicz, eds. *Commodity Chains and Global Capitalism.* Westport, CT: Greenwood Press, 1994.

Hobsbawm, Eric, and Terence Ranger. *The Invention of Tradition.* Cambridge, UK: Cambridge University Press, 1983.

Maguire, Joseph. *Global Sport: Identities, Societies, Civilizations.* London: Polity Press, 1999.

Smart, Barry. *The Sport Star: Modern Sport and the Cultural Economy of Sporting Celebrity.* London: Sage Publications, Ltd, 2005.

Snyder, Rachel Louise. *Fugitive Denim: A Moving Story of People and Pants in the Borderless World of Global Trade.* New York: W. W. Norton & Co., 2008.

Wagg, Stephen, and David L. Andrews, eds. *East Plays West: Sport and the Cold War.* London: Routledge, 2007.

Wilkinson, James, and H. Stuart Hughes, *Contemporary Europe: A History,* 9th ed. Upper Saddle River, NJ: Prentice Hall, 1998.

NOMADIC HOMES, POSTMODERN TRAVEL, AND THE GEOPOLITICAL IMAGINARY IN THE POST-TOTALITARIAN CULTURES OF POLAND AND UKRAINE

IRENE SYWENKY

Human beings are intricately connected, individually and collectively, to the workings and articulations of space, both physical and symbolic. In the context of the collapse of the totalitarian regimes in Europe and radical restructuring and unification of Europe in 1992, post-totalitarian Central and Eastern Europe is one of the most rapidly evolving and changing regions today. In the world of shifting borders and continuous redefinition of collective identities, this geopolitical and geocultural space belongs to one of the most debated and contested designations.

The geopolitical body of Europe has long been viewed as a more coherent and unified entity than it has ever been. Ironically, it was the emergence of the discourse of postcolonial studies that inadvertently contributed to the formulation of this unity through the conceptualization of European imperial otherness. The homogenization of Europe was brought about by

> the way in which the political and disciplinary collisions between the Eurocentric premises of traditional comparative approaches to literary and cultural study and the inherently and necessarily anti-Eurocentric stance of postcolonial politics and theory appear to have colluded towards a subtle yet unmistakable reinforcement of a monolithic and monologic "European" identity, in which the ideal notion of "Europe as Subject,"[1] devoid of historical and geopolitical determinants of its own, is mirrored by the oppositional construct of Europe as Object, a staunchly self-identical metropolitan Other to the richly fragmented (post)colonial Self.[2]

It is the evolution of postcolonial studies since its inception in the middle of the twentieth century together with the radical restructuring of Europe—set in train, at the end of the 1980s and beginning of the 1990s, by the collapse of the Soviet bloc—that, among other developments, brought into focus Europe's perpetual re-hierarchization through continuous socio-political and economic power play and through the revision of the concept of "monologism" of European identity.

Representing identity and selfhood in the context of this region is a political and ideological enterprise as it inevitably involves the negotiation of the "center"/"periphery" dynamics intricately linked to the ideological representations of space. Radical devaluation of the area during the years of the Soviet empire gave rise to two important processes in the post-totalitarian period: 1) centrifugal reorientation towards the West, which meant a positioning of these cultures in relation to the Western "center." Although always prominent historically, this impetus gained more significance, politically and otherwise, over the last two decades; 2) centripetal drive towards the exploration and articulation of the national selfhood. Both developments manifest a deeply internalized "otherness," which remains to be a long-term effect of the historical construction of the geopolitical peripherality of this zone. Commenting on the concept of the "new" Europe and the ever "in-progress" construction of European myth ("a certain Europe [that] does not yet exist"), Jacques Derrida reflected that "there is no self-relation, no relation to oneself, no identification with oneself, without culture, but a culture of oneself *as* a culture *of* the other, a culture of the double genitive and of the *difference to oneself.*"[3]

Both Poland and Ukraine are important loci of cultural displacement through the change of political regimes and borders: Poland as a self-defined Central European state and a EU member, a culture that has always been historically conscious of its peripherality; Ukraine as a postcolonial space *par excellence* that has historically occupied the position of an ambivalent mediator between the West and the East. The two cultural sites provide representative material in that they foreground an ongoing dialogue on the issues of national identity and national space, on the problem of history and national past, and on the process of globalization and construction of meaning in and about today's world. If we agree that "[m]odernity [is] a central universalizing theme"[4] of today's culture globally, the figurations of identity capture the struggles with the anxieties of the modern world generally and articulate the concerns related to more specific socio-political contexts.

For all its universalizing claims, the era of globalization has not diminished the significance of space and spatial behavior in the articulation of the structures of identity, home, belonging, and the role meaning and social values play in the many aspects of spatial practices. Globalization is intricately involved in the processes of displacement, in the increasing importance of personal mobility, and in the ever more prominent diffusion and indeterminacy of borders. As some scholars argue, "'globalization' refers to far too complex a set of phenomena to reduce to a single, simple spatial metaphor. The spatial dynamics of these phenomena are highly complex, involving a continuation of capitalism's historical tendency of destabilizing some places while creating others, plus the development of new kinds of places...and new kinds of flow between and across places."[5] In other words, globalization does not create a uniform, global, homogenous space/place but rather increases the tension between the local and the global and enhances local self-awareness. Moreover, while we tend to postulate the existence of an abstract globality as a physically delineated, material space, "'global' space is almost always also concrete, local space.... There is no inhabited, tangible, purely global space."[6] Globality cannot have any other manifestation but through locality and thus inherently posits questions not only about the ways the global impacts the local but also about how the local articulates its relationship to the global and legitimates, integrates, or subverts it. Seeing globalization as the only force that shapes today's distribution of political and economic power and conceptualization of space internationally "might distract us from the ways in which capitalist processes and ideologies shape space intra*national*ly."[7] Along the lines of this argument, it is of interest to see how postmodern nomadism and mobility shaped in the context of a consciousness of globalization impact the way peripheral cultures articulate themselves in relation to geopolitical hierarchies.

Arguably, Central and Eastern Europe as a geopolitical space involves the problematics attributed to mobility and cultural cross-fertilization in the globalized world irrespective of the historical period:

> [T]he region is intuitively "comparative." In Eastern Europe, one town would commonly speak several native languages, belong to two or three empires in the course of a single generation, and assume most of its residents to be hybrids who carried the dividing-

lines of nationality within themselves.... Exile, displacement, multi-languagedness, heteroglossia, outsideness to oneself and thus a taste for irony, the constant crossing of borders and the absence of a tranquil, organic, homogenized center that belongs to you alone: all these Bakhtinian virtues and prerequisites for genuine dialogue have long been endemic to Central Europe.[8]

Today's body of Polish and Ukrainian writing presents persistent concerns with the representation of space and reorientation of collective identities in the context of the geopolitical changes in Europe. The works of such key writers as Andrzej Stasiuk, Manuela Gretkowska, Olga Tokarczuk (Poland), Yuri Andrukhovych, and Yuri Vynnychuk (Ukraine), to name just a few, are defined by the trope of travel and by the practice of what can be described as literary cartography. I will argue that this "geographicity" itself lays bare a distinct problematic, where articulations of spatiality reference real places but also conceptualize them as fictions, mythologies, narratives, and loci of geopolitical desire, thus participating in the discourses of redistribution of power and geopolitical revisionism. Central Europe in particular sets forth a geo-political imaginary that serves as a political tool to rewrite these collective identities and reorient them toward the ambivalent, "global" Western center. While the original designation of *Mitteleuropa* was associated with the rise of German interests in the eighteenth-century Europe, today's concept of Central Europe presents a set of different implications. Under the Soviet empire, the region's cultures underwent a radical depreciation, and the geopolitical space of "Eastern Europe" acquired the stigma of political, economic, and cultural difference that, to this day, has remained powerfully determinant with regard to how the whole area is perceived by the rest of the Continent. In postcommunist East European societies, the idea of Central Europe can be conceptual-ized primarily as a strategic tool used to reorient these cultures away from the Russian "East" and to realign them with the Western "center." Thus, the concept of Central Europe can be set up as an intermediary space negotiating politically and culturally the constructs of the West/East dichotomy. The idea is particularly vital in Poland and (West-ern) Ukraine, which have been historically connected to the Habsburg Empire and whose cultures, as a result, often indulge in ambivalent imperial nostalgia.

Culturally and geopolitically circumscribed as it may be, today's Polish and Ukrainian discourse of the geographical imagination also participate in the broader, postmodern rediscovery of and fascination with travel. Because of the inherent fluidity and elusiveness of the changing geopolitical structures of "new" Europe, emphasis on nomadism, migrancy, and unhomeliness constitutes one of the defining features of these narratives. The phenomenon of "nomadism," to begin with, can be defined as an alternative mode of existing, an inherent condition of non-belonging in today's world, and an embodiment of postmodern subjectivity[9]; for Deleuze and Guattari, nomadism, fundamentally rhizomic and unrooted, foregrounds the "deterritorialized" state of being. Nomadism is always marginal, decentered, and displaced; it is at the core of the center-periphery movement and of the renegotiation of the relationship between Europe and its geographical, economic, political, cultural margins. In this context, the inclusion of cyberdiscourse in this study serves as a logical extension of the discussion of spatiality and its representations. An alternative space that redefines and subverts traditional space, virtual reality is symptomatic of the evolving resistance to the physical and organic boundaries that constitute our material culture, but also of the growing desire to reshape and rewrite these boundaries, if only through elusively cyber-signified reality. According to Louis Schein's notion of "imagined cosmopolitanism," media consumers, who are exposed today to various types of global communications including virtual computer technologies, construct (or "imagine") themselves as participants in the global culture.[10] Although the above-mentioned centrifugal drive is undoubtedly present in this type of global discourse, the centripetal impetus towards the center and the exploration of identity, home, and belonging are also strongly represented in the discourses of post-totalitarian Eastern Europe.

The last couple of decades have witnessed an unprecedented development of the theories and the practices of space as a socially and ideologically conditioned activity. As Michel Foucault has envisioned much earlier in 1967, "[t]he present epoch will perhaps be above all the epoch of space."[11] Today's interest in spatiality can be located at the crossroads of various disciplinary and methodological concerns such as history, anthropology, sociology, gender studies, postcolonial studies, cultural studies, and urban and ecocritical discourses, among others. One of the central foci of these inquiries is the examination of the historical process of the geopolitical production and formation of otherness, where articulation of spatiality is linked to the generation of social meaning and the workings of power and knowledge. The notable attempts to deconstruct the positivistic conceptions of space and theorize it as a fluid and pluralistic discursive and semiotic continuum that reflects complex gradations of power and is a product of socio-historical and political forces are the Foucauldian heterotopologies, the "triple dialectic" of Lefebvre's spatial theoretical imagination, the multiple hybridities of Homi Bhabha's rethinking of the postcolonial binary problematic, and Edward W. Soja's "thirdspace."[12] These theories lay ground for the postmodern rethinking of spatiality and of the complex relationship of human beings in conjunction with the practical workings of concepts such as "home," "place," "location," and "territory." The "thirdspace" of today's narrativized literary "geographies" represents a negotiation between the reality of the material, lived geophysical space and the changing conceptions and constructions of the geopolitical ideological structures reflecting the fluctuating gradation of power within European political and cultural space.

One of the evolving ways of negotiating borders, geopolitical domains, and established hierarchies, as well as of engaging in simulated geographic mobility are virtual communities and spaces. "Cyberculture," it has been pointed out, "ceaselessly redefines the outlines of a mobile and expanding labyrinth that can't be mapped, a universal labyrinth.... I refer to this universality without any centralized meaning, this system of disorder and labyrinthine transparency, as the *universal without totality*."[13] Although cyberspace is a powerful factor in globalization, it does not eliminate local centers, and it is within this new utopian realm that the reinvention and mythologizing of Central European space are taking place. It is significant that, even though the virtual medium satisfies the post-material desires of today's producers and consumers of virtual culture, this medium attempts, at the same time, to recreate and reshape some of the more tangible elements of material culture. Virtual place becomes a new ambivalent utopia where borders are rewritten, maps redrawn, and cultural identifications redefined according to the whim and taste of its visitors/consumers.

The literary and socio-political, multicultural virtual journal such as *Potiah 76* (Train 76) is a good example of a narrative consistently foregrounding the problems of belonging and exclusion, shifting and elusive borders, and interrupted and fragmented identities; it is one of the representative instances of participation in imaginary cosmopolitanism while redefining and reaffirming local center(s). *Potiah 76* was created by the Ukrainian writer Yuri Andrukhovych in June 2003 and described by its author as "dedicated to the newest literature of Central and Central Eastern Europe," as well as to the issues of "polytology, socio-cultural anthropology, journalism, socio-political and artistic life."[14] Through its emphasis on the geopolitical context of the project, the broad spectrum of the post-Soviet societies represented on the site (from the Balkans to the Baltic states, from the Czech Republic to Belarus and Ukraine) and the scope of genres and discourses (fiction, political essays, cultural analyses, among others), the journal attempts to make a statement in terms of a coherent cultural narrative. This digital space, which serves as another way of mapping the new Central Europe, showcases, through its participation in a global discourse and creation of an alternative cartography, the universalizing claim of virtuality combined with the localizing impetus and the precision of the geopolitical desire aimed at rewriting the historical narrative of Eastern Europe. The representation of space in *Potyah 76* is significant both in terms of content and visuals. The trope of movement and travel dominates both spheres: the journal invites you to experience the new Central Europe by means of a journey through the area's literature and, more generally, culture, but also via a more immediate effect of the cartographic plays the editorial team engages in. The visual motto of the journal is a train (which hints at the meaning of the Ukrainian word "potyah/потяг") running across the screen in perpetual motion. The name of the train route refers to an actual international express existing earlier in the 1960s; the itinerary symbolically united the region while also including Ukraine as part of the geopolitical space it mapped. The gradual dissolution of itinerary 76 was perceived back then as representative of the growing isolation of the cultures of this region from each other and from Europe's "core." The cartographic representation of route 76 on the site homepage is clearly playful, yet it is also intended to put forward a specific message: the trajectory is non-linear, as its sequence of urban points/place names has no reference to actual geophysical reality and so does not reflect any real cartographic "order." The itinerary is inclusive rather than exclusive in its non-linearity and subversive in its rewriting of earlier, historical and political models of Central Europe (such as the Austro-Hungarian, Polish, and

Soviet imperial spaces). It is an imaginary space, yet, in its invented un-reality, it is also a projection of a collective desire that comprises both imperial nostalgia and the propensity for a new geopolitical order. A virtual, secondary ontology like *Potyah 76* then destabilizes existing borders, subverts normative and normalizing socio-political spatial practices, and offers an alternative vision, both as a ready-made product of popular consumption and as a vision to be shaped, refined, and used to cultivate an idea of community.

The sense of "unhomeliness" of the new Europe, the continent's spatial instability and fluidity, is projected with unique force in the inaugural issue of the journal, specifically by Andrzej Stasiuk, one of the major contemporary authors in Poland today. His brief essay "Right of the Seventeenth Degree" is a reflection on the elusive and shifting geopolitical imaginary of Central/new Europe. Although every place is potentially a palimpsest layered with multiple histories, stories, myths, and memories,[15] the indeterminate, evolving narrative of Europe of the last decades is particularly rich with historical intertexts and ideological manipulations and is reminiscent of Borgesian, discursively fashioned constructs:

> It's an invention, a legend, a myth.... This Europe does not really exist. It's only a dream, which is being dreamt. Moreover, it's a dream that is being dreamt only by some, select people.
>
> Her borders are unclear, interwoven and whimsical. They stretch in space, take shape in time, consciousnesses, hearts, memories, blood and bodies; they cut in half the wholes and unite the divided segments. Nobody knows where the beginning and the end are and if there ever have been a beginning and an end...
>
> The grounds for the existence of this Europe are a guess, a suspicion, a fantasy and an invention.... Accustomed to non-existence, Europe is here used to wearing masks.... This world east of the 17th degree latitude is still in the process of completion and hence so mesmerizing.... Life here manifests itself in unstructured, anarchic forms; it still bears the memory of its own dark, violent beginnings.[16]

Like Foucauldian heterotopia,[17] this Europe is here and elsewhere; it is a plurality, an intersection of different historical planes, a multivoiced narrative. Europe itself is a perpetual nomad that has been historically homeless. Stasiuk's reference to Europe's violent beginnings[18] contains an allusion to the narrative of Europa, the foundational myth of Europe. The Phoenician princess, Europa, was daughter of the King of Tyre. Kidnapped by Zeus, taken to the island of Crete, and raped, she gave birth to three sons, whose empires were the mythic origins of modern Europe. The relevance of this myth to today's negotiation of the space of Central Europe along the West/East continuum inheres in the fact that the story of Europa "is not set at the centre of Europe—wherever that may be—but takes place at its outer margins…it is a liminal story…situated in in-between spaces."[19] Analogous to the narrative of Europe, originating as the latter did, in Asia Minor, outside the traditional space of modern Europe and thus reminding us that its relation to the "other" is less than clear-cut, the contributors to *Potyah 76* engage in rewriting the narrative of today's Europe from the continent's margins, questioning its traditional center and constructing a new European cultural identity. Curiously enough, the Ukrainian word "potyah" combines two distinct meanings: "train" and "longing," "desire" (which was noted in an online Polish review of the journal[20]); while the trope of movement here emphasizes the opening up of the space of Central Europe, the space of the site itself can be conceptualized as a locus of desire.

Another representative example of such a geopolitically oriented online community is the Polish online magazine *Panorama Kultur—Europa Mniej Znana* (Panorama of Cultures—The Less-Known Europe), established in 2002-2003. The title's reference to a Europe "less known" foregrounds the perspective of the "center" and reinforces the process of "othering" of the region. At the same time, otherness is here assumed with a sense of pride and as a tool of constructing and reappropriating the space referred to as "our Europe." Although the magazine is devoted to the discussion and popularization of what is designated as "Central East European" culture across all media, the editorial group also states that they "consider as [their] duty building and promoting Central European identity."[21] The shift from the more specific designation of Central Eastern Europe to the indeterminate space of Central Europe is notable as it is primarily a shift from a more geographically defined criterion to a cultural one. Just as with *Potyah 76*, an important part of *Panorama*'s engagement with its audience involves cultivating a sense of collective identity and belonging. The geographic scope of featured cultures—the

Balkans, the Baltic states (Estonia), (East) Germany, the Czech Republic, Hungary, Romania, Bulgaria, Ukraine, Belarus—clearly indicates that Central Europe is defined here very loosely, primarily in the context of the former Soviet empire.[22] The politically emancipatory impetus behind such a project is hard to ignore. In his "Short Story of Identity," Zygmunt Bauman proposes that "countries previously labeled as 'outside Europe' are in the process of rewriting their national history. For some of these countries rewriting history means establishing a relationship with Europe, that is to say, claiming a European history. Yet establishing such a relationship is also a political act, for it entails crossing a boundary"; for them, "Europe becomes a pervasive concept."[23] It is of interest that the editorial team of the magazine consists mostly of academically trained individuals, fully conversant with the theoretical assumptions underpinning the discourse of their publication (notably, the idea of the creation of *Panorama Kultur* came from the students of the School of Eastern Europe and Institute of Slavic Language and Literature Studies of the Warsaw University). The scope of materials featured by the journal is very broad, ranging from an update on the academic and cultural events both in Poland and abroad to an archive of articles to an excellent source on the newest film releases (PK Film) to a list of blogs relevant to the discussion of Central European culture.

The post-totalitarian literary production in Poland shows similar concerns with the problems of identity formation in the period of changing epistemic paradigms and with the role space construction plays in making meaning in and of today's world. If authors such as Andrzej Stasiuk, both in his fictional and essayistic writing, thematize travel and celebrate postmodern mobility in the new Europe while also remaining aware of how this mobility shapes domestic space (cf. his *Moja Europa*; *Jadąc do Babadag*; *Fado*, 2006), other writers focus on the meaning-generating significance of local places such as small provincial towns and on their role in the broader, spatial construction of history and ethnicity. Stasiuk himself acknowledges different aspects and modes of travel and their relation to the conceptualization of the space of home and, ultimately, to self-identification: "Central Europe never gave birth to great travelers. She was preoccupied with journeying inside herself. To travel out of curiosity? Such a thought may occur to someone who is certain of the immobility of his own home, who altogether does not wonder whether upon his return he will find his house still in the same place. It's quite possible that this deceptive perception of being settled, this immobility of the home, is a consequence of a profound feeling of unhomeliness in an inner, mental sense."[24] In this context, of relevance is *Dom dzienny, dom nocny* (House of Day, House of Night, 1988-2002), one of the novels of Olga Tokarczuk, a bestselling writer of today's Poland, who explores the space of Silesia, a quintessential palimpsest of histories, discourses, ideologies, and meanings. The south-western part of the country has been part of Germany, former Czechoslovakia, and Poland, and is thus a commentary on all of Europe, an embodiment of the impossibility of any real origin, purity, and monologism. Although the narrative of the novel never moves beyond the small town of Nowa Ruda, has only a residual plot with virtually no action, and produces a closed, almost claustrophobic effect, space is here inherently "unsettled" (in Stasiuk's sense), open and looking outward, seeking out hidden connections, and aware of its own potentialities: "It's a town dreaming that it's in the Pyrenees, that the sun never sets on it, that all the people who've left will be back one day, and that there are underground tunnels from the German era leading to Prague, Wrocław, and Dresden. It's a fragment town, a Silesian, Prussian, Czech, Austro-Hungarian, and Polish town, a town on the outskirts."[25] In the novel, the communal desire for home is elusive and hard to articulate; the possibility of a specific, local home can be actualized only through a reconciliation with the global, universal home we all belong to and through the acceptance of this "other" home. As Tokarczuk's narrator comments, "each of us has two homes—one actual home with a fixed location in time and space, and a second that is infinite, with no address and no chance to be immortalized in architectural plans—and...we live in both of them simultaneously."[26] The potential of each place and space, of belonging simultaneously here and elsewhere, of being part of a broader context, underpins the tension between center and periphery, the global and the local.

As opposed to Tokarczuk's introspective, unrushed prose, Manuela Gretkowska's writing represents a different face of the Polish post-totalitarian postmodernism. Much lighter and accessible, geared towards the mass audience (she is one of the commercially successful authors), with elements of autobiography and documentary non-fiction, Gretkowska's books present a diverse mosaic of contemporary European culture and society. Streets, people, a circle of friends brought together by circumstances, casual conversations render her narratives fragments of different people's lives, interspersed with reflections on art, religion, literature, historiography, and the like. Even though most of her characters live outside Poland, the author's cosmopolitan experiences in Western Europe paradoxically—and inevitably—resound with Polish subtexts. Her earlier books (*My zdies' emigranty* [We Are Here Immigrants], 1991; *Tarot paryski* [The Parisian Tarot], 1993; *Kabaret metafizyczny* [Metaphysical Cabaret],1995; *Podręcznik do ludzi* [A Textbook on People], 1996; *Światowidz* [Worldview], 1998), as well as the more recent (*Polka* [Polish Woman], 2001; *Europejka* [European Woman], 2004; *Obywatelka* [Citizen], 2008, to name a few) explore the experience of being Polish in a Europe with open borders and in the global world, as well as what it means to see one's own culture through the eyes of others. This continuous, askance glance and the ironic attitude Gretkowska adopts foreground the process of negotiating the collective self-definition: although Poland as such may not necessarily be present in her books, Polish cultural space and identity form an implicit background for most of her writing.

The author's/narrator's extensive travel experiences captured in fragmented vignettes echo the postmodern narrative techniques she uses to mirror the disconnected and unhomely world of today's Poles whether in diaspora or in their home country. Thus, *Kabaret metafizyczny* is structured as a series of footnotes where each brief segment of writing serves as a gloss to the previous one, that is, forms a subordinate level, unfolding into a Chinese box structure. The catch, however, is that the chain-like development of the succession of footnotes lacks the traditional (and commonly expected) dependence of a regular note on the main narrative; here, the relation between the footnote and the footnoted text is built mostly on the associative link to an arbitrary word in the text, which word also happens to be placed in the opening sentence of the next footnote. The very idea of footnotes, of course, is implicit of the "main" narrative in the background; the absence of such a metanarrative forms an explicit gap, inviting the reader to fill it in at his/her own discretion, and, at the same time, emphasizing the arbitrariness of such an operation. Although without the usual footnote graphic markers, the "footnoted" narrative style is characteristic of other Gretkowska's writing. Just like the missing frame narrative in most of her novels, the nomadic lifestyle of the characters inhabiting her semi-fictional stories lacks the master "home" narrative. Gretkowska's attempts to write such a home narrative takes up various forms. Thus, in *Podręcznik do ludzi*, she casts herself as the author of *Rękopis nieodnaleziony* (The Undiscovered Manuscript), a creative extension of Jan Potocki's original work. Count Jan Potocki (1761-1815) was a famous Polish historian and archeologist who was educated in Switzerland and France. Potocki traveled and researched extensively in Northern Africa, the Middle East, and Asia. His *Rękopis znaleziony w Saragossie* (The Manuscript Found in Saragossa, 1804-05) was written and published originally in French under the title of *Le manuscrit trouvé à Saragosse*. Written in the tradition of *The Arabian Nights*, Chaucer, and Boccaccio, it is a metafictional and self-reflexive narrative that is as much about an eclectic collection of adventure and mystery stories as it is about the act and tradition of storytelling itself. Using Potocki intertextually, Gretkowska playfully decontextualizes him and places his work in the framework of contemporary Polish society. The irony of this move is that if the eighteenth-century Potocki traveled and wrote as a European in the Orient, the contemporary Potocki, coming from the peripheries of today's Europe, would himself be subjected to neo-Orientalist attitudes.[27] One of the more interesting aspects of Gretkowska's work is exposing the historical ironies of travel and "being" in the world, as a way of exploring the shaping of identity in contemporary Poland.

In the post-totalitarian literature of Ukraine now, Yuri Andrukhovych's oeuvre expresses particularly strong awareness of the ambivalence of the Ukrainian geopolitical space along the West/East continuum. One of the key literary figures of today's Ukraine, Andrukhovych is also, in a narrower sense, a Western Ukrainian author who works with the rich, historical heritage of the region that has been multiethnic, cosmopolitan by nature, and sharing the legacies of three different empires. His collections of essayistic non-fiction *Dezorientacija na miscevosti* (Disorientation on Location, 1999) and *Moia Ievropa* (My Europe, 2001, co-authored with Andrzej Stasiuk), where the titles themselves are indicative of the scope of the problematic, deal with a wide range of geocultural issues and with what he defines as "geopoetics," including the way spatial cultural representations mediate our relationship with the natural space we inhabit and form a quintessential part of our identity. His essay "Carpathologia cosmophilica," in whose subtitle he identifies the piece as an attempt at a fictional study in local geography, can be designated as a programmatic text that defines the writer's vision of (Western) Ukraine as a Central European space. For Andrukhovych, the Carpathians are simultaneously a natural object and an object of a centuries-long historical, political, and ideological inscription. As opposed to the urban imaginaries of Gretkowska, Tokarczuk, and Vynnychuk (the latter will be discussed below), Andrukhvych's Central Europe begins even further away in the continent's margins, in the depths of the mountain range that spans the territory of several countries and endows them with shared cultural characteristics. The Carpathians are at the very roots of the modern divisions that separate the continent—Roman versus Byzantine Empires, West versus East—and home to the unique socio-ethnic niches (Bukovyna, Transylvania, the Hutzul country) that are the very core of what he conceptualizes as Central Europe. The Carpathians are a dreamscape, a "structure-myth beyond which there is no deconstruction."[28] In Andrukhovych, the Carpathian landscape often incorporates, harmoniously and aesthetically, eclectic glimpses of post-apocalyptic scenery, with abandoned and half-ruined architectural and industrial structures bearing witness to several lost empires and civilizations. The mountains are a remnant of the mythical "L'viv-Warsaw-Vienna-Paris" vector, of which only gossips and guesses have reached us,"[29] and thus themselves become mere ghosts of history.

The topos of the Carpathians is also featured prominently in Andrukhovych's novel *Dvanadciat' obruchiv* (The Twelve Rings, 2003). In his afterword to the novel, "A Chronic Orpheus: An Attempt at an Autocommentary," the writer states—perhaps tongue-in-cheek—that "the mountains are the main hero of this novel."[30] *The Twelve Rings* is a narrative of an Austrian citizen, Karl-Joseph Zumbrunnen (whose name immediately associates with Karl Franz Joseph von Habsburg—Charles I, the Emperor of Austria), who is obsessed with traveling to the post-Soviet Western Ukraine, the territory formerly belonging to Austro-Hungarian Empire. Zumbrunnen's hermeneutic "quest" for understanding this country as well as digging up his family roots there has the distinct touch of a neo-colonial gaze. Andrukhovych's use of the elements of the literary genre of travelogue—"*notatky podorozhnioho*"[31]—and of the epistolary form are highly significant. These are first-hand accounts of a traveler's (re)discovery of a mysterious, lost Europe hidden in the depths of the continent. Andrukhovych too lays out a strong parodic context by linking Zumbrunnen's epistolary records to the tradition of early travelogues and explorers' documents. The discourse of cartography constitutes an indispensable part of Zumbrunnen's story, for this discourse is indeed an exercise in orientation on location: ironically, and rather symbolically, the Austrian traveler orients himself with help from old Viennese maps of Galicia, dubious tourist guides providing a wealth of familiar stereotypes and assumptions about Eastern Europe. The mountains are a quintessential liminal territory, a space of becoming for Zumbrunnen in search for his ancestral history. The Austrian's subliminal longing "to disappear in the depths" and "never to return"[32] appears earlier in the novel and foreshadows his own, future undoing. Here, Andrukhovych is unmistakably engaging in an intertextual play with Joseph Conrad's *Heart of Darkness*. Zumbrunnen's death in the mountains serves as a metaphor of his all-absorbing, self-annihilating desire "[to become] one with the Other,"[33] and the Carpathians transform into a blind, irrational force, but also into a space of resistance to neo-colonial reappropriation:

> The forest is such a nightmarish labyrinth, a great green monster, especially this forest, a primordial thicket that was not planted by a human hand, it lets in light-headed Viennese tourists, who are used only to waltzing on palace parquets, and refuses to let them go. But it's not Vienna here, and not even Viennese woods, where all the paths are asphalted. The forest is green, and *the green* swallows you.[34]

In *The Twelve Rings* the natural world forms a central part of the socio-cultural sphere; the two cannot be separated, and resistance of the one becomes resistance of the other. In his article "Choosing a Europe," Marko Pavlyshyn argues that the writers of the post-Soviet Ukrainian literature such as Andrukhovych and Izdryk attempt to reorient collective national identity toward Europe, constructing, more specifically, a particular model of Europe. This is convincingly demonstrated by Andrukhovych's oeuvre, in which such a model is not only proposed but also appropriated for specific geopolitical goals in the negotiation of the East/West binary. As Pavlyshyn rightly notes,

> Andrukhovych chooses a Europe which allows him to view his native landscape—the foothills of the Carpathians—and his favourite city, L'viv with its Habsburg history, as part of a continuum that

stretches to Venice and Munich, encompassing much that is picturesque and visually comfortable. The physical existence of the
landscape appears to render this Europe tangible, but as a cultural
object it is the fruit of selective vision, nostalgic introspection and
imagination.[35]

Although there is no doubt that both Habsburg aesthetic nostalgia and an
alternative model of the non-urban Central Europe play an important
role in Andrukhovych's conceptualization of this geopolitical space, it
would not be fair to say that such a position offers no "socio-political
challenges."[36] What Andrukhovych constructs, both in his fiction and
non-fiction, is a different concept of both Central European and European culture, which rewrites the traditional understanding of the region
from its margins and subverts the historical idea of European "civilization," thus also accommodating the "other," non-urban Europe as key to
articulating collective identity in his own culture.

Another prominent Ukrainian literary figure of today, Yuri
Vynnychuk, who is a prolific fiction writer, has also been involved in the
research and retrieval of the history of Ukraine's urban space. His
loosely culturological *Knajpy L'vova* (The Pubs and Eateries of L'viv)
quickly became a bestseller. Specifically, of interest is his focus on
geography and its relation to the processes of nation building and identity formation, as well as the representation of urban space as a fluid
signifier, a cartographic game, and a nostalgic desire for elusive,
mythological "home." Although Vynnychuk's book does not concern
itself with travel as such—that is, it does not thematize travel and can be
marketed primarily as a reference book focusing on the history of coffee
houses and popular eateries in L'viv—it implies travel throughout, inviting those who are unfamiliar with the city to imagine it and those who
know it to revisit it in a less familiar context. What with the flourishing
of domestic and international tourism in the post-Soviet period, urban
space becomes a highly marketable commodity, an open-ended narrative, and a domain to be reimagined, reinvented, and constructed to
anyone's taste and liking. It is worth recalling, along these lines, that, in
her study of the history of tourism as a global cultural practice, Maxine
Feifer conceptualizes our new relation to experiencing the world as
"post-tourism." "Above all," she argues, "the post-tourist knows that he
is a tourist: not a time traveller when he goes somewhere historic; not an

instant noble savage when he stays on a tropical beach; not an invisible observer when he visits a native compound. Resolutely 'realistic,' he cannot evade his condition of outsider."[37] This condition of postmodern outsidedness as well as the awareness of oneself's construction as an observer of history and urban space are well exemplified by Vynnychuk's text, which, pointedly, transgresses any fixed generic classification. *Knajpy L'vova* is an extremely well-researched study drawing on archival materials but also one deliberately avoiding the conventions of the academic discourse. The volume may be seen as a popular reference book that constitutes entertaining reading given that a lot in it appears to be purely anecdotal information, but it is also an intellectual and scholarly project that undoubtedly engages in an ideologically informed construction of a cultural space. *Knajpy L'vova* combines text with visuals (drawings, old postcards, posters, advertisements, photos, and maps), retraces historical architectonics, and rebuilds topographies. It is eclectic enough to appeal to tourists, fiction readers, and cultural analysts.

It is useful to recall here Michel de Certeau's study of spatiality, where he distinguishes between the concept of "place" (which "implies an indication of stability") and "space," which "occurs as the effect produced by the operations that orient it, situate it, temporalize it, and make it function in a polyvalent unity of conflictual programs...[s]pace is like the word when it is spoken, that is, when it is caught in the ambiguity of an actualization,...situated as the act of a present...and modified by the transformations caused by successive contexts."[38] In short, *"space is a practiced place"*[39] continuously changed by actions of historical subjects. Among spatializing practices are "narrative actions...as forms of practices organizing space."[40] Vynnychuk's *Knajpy L'vova* is an example of such a space-organizing narrative that documents evolution of the culture of public consumption in the city (specifically, in its coffee houses and popular restaurants) and constitutes an interpretive project focused on the urban identity of its population. In one of the interviews, the author readily admits that what he was interested in was not so much the history of the city as the everyday social practices of its inhabitants.

One of the underlying geopolitical tensions that becomes immediately apparent in Vynnychuk's study is the continuous negotiation of the East/West dichotomy that defines the identity of L'viv's urban space. Tracing the history of the coffee culture in L'viv (and thus promoting its Western-oriented identity), the author refers to the seventeenth-century successful Galician enterprises in Vienna (owned by Kul'chyc'kyj) and to the first coffee houses in Kam'janec'-Podil'skyj (in 1672, during the Ottoman Empire, and later, in 1699, during Rzeczpospolita), which were opened and operated by the Turks. The true obsession with the coffee culture started in the eighteenth century and thus included influences from the Austrian and Ottoman cultures alike. Vynnychuk takes the reader through a multitude of coffee houses, eateries, and pubs that have been defining the identity of the city for the last 300 years. The narrative of changing place-names, street-names, reconstructed buildings, and languages reflects the fluid historical architectonics of the city. The long list of *knajpas* would resemble a postmodern inventory where the object itself precedes its context if it were not for the vividly populated, lived spaces they represented. Vynnychuk's exploration of the development of modern urban consumer culture in L'viv centers on the changing modes of reproduction and representation, and on the relationship between cultural operations and their participants through the city's centuries of changing imperial subordination.

According to Walter Benjamin, "history is the subject of a structure whose site is not homogenous, empty time, but time filled by the presence of the now,"[41] and Vynnychuk is indeed keen on creating the feeling of the presence of the now. His city is not an artifact but a living space populated with discourses; it is a pluralized city, a migratory and migrating city, and new topographies and landscapes emerge with every new story. Here L'viv is a radically "other" city, experienced through a detached, outside perspective of a postmodern storyteller and reader, a space of continuous unhomeliness where the center is always elsewhere. In his reading of urban culture, Certeau comments on this condition of necessary historical displacement:

> Where is the fiction? Where is the real? The link between the "events" and "order" engages the relation that we have with ourselves, both individually and collectively. To let go [of the past] means choosing and selecting once again.... It is tantamount to pronouncing a judgment, but without a trial, cutting into our history in order to make a division between truth on one side and illusion on the other....[42]

In Vynnychuk truth and illusion become deliberately displaced. His eclectic "textualization" and "reading" of city life captures the essence of Benjamin's critique of urban space as an ultimate site of consumer seduction and pleasure. More importantly, this reading also offers insightful commentary on the development of the concept of modernity and the consolidation of the modern Ukrainian intelligentsia, both a critic and an avid consumer of the newly evolving modern urban culture, which served as a hotbed for the developing discourse of modernism. The writer, who is a narrator/investigator/analyst/reader, assumes the stance of a *flâneur*, both an observer and a participant, someone who maintains critical distance while becoming a part of urban life. Thus, one discerns in the book a voyeuristic enjoyment as the author constructs the simulacrum of the historical present.

As Charles Baudelaire, arguably the first painter of modern life, commented in *Paris Spleen*, "[t]he solitary and thoughtful stroller finds a singular intoxication in this universal communion [with the crowd]. The man who loves to lose himself in the crowd enjoys feverish delights that the egoist misses.... What men call love is a very small, restricted, feeble thing compared with this ineffable orgy, this divine prostitution of the soul giving itself entire, all its poetry and all its charity, to the unex-pected as it comes along, to the strange as he passes."[43] In the *Arcades Project*, Benjamin argues that modern urban culture "opens a phantas-magoria which a person enters in order to be distracted. The entertain-ment industry makes this easier by elevating the person to the level of commodity. He surrenders to its manipulations while enjoying his alien-ation from himself and others."[44] Throughout his historical excursus, the writer does exactly that, namely, opens a phantasmagoria of public urban encounters in a clash of high and low cultures within the symbolic space of the city where histories collide. To him, this is primarily a city of entertainment, of enjoyment, of seduction, and of erotic allure, a space of performativity, of "happening," beyond any traditional rigid binaries.

Together with the reconstruction of places and their histories, the author inevitably populates them with a mixture of aristocracy, local gentry, and, increasingly more prominent, intelligentsia. Among other things, Vynnychuk specifically zeroes in on the emergence of national modernity against the background of the evolving urban consumer cul-ture. In Benjamin's words, "in the *flâneur*, the intelligentsia sets foot in the marketplace—ostensibly to look around, but in truth to find a buyer.... The crowd is the veil through which the familiar city beckons to the *flâneur* as phantasmagoria—now a landscape, now a room. In this intermediate stage, in which it still has patrons but is already beginning to familiarize itself with the market, it appears as the *bohème*. To the uncertainty of its economic function corresponds the uncertainty of its political function."[45] In Vynnychuk's *fin-de-siècle* L'viv, the sold and bought commodities included everything from fashion to the latest trends in entertaining to intellectual ideas, in other words, a complex network of social practices that defined the evolving identity of the modern, urban nation.

Speaking of Ukrainian intelligentsia, one of the contemporaries, Myxajlo Rudnyc'kyj, noted: "Ukrainian writers of earlier generations could not even imagine that it was possible to think and write in a coffee house.... In the era of modernism, an unstructured, spontaneous life outside one's home acquired the taste and appeal of the exotic."[46] Commenting on the growth of the coffee culture at the turn of the nineteenth and twentieth centuries, Petro Karmans'kyj wrote about the role of coffee houses in fostering a community within Ukrainian intelligentsia and artistic circles and in providing a free, uncensored environment for an exchange of ideas: "All that's left for our fellow poor poets or publicists is the modern, inexpensive, quiet, discrete coffee house, where they can find a source of creative impetus and new concepts. For a price of several coins, paid for tea or coffee he could feel like a real human being and could do intellectual work for several hours."[47] In fact, the very existence of Moloda Musa (The Young Muse), a L'viv-based modernist group, cannot be separated from the evolving urban space and the culture of such venues: "Coffee places allowed our fellow poets and artists to forget about reality [impoverished], they gave us an illusion of well being and, what is more important, they made us into a fellowship of brothers of similar thinking and similar aspirations.... The real life was happening in the coffee house. We talked about the essence and goals of art, debated, and discussed new ideas...."[48] The coffee house was an ultimate democratic space that allowed for development of alternative discourses and practices. Here, modern urban space performed as an ideology—rather than as a geophysical space—that participated in and contributed to many aspects of the formation of modern national identity. Echoing de Certeau, Alison Russell comments that "space is never neutral, neither is our mapping of space, whether that mapping is verbal or cartographic"; rhetorical reading of space reveals the reader's positioning practice and "hierarchization of space."[49] In Vynnychuk, successive pages of the imperial history are reappropriated and integrated as part of the identity he constructs, that is to say, fluid and migratory identity, where belonging/non-belonging itself becomes tenuous and binaries disappear. Although Vynnychuk's book may appear to be addressed to tourists, in reality it is meant for those who know the city well, "practice" it on an everyday basis, and may appreciate the community-building value of this narrative. Behind Vynnychuk's impetus to reconstruct the historical L'viv lies primarily the desire to reconstruct and document the city's long alignment with what can be defined as a model of Western urban culture.

To conclude, the persistent trend toward literary "geographicity" in today's Polish and Ukrainian writing can be fully understood if one takes into account the historically constructed marginality of these cultures. Periphery inherently implies, critics have insisted, a power relation that potentially excludes its member(s) from the position of subjects endowed with hierarchy-changing agency:

> The geographical and social conception of periphery is an inherently dyadic, relativistic one, predicated upon explicit or implicit, binary contrasts between two constructed spheres of contrasted spatial and social difference. Moreover, these spheres of spatial difference have normally been constructed and defined by agents deriving their perspectives, self-definition, and not infrequently, their power and authority from membership of the constructed core sphere, rather than from membership of the constructed peripheral one.[50]

In the context of the historically fashioned "spheres of spatial differences," questioning the global and European geopolitical balance by revising the narratives of local places and spaces, by speaking from the margins, and by re-centering these margins constitutes an act of agency that redefines our views of new Central and Eastern Europe in the second decade of its making.

NOTES

1. Gayatri Chakravorty Spivak, "Can the Subaltern Speak?" in *Marxism and the Interpretation of Culture*, eds. C. Nelson and L. Grossberg (Macmillan Education: Basingstoke, 1988), 271.

2. Anna Klobucka, "Theorizing the European Periphery," *symplokē* 5.1-2 (1997): 126.

3. Jacques Derrida, "The Other Heading: Memories, Responses, and Responsibilities," *PMLA: Publications of the Modern Language Association of America* 108.1 (1993): 90, emphasis in the original.

4. Immanuel Wallerstein, *Geopolitics and Geoculture* (Cambridge: Cambridge University Press, 1991), 175.

5. Alexandra Kogl, *Strange Places: The Political Potentials and Perils of Everyday Spaces* (Lanham, MD: Lexington Books, 2008), 1.

6. *Ibid.*, 45.

7. *Ibid.*, 2, emphasis in the original.

8. Caryl Emerson, "Answering for Central and Eastern Europe," in *Comparative Literature in an Age of Globalization*, ed. Haun Saussy (Baltimore, MD: The Johns Hopkins University Press, 2006), 203-4.

9. Ewa Mazierska and Laura Rascaroli, *Crossing New Europe: Postmodern Travel and the European Road Movie* (London and New York: Wallflower Press, 2006), 111, 137.

10. Louisa Schein, "Of Cargo and Satellites: Imagined Cosmopolitanism," *Postcolonial Studies* 2 (1999): 345-75.

11. Michel Foucault, "Des Espaces Autres," 1967, *Architecture/Mouvement/ Continuité* October, 1984; "Of Other Spaces," trans. Jay Miskowiec, 1998, http://www.foucault.info/documents/heteroTopia/foucault.heteroTopia.en.html (accessed August 22, 2008).

12. Foucault, "Des Espaces Autres"/"Of Other Places"; Henri Lefebvre, *La production de l'espace* (Anthropos: Paris, 1974); Homi Bhabha, *The Location of Culture* (London and New York: Routledge, 1994); Edward W. Soja, *ThirdSpace* (Oxford: Blackwell, 1996), *Postmodern Geographies: The Reassertion of Space in Critical Social Theory* (London: Verso, 1989).

13. Pierre Levy, *Cyberculture*, trans. Robert Bonnono (Minneapolis, MN: University of Minnesota Press, 2001), 91-92, emphasis in the original.

14. *Potyah 76*, http://www.potyah76.org.ua (accessed July 17, 2008). All translations from *Potiah 73* are mine.

15. Nedra Reynolds, *Geographies of Writing*, (Carbondale, IL: Southern Illinois University Press, 2004), 2.

16. Andrzej Stasiuk, "Right of the Seventeenth Degree" http://www.potyah76.org.ua/potyah/?t=42 (accessed February 12, 2009).

17. Foucault, "Des Espaces Autres"; "Of Other Spaces."

18. In the original, "violent" beginnings (гвалтовні початки) has a clear implication of violent rape.

19. Manfred Pfister, "Europa/Europe: Myths and Muddles," in Richard Littlejohns and Sara Soncini, eds., *Myths of Europe* (Amsterdam: Rodopi, 2007), 24.

20. Tadeusz Iwański, "Pociąg do literatury," *Panorama kultur* http://www.pk.org.pl/artykul.php?id=189 (accessed January 13, 2009).

21. *Panorama kultur*, http://www.pk.org.pl/dzial.php?idd=62&id=8 (accessed January 27, 2009).

22. The site link entitled "Dossier" gives a comprehensive list of the countries covered by this project. It should be noted that Russia is also included in some of the journal's materials, as well as Turkey.

23. Jaro Stacul, Christina Moutsou, and Helen Kopnina, eds., "Crossing European Boundaries: Beyond Conventional Geographical Categories," in *Crossing European Boundaries: Beyond Conventional Geographical Categories* (New York: Berghahn Books, 2006), 3.

24. Andrzej Stasiuk, "Korabel'nyj shchodennyk" ["A Ship Diary"], in Andrzej Stasiuk and Yuri Andrukhovych, *Moia Ievropa* [*My Europe*] (L'viv: Klasyka, 2001), 30, my translation.

25. Olga Tokarczuk, *House of Day, House of Night*, trans. Antonia Lloyd-Jones (Evanston, IL: Northwestern University Press, 2002), 285.

26. *Ibid.*, 204.

27. In today's literature of Ukraine and Poland, Neo-Orientalism is a very common approach to conceptualizing the perception of Eastern Europe in broader, European and global contexts. Thus, for example, Stasiuk, in the essay from *Potyah 76* quoted above, alludes heavily to the classical Orientalist vocabulary of the early travelers to the East.

28. Yuri Andrukhovych, "Carpathologia cosmophilica," in his *Dezorientacija na miscevosti*. [Disorientation on Location], 1999 (Ivano-Frankivs'k: Lileja, 2006), 17. The original word for "deconstruction" (деструкція) also implies "destruction."

29. *Ibid.*, 16.

30. Yuri Andrukhovych, *Dvanadciat' obruchiv* [The Twelve Rings], 2003 (Kyiv: Krytyka, 2004), 326. Here and further my translation.

31. *Ibid.*, 16, emphasis in the original.

32. *Ibid.*, 20.

33. *Ibid.*, 27.

34. *Ibid.*, 212, emphasis in the original.

35. Marko Pavlyshyn, "Choosing a Europe: Andrukhovych, Izdryk and the New Ukrainian Literature," *New Zealand Slavonic Journal* 35 (2001): 43.

36. *Ibid.*

37. Maxine Feifer, *Tourism in History: From Imperial Rome to the Present* (New York: Stern and Day, 1986), 271.

38. Michel de Certeau, *The Practice of Everyday Life*, trans. Steven F. Rendall (Berkeley, CA: University of California Press, 1984), 117.

39. *Ibid.*

40. *Ibid.*, 116.

41. Walter Benjamin, *Illuminations*, trans. H. Zohn (New York: Schocken Books, 1969), 261.

42. *The Certeau Reader*, Ed. Graham Ward (New York: Blackwell, 2000), 61-62.

43. Charles Baudelaire, *Paris Spleen*, trans. Louise Varése (New York: New Directions Publishing, 1970), 20.

44. Walter Benjamin, *Selected Writings*, ed. M. Jennings (Cambridge, MA: Harvard University Press, 2002), 37.

45. *Ibid.*, 40.

46. Yuri Vynnychuk, *Knajpy L'vova* [The Pubs and Eateries of L'viv] (L'viv: Piramida, 2005), 16. Here and further translation is mine.

47. *Ibid.*, 15.

48. *Ibid.*, 16.

49. Alison Russell, *Crossing Boundaries: Postmodern Travel Literature* (New York: Palgrave, 2000), 13.
50. A. V. Seaton, "The Worst of Journeys, the Best of Journeys: Travel and the Concept of Periphery in European Culture," Mike Robinson and Phil Long, eds., *Expressions of Culture, Identity and Meaning in Tourism* (Sunderland: Center for Travel and Tourism, 2000), 322-23.

BIBLIOGRAPHY

Andrukhovych, Yuri. "Carpathologia cosmophilica." In Andrukhovych, *Dezorientacija na miscevosti*, 15-24.

_____. *Dezorientacija na miscevosti [Disorientation on Location]*. 1999. Ivano-Frankivs'k: Lileja, 2006.

_____. *Dvanadciat' obruchiv*. *[The Twelve Rings]* 2003. Kyiv: Krytyka, 2004.

Baudelaire, Charles. *Paris Spleen*. Trans. Louise Varése. New York: New Directions Publishing, 1970.

Bauman, Zygmunt. "From Pilgrim to Tourist—or a Short Story of Identity." In *Questions of Cultural Identity*, edited by Stuart Hall and Paul Du Gay. London: Sage, 1996. 18-35.

Benjamin, Walter. *Illuminations*. Trans. H. Zohn. New York: Shocken Books, 1969.

_____. *Selected Writings*. Edited by M. Jennings. Cambridge, MA: Harvard University Press, 2002.

Bhabha, Homi. *The Location of Culture*. London and New York: Routledge, 1994.

Binnie, Jon, Julian Holloway, Steve Millington, and Craig Young, eds. *Cosmopolitan Urbanism*. London and New York: Routledge, 2006.

Certeau, Michel de. *The Practice of Everyday Life*. Trans. Steven F. Rendall. Berkeley, CA: University of California Press, 1984.

The Certeau Reader. Ed. Graham Ward. New York: Blackwell, 2000.

Derrida, Jacques. "The Other Heading: Memories, Responses, and Responsibilities." *PMLA: Publications of the Modern Language Association of America* 108.1 (1993): 89-93.

Emerson, Caryl. "Answering for Central and Eastern Europe." In *Comparative Literature in an Age of Globalization*, edited by Haun Saussy. Baltimore, MD: The Johns Hopkins University Press, 2006. 203-11.

Feifer, Maxine. *Tourism in History: From Imperial Rome to the Present*. New York: Stern and Day, 1986.

Foucault, Michel. "Des Espaces Autres." 1967. *Architecture/Mouvement/Continuité*. October, 1984.

_____. "Of Other Spaces." Trans. Jay Miskowiec, 1998. http://www.foucault.info/documents/heteroTopia/foucault.heteroTopia.en.html (accessed August 22, 2008).

Gretkowska, Manuela. *My zdies' emigranty [We Are Here Immigrants]*. 1991. Warszawa: Wydawnictwo W.A.B., 1995.

_____. *Kabaret metafizyczny*. Warszawa: Wydawnictwo W.A.B., 1995.

_____. *Podręcznik do ludzi*. Warszawa: Beba Mazeppo & Company, 1996.

_____. *Tarot Paryski*. Warszawa: Wydawnictwo W.A.B., 1995.

Iwański, Tadeusz. "Pociąg do literatury." *Panorama kultur*. http://www.pk.org.pl/artykul.php?id=189 (accessed January 13, 2009).

Klobucka, Anna. "Theorizing the European Periphery." *symplokē* 5.1-2 (1997): 119-35.

Kogl, Alexandra. *Strange Places: The Political Potentials and Perils of Everyday Spaces.* Lanham, MD: Lexington Books, 2008.

Lefebvre, Henri. *La production de l'espace.* Paris: Anthropos, 1974.

Levy, Pierre. *Cyberculture.* Trans. Robert Bonnono. Minneapolis, MN: University of Minnesota Press, 2001.

Mazierska, Ewa, and Laura Rascaroli. *Crossing New Europe: Postmodern Travel and the European Road Movie.* London and New York: Wallflower Press, 2006.

Panorama kultur. http://www.pk.org.pl/dzial.php?idd=62&id=8 (accessed January 27, 2009).

Pavlyshyn, Marko. "Choosing a Europe: Andrukhovych, Izdryk and the New Ukrainian Literature." *New Zealand Slavonic Journal* 35 (2001): 37-48.

Pfister, Manfred. "Europa/Europe: Myths and Muddles." In *Myths of Europe*, edited by Richard Littlejohns and Sara Soncini. Amsterdam: Rodopi, 2007. 21-33.

Potyah 76. http://www.potyah76.org.ua (accessed July 17, 2008).

Robyn, Richard. *The Changing Face of European Identity.* London and New York: Routledge, 2005.

Reynolds, Nedra. *Geographies of Writing.* Carbondale, IL: Southern Illinois University Press, 2004.

Russell, Alison. *Crossing Boundaries: Postmodern Travel Literature.* New York: Palgrave, 2000.

Schein, Louisa. "Of Cargo and Satellites: Imagined Cosmopolitanism." *Postcolonial Studies* 2 (1999): 345-75.

Seaton, A. V. "The Worst of Journeys, the Best of Journeys: Travel and the Concept of Periphery in European Culture." In *Expressions of Culture, Identity and Meaning in Tourism*, edited by Mike Robinson and Phil Long. Sunderland: Center for Travel and Tourism, 2000.

Soja, Edward W. *ThirdSpace.* Oxford: Blackwell, 1996.

_____. *Postmodern Geographies: The Reassertion of Space in Critical Social Theory.* London: Verso, 1989.

Spivak, Gayatri Chakravorty. "Can the Subaltern Speak?" In *Marxism and the Interpretation of Culture*, edited by C. Nelson and L. Grossberg. Macmillan Education: Basingstoke, 1988. 271-313.

Stacul, Jaro, Christina Moutsou, and Helen Kopnina, eds. "Crossing European Boundaries: Beyond Conventional Geographical Categories." In their *Crossing European Boundaries: Beyond Conventional Geographical Categories.* New York: Berghahn Books, 2006. 1-19.

Stasiuk, Andrzej. "Right of the Seventeenth Degree." http://www.potyah76.org.ua/potyah/?t=42 (accessed February 12, 2009).

_____. "Korabel'nyj shchodennyk" ["A Ship Diary"]. In Andrzej Stasiuk and Yuri Andrukhovych, *Moia Ievropa* [My Europe]. L'viv: Klasyka, 2001. 7-68.

Andrzej Stasik and Yuri Andrukhovych. *Moia Ievropa* [My Europe]. L'viv: Klasyka, 2001.

Tokarczuk, Olga. *Dom dzienny, dom nocny.* Wałbrzych: Wydawnictwo "Ruta," 1998.

_____. *House of Day, House of Night.* Trans. Antonia Lloyd-Jones. Evanston, IL: Northwestern University Press, 2002.

Wallerstein, Immanuel. *Geopolitics and Geoculture.* Cambridge: Cambridge University Press, 1991.

CONTRIBUTORS

CHRISTIAN MORARU is Professor of English at University of North Carolina, Greensboro. He specializes in critical theory and 20th-century American and comparative literature, with particular emphasis on narrative and narrative theory, postmodernism in cross-cultural perspective, and the relations between globalism and culture. His latest books include *Rewriting: Postmodern Narrative and Cultural Critique in the Age of Cloning* (SUNY Press 2001), *Memorious Discourse: Reprise and Representation in Postmodernism* (Fairleigh Dickinson University Press, 2005), and *Cosmodernism: American Narrative, Late Globalization, and the New Cultural Imaginary* (forthcoming, 2010). A chapter of his earlier book on 20th–century mimetic ideologies, *Poetics of Reflection: An Archeology of Mimesis*, has been reprinted in the SUNY Press anthology, *The Play of the Self* (1994). *Utopian Studies, LIT: Literature Interpretation Theory, The Comparatist, Canadian Review of Comparative Literature, Studies in the Novel, Modern Fiction Studies, College Literature, American Book Review, The Journal of Narrative Technique*, and *Names* are among the journals that have published his essays.

AARON CHANDLER is Lecturer at University of North Carolina Greensboro, Department of English. His research interests include post-Cold War literature, theories of affect, globalization, and cosmopolitanism. He has recently published essays in *Critique: Studies in Contemporary Fiction* and *LIT: Literature Interpretation Theory*. He is currently finishing a book-length study of postmodern revisions of eighteenth- and nineteenth-century sentimentalism.

MARCEL CORNIS-POPE is Professor of English and Director of the interdisciplinary Ph.D. in Media, Art, and Text at Virginia Commonwealth University. His publications include *Anatomy of the White Whale: A Poetics of the American Symbolic Romance* (1982), *Hermeneutic Desire and Critical Rewriting: Narrative Interpretation in the Wake of Poststructuralism* (1992), *The Unfinished Battles: Romanian Postmodernism before and after 1989* (1996), and *Narrative Innovation and Cultural Rewriting in the Cold War Era and After* (2001). He has also co-edited with Ron Bogue the collection *Violence and Mediation in Contemporary Culture* (1995) and has published numerous articles on contemporary fiction, narrative studies, and critical theory in journals and collective volumes. His current project is a multi-volume work (co-edited with John Neubauer) entitled *History of the Literary Cultures of East Central Europe: Junctures and Disjunctures in the 19th and 20th Century*, which explores East Central European literatures from a comparative-intercultural perspective. Vol. 1 of this work, on "Nodes of Political Time" and "Histories of Literary Form," vol. 2, on "Literary Topographies," and vol. 3, on "Literary Institutions," were published by John Benjamins Press in 2004, 2006, and 2007, respectively. Vol. 4, focused on "Figures and Types," will be published in 2009. In 1996, Cornis-Pope received the CELJ Award for Significant Editorial Achievement for his work as editor of *The Comparatist*, and last year, VCU's Award of Excellence for his teaching, scholarship, and service. His other awards include the Romanian Writers' Award for best book translation into English (1975), the Romanian Writers' Award for best book of criticism (1982), a Fulbright teaching and research grant (1983-85), an Andrew Mellon Faculty Fellowship at Harvard University (1987-88), and the VCU College of Humanities and Sciences Scholarship Award and Elske Smith Lecturer Award (1991; 1993).

ALEXANDER KIOSSEV is Associate Professor of History of Modern Culture at the University of Sofia. His research interests cover the cultural history of space, imaginary geographies, construction of identities, and space and visual culture. He has published a book on the history of Bulgarian literature and two others on the cultural history of the postcommunist transition period in Eastern Europe. He has edited the collective volume *Post-Theory, Games, and Discursive Resistance* (Albany, NY: SUNY Press, 1995). Since 2000, he has been a leading researcher in several international projects including "The Visual Seminar," which focuses on the changes in the visual environment of postcommunist-era Sofia.

ALMANTAS SAMALAVICIUS was born in Vilnius in 1963 and graduated from Vilnius Pedagogical University in 1985. He holds a Ph.D. in Art History and Theory, has taught cultural history and Lithuanian literature at Vilnius University, and has been a visiting lecturer at University of Illinois at Chicago and Helsinki University. He has given lectures at Florence University and University of the Basque Country. During the last decade, he has been an Associate Professor at the Department of Architectural Fundamentals and Theory at Vilnius Gediminas Technical University and has also been teaching in Vilnius University's Department of English. An author of more than 70 essays on architecture, culture, and literature, he has also published 6 books in Lithuanian. Among them: *Visionaries of the 20th Century* (1997) and *Ideas and Structures in the History of Architecture* (2004). He is an associate editor of the *Kulturos barai* journal and president of the Lithuanian PEN Club.

MARCELA KOSTIHOVÁ is Assistant Professor of English at Hamline University in St. Paul, Minnesota, where she teaches a range of courses in literature, as well as cultural, gender, and film studies. Her research investigates changing structures of identity formation in Central Eastern Europe's post-communist cultural sphere, ranging from literature and theater to film. She has published in national and international journals, and her first book, *Shakespeare in Transition: Political Appropriations in the Post-communist Czech Republic*, is forthcoming from Palgrave Macmillan.

PETER MORGAN is Professor and, currently, Convenor of European Studies at the University of Western Australia. His publications include *The Critical Idyll: Traditional Values and the French Revolution in Goethe's* Hermann und Dorothea (Columbia, SC: Camden House, 1990) and *Ismail Kadare: The Writer and the Dictatorship, 1957-1990* (Oxford: Legenda, 2009), as well as numerous articles and chapters on classical, 19th-century, and contemporary German and Austrian literature, on comparative literature, and on the teaching of German and European Studies. Peter Morgan's research has been supported by the Alexander von Humboldt Foundation (1992), the Australian Research Council (2003), and the Camargo Foundation (2004). In 2010, Peter Morgan will take up the position of Foundation Professor of European Studies at the University of Sydney.

JENNIFER RUTH HOSEK is Assistant Professor of German at Queen's University, Ontario, Canada. She holds a Ph.D. in Comparative Literature from UC Berkeley and has been a Stanford Fellow. She has published on literature, film, critical theory and neuroscience, information technology, and women's movement. Her book manuscript, which considers cultural influences of the global South on the North through the example of Cuba and the Germanies, has received support from the Studienstiftung des Abgeordnetenhauses von Berlin, DAAD, Humboldt and Mellon Foundations, UC Berkeley, and Queen's University. In 2008, "*Buena Vista* Deutschland: Nation and Gender in Wenders, Gaulke and Eggert," which has been published in three languages, won the National Coalition of Women in German Best Article Prize.

MATEVŽ KOS (1966) is Associate Professor in the Department of Comparative Literature and Literary Theory, Faculty of Arts, University of Ljubljana, Slovenia. He has published five books: *Prevzetnost in pristranost: Literarni spisi* (Pride and Prejudice: Literary Essays, 1996), *Kritike in refleksije* (Reviews and Reflections, 2000), *Poskusi z Nietzschejem: Nietzsche in ničejanstvo v slovenski literaturi* (Experimenting with Nietzsche: Nietzsche and Nietzscheanism in Slovenian Literature, 2003), *Branje po izbiri* (Reading by Choice, 2004), and *Fragmenti o celoti* (Fragments Describing the Whole, 2007). He has prepared and annotated a number of anthology selections (V. Taufer, S. Kosovel, M. Dekleva, F. Nietzsche, *The Slovenian Essay of the Nineties*, *Mi se vrnemo zvečer: Antologija mlade slovenske poezije 1990–2003* [We Are Coming Back in the Evening: An Anthology of Young Slovenian Poetry *1990–2003*]). His fields of research include Nietzsche and his impact on Slovenian literature; literature and philosophy; modernism and postmodernism; contemporary Slovenian literature.

NATAŠA KOVAČEVIĆ is Assistant Professor of Global Literature and Postcolonial Theory at Eastern Michigan University. Her recent book, *Narrating Post/Communism: Colonial Discourse and Europe's Borderline Civilization* (Routledge 2008), investigates the role of anti-communist dissident literature in both shaping and undermining an Orientalist discourse about post/communist Eastern Europe. She has also published an essay on Milan Kundera in *Modern Fiction Studies*, an essay on Virginia Woolf in *LIT: Literature Interpretation Theory*, and an interview with Dubravka Ugrešić in *Women and Performance: A Journal of Feminist Studies*. Her current work interrogates concepts of community and difference in supranational entities such as the European Union in an attempt to rethink the legacy of postcolonial and Marxist theories in the era of globalization.

ANIKÓ IMRE is Assistant Professor of Critical Studies in the School of Cinematic Arts of the University of Southern California. Her publications on media globalization, media education, consumption and mobility, and identity and play have appeared in *Screen, Camera Obscura, Framework, Third Text, CineAction, Signs, The European Journal of Cultural Studies, Feminist Media Studies,* and numerous book collections. She is the author of *Identity Games: Globalization and the Transformation of Post-Communist Media Cultures* (MIT Press, 2009), editor of *East European Cinemas* (AFI Film Readers, Routledge, 2005), co-editor of *Transnational Feminism in Film and Media* (Palgrave, 2007), guest co-editor of a special issue of the *European Journal of Cultural Studies* on "Media Globalization and Post-Socialist Identities" (May

2009), and guest co-editor of a special issue of *Feminist Media Studies* entitled "Transcultural Feminist Mediations" (December 2009).

PHYLLIS WHITMAN HUNTER is Associate Professor of history at University of North Carolina, Greensboro. She is the author of *Purchasing Identity in the Atlantic World* (Cornell University Press, 2001). Her scholarship centers on the cultural effects of capitalism in the seventeenth through early nineteenth centuries. She has two books in progress. One is tentatively titled "Geographies of Capitalism: Encountering Asia in Early America." The other focuses on the first merchant voyage from America to China and is forthcoming in Oxford's "Pivotal Moments in American History" series.

IRENE SYWENKY holds a Ph.D. in Comparative Literature (2005) and is currently Assistant Professor in the Comparative Literature Program and Department of Modern Languages and Cultural Studies at the University of Alberta. She has published on the post-totalitarian East European cultures and Canadian Asian diasporic writing. Her research areas include postmodernism; postcolonialism; cultural peripherality; Central and East European literatures and cultures; Canadian diaspora writing; comparative fantasy, science fiction, and popular culture; literature and science. She is at work on a monograph on liminal postmodernisms and is also completing a project on the processes of identity formation in Central Europe.